D1409433

CLASSIC FIGHTERS
The Inside Story

CLASSIC FIGHTERS
The Inside Story

Ray Bonds

CHARTWELL
BOOKS, INC.

This edition published by

CHARTWELL BOOKS, INC.
A Division of
BOOK SALES, INC.
276 Fifth Avenue Suite 206
New York, New York 10001

Reprinted 2011.

ISBN: 978-0-7858-2785-6

© 2005 by Compendium Publishing Ltd., 43 Frith Street, London
W1D 4SA, United Kingdom

Cataloging-in-Publication data is available from the Library of
Congress

All rights reserved. No part of this publication may be repro-
duced, stored in a retrieval system or transmitted in any form or
by any means, electronic, mechanical, photocopying, recording
or otherwise, without the prior permission of Compendium
Publishing Ltd. All correspondence concerning the content of
this volume should be addressed to Compendium Publishing
Ltd.

The Author
Ray Bonds has been a defense journalist, editor, and publisher
during a career spanning over thirty-five years, covering periods
and subjects as wide-ranging as the American Civil War, anti-
ballistic missile systems, stealth warfare, and modern military
intelligence gathering. He has written and edited scores of well-
respected titles on military aviation, and the world's major
armed forces, their battles, weapons, and organization.

Designer: Tony Stocks/Compendium Publishing

Cutaway drawings on the following pages © Mike Badrocke
2004: 9, 11, 13, 41, 45, 49, 53, 55, 115, 127, 209, 223, 231, 235,
239
All other cutaway drawings: courtesy Amber Books

Printed and bound in China

Page 1: The Messerschmitt Bf 109F-4/Trop in desert colors adopted by at least one Luftwaffe unit in 1942. The Bf 109 was Germany's most ubiquitous and prolific fighter during World War II.

Above: Lockheed Martin's stealthy YF-22 (development aircraft for the F-22A Raptor) releases an AIM-120 Amraam air-to-air missile during trials.

Pages 4-5: A Royal Air Force Tornado F.3 dispenses chaff and flares countermeasures over the North Sea. This interceptor with variable-sweep wings was developed from the earlier Tornado IDS (Interdictor Strike) aircraft produced by the European consortium (Britain, Germany and Italy) known as Panavia.

CONTENTS

INTRODUCTION

As they thunder through the skies, performing often unbelievable gyrations, the stars of air shows throughout the world are undeniably the fighters. But they are more than this; they represent the peak of national technology, the ultimate expression of national pride, and often the first line of defense of national freedom. Today, they carry detection systems of fantastic complexity and weapons of awesome capability.

Whereas warfare is as old as the history of mankind, the fighter is very much of the last hundred years. It was born in the stick-and-string era of the second decade of the 20th Century, and honed in the crucible of battle during World War I. In previous centuries, warfare was a two-dimensional combination of fire and movement, with the advantage going to the general who could out-maneuver his adversary. With the advent of the repeating rifle and the machine gun the advantage passed to the defensive, and the Great War bogged down in the trenches. Movement was no more, and tens of thousands of lives were sacrificed to gain a few hundred yards. With the trenches stretching from the Swiss border to the North Sea, no outflanking moves were possible. Except one. The new-fangled flying machines could overfly the wire-strewn and bullet-swept front lines with ease.

Given that wars were won by surface forces, the most valuable roles for aircraft were reconnaissance and artillery spotting. This was closely followed by the dropping of primitive bombs, and machine-gunning enemy troops in the trenches. The fighter arose from the need to deny similar facilities to the enemy, and to protect friendly aircraft going about their routine tasks. At a later date this was called air superiority, and was defined as the ability to create favorable conditions for the conduct of surface operations, and the air operations which directly support them.

In practice, air superiority was both local and temporary, but the fighter pilots who gained it took on another aspect. The successful ones became heroes, not only defying the inherent dangers of flight, but assuming the mantle of the single-combat champions of times long gone. The world needed heroes; it also needed glamor. The first fighter pilots provided both, to become an inspiration to nations sickened by the apparently useless slaughter in the mud of the battlefields.

Even as the champions of old needed legendary weapons and enchanted armor to conquer, so the new knights of the air needed ever-improved machines in which to fight. Aircraft were designed to fill these needs; higher, faster, more powerful, more agile. Thus began the race for the best, culminating in the modern fighter and its weaponry.

Along the way many classic fighters have been designed and have seen service with air forces throughout the world. Sixty of them have been laid bare in these pages, in incredibly detailed cutaway drawings, supplemented by dramatic photographs and concise descriptions. They include warplanes that between them have notched up various "firsts" as well as records for speed and other performance characteristics. While many did not see combat action, and some have not yet even seen squadron service, nevertheless they are all part of the development story of the most exciting fighting machines ever built.

ABOVE: Bristol F.2B Fighters (commonly called "Brisfits") of 141 Squadron lined up at Biggin Hill, southern England, in 1918. A two-seat biplane of wooden construction, it made real impact against German fighters over the Western Front once the pilots began to fly them as if they were single-seaters.

OPPOSITE: High over the Northern Hemisphere, a pair of USAF F-15 Eagles "intercepts" a Russian Tu-95 Bear long-range bomber in the mid-1980s, during the Cold War. In various versions, the Eagle has had an extremely successful combat record – more than a hundred enemy aircraft destroyed for no losses.

ALBATROS D V

Germany's Albatros series of single-seat, single-engined tractor biplane fighters first entered service in the fall of 1916. Although the series exhibited serious structural weaknesses, as well as various deficiencies in performance and firepower, they were nevertheless numerically the most important German fighters of World War I.

Aerial control of the battlefronts in France changed hands frequently during 1916 and 1917 as first one side and then the other fielded aircraft that were superior in maneuverability, or speed, or endurance, or weaponry, or a combination of these, and also as tactics and organization of the air services evolved. By early 1916, the so-called "Fokker Scourge" had spread like a blight across the fighting areas above the Western Front, where the British and French flying services suffered rapidly increasing loses to the agile German Eindeckers. The almost defenseless Allied reconnaissance machines were no match for an armed Fokker scout against which they were unable to maneuver quickly when attacked. But more agile and better-armed Allied aircraft entered the fray and got into their stride by the summer of 1916, and the Fokker menace soon abated.

The Allies' aerial supremacy was short-lived, however, for in late 1916 new fighting machines began to appear in German *Jagdstaffeln* (literally, Hunting Squadrons) – among them the Albatros D I and D II scouts. Of streamlined shape, with a plywood-skinned fuselage, the Albatros carried twin synchronized machine guns firing through the propeller arc – an armament arrangement that was to become classic in fighter aircraft for the remainder of the war and, indeed, for nearly twenty years after.

The D I's semi-monocoque wooden fuselage differed radically from the fabric-skinned, braced box-girder type fuselages that were used on almost all other aircraft of the period. The wings were conventional wooden structures, fabric-covered. The D Is were delivered to the Front by November 1916, but were almost immediately phased out in favor of the D II, which was an improvement over the D I in that the upper wing was lowered in height and the cabane in front of the cockpit modified, thus improving one of the greatest faults of this fighter – the forward and upward view from the cockpit.

The D III was the result of further improvements: it still featured the semi-monocoque fuselage and tail surface, but the lower wing was made narrower, improving pilot visibility, wingspan was increased, and a single spar connected it to the upper wing by a V-strut.

The D II and D III were largely responsible for giving the

Central Powers air supremacy over the Allies, but this lasted really for only a few months. By spring 1917 better British and French designs – S.E. 5as, Sopwith Camels, and the latest SPADS and Nieuports – with improved maneuverability and performance entered service, whereas the Albatros designers rested on their laurels. The few improvements that led to the D V were related mainly to drag reduction: the fuselage was made more oval, with a new longeron on each side; a large spinner was fitted; and the rudder was made rounder.

Some 900 D Vs were built but the new aircraft became outclassed and outfought by the Allies' fighters while a thorough structural reappraisal was undertaken. The D III had shown a tendency to lose its wings as speed built up in a prolonged dive, and this ghastly fault also afflicted the D V early in its service life. A partial solution was to fit a short strut from the leading edge to the front of the V-strut, while pilots were instructed not to sustain dives for too long, which severely restricted them in attack and evasion. The end product of the reappraisal was the D Va, with stronger spars, heavier ribs, and additional fuselage members, but without commensurate power increase, resulting in performance degradation. Nevertheless, 1,612 were built, with 928 serving at the Front at the end of April 1918 – almost half the fighter strength available to the Germans in their spring offensive of that year.

Specifications for Albatros D V

Dimensions:	wingspan 29 feet 8 inches, length 24 feet 0.5 inches, height 8 feet 10.25 inches
Power:	one Mercedes inline engine, 180hp
Weights:	empty 1,515lb, max takeoff 2,066lb
Speed:	max 115mph at 3,281 feet
Ceiling:	20,506 feet
Range:	endurance 2 hours
Armament:	two fixed belt-fed 7.92mm Spandau machine guns firing through propeller disc
Crew:	pilot

Albatros D 5a cutaway key

1 Starboard fabric-covered aileron
2 Wing panel fabric covering
3 Aileron hinge control
4 Interplane V struts
5 Starboard lower wing panel
6 Leading edge auxiliary bracing strut
7 Propeller tip metal sheathing
8 Aileron control cables
9 Flying wires
10 Lifting wires
11 Plywood-covered leading edge
12 D-section leading edge member
13 Compression struts
14 Wing panel internal wire bracing
15 Trailing edge rib structure
16 Trailing edge auxiliary spar
17 Radiator
18 Radiator header tank and filler
19 Center section cabane N struts
20 Water coolant pipes
21 Exhaust pipe
22 Two-bladed laminated wooden propeller
23 Light alloy spinner
24 Propeller hub attachment bolts
25 Fuselage lower main longeron
26 Undercarriage front strut anchorage
27 Engine mounting deck
28 Upper main longeron
29 Bolted engine mounts
30 Mercedes D.111a engine
31 Carburetor and access hatch
32 Inlet manifolds
33 Twin magnetos
34 Machine gun barrels
35 Fuel tank
36 Engine bay/cockpit dividing bulkhead
37 Stub wing and lower wing panel attachment joint
38 Rudder pedal bar
39 Undercarriage rear strut anchorage
40 Cockpit floor panel
41 Control column mounting and cable pulleys
42 Cartridge case collector box
43 Ammunition magazines
44 Twin Spandau 7.92mm machine guns
45 Transverse gun mounting
46 Airspeed indicator
47 Altimeter
48 Windscreen panel
49 Port center section cabane struts
50 Pilot's seat
51 Seat belt
52 Seat mounting
53 Boarding step
54 Box-section wing spars
55 Fabric-covered bulkhead/fuselage dust cover
56 Padded cockpit coaming
57 Trailing edge cut-out, upward vision
58 Fuselage plywood skin paneling
59 All-wood fuselage monocoque structure
60 Plywood fuselage formers
61 Starboard tailplane
62 Fin and tailplane support frames
63 All-wood fin structure, integral with fuselage
64 Sternpost
65 Rudder horn balance
66 Welded steel tube elevator structure, fabric-covered
67 Elevator cable control horns
68 Single elevator
69 Welded steel tube elevator structure, fabric-covered
70 Elevator hinge mountings
71 Port tailplane all-wood structure
72 Ventral fin
73 Steel-shod tailskid
74 Elastic cord shock absorber
75 Tailplane attachment bolted joint
76 Aft fuselage tie-down fitting
77 Tail control cables
78 Steel wire wing trailing edge
79 Aileron mounting auxiliary spar
80 Aileron cable-operated rocking-arm hinge control
81 Welded steel tube aileron structure, fabric-covered
82 Aileron hinge fittings
83 Plywood-covered wing tip edge member
84 Plywood wing ribs with spruce capping strips
85 Steel strut attachment fittings
86 Port interplane V struts
87 Leading edge auxiliary bracing strut
88 Aileron control cables
89 Lower wing panel rib structure
90 Leading edge compression struts
91 Lower wing panel box-section main spar
92 Port lifting and flying wires
93 Auxiliary rear spar
94 Plywood-covered leading edge
95 Main undercarriage V struts
96 Diagonal bracing wires
97 Port mainwheel
98 Light allow wheel hub cover with tire valve access
99 Axle spreader beam
100 Light alloy axle fairing
101 Elastic cord shock absorber
102 Starboard mainwheel

ABOVE: One of the sleekest fighters of the Great War, the Albatros D V entered service in mid-1917. Dogged by frequent wing failures, it was replaced from October 1917 by the improved D Va. The D V shown is being examined by fascinated Allied soldiers, it having force-landed behind British lines.

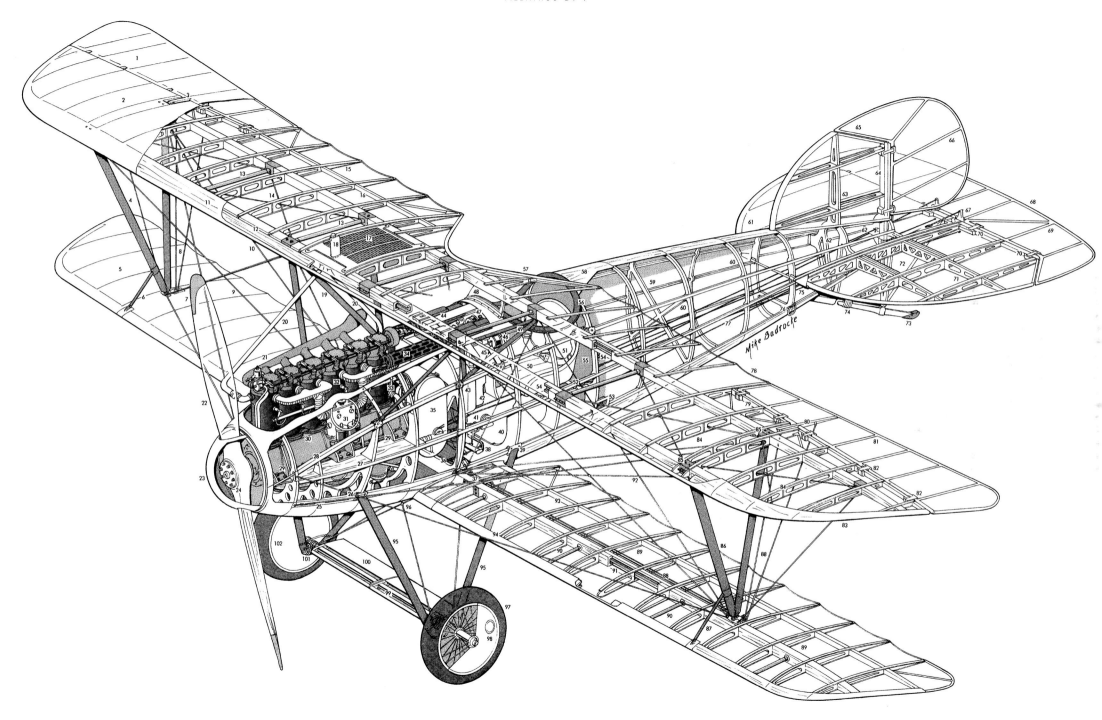

Copyright Mike Badrocke – 2004

AVRO CANADA CF-100 CANUCK

Immediately after World War II, Canada had taken on three important commitments: defense of its homeland, participation in the newly formed North Atlantic Treaty Organization (NATO), and United Nations operations. The Royal Canadian Air Force was equipped with combat aircraft such as the North American P-51 Mustang and de Havilland Vampires, both stopgap aircraft that were essentially obsolete with the threat of the Cold War looming.

When the initial design for the CF-100 transonic night and all-weather long range interceptor was created for the RCAF in October 1946, the aircraft faced a formidable task in extremely difficult conditions. The main threat was perceived to be Russian strategic bombers coming in their droves into North America over the North Pole. The CF-100 would have to operate over the enormous land mass of its homeland in frequently terrible weather conditions, and in areas above the Arctic Circle that seldom if ever saw daylight during the long winter months. This called for a large aircraft to carry a two-man crew with radar, and voluminous fuel tanks to provide extended endurance.

The Avro Canada CF-100 Canuck, affectionately called the "Clunk" by its aircrews, was the first all-Canadian designed and built combat aircraft, and one of the largest fighters ever produced. The fuselage was flanked by engine nacelles; the straight wings were low-set, and had ailerons and double-slotted flaps on the trailing edge. The fin was plain, with horizontal tail surfaces set high on it. The crew sat in tandem behind the nose radar.

The first of two prototypes (CF-100 Mk 1) was flown on January 1950, powered by 6,500lb Rolls-Royce-Avon RA 3 turbojets. Ten unarmed pre-production aircraft (CF-100 Mk 2) followed. The first of these flew on June 20, 1951, with 6,000lb Orenda 2 engines produced by Avro Canada. The initial production model (CF-100 Mk 3) had Orenda 8 engines of similar power rating, together with APG-33 nose-mounted radar and eight 0.5 inch Colt-Browning machine guns in a ventral pack. Some seventy Mk 3s were built, and the first were delivered in September 1952. Of these, fifty were ultimately converted to Mk 3CT and 3D trainers.

A prototype Mk 4, the tenth and last Mk 2, flew on October 11, 1952, followed on October 24, 1953, by the CF-100 Mk 4A which was the result of major structural redesign. It had an APG-40 radar linked to a Hughes MG-2 fire control system, and more powerful 6,500lb Orenda 9 engines offsetting significant weight increase. Armament comprised 48 unguided missiles in a ventral pack and 29 similar missiles in each of two wingtip pods. The ventral

pack was interchangeable with one containing eight 0.5 inch guns. Wingspan was increased by 19 inches over the Mk 3. The CF-100 4B was an improved model powered by Orenda 11 engines of 7,275lb. The Mk 5 was also powered by Orenda 11s or Orenda 14s, of similar rating, and featured weight savings, a 6ft increase in wingspan, and an extended tailplane. The first production Mk 5 flew on October 12, 1955. On this, the final model, the ventral gun or missile tray was eliminated, and armament was confined to the wingtip missile pods. With these, wingspan became 60ft 10in.

A total of 692 aircraft of all marks (1 to 5) were built up to 1957, some 53 (Mk V standard) being supplied to *Force Aérienne Belge*.

Specifications for CF-100 Mk 5

Dimensions:	wingspan 58 feet, length 54 feet 1 inch, height 15 feet 6.5 inches
Power:	two Orenda 11 or 14 single-stage axial flow turbojets rated at 7,275lb thrust
Weights:	empty 23,100lb, notmal takeoff 37,000lb, max takeoff 45,000lb
Speed:	650mph at 10,000 feet
Ceiling:	54,000 feet
Armament:	106 x 2.75in folding fin rockets in ventral pack (or ventral gun pack) and wingtip pods
Crew:	pilot and weapon systems officer (WSO)

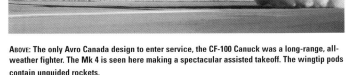

ABOVE: The only Avro Canada design to enter service, the CF-100 Canuck was a long-range, all-weather fighter. The Mk 4 is seen here making a spectacular assisted takeoff. The wingtip pods contain unguided rockets.

CF-100 Mk 4B cutaway key

1 Starboard tailplane construction
2 Starboard elevator
3 Trim tab
4 Rudder upper section
5 Communications aerial
6 Fin construction
7 Port tailplane
8 Rudder lower section
9 Rudder trim tab
10 Tail navigation lights
11 Tailcone
12 Leading edge de-icing
13 Fin spar joints
14 Tailcone attachment frame
15 Tail bumper
16 Fuselage skinning
17 Rear fuselage construction
18 Fuselage frames
19 Air intake
20 Air conditioning plant
21 Radio equipment bay
22 Jet efflux
23 Nacelle tailpipe
24 Nacelle construction
25 Wing rear spar fixing
26 Starboard wing flap
27 Flap hydraulic jack
28 Herringbone airbrake
29 Aileron trim tab
30 Starboard aileron
31 Wing-tip rocket pod
32 292-gallon wing-tip fuel tank
33 Tip tank navigation light
34 Rocket pod navigation light
35 Wing-tip attachment
36 29 folding fin 2.75in (70mm) rockets
37 Rocket pod frangible nosecone
38 Wing construction
39 Wing inner skin
40 Wing stringers
41 Main spar
42 Wing fuel tanks
43 Leading edge construction
44 Leading edge de-icing
45 Twin mainwheels
46 Undercarriage leg door
47 Main undercarriage leg
48 Main spar fixing
49 Undercarriage leg pivot
50 Retraction jack
51 Nacelle center section construction
52 Jet pipe shroud
53 Engine mounting struts
54 Orenda 11 turbojet engine
55 Fuselage fuel tanks
56 Control duct along top of fuselage
57 Port engine nacelle
58 Airbrake hydraulic jack
59 Port airbrake
60 Port wing flap
61 Aileron trim tab
62 Port aileron
63 Aileron hydraulic jack
64 Wing-tip rocket pod
65 Landing la,p
66 Wing inner skin
67 Leading edge de-icing boots
68 Pitot head
69 Port wing fuel tanks
70 Port engine cowlings
71 Sliding canopy cover
72 Canopy rails
73 Air intake
74 Engine mounting frame
75 Firewall
76 Engine-driven gearbox
77 Engine bay construction
78 Nacelle lower fairing
79 Ventral gun pack
80 Ammunition boxes
81 Spent cartridge deflector plates
82 Eight 0.50in (12.7mm) Browning machine guns
83 Gun muzzle fairings
84 Gun port
85 Starboard intake guard
86 Engine air intake
87 Intake anti-ice spray
88 Ammunition bay
89 Navigator's ejection seat
90 Radar display
91 ADF loop aerial
92 Port engine intake
93 Pilot's ejector seat
94 Nosewheel bay
95 Nosewheel door
96 Pressurised cockpit structure
97 Control column
98 Engine throttles
99 Windscreen frme
100 Gun sight
101 Nose electronics compartment
102 Rudder pedals
103 Nose undercarriage pivot
104 Nosewheel leg
105 Twin nosewheels
106 Nosewheel leg door
107 Nose radar bay construction
108 Hughes APG-40 radar
109 Fire control ad interrogation radar
110 Radar scanner
111 Radome

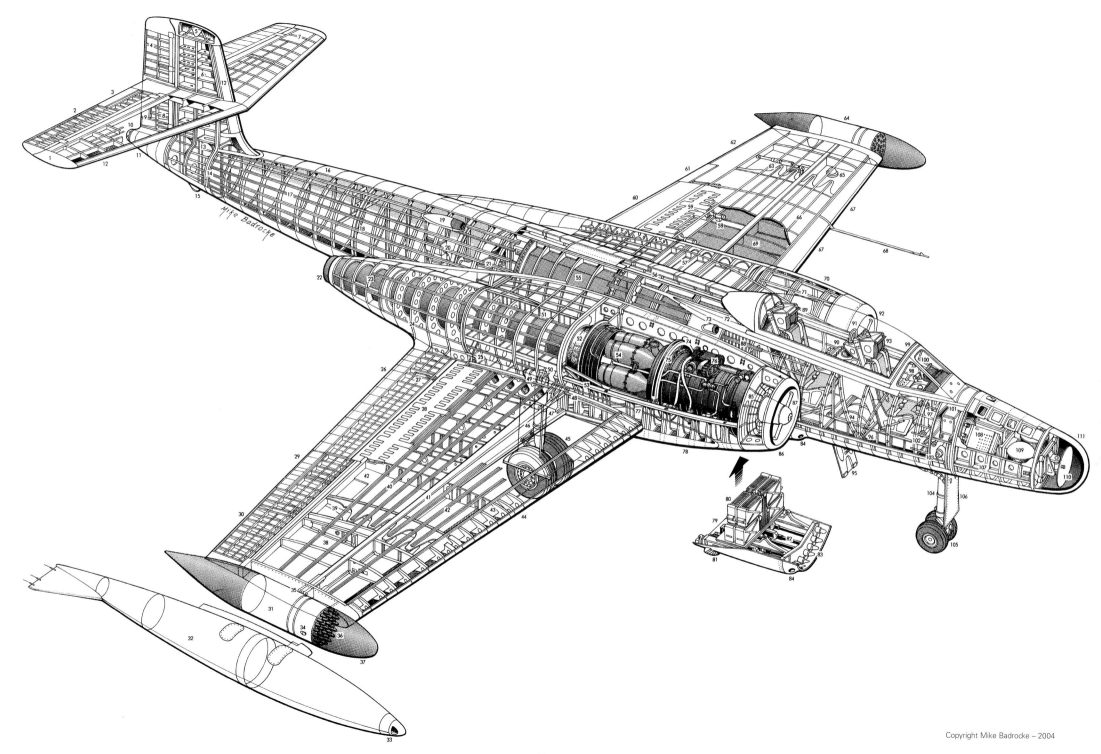

Copyright Mike Badrocke – 2004

BRISTOL F.2B FIGHTER

LEFT: The first truly successful two-seater fighter, the Bristol F.2B followed the F.2A into service in April 1917. Although large, it was a match for most German single-seaters. It remained in RAF service until 1932.

The Bristol Fighter (in its F.2A single-seat and evolved F.2B two-seat versions) was a truly great and successful World War I British design, once the pilots had become more tactically aware. In particular, pilots of the two-seaters learned to fly them like single-seaters, using their synchronized Vickers fixed machine guns as their main weapons, and leaving the observers/gunners to guard their tails with their Lewis MGs. The Lewis guns could be elevated or depressed easily, and the observers had spacious cockpits with sliding seats, both of which gave them relative freedom of movement.

Compared to the F.2A, the F.2B two-bay biplane, of wooden construction and with two main spars in both upper and lower planes, afforded the pilot improved visibility, greater fuel capacity, and more ammunition for the Vickers. With the larger engine (see below), the F.2B was as agile as most single-seat fighters it opposed, and could achieve a time to climb rate of ten minutes to 6,500 feet.

The most successful F.2B pilot during World War I was Andrew McKeever, a Canadian who joined Britain's Royal Flying Corps No. 11 Squadron in May 1917. He was a superb marksman and natural flier, achieving thirty victories between June 20, 1917, and January 1918 to prove it. His observers/gunners claimed a further eleven victories.

A phenomenal total of 4,747 F.2Bs were completed between April 1917 and September 1919, most with Rolls-Royce Falcon I (190hp), II (220hp), or III (275hp) engines, while some of the later production batches had other powerplants installed: 153 aircraft with 200hp Sunbeam Arabs and 19 aircraft with 230hp Siddeley Pumas. Having outperformed most enemy aircraft types during World War I, the Bristol Fighter was used for Army co-operation after the war, being reinstated into production as the Mk II, while others were refurbished to similar standards. In 1926, fifty aircraft with structural revisions were delivered as Mk IIIs, and all survivors of this version were converted as Mk IVs in 1928. Many Bristol Fighters remained in service until 1932. The type was widely exported in a variety of modified versions.

Specifications for Bristol F.2B Fighter

Dimensions:	wingspan 39 feet 4 inches, length 25 feet 10 inches, height 9 feet 6 inches
Power:	one Rolls-Royce Falcon I engine of 190hp, or 1 x Falcon II of 220hp, or 1 x Falcon III of 275hp
Weights:	empty 1,930lb, normal takeoff 2,848lb
Speed:	123mph at 5,000 feet (with Falcon III engine, 1918)
Ceiling:	20,000 feet
Range:	endurance 3 hours
Armament:	one .303in Vickers belt-fed machine gun, fixed, and one Scarff-mounted .303in Lewis drum-fed machine gun, swiveling, in rear cockpit
Crew:	pilot and observer/gunner

Bristol F.2B Fighter cutaway key

1 Wing-tip edge member
2 Starboard upper aileron
3 Aileron control horn
4 Fixed trailing-edge ribs
5 Compression ribs
6 Wing panel internal wire bracing
7 Leading-edge stiffeners
8 Outboard interplane struts
9 Diagonal wire bracing
10 Lower wing panel fabric covering
11 Aileron operating cable
12 Inboard interplane struts
13 Upper engine cowling panels
14 Machine gun barrel
15 Blast tube vent
16 Machine gun muzzle blast tube
17 Radiator filler cap
18 Radiator shutters
19 Shuttle control lever
20 Two-bladed laminated wooden propeller
21 Anti-corrosion metal-bound propeller leading edge
22 Propeller hub
23 Propeller hub fixing bolts
24 Radiator
25 Radiator drain cock
26 Lower engine cowling panels
27 Engine bearer struts
28 Main engine mountings
29 Rolls-Royce Falcon III liquid-cooled 12-cylinder Vee-engine
30 Engine magneto
31 Exhaust pipe
32 Engine bay rear bulkhead
33 Rudder pedals
34 Cockpit floor paneling
35 Seat mounting longeron
36 Sloping upper longeron
37 Control column
38 Cartridge case ejector chute
39 Upper (main) fuel tank, total fuel capacity 52.8 gallons
40 Center section front strut
41 Gunsight ring
42 Upper wing panel center section
43 Compass
44 Windscreen panel
45 Aldis gunsight
46 Wing spar/center section attachment joint
47 0.303in (7.7mm) Vickers machine gun
48 Machine gun mounting struts
49 Instrument panel

50 Engine throttle and mixture control levers (postwar port-side position)
51 Lower fuel tank
52 Observer's cockpit floor paneling
53 Observer's emergency control column (offset to starboard)
54 Pilot's seat
55 Center section rear strut
56 Cockpit coaming
57 Scarff-ring machine gun mounting
58 Gun elevating mchanism
59 Ammunition drum
60 0.303in (7.7mm) Lewis machine gun
61 Swiveling gun mounting
62 Spare ammunition drums
63 Observer's sliding seat
64 Seat mounting rail
65 Diagonal fuselage braces
66 Upper longerons
67 Fuselage internal wire bracing
68 Fabric top decking
69 Starboard tailplane
70 Starboard elevator
71 Fin construction
72 Sternpost
73 Rudder construction
74 Tailplane bracing cables
75 Rudder control horn
76 Port elevator construction
77 Elevator control horn
78 Tailplane construction
79 Elevator control cables
80 Ventral fin segment
81 Trimming tailplane incidence control linkage
82 Rear fuselage bulkhead
83 Rudder control cables
84 Tailskid steering linkage
85 Fuselage lower longeron
86 Tailskid mounting struts
87 Steerable tailskid
88 Elastic cord shock absorber
89 Vertical spacers
90 Fuselage fabric coverng
91 Fabric lacing
92 Horizontal spacers
93 Wing trailing-edge ribs

94 Rear spar
95 Compression ribs
96 Front spar
97 Wing panel internal wire bracing
98 Rib support stringers
99 Aileron balance cable
100 Aileron control horn
101 Port upper aileron
102 Wing-tip edge member
103 Aileron interconnecting cable
104 Port lower aileron
105 Ventral wing-tip slid
106 Aileron operating cable
107 Outboard interplane struts
108 Pitot tube
109 Lower wing panel rib construction
110 Leading-edge stiffeners
111 Inboard interplane struts
112 Boarding steps
113 Lower wing panel center section attachment struts
114 Ventral bomb racks (6)
115 Wing spar/center section attachment joint
116 Wind-driven fuel pump
117 Main undercarriage V-struts
118 Diagonal wire bracing
119 Axle beam
120 Starboard mainwheel
121 Elastic cord shock absorbers
122 Wheel spokes
123 Tire inflation valve
124 Wheel disc fabric cover
125 Port mainwheel
126 25lb (11kg) Cooper bomb (12)

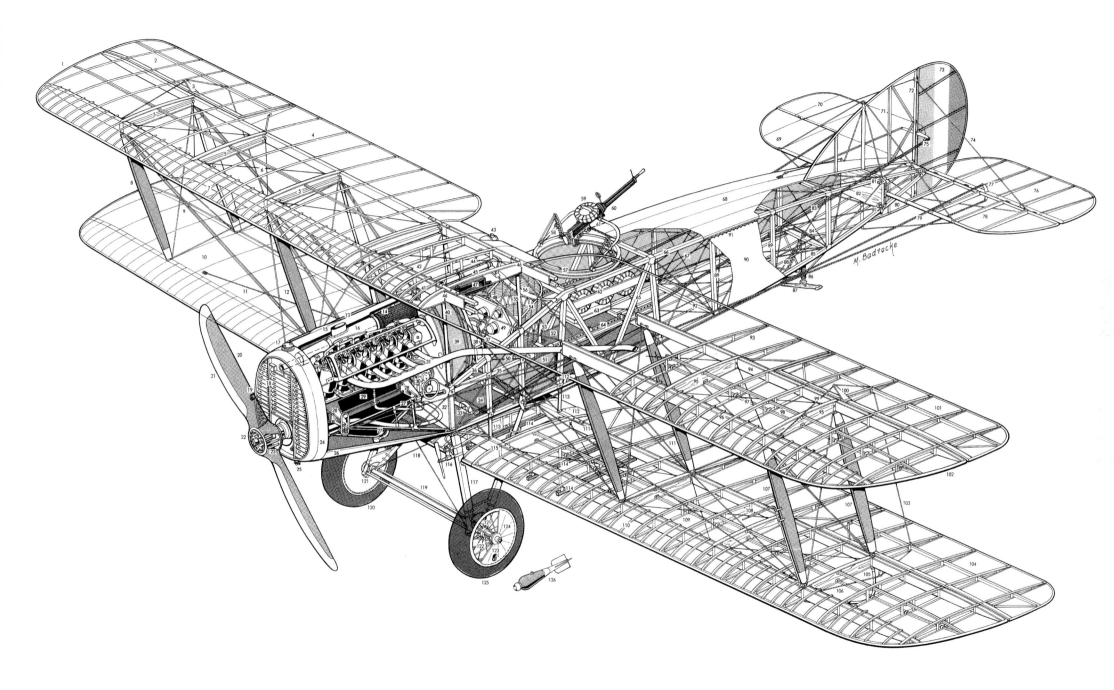

Copyright Mike Badrocke – 2004

BRISTOL BEAUFIGHTER

LEFT: Developed from the inadequate Beaufort torpedo bomber, the Bristol Beaufighter first made its name as a night fighter. This Mk X, armed with air-to-surface rockets, was a very effective strike fighter with the RAF's Coastal Command.

As the first ever effective radar-equipped night fighter (the IF version), the British Beaufighter has assured its place in the hall of fame. Big enough to carry on-board radar, it also had the performance to catch German night raiders during the first years of World War II, and armament heavy enough to destroy them with a single short burst.

The Beaufighter was developed in haste, the first flight of the prototype (Type 156) occurring on July 17, 1939, using wings, fuselage and empennage from the Beaufort torpedo bomber. The aircraft's handling qualities left much to be desired, tending to swing on takeoff or landing, and it was laterally unstable at low speeds. But evolved aircraft were surprisingly maneuverable, and extremely strong, had a maximum speed of over 320mph, and a murderous armament of four 20mm cannon and six wing machine guns. Originally the 20mm cannon were drum-fed, but this was later changed to belt-feeding. Tough and versatile, the Beaufighter served in many other roles. It was successfully developed into an anti-shipping strike aircraft, carrying rockets or a torpedo. The advent of the air-to-ground rocket added more punch to the fighter-bomber such that a salvo of rockets from a Beaufighter could blow a ship out of the water.

The first production Beaufighter IF was cleared for RAF service on July 26, 1940, powered by two 1,400hp Bristol Hercules III radial engines, which were replaced later in the production run by the more powerful 1,500hp Hercules XIs. The AI Mk IV radar was fitted to the Beaufighter IF from September 1940. Within three months the 100th aircraft was completed, and the 200th rolled out just five months later. The *Luftwaffe* certainly feared the Beaufighter, even when it was serving 500 miles out in the Atlantic. Equipped with radar, the night fighter hit back hard at Germany's bombers and fighter-bombers, and were credited as being one of the main reasons for the *Luftwaffe* abandoning its *Blitz* on Britain.

The British AI (Airborne Interception) Mk IV was the first radar for night fighters to go into large-scale service. The arrow-shaped aerial on the nose of Beaufighter IFs belonged to the transmitter, while the pairs of aerials on the wings belonged to the receiver. When the signals picked up by each of the wing aerials were equal in strength, the target was dead ahead. Range was about three-and-a-half miles at 18,000 feet.

Total production of the IF was 914. There followed the IIF in March 1941. This had two Rolls-Royce Merlin XX V-12 engines of 1,260hp rating; 450 were built. A further variant, the VIF, had two 1,635hp Hercules engines, and was fitted

with AI Mk VII radar, which entered service in 1942. The Beaufighter served in all theaters (the Japanese nicknamed it "Whispering Death," for the quietness of its engines) and in a variety of roles. One variant, the IC, was evolved specifically for RAF Coastal Command for shipping strikes and protection of coastal shipping. Some 5,564 Beaufighter were built in England, and a further 364 in Australia. The last fighter and torpedo versions served with Coastal Command, the Far East Air Force and the Royal Australian Air Force until 1960.

Specifications for Bristol Beaufighter IF

Dimensions:	wingspan 57 feet 10 inches, length 41 feet 8 inches, height 15 feet 10 inches
Power:	two Bristol Hercules XI 14-cylinder radial engines of 1,500hp
Weights:	empty 14,069lb, max loaded 21,100lb
Speed:	306mph at sea level, 323mph at 15,000 feet
Ceiling:	28,900 feet
Range:	1,170 miles
Armament:	four fuselage-mounted 20mm Hispano cannon and (from 50th aircraft) six wing-mounted 0.303in Browning machine guns
Crew:	pilot and radar operator/observer

Beaufighter Mk 1 cutaway key

1 Starboard navigation light (fore) and formation-keeping light (aft)
2 Wing structure
3 Aileron adjustable tab
4 Starboard aileron
5 Four Browning 0.303in (7.7mm) machine-guns
6 Machine-gun ports
7 Starboard outer wing fuel tank, capacity 104.4 gallons
8 Split trailing-edge flaps, hydraulically actuated
9 Starboard flap
10 Flap-operating jack
11 Starboard nacelle tail fairing
12 Oil tank capacity 20.4 gallons
13 Starboard inner wing fuel tank, capacity 225.6 gallons
14 Cabin air duct
15 Hinged leading-edge sections
16 Engine bulkhead
17 Engine bearers
18 Auxiliary intake
19 Supercharger air intake
20 Engine cooling flaps
21 1,560hp (1164-kW) Bristol Hercules III radial engine
22 de Havilland Hydromatic propeller
23 Propeller spinner
24 Lockheed oleo-pneumatic shock absorber
25 Starboard mainwheel, with Dunlop brakes
26 Forward identification lamp in nose cap
27 Rudder pedals
28 Control column
29 Cannon ports
30 Seat adjusting lever
31 Pilot's seat
32 Instrument panel
33 Clear vision panel
34 Flat bulletproof windscreen
35 Fixed canopy (sideways-hinged on later aircraft)
36 Spar carry-through step
37 Nose center-section attachment point
38 Fuselage/center-section attachment point
39 Pilot's entry/emergency escape hatch
40 Underfloor cannon blast tubes
41 Fuselage/center-section attachment points
42 Center-section attachment longeron reinforcement
43 Cabin air duct
44 Cannon heating duct
45 Rear spar carry-through

46 Bulkhead cutout (observer access to front hatch)
47 Bulkhead
48 Hydraulic header tank
49 Aerial mast
50 Monocoque fuselage construction
51 Starboard cannon (two 20mm)
52 Floor level
53 Steps
54 Observer's swivel seat
55 Radio controls and intercom
56 Observer's cupola
57 Hinged panel
58 Aerial
59 Oxygen bottles
60 Vertical control cable shaft
61 Sheet metal bulkhead
62 Control cables
63 Tailplane structure
64 Elevator
65 Elevator balance tab
66 Fin structure
67 Rudder balance
68 Rudder framework
69 Tail formation keeping (upper) and navigation lamps
70 Rudder
71 Rudder trim tab
72 Elevator trim tab
73 Elevator balance tab
74 Elevator structure
75 Port tailplane (12° dihedral on later aircraft)
76 Rudder hinge (lower)
77 Tailwheel retraction mechanism
78 Retracting tailwheel
79 Tailwheel bay
80 Tail unit joint ring
81 Control cables
82 Parachute flare chute
83 Fuselage skinning – flush-riveted Alclad
84 Observer's entry/emergency escape hatchway
85 Lower fuselage longeron
86 Entry ladder/emergency exit chute
87 Wing root fairing fillet
88 Port cannon breeches and magazine drum

89 Dinghy location – multi-seat "H" or "K" type in blow-out stowage
90 Flap (inner section)
91 Flap operating jack
92 Wing center/outer-section attachment point
93 Two 0.303in (7.7mm) machine guns
94 Flap (outer section)
95 Rear spar
96 Aileron control rod and linkage
97 Port aileron
98 Aileron trim tab
99 Port wingtip
100 Port navigation light (forward) and formation-keeping lamp (rear)
101 Front spar
102 Pitot head
103 Twin landing lights (port wing only)
104 Machine gun ports
105 Oil cooler
106 Port outer wing fuel tank
107 Mainwheel well
108 Engine bearers
109 Front spar/undercarriage attachment
110 Engine cooling flaps
111 Supercharger air intake
112 Engine mounting ring
113 Cowling nose ring
114 Non-feathering (early) or feathering constant-speed (late) propellers
115 Mainwheel leg
116 Port mainwheel
117 Retraction jack
118 Undercarriage door

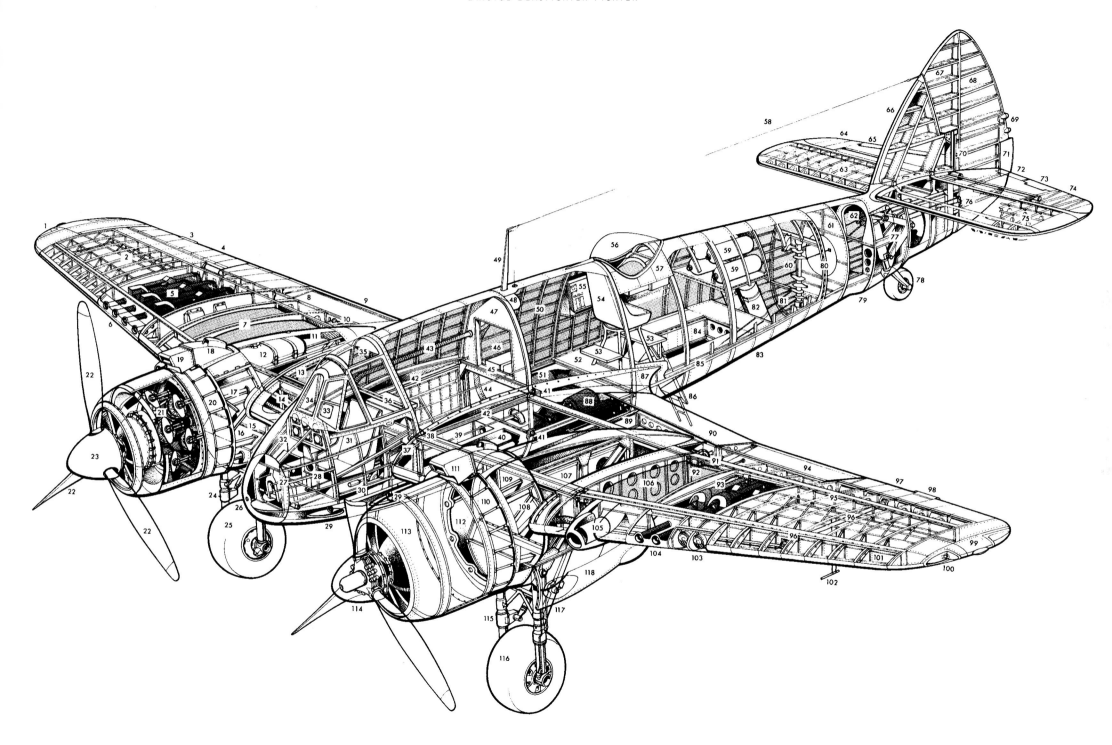

BAe/McDONNELL DOUGLAS AV-8B HARRIER II

LEFT: The final development of the Harrier is the BAe/McDonnell Douglas Harrier II Plus. The APG-65 multi-mode radar and AIM-120 Amraam missiles give it a true fighter capability. This USMC aircraft is shown leaving the USS *Peleliu* for Afghanistan.

The AV-8B Harrier II is a direct descendant of the British Hawker P.1127 that was first flown on October 21, 1960. This was developed into the Royal Air Force's Harrier which entered service as the world's first operational V/STOL (Vertical/Short Take Off and Landing) aircraft on April 1, 1969. It was built around the Rolls-Royce Pegasus engine, a large and powerful turbofan with four thrust-vectoring nozzles to power the aircraft in both vertical and horizontal regimes. As well as the RAF's Harrier, the evolving program spawned the Royal Navy's Sea Harrier FRS 1 (first flight August 20, 1978) which, optimized for the fleet air defense role, overcame theoretically superior Argentinean supersonic Mirages and Daggers in the Falklands War of 1982 (23 combat successes for no losses), and the F/A 2 (first flight September 19, 1989).

The U.S. Marine Corps, seeking organic air cover for amphibious operations, became interested in the project at an early stage and in the early 1970s ordered 102 single-seat Harriers as AV-8As, together with eight TAV-8A two-seat trainers, produced under license by McDonnell Douglas. The AV-8A Harrier was a strike aircraft that was designed to take off and land from either very short rough strips or even vertically from clearings or amphibious assault ships, which had previously been able to carry only helicopters. There was no need for any form of catapult that was required for all other fixed wing aircraft. The first AV-8A was delivered in 1971 and VMA-513 became the first squadron to receive them later that year.

In 1975 designs for the AV-8B emerged. Superficially similar to the AV-8A, this was actually a new aircraft, having a larger wing and with a cockpit that gave the pilot better all round visibility than its predecessor. With a new, more reliable engine and increased fuel capacity, greater ranges and ordnance carrying capabilities could be achieved. The AV-8B entered service in 1985 and features seven weapon stations plus two belly packs, one of which carries a 25mm cannon while the other houses the ammunition. Over 13,000lb of ordnance can be carried, including bombs, air-to-air and air-to-surface missiles and rockets, as well as external fuel tanks.

Improvements to the USMC AV-8s have resulted in remanufacture of the airframes to produce sub-variants optimized for specific roles. The Marines now fly four versions: the AV-8B Day Attack (DA) with Hughes ASB-19 Angle-Rate Bombing Set (ARBS); the AV-8B Night Attack (NA) with night-vision goggle compatible cockpit controls, Navigation Forward Looking Infra-red (NAVFLIR), plus the ARBS with laser spot tracker; the AV-8B Night Attack/Radar

(NA/R), also known as Harrier II Plus, with additional air-ground and air-to-air defense capabilities; and finally the TAV-8B trainer.

It was realized that the AV-8B's single cannon and two Sidewinder missiles afforded it marginal air defense capabilities, so a dedicated fighter version was created for the Marines as the AV-8B Harrier II Plus, first flying on September 22, 1992. It has the APG-65 radar as used on the Hornet, and typical air-to-air armament consists of up to six AIM-120 Amraams or two Amraams and four Sidewinders, while it can still double in the air-to-ground role. The Harrier II Plus serves with the Italian and Spanish navies as a fleet air defense fighter.

It is anticipated that versions of the AV-8 will remain in service until around 2015, by which time it will have been replaced by the Joint Strike Fighter.

Specifications for BAe/McDonnell Douglas AV-8B Harrier II Plus

Dimensions: wingspan 30 feet 4 inches, length 47 feet 9 inches, height 11 feet 8 inches

Power: one Rolls-Royce Pegasus F402-RR-408 twin-spool unaugmented turbofan with vectoring nozzles rated at 23,800lb thrust

Weights: empty 14,867lb, normal takeoff 23,650lb, max takeoff 31,000lb

Speed: max 674mph at sea level, 600mph at 30,000 feet

Ceiling: 45,000 feet

Range endurance two hours at 115 miles radius with six AAMs and two drop tanks:

Armament: one 25mm GAU-12 cannon with 300 rounds, six AIM-120 Amraam and two AIM-9 Sidewinder air-to-air missiles, plus a range of air-to-surface ordnance

Crew: pilot

AV-8B Harrier II cutaway key

1 Glass-fiber radome
2 Planar radar scanner
3 Scanner tracking mechanism
4 Radar mounting bulkhead
5 Forward-Looking Infra-Red (FLIR)
6 APG-65 radar equipment module
7 Forward pitch control reaction air nozzle
8 Pitot head, port and starboard
9 Cockpit front pressure bulkhead
10 Pitch feel unit and trim actuator
11 Yaw vane
12 Single-piece wrap-round windscreen
13 Instrument panel shroud
14 Rudder pedals
15 Underfloor avionics bay, air data computer and inertial navigation equipment
16 Electro-luminescent and covert night vision goggle (NVG) formation lighting strips
17 Control column
18 Engine throttle and nozzle angle control levers
19 Instrument panel with full-color multi-function CRT displays
20 Pilot's head-up display (HUD)
21 Sliding cockpit canopy with miniature detonating cord (MDC) emergency breaker
22 UPC/Stencil I lightweight ejection seat
23 Cockpit section framing, all-composite forward fuselage structure
24 Sloping seat mounting rear pressure bulkhead
25 Intake boundary layer separator
26 Port air intake
27 Landing/taxiing light
28 Levered suspension nosewheel, shortens on retraction
29 Intake suction relief doors, free-floating
30 Hydraulic nosewheel retraction jack
31 Hydraulic system accumulator
32 Demountable flight-refueling probe
33 Cockpit air-conditioning pack
34 Intake boundary layer air spill duct
35 Heat exchanger ram air intakes
36 Rolls-Royce F402-RR-408A Pegasus 11-61 turbofan engine
37 Full-authority digital engine control (FADEC) unit
38 Upper formation lighting strips
39 Accessory equipment gearbox
40 Alternator
41 Engine oil tank
42 Forward fuselage fuel tank
43 Hydraulic system ground connectors and engine monitoring and recording equipment

44 Fuselage lift-improvement device (LID), lateral strake
45 Forward zero-scarf (fan air) swiveling exhaust nozzle
46 Center fuselage fuel tank
47 Nozzle bearing
48 Gas turbine starter/ auxiliary power unit
49 Leading-edge root extension (LERX)
50 Wing center-section integral fuel tank
51 Wing center-section integral fuel tank
52 Starboard wing integral tank
53 Fuel feed and vent piping
54 Starboard weapons pylons
55 RWR antenna
56 Starboard navigation light
57 Roll control reaction air valve, upper and lower surface vents
58 Wingtip formation lights
59 Fuel jettison
60 Starboard aileron
61 Outrigger wheel fairing
62 Starboard outrigger wheel, retracted position
63 Slotted flap
64 Articulated flap vane
65 VHF/UHF antenna
66 Anti-collision beacon
67 De-mineralised water tank
68 Engine fire suppression bottle
69 Water filler
70 Rear fuselage fuel tank
71 Electrical system distribution panels, port and starboard
72 Chaff/flare launchers
73 Heat exchanger ram air intake
74 Rudder hydraulic actuator
75 Starboard all-moving tailplane
76 Formation lighting strip
77 Fin conventional light alloy structure
78 MAD compensator
79 Temperature probe
80 Broad-band communications antenna
81 Glass fiber fintip antenna fairing
82 Radar beacon antenna
83 Rudder
84 Honeycomb composite rudder structure
85 Yaw control reaction air valve, port and starboard nozzles
86 Rear RWR antennas
87 Rear pitch-control reaction air nozzle

88 Port all-moving tailplane
89 Carbon fiber composite multi-spar tailplane structure
90 Tail bumper
91 Lower broad-band communications antenna
92 Tailplane hydraulic actuator
93 Heat exchanger exhaust
94 Avionics equipment air-conditioning pack
95 Tailplane control cables
96 Conventional rear fuselage light alloy structure
97 Rear fuselage avionics equipment bay
98 Avionics bay access hatch, port and starboard
99 Formation lighting strip
100 Ventral airbrake panel
101 Airbrake hydraulic jack
102 Port slotted flap
103 Carbon fiber composite flap structure
104 Flap hydraulic jack
105 Exhaust nozzle shroud
106 Outboard flap hinge and interconnecting link
107 Port outrigger fairing
108 Port aileron
109 Aileron carbon-fiber composite structure
110 Fuel jettison
111 Port wingtip formation lights
112 Roll control reaction air valve, upper and lower surface vents
113 Port navigation light
114 RWR antenna
115 Port wing stores pylons
116 Port outrigger wheel
117 Pylon attachment hardpoints
118 Outer wing panel dry bay
119 Aileron hydraulic actuator
120 Outrigger wheel strut
121 Hydraulic retraction jack
122 Port wing integral fuel tank
123 Aileron control rod
124 Intermediate missile pylon
125 AIM-9L/M Sidewinder air-to-air missile
126 Missile launch rail
127 Wing leading-edge fence
128 Carbon fiber composite 'sine wave' multi-spar structure
129 Rear, hot steam, swiveling exhaust nozzle
130 Rear nozzle bleed-air cooled bearing housing

131 Hydraulic reservoir, dual system, port and starboard
132 Pressure refuelling connection and control panel
133 Reaction-control air ducting
134 Aft retracting twin-wheel main undercarriage
135 Inboard "wet" stores pylon
136 External fuel tank
137 Ventral gun pack, replaces fuselage LID strakes
138 Gun pneumatic drive unit
139 Ammunition cross-feed and link return chute
140 Ammunition magazine, 300 rounds
141 Retractable LID cross dam and hydraulic jack
142 Cannon muzzle aperture
143 Gun gas vent
144 Forward recoil mounting
145 GAU-12/U 25-mm five-barreled rotary cannon
146 Gun pack LID strake
147 AGM-65A Maverick, laser-guided air-to-surface missile
148 AIM-120 Amraam, air-to-air missile
149 CBU-89B Gator, submunition dispenser
150 Triple ejector rack
151 Mk 82 LDGP 500lb (227kg) bomb
152 Mk 82SE Snakeye, retarded bomb
153 AGM-84A-D Harpoon, air-to-surface anti-ship missile

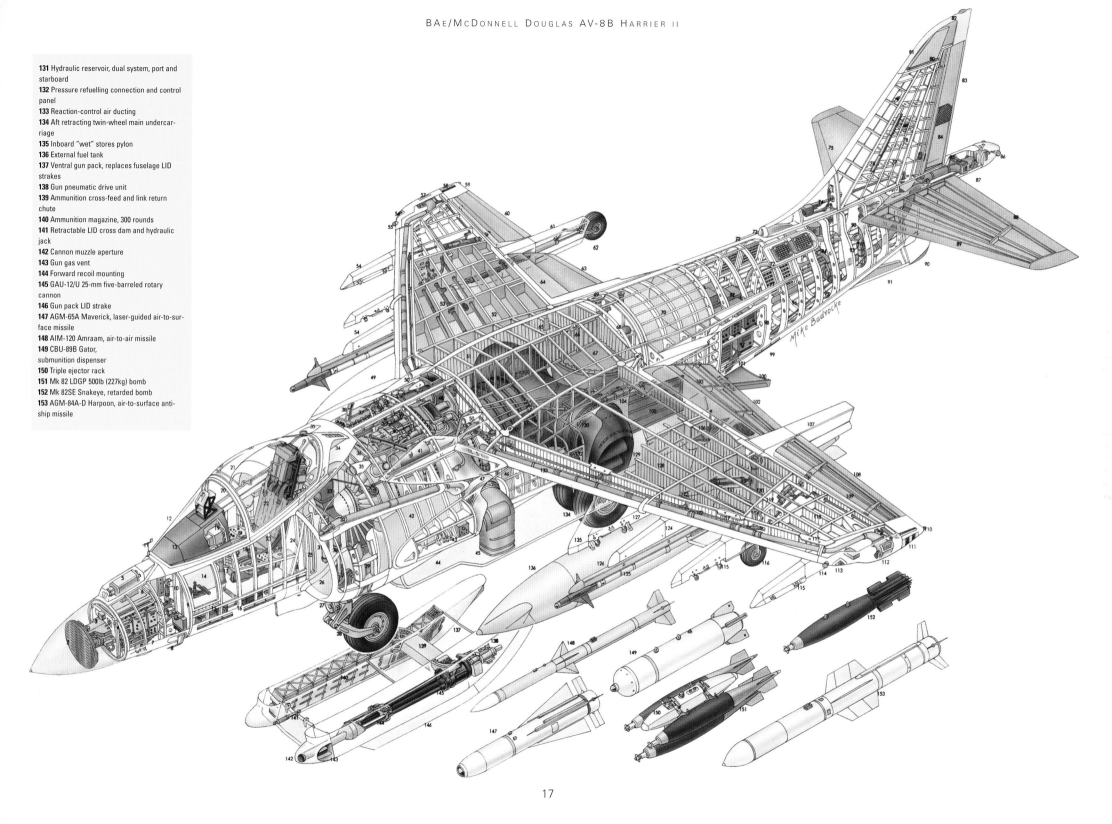

17

RIGHT: The Harrier II Plus was the first aircraft in service to feature "fly-by-light," rather than fly-by-wire, the control surfaces being commanded by light impulses via fiber optics.

ABOVE: About two-thirds of all US Marine Harrier II Plus were remanufactured from the AV-8B attack variant. Visually the main difference lies in the radome, which has been slightly bulged to hold the cropped APG-65 antenna.

RIGHT: The Harrier II Plus has been exported in small numbers to two countries, Spain and Italy. This is an Italian aircraft of the *Marina*, operating from the aircraft carrier *Giuseppe Garibaldi*.

CONVAIR F-102 DELTA DAGGER

The world's first supersonic all-weather jet interceptor to fly, the Convair F-102 Delta Dagger was the first delta-wing aircraft to become operational with the U.S. Air Force. Although it had a relatively short production life, the first prototype flying on October 24, 1953, and the last example, the 875th, rolling out in April 1958, the Delta Dagger had many claims to fame as well as its tail-less delta shape.

Marking perhaps the biggest jump in fighter history, it was also the first fighter to dispense completely with guns in favor of an all-missile armament, carrying six Falcon air-to-air missiles (usually three heat-homing and three radar-guided) in an internal bay – another first. In addition, it was the first fighter to be equipped with a semi-automatic interception system. In combat, once its electronic equipment had located the target (with the pilot positioning his head in a radar viewing hood, with one hand on the control column and the other on the radar control stick), the radar would guide the interceptor into position for attack and at the correct moment the electronic fire control system would automatically fire the air-to-air spin-stabilized rockets or missiles. Most of the fuselage ahead of the wing was filled with avionics, including the black boxes for the collision-course interception system.

The delta wing configuration offered a combination of light but rigid structure, a low thickness:chord ratio, large wing area for low wing loading, and plenty of room for internal fuel. But when the first YF-102 prototype flew, it displayed serious performance deficiencies, including poor handling and subsonic speed, and this led to a major redesign. This included a conical camber on the wing leading edge, a sharp-edged V-shape windshield, and the application of the "area rule" concept. This was a principle developed by NACA Langley's Richard Whitcomb to give it supersonic performance. Essentially, this required that a plot of cross-sectional area from nose to tail should be a smooth curve.

Alterations included adding almost 16 feet to the length of the fighter, making the triangular fin taller, and adding large fairings to the rear fuselage. Thus developed, the YF-102A reached Mach 1.2 on December 21, 1954.

The F-102A – popularly known as the "Deuce" – entered service with USAF Air Defense Command (ADC) from mid-1956, and toward the end of the 1950s, at the peak of its service, the interceptor was deployed with more than twenty-five ADC squadrons. The USAF also bought 111 TF-102s as combat trainers with side-by-side seating.

"Deuces" did not see much combat action. One was shot down by a MiG over Vietnam, and it is believed that Turkish and Greek F-102s clashed over Cyprus in 1974.

LEFT: The Convair F-102 Delta Dagger was the first fighter to abandon guns in favor of all-missile armament. Designed as a pure air defense interceptor, it entered service in mid-1956. This is the first YF-102A pre-production aircraft.

Specifications for Convair F-102A Delta Dagger

Dimensions:	wingspan 38 feet 1.5 inches, length 68 feet 4.67 inches, height 21 feet 2,5 inches
Power:	one Pratt & Whitney J57-P-23 two-spool afterburning turbo jet of 17,200lb maximum and 11,700lb military thrust
Weights:	empty 19,050lb, normal takeoff 27,765lb, max 31,500lb
Speed:	max Mach1.25 at 40,000 feet
Ceiling:	54,000 feet
Range:	1,350 miles (with external tanks)
Armament:	twenty-four Mighty Mouse 2.75in folding-fin unguided rockets in the weapons bay doors; six AIM-4 Falcon air-to-air missiles, three radar-guided, three heat-homing in an internal bay; later, two AIM-26B Nuclear Falcons or one AIM-26B and three AIM-4s
Crew:	pilot

F-102A cutaway key

1 Pitot head
2 Radome
3 Radar scanner
4 Scanner tracking mechanism
5 ILS glideslope aerial
6 Radar mounting bulkhead
7 Radar pulse generator and modulator units
8 Nose compartment access doors
9 Static port
10 Lower IFF aerial
11 Angle of attack transmitter
12 TACAN aerial
13 MG-10 fire control system electronics
14 Nose compartment longeron
15 Infra-red detector
16 Electronics cooling air duct
17 Windscreen panels
18 Central vision splitter
19 Instrument panel shroud
20 Rudder pedals and linkages
21 Cockpit front pressure bulkhead
22 Air-conditioning system ram air intake
23 Boundary layer splitter plate
24 Electrical system equipment
25 Port air intake
26 Nosewheel door
27 Taxiing lamp
28 Nosewheel, forward-retracting
29 Nose undercarriage leg strut
30 Torque scissor links
31 Intake duct framing
32 Nose undercarriage pivot mounting
33 Cockpit pressure floor
34 Port side console panel
35 Engine throttle lever
36 Two-handed control grip, radar and flight controls
37 Pilot's ejection seat
38 Canopy handle
39 Starboard side console panel
40 Radar display
41 Optical sight
42 Cockpit canopy cover, upward-hinging
43 Ejection seat headrest
44 Boundary layer spill duct
45 Sloping cockpit rear pressure bulkhead
46 Air-conditioning plant
47 Canopy external release
48 Canopy jack
49 Air exit louvers
50 Equipment bay access hatches, port and starboard

51 Canopy hinge
52 Radio and electronics equipment bay
53 Forward position light
54 Intake trunking
55 Missile bay cooling air duct
56 Missile bay door pneumatic jacks
57 Canopy emergency release
58 Liquid oxygen converter
59 Electrical system equipment bay
60 Fuselage upper longeron
61 Upper IFF aerial
62 Wing front spar attachment bulkhead
63 Pneumatic system air bottles
64 Bifurcated intake duct
65 Close-pitched fuselage frame construction
66 Engine bleed air duct
67 Anti-collision light
68 Starboard wing forward main fuel tank, total internal capacity 1,085 gallons
69 Inboard wing fence
70 Fuel system piping
71 Center-section wing dry bay
72 Wing pylon mountings and connectors
73 Starboard main undercarriage pivot mounting
74 Dorsal spine fairing
75 Intake duct mixing chamber
76 Engine intake centre-body fairing
77 Wing main spar attachment bulkheads
78 Intake compressor face
79 Forward engine mounting
80 Pratt & Whitney J57-P-23A afterburning turbojet engine
81 Engine oil tank, capacity 5.5 gallons
82 Oil filler cap
83 Starboard wing aft main fuel tanks
84 Fuel feed and vent piping
85 Ventral actuator fairing
86 Outboard wing fence
87 Cambered leading edge
88 Wing tip camber wash-out
89 Starboard navigation light
90 Fixed portion of trailing edge
91 Starboard outer elevon
92 Elevon hydraulic actuator

93 Trailing-edge dry bay
94 Fin leading-edge rib construction
95 Aerial tuning units
96 Fin attachment joints
97 Tailfin construction
98 Artificial feel system pitot intakes
99 Sloping front spar
100 Upper fin multi-spar construction
101 Fintip aerial fairing
102 UHF aerials
103 VOR localiser aerial
104 Rudder
105 Honeycomb core rudder construction
106 Split airbrake panels
107 Airbrake pneumatic jacks
108 Airbrake, open position
109 Variable-area afterburner exhaust nozzle
110 Aft fuselage aerodynamic (area-rule) fairing
111 Exhaust nozzle control jacks (eight)
112 Tailcone attachment joint frame (engine removal)
113 Rear position lights
114 Afterburner duct
115 Engine bay internal heat shield
116 Brake parachute housing
117 Rudder hydraulic actuator
118 Rudder trim and feel force control units
119 Afterburner fuel manifold
120 Rear engine mounting
121 Inboard elevon hydraulic actuator
122 Engine turbine section
123 Bleed air connections
124 Bleed air blow-off valve
125 Engine accessory equipment gearbox
126 Wing spar/fuselage frame pin joints
127 Wingroot rib
128 Port wing aft integral fuel tanks
129 Fuel tank dividing rib
130 Rear spar
131 Trailing-edge ribs
132 Runway emergency arrester hook, lowered
133 Elevon spar
134 Inboard elevon
135 Elevon rib construction
136 Outboard elevon

137 Trailing-edge honeycomb
138 Wingtip fairing construction
139 Port navigation light
140 Cambered leading-edge rib construction
141 Outboard wing fence
142 Wing rib construction
143 Main undercarriage mounting rib
144 Twin main spars
145 Main undercarriage side strut
146 Hydraulic retraction jack
147 Main undercarriage leg pivot mounting
148 Drag strut and pneumatic brake reservoir
149 Landing lamp
150 Port wing dry bay
151 Wing pylon mountings and connectors
152 Main undercarriage leg door
153 Port mainwheel
154 Torque scissor links
155 Port wing forward integral fuel tank
156 Inboard wing fence
157 Mainwheel door
158 Hydraulic reservoirs
159 Position of ram air turbine on starboard side
160 Missile bay aft section doors
161 Retractable over-run barrier probe
162 Wing front spar
163 Port missile bay doors
164 Pantographic action missile displacement
gear
165 Displacement gear hydraulic jack
166 Missile launch rail
167 Missile bay door integral rocket launch
tubes
168 Center missile bay door
169 2.75in (70mm) FFAR folding-fin rockets (24)
170 AIM-4D Falcon air-to-air missile (6)
171 Port wing fuel tank pylon
172 215-gallon external fuel tank

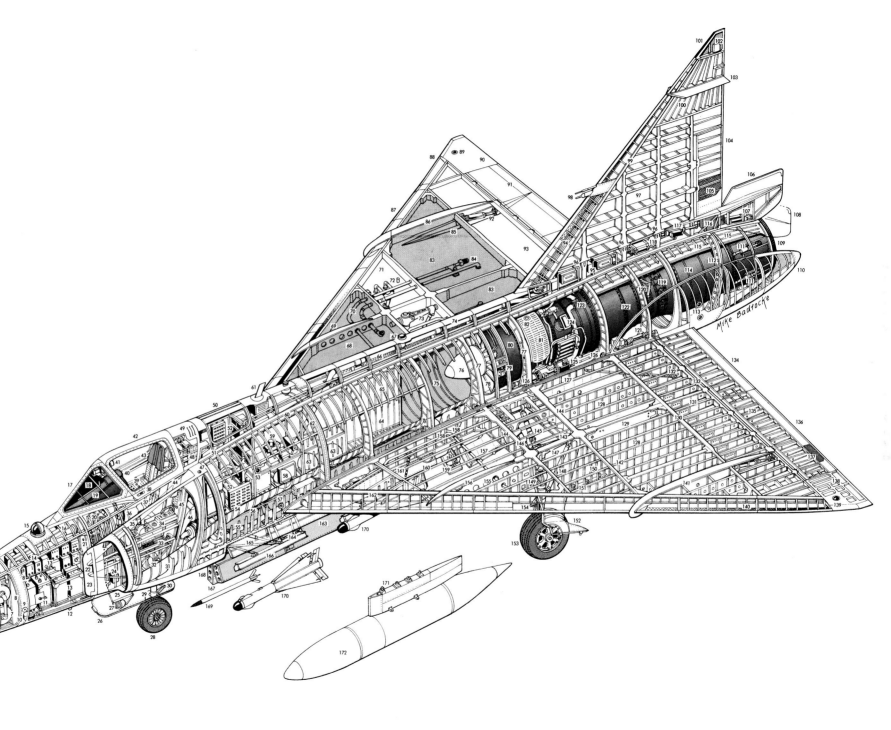

CONVAIR F-106 DELTA DART

The F-106 Delta Dart was a development of the Delta Dagger, being initiated as the F-102B and later redesignated. The first trials aircraft flew on December 26, 1956, and the type entered service with the USAF Air Defense Command in July 1959, with initial operating capability occurring in October 1960. The "Six," as it became known, was nearly twice as fast as the F-102 "Deuce" and it completely met the requirements of Air Defense Command for a manned interceptor to defend the continental United States. It was linked via its complex and bulky Hughes MA-1 electronic fire-control system through a digital data link into the nationwide SAGE (Semi-Automatic Ground Environment) system, which included autopilot.

With this system the F-106 could be flown by computer through most of its mission, the pilot being required only for takeoff, landing, or in case of a malfunction with the system. During the automated intercept, the MA-1 would take over control of the interceptor shortly after takeoff and guide it to the proper altitude and attack position, where the fire-control system would lock on and fire the F-106 weapons at the target intruder. The pilot used a Tactical Situation Display (TSD), also called Tactical Display Indicator (TDI), located low on the instrument panel, with which to observe this entire intercept. The TSD would use map projections and small symbols, one for the Delta Dart, the other for the enemy aircraft, to represent the intercept mission.

The F-106 incorporated a delta wing with a cambered leading edge extending from wing root to wing tip and swept tail surface, with control surfaces power-operated. Significant changes over the F-102 included a redesigned fuselage from which the Deuce's fairings were removed, a broad-chord and flat-topped fin, and inlets set behind the cockpit.

Armament, which could be fired manually or automatically, was located in a bay in the bottom of the fuselage. Two AIM-4F plus two AIM-4G Falcon air-to-air missiles were extended below this section for firing and the two AIR-2A or AIR-2G Genie unguided nuclear-tipped missiles were ejected from the bay by an explosive charge. This array was supplemented from 1973 by a return to the gun – a 20mm M-61 multi-barrel rotary cannon, in a neat installation in the missile bay, causing a slight ventral bulge.

Apart from the gun, there were several other upgrades during the Delta Dart's service life, including improved avionics, a highly sensitive infrared sensor facing ahead for detecting heat from hostile aircraft and assisting the lock-on of missiles, and a flight-refueling boom receptacle.

Total production, which was completed in July 1961, was made up of 277 single-seat F-106As and 63 two-seat F-106B armed trainers, which were fully combat-capable. The aircraft remained in USAF Air National Guard service until August 1988, being finally replaced by the F-15 Eagle and F-16 Fighting Falcon. At least one flew with NASA on storm hazard research, while from 1986 some 194 F-106A/Bs were taken out of mothballs and converted to QF-106 target drones, which flew their final mission on January 28, 1998.

Specifications for Convair F-106 Delta Dart

Dimensions:	wingspan 38 feet 3.5 inches, length 70 feet 8.75 inches, height 20 feet 3.67 inches
Power:	one Pratt & Whitney J75-P-17 two-spool afterburning turbo jet rated at 24,500lb maximum and 17,200lb military thrust
Weights:	empty 24, 315lb, normal takeoff 35,000lb, maximum 39,915lb
Speed:	max Mach 2.01 at altitude
Ceiling:	57,000 feet
Range:	combat radius (without external fuel) 575 miles
Armament:	four AIM-4 Falcon air-to-air missiles and two AIR-2 Genie AAMs with nuclear warheads in an internal weapons bay, plus one 20mm M-61 multi-barrel rotary cannon
Crew:	pilot

LEFT: The Delta Dart retained the tail-less delta configuration of the Delta Dagger: from this angle only the rearward location of the engine inlets and the absence of the Yellow Canary fuselage fairings distinguish the F-106 from its F-102 predecessor.

F-106A Delta Dart cutaway key

1 Pitot head
2 Radome
3 Radar scanner dish
4 Radar tracking mechanism
5 Hughes MA-1 weapons system radar unit
6 Radar mounting bulkhead
7 Pulse generator units
8 TACAN aerial
9 Angle of attack transmitter
10 MA-1 weapons system electronics units
11 Electronics bay access door
12 Infra-red detector fairing
13 Retractable infra-red detector
14 Knife-edged windscreen panels
15 Central vision splitter
16 Instrument panel shroud
17 "Head down" tactical display panel
18 Canopy external release
19 Rudder pedals
20 Cockpit front pressure bulkhead
21 Electrical relay panel
22 Nose undercarriage wheel bay
23 Nosewheel door
24 Taxiing lamp
25 Twin nosewheels
26 Torque scissor links
27 UHF aerial
28 Nose undercarriage leg strut
29 Oxygen filler point and gauge
30 Nosewheel leg pivot fixing
31 Liquid oxygen converter
32 Cockpit air-conditioning ducting
33 Cockpit pressure floor
34 Control column
35 Two-handed control grip, radar and flight controls
36 Engine throttle lever
37 Pilot's ejection seat
38 Radar display
39 Optical sight
40 Cockpit canopy cover
41 Ejection seat headrest
42 Ejection seat launch rails
43 Cockpit rear pressure bulkhead
44 Side console panel
45 Ground power supply connections
46 Doppler navigation unit
47 Aft lower electronics compartment
48 Aft upper electronics equipment bays, port and starboard
49 Electronics bay door
50 Cockpit rear decking
51 Over pressurisation relief valve

52 Canopy pneumatic jack
53 Canopy hinge
54 Air exit louvers
55 Starboard engine air intake
56 Fuel tank access panel
57 Upper longeron
58 Fuselage fuel tank, total internal capacity, 1,514 gallons
59 Fuselage frame construction
60 Ventral weapons bay
61 Missile pallet hinge arms
62 Bottom longeron
63 Boundary layer splitter plate
64 Port engine air intake
65 Variable area intake ramp
66 Ramp bleed air louvers
67 Air-conditioning system intake duct
68 Intake duct framing
69 Starboard side pressure refueling connection
70 Forward missile pallet pneumatic jack
71 Air-conditioning plant
72 De-icing fluid reservoir
73 Heat exchanger air exit duct
74 Air refueling ramp door, open
75 Pneumatic system air bottles
76 Bifurcated intake ducting
77 Aft missile pylon pneumatic jacks
78 AIR-2 Genie air-to-air missile housing
79 Hydraulic accumulators
80 Hydraulic reservoirs, duplex systems
81 Intake trunking
82 Wing spar attachment fuselage main frames
83 Oil cooler air duct
84 Intake center-body fairing
85 Engine intake compressor face
86 Bleed air ducting
87 Dorsal spine fairing
88 Fuel boost pump
89 Starboard main undercarriage pivot fixing
90 Wing forward fuel tank
91 Dry bay
92 Wing pylon mountings and connectors
93 Fuel system piping
94 Starboard wing main fuel tank
95 Leading-edge slot

96 Cambered leading edge
97 Wingtip fairing
98 Starboard navigation light
99 Outboard elevon
100 Elevon hydraulic jack
101 Elevon jack ventral fairing
102 Inboard elevon
103 Starboard wing aft fuel tank
104 Fuel system vent piping
105 Engine oil tank, 45 gallons
106 Pratt & Whitney J75-P-17 turbojet engine
107 Forward engine mounting
108 Ventral accessory equipment compartment
109 Cooling air ducting
110 Wing and fin spar attachment main frame
111 Inboard elevon hydraulic jack
112 Engine turbine section
113 Exhaust pipe heat shroud
114 Rear engine mounting
115 Aerial tuning units
116 Artificial feel system pitot intakes
117 Fin leading edge
118 Tailfin construction
119 Air-to-air identification (AAI) aerial
120 Fin tip aerial fairing
121 UHF/TACAN aerial
122 Tail navigation light
123 Rudder
124 Rudder honeycomb construction
125 Split air brake panels
126 Airbrake pneumatic jacks
127 Brake parachute housing
128 Rudder hydraulic jack
129 Rudder trim and feel force control units
130 Air brake, open position
131 Divergent exhaust nozzle
132 Variable-area afterburner exhaust nozzle
133 Detachable tailcone (engine removal)
134 Afterburner nozzle control jacks
135 Afterburner ducting
136 Sloping fin mounting bulkheads
137 Afterburner fuel spray manifold
138 Engine withdrawal rail
139 Port inboard elevon
140 Runway emergency arresting hook, lowered
141 Port outboard elevon

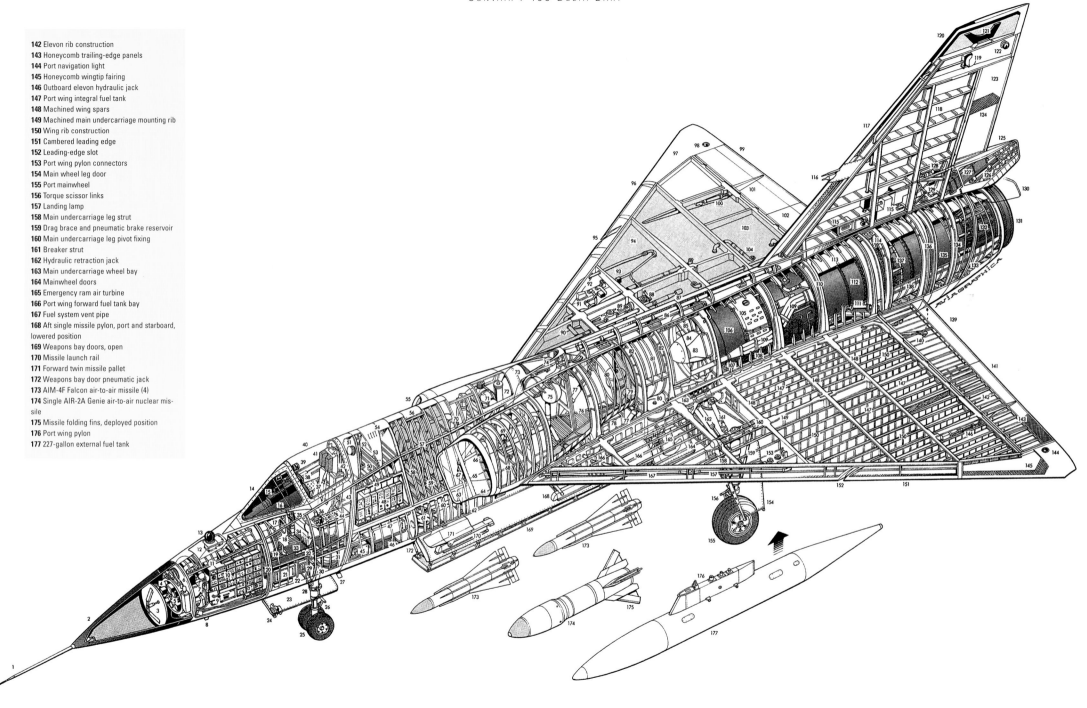

142 Elevon rib construction
143 Honeycomb trailing-edge panels
144 Port navigation light
145 Honeycomb wingtip fairing
146 Outboard elevon hydraulic jack
147 Port wing integral fuel tank
148 Machined wing spars
149 Machined main undercarriage mounting rib
150 Wing rib construction
151 Cambered leading edge
152 Leading-edge slot
153 Port wing pylon connectors
154 Main wheel leg door
155 Port mainwheel
156 Torque scissor links
157 Landing lamp
158 Main undercarriage leg strut
159 Drag brace and pneumatic brake reservoir
160 Main undercarriage leg pivot fixing
161 Breaker strut
162 Hydraulic retraction jack
163 Main undercarriage wheel bay
164 Mainwheel doors
165 Emergency ram air turbine
166 Port wing forward fuel tank bay
167 Fuel system vent pipe
168 Aft single missile pylon, port and starboard, lowered position
169 Weapons bay doors, open
170 Missile launch rail
171 Forward twin missile pallet
172 Weapons bay door pneumatic jack
173 AIM-4F Falcon air-to-air missile (4)
174 Single AIR-2A Genie air-to-air nuclear missile
175 Missile folding fins, deployed position
176 Port wing pylon
177 227-gallon external fuel tank

OPPOSITE: A broad-chord fin with a cropped tip is another external difference between the F-102A and F-106A. Aerodynamic and propulsion advances made the Six a far more potent bird than the Deuce, which it started to replace from July 1959.

BELOW: A Six launches what appears to be an AIR-2 Genie unguided nuclear air-to-air missile, presumably with a dummy warhead. The Genie was armed with a lanyard, which sometimes made results rather interesting.

LEFT: Only 340 F-106s were built, of which 63 were F-106B two-seater conversion trainers which however retained full combat capability. With a cannon added to the missiles, the Six remained in service until August 1988.

RIGHT: The racks of black boxes that gave the Delta Dart its automatic interception capability, plus weaponry. In the front is a Nuclear Falcon; on one side three AIM-4 Falcons, two IR and one radar-homing, with a Genie on the other side.

DASSAULT MIRAGE III

LEFT: Dassault's Mirage IIIC was a response to the Cold War threat of the fast, high-flying, nuclear-armed bomber. The tailless delta configuration offered low wing loading, low supersonic drag, and structural simplicity.

The Dassault Mirage III has been a great success in terms of sales to the French air Force, l'Armée de l'Air, and to export customers, and also in combat, particularly in the Middle East where it built its reputation fighting for Israel in the Arab-Israeli Wars of the 1960s and '70s, scoring heavily against Russian-built aircraft flown by admittedly less-well-trained Arab pilots.

The Mirage started life as the MD 550 Mirage I, originally called Mystere-Delta, that was designed to meet requirements of a 1954 specification for a small, all-weather interceptor fighter that could reach 59,000 feet in just six minutes and sustain a speed of more than Mach 1 in level flight. Dassault chose the tail-less delta configuration, which offered low wave drag with good fuel volume, while permitting traditional construction methods. There were penalties with pure delta geometry, however, including the fact that with no tail, no trailing edge flaps could be fitted, so that approach speeds were high and landing performance was relatively poor. In addition, sustained turn was compromised by high induced drag resulting from low aspect ratio, and excessive trim drag also adversely affected maneuverability.

The Mystere-Delta first flew on June 25, 1955, and after some alterations it became the Mirage I, which attained Mach 1.3 in level flight on December 17, 1956. It was decided that this was too small to carry an effective mix of armament and fuel for combat, so a slightly larger version, a Mirage II, with more powerful engines, was mooted, but this proposal was discarded in favor of the even larger Mirage III design. This was an enlarged development of the Mirage I, and was some 30 percent heavier, but had much more powerful engines (9,700lb thrust each with afterburning, compared to the Mirage I's pair of turbojets rated at 2,160 thrust each with afterburning supplemented by a 3,307lb thrust rocket motor). The prototype first flew on November 17, 1956, and over the next couple of months reached a speed of Mach 1.52; fitted with a rocket motor, and altered slightly in other respects, it reached a speed of Mach 1.8.

Testing and development continued through the late 1950s with Mirage IIIAs, and then the derived Mirage IIIB two-seat trainer and Mirage IIIC interceptor fighter went into production, and service entry with l'Armée de l'Air began in July 1961, with exports starting almost immediately.

That same year saw the first flights of prototypes of a further version, the Mirage IIIE multi-role aircraft that was again successful around the world. With the emphasis on strike capability, the Mirage IIIE had an extension to the forward fuselage which allowed for enlargement of the avionics bay behind the cockpit; it carried dual-role radar. First deliveries to l'Armée de l'Air occurred in January 1964, while versions were license-built by Australia (Mirage IIIO) and Switzerland (Mirage IIIS).

Israel produced its own un-licensed version, the Neshr, when France put an embargo on deliveries of Mirages to that nation in never-ending conflict. They were essentially Mirage 5s (Mirage IIIs with a longer nose) fitted with home-built engines and avionics. Deliveries to the Israeli Air Force began in 1971, and some 61 were produced, including two two-seat versions. Israel Aircraft Industries also created the Kfir by fitting the license-built General Electric J79 engine into a Mirage airframe, but it was longer and heavier than the Mirage IIIC. It was first flown in October 1970, and underwent various development stages, one of which (the Kfir C 2 onwards) saw the installation of nose strakes, dogtooth wing leading edges, and canard foreplanes. Some Kfirs even served with U.S. forces – with the Navy and Marine Corps as aggressor aircraft in pilot air combat training.

Specifications for Dassault Mirage IIIC

Dimensions:	wingspan 27 feet, length 48 feet 4 inches, height 13 feet 11.5 inches
Power:	one SNECMA Atar 9B twin-spool turbojet rated at 13,320lb maximum and 9,460lb military thrust, plus optional 3,307lb thrust SEPR 84 rocket motor
Weights:	empty 13,040lb, normal takeoff 19,000lb, max 21,444lb
Speed:	max Mach 2.15 at altitude, Mach 1.14 at sea level
Ceiling:	54,137 feet (without rocket motor)
Range:	operational radius (internal fuel only) 180 miles
Armament:	two 30mm DEFA 552 cannon with 125 rounds per gun (without rocket motor fitted); one Matra R 511 or R 530 air-to-air missile; two R 550 Magic, Shafrir or Sidewinder missiles
Crew:	pilot

Mirage IIIE cutaway key

1 Glass-fiber fintip aerial fairing
2 VHF aerial
3 Tail navigation and anti-collision lights
4 Tail radar warning antenna
5 Rudder construction
6 Fin main spar
7 Passive radar antenna
8 UHF aerial
9 Rudder hydraulic actuator
10 Magnetic detector
11 Parachute release link
12 Brake parachute housing
13 Parachute fairing
14 Exhaust nozzle shroud
15 Variable-area exhaust nozzle flaps
16 Nozzle jacks
17 Cooling air louvers
18 Jet pipe
19 Rear fuselage frame and stringer construction
20 Wingroot trailing-edge fillet
21 Fin attachment main frame
22 Fin spar attachment joint
23 Control cable runs
24 Engine bay/jet pipe thermal lining
25 Afterburner duct
26 Elevon compensator hydraulic jack
27 Ventral fuel tank
28 Main engine mounting
29 Wing spar/fuselage main frame
30 Main spar joint
31 Engine gearbox driven generator
32 Engine accessory compartment
33 SNECMA Atar 9C afterburning turbojet
34 Cooling system air intakes
35 Heat exchanger
36 Engine oil tank
37 IFF aerial
38 Port wing integral fuel tank, total internal capacity 879.6 gallons
39 Inboard elevon
40 Outboard elevon
41 Port navigation light
42 Cambered leading-edge ribs
43 Port wing pylon fixing
44 Leading-edge notch
45 Port leading-edge fuel tank
46 Main undercarriage pivot fixing
47 Fuselage dorsal systems ducting
48 Air system piping
49 Turbojet intake
50 Engine starter housing
51 Fuselage fuel tanks
52 Equipment cooling system air filter
53 Computer system voltage regulator
54 Oxygen bottles
55 Inverted flight fuel system accumulator
56 Intake ducting
57 Matra 530 missile computer
58 VHF radio transmitter/receiver
59 Gyro platform multiplier
60 Doppler transceiver
61 Navigation system computer
62 Air data computer
63 Nord missile encoding supply
64 Radio altimeter transceiver
65 Heading and inertial correction computer
66 Armament junction box
67 Radar program controller
68 Canopy external release
69 Canopy hinge
70 Radio and electronics bay access fairing
71 Fuel tank stabilising fins
72 343.2-gallon auxiliary fuel tank (448.8-gallon alternative)
73 164.4-gallon drop tank
74 Cockpit canopy cover
75 Canopy hydraulic jack
76 Ejection seat headrest
77 Face blind firing handle
78 Martin-Baker (Hispano license) RM4 ejection seat
79 Port side console panel
80 Canopy framing
81 Pilot's head-up display
82 Windscreen panels
83 Instrument panel shroud
84 Instrument pressure sensors
85 Thomson-CSF Cyrano II fire control radar
86 Radar scanner dish
87 Glass-fiber radome
88 Pitot tube
89 Matra 530 air-to-air missile
90 Doppler radar fairing
91 Thomson-CSF Doppler navigation radar antenna
92 Cockpit front pressure bulkhead
93 Rudder pedals
94 Radar scope (head-down display)
95 Control column
96 Cockpit floor level
97 Starboard side console panel
98 Nosewheel leg doors
99 Nose undercarriage leg strut
100 Landing/taxiing lamps
101 Levered suspension axle unit
102 Nosewheel
103 Shimmy damper
104 Hydraulic retraction strut
105 Cockpit rear pressure bulkhead
106 Air-conditioning ram air intake
107 Movable intake half-cone center-body
108 Starboard air intake
109 Nosewheel well door (open position)
110 Intake center-body screw jack
111 Air-conditioning plant
112 Boundary layer bleed air duct
113 Center fuselage bomb rack
114 882lb (400kg) HE bombs
115 Cannon barrels
116 30mm DEFA cannon (2), 250 rounds per gun
117 Ventral gun pack
118 Auxiliary air intake door
119 Electrical system servicing panel
120 Starboard 30mm DEFA cannon
121 Front spar attachment joint
122 Fuel system piping
123 Airbrake hydraulic jack
124 Starboard airbrake, upper and lower surfaces (open position)
125 Airbrake housing
126 Starboard leading-edge fuel tank
127 AS37 Martel, radar-guided air-to-ground missile
128 Nord AS30 air-to-air missile
129 Starboard mainwheel
130 Mainwheel leg door
131 Torque scissor links
132 Shock absorber leg strut
133 Starboard main undercarriage pivot fixing
134 Hydraulic retraction jack
135 Main undercarriage hydraulic accumulator
136 Wing main spar
137 Fuel system piping
138 Inboard pylon fixing
139 Leading-edge notch

140 Starboard inner stores pylon
141 Control rod runs
142 Missile launch rail
143 AIM-9 Sidewinder air-to-air missile
144 JL-100 fuel and rocket pack, 66 gallons of fuel plus 18 x 68mm unguided rockets
145 Outboard wing pylon
146 Outboard pylon fixing

147 Front spar
148 Starboard navigation light
149 Outboard elevon hydraulic jack
150 Starboard wing integral fuel tank
151 Inboard elevon hydraulic actuator
152 Wing multi-spar and rib construction
153 Rear spar
154 Outboard elevon construction

155 Inboard elevon construction
156 Elevon compensator
157 132-gallon auxiliary fuel tanks

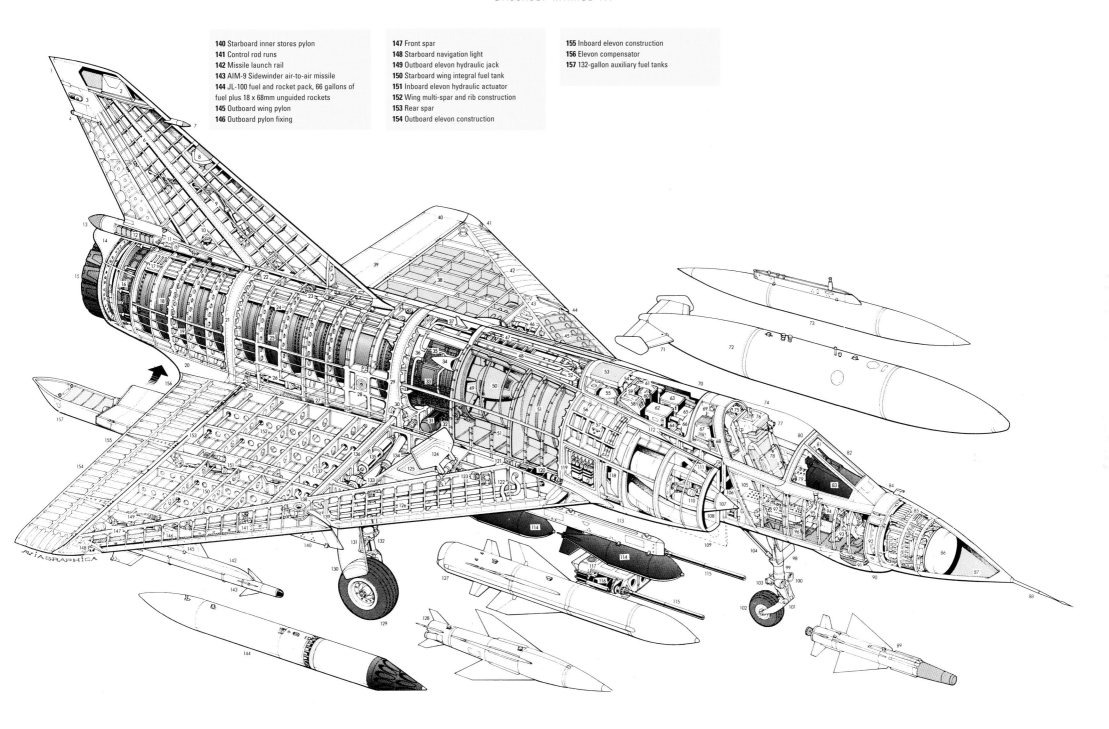

MAIN PICTURE: Success in Israeli service in the Six Day War of 1967 saw various Mirage III exports boom, with over 20 nations operating the type. This factory-fresh Mirage IIIEL was one of a small batch bought by Lebanon, but little used.

LEFT: This is the Mirage IIIEX. Offered as an affordable attack fighter in 1989, it features a basic range-only radar in a fined-down nose, a flight refueling probe, and canard surfaces on the intake ducts.

MAIN PICTURE: The 5/50 series were essentially Mirage IIIs, with downgraded avionics. Intended primarily for export, they had varying degrees of success. But the Mirage IIING (Nouvelle Génération) launched in 1983, found no takers.

BELOW: The Mirage IIIE was conceived as a multi-role aircraft with the emphasis on attack. For this it was given improved avionics, including dual-role radar, and a Doppler navigation system, the housing for which can be seen under the nose.

DASSAULT MIRAGE F1

Left: Dassault turned to an orthodox layout for the Mirage F1 to get away from the failings of the tail-less delta - its high takeoff and landing speeds, and its tendency to bleed off speed in hard turns at an alarming rate.

When the French company Dassault designed a replacement for the Mirage III it moved away from the tail-less delta concept, with its attendant problems of excessive takeoff and landing speeds, unsatisfactory ride qualities at high speeds and low altitudes and maneuvering shortcomings. Instead, Dassault reverted to a more conventional arrangement of moderately swept, shoulder-mounted wing trimmed by a horizontal tail, with all-moving, low-set horizontal tail surfaces and twin ventral fins beneath the tail. Although the F1 had virtually nothing in common with the Mirage III, the company decided to retain the name "Mirage" for the new warplane.

Dassault received a contract early in 1964 to develop the III's successor with emphasis on the low-altitude penetration role, and the F2 emerged as a single prototype of a tandem two-seat aircraft that first flew on June 12, 1966. While flight trials continued, work had begun on a single-seat version, the F3, but revised l'Armée de l'Air requirements resulted in interest focussing on a scaled-down and simplified version of the basic design, the Mirage F1, that the French company had been developing alongside the F2 as a private venture. The first of three pre-series aircraft flew on March 20, 1969, and later that year Dassault received the initial production order from l'Armée de l'Air for what was designated F1C which, with emphasis on the all-weather intercept mission, became the standard French fighter before the Mirage 2000 entered service.

Although the F1C's wing loading was much more than on the Mirage III - almost double - the potential adverse effects of this in handling and performance were overcome by high-lift devices and double-slotted trailing edge slats. Consequently, the F1C could out-turn the Mirage III, suffering less speed loss, and also approach speed was much reduced compared to that of the III - from 210mph for the delta-wing fighter down to 160mph for the F1C.

L'Armée de l'Air ordered 161 Mirage F1C interceptors, plus 20 two-seat trainers (F1B) and 64 reconnaissance (F1CR) aircraft. Initial operational capability was achieved in 1974. From 1979, some of these aircraft were retroactively modified to, or delivered in, F1C-200 standard with a 3.15-inch plug in the slender fuselage to accommodate a removable flight-refueling probe.

The basic Mirage F1 was popular in export markets and, apart from the F1C, was offered in variants including F1A (with simplified avionics) and F1E multi-role air-superiority/ground attack/recce versions. Customers were Ecuador, Greece, Iraq, Jordan, Kuwait, Libya, Morocco, Qatar, South Africa, and Spain. Production ended in 1990,

with 731 of all types built, although the following year work began on adapting 30 F1C-200 aircraft as F1CT ground attack fighters.

Mirage F1s were involved in air combat in the 1980s during the Iran/Iraq War, and later in the Gulf War of 1991, but they were no match for Coalition fighters. South Africa, which purchased 32 F1AZs and 16 F1CZs, flew them against Angola.

Specifications for Dassault Mirage F1C

Dimensions: wingspan 27 feet 6.75 inches, length 50 feet 2.5 inches, height 14 feet 9 inches

Power: one SNECMA Atar 9K50 two-stage turbojet rated at 15,873lb maximum and 11,060lb military thrust

Weights: empty 16,315lb, normal takeoff 25,353lb, max 35,714lb

Speed: max Mach 2.2 at 39,372 feet, Mach 1.2 at sea level

Ceiling: 65,620 feet

Range: combat air patrol endurance (armed with two Super 530 AAMs and ventral tank) 2.25 hours

Armament: two 30mm DEFA 553 cannon with 135 rounds per gun; two Matra Super 530F SARH and two Matra R 550 Magic IR air-to-air missiles

Crew: pilot

Mirage F1CT cutaway key

1 Pitot head
2 Glass-fiber radome
3 Radar scanner housing
4 Inflight-refuelling probe
5 Dynamic pressure sensor
6 Thomson-CSF Cyrano IVMR radar equipment module
7 Incidence probe
8 TMV 630A laser rangefinder
9 Rudder pedals
10 Control column
11 Instrument panel shroud
12 Windscreen panels
13 Thomson VE120 head-up display
14 Upward-hinging cockpit canopy cover
15 Martin-Baker F10M zero-zero ejection seat
16 Engine throttle lever
17 Side console panel
18 Nose undercarriage hydraulic retraction jack
19 Twin nosewheels, aft-retracting
20 Hydraulic steering mechanism
21 TACAN aerial
22 Cockpit sloping rear pressure bulkhead
23 Canopy jack
24 Canopy emergency release
25 Central intake control actuator
26 Movable half-cone intake center-body
27 Port air intake
28 Air-conditioning equipment bay
29 Intake center-body screw jack
30 Intake suction relief door
31 Pressure refueling connection
32 Port airbrake panel
33 Airbrake hydraulic jack
34 Retractable landing lamp
35 Forward fuselage integral fuel tank
36 Boundary layer spill duct
37 Avionics equipment bay
38 Power amplifier
39 Strobe light (white) and anti-collision beacon (red)
40 Fuel system inverted flight accumulator
41 30mm DEFA cannon, starboard side only
42 Ammunition magazine, 135 rounds
43 External fuel tank
44 Starboard wing integral fuel tank
45 Forged steel wing attachment fitting
46 Inboard pylon attachment hardpoint
47 MATRA-Philips Phimat chaff/flare pod

48 Leading-edge flap
49 Starboard navigation light
50 Wingtip missile launch rail
51 MATRA Magic air-to-air missile
52 Starboard aileron
53 Two-segment double-slotted flaps
54 Spoiler panel (open)
55 Wing panel attachment machined fuselage main frame
56 Fuel system filters
57 Engine intake center-body/starter housing
58 Wing panel attachment pin joints
59 Engine accessory equipment gearbox
60 SNECMA Atar 9K-50 afterburning engine
61 Engine bleed air pre-cooler
62 Rear spar attachment joint
63 Rear fuselage integral fuel tank
64 Engine turbine section
65 Engine bay thermal lining
66 Fin spar attachment joint
67 Starboard all-moving tailplane
68 Forward SHERLOC ECM antenna fairing
69 UHF antenna
70 VOR aerial
71 Fin-tip aerial fairing
72 IFF/VHF 1 aerial
73 Rear navigation light and anti-collision beacon
74 Aft SHERLOC ECM antenna
75 Rudder
76 Rudder hydraulic actuator
77 Rudder trim actuator
78 VHF 2 aerial
79 Brake parachute housing
80 Variable-area afterburner nozzle
81 Nozzle control jacks
82 Port all-moving tailplane
83 Honeycomb trailing-edge panel
84 Multi-spar tailplane construction
85 Tailplane pivot fitting
86 Tailplane hydraulic actuator
87 Autopilot controller
88 Port ventral fin
89 Inboard double-slotted flap segment

90 Flap hydraulic jack
91 Spoiler hydraulic jack
92 Port spoiler housing and actuating linkage
93 Port aileron hydraulic actuator
94 Outboard double-slotted flap segment
95 Port aileron
96 Wingtip missile interface unit
97 Port navigation light
98 Leading-edge flap
99 Port MATRA Magic air-to-air missile
100 68mm rocket projectile
101 MATRA 18-round rocket launcher
102 Thomson-CSF ECM pod
103 Outer pylon attachment hardpoint
104 Wing panel multi-spar construction
105 Port wing integral fuel tank
106 Main undercarriage hydraulic retraction jack
107 Shock absorber strut
108 Twin mainwheels
109 Levered suspension axle
110 Mainwheel leg strut and leg rotating linkage
111 Leading-edge flap hydraulic jack
112 Main undercarriage wheel bay
113 Port ammunition bay, unused
114 Center fuselage weapon pylon
115 881lb (400kg) HE bombs
116 Underwing MATRA-Corral conformal chaff/flare dispenser
117 Multiple bomb-carrier
118 Thomson-Brandt BAP-100 runway-cratering bomb or BAT-120 area denial/anti-armor munition
119 MATRA Belouga submunition dispenser
120 MATRA Durandal retarded concrete-piercing bomb

DASSAULT MIRAGE 2000

LEFT: The Mirage 2000 at first appeared to be a retrograde step, but advances in technology, specifically relaxed stability and fly-by-wire, had made it possible to overcome the worst faults of the tail-less delta. This is the -5 variant.

When Dassault designed the single-seat, single-engined air superiority and multi-role fighter Mirage 2000 in the early 1970s the company reverted to the tail-less delta planform featured on the Mirage III. France's air force, l'Armée de l'Air, had announced a requirement for an avion de combat futur (ACF), which came to be called the Super Mirage, which was to be a twin-engined, very agile Mach 3 fighter that could climb higher than 59,000 feet with a large multi-mode radar and with the performance of the U.S. F-15 Eagle, to counter the Russian MiG-25 Foxbat. However, Dassault soon realized this posed insurmountable technical difficulties, and was also unaffordable, so in 1972 began development studies for a simpler, more lightweight fighter and, when the ACF was inevitably canceled in 1975, the basic concept of the alternative proposal was ready and waiting, and l'Armée de l'Air wrote their revised requirement around it.

The tail-less delta offers low wing loading, low thickness:chord ratio for supersonic flight, simplicity and relative lightness of weight, as well as ample space for fuel. The drawbacks of the delta planform – including excessive take-off and landing speeds, the need for long runways, poor ride at high speeds and low altitudes, rapid bleed-off of energy during hard maneuvering – have been largely overcome in the Mirage 2000 by moving the center of gravity aft to give relaxed stability, using computer-controlled fly-by-wire, and a variable camber wing. The latter is formed by a combination of full-span leading edge slats and two-piece trailing edge elevons, permitting safe operation up to high angles of attack, as when landing and maneuvering. The fuselage is shaped like a tube with a pointed nose and a large exhaust that protrudes beyond the tail. The wings are mounted low on the fuselage, and the fin is swept back. There are semi-circular air intakes on the fuselage forward of the wings, and small strakes on the outside of the intakes that produce vortices to clean up the airflow over the wings.

The first prototype flew on March 10, 1978, with that of a two-seat conversion trainer following on October 11, 1980. Powered by a 19,840lb thrust SNECMA M53-5 afterburning single-spool turbofan, more appropriately described as a continuous bleed turbojet optimized for high speed at high altitude, the first production Mirage 2000C took to the air on November 20, 1982. Later production aircraft have been fitted with the improved M53-P2 power-plant rated at 21,400lb maximum and 14,400lb military thrust. Deliveries to l'Armée de l'Air commenced in 1983 and initial operational capability was achieved in 1984.

A family of variants followed, including the Mirage 2000N two-seat penetrator optimized for nuclear strike; the Mirage 2000E multi-role export variant; the two-seat, all-weather, day and night, air-to-surface attack Mirage 2000D; and trainer and recce versions.

An advanced "glass cockpit" (with five multi-function display screens) was installed in 1991, as well as hands-on-throttle-and-stick (HOTAS) pilot controls. Together with other upgrades, particularly regarding radar and avionics, this gave the Mirage 2000-5 multi-role fighter, and later came the 2000-9, with improved avionics.

Dassault has always fielded an aggressive sales force, and the Mirage 2000 was a hot machine that attracted many export orders, including those from Abu Dhabi, Egypt, Greece, India, Peru, Qatar, Taiwan, and the United Arab Emirates.

Specifications for Dassault Mirage 2000C

Dimensions:	wingspan 29 feet 11 inches, length 47 feet 1.5 inches, height 17 feet 1 inches
Power:	one SNECMA M53-P2 single-spool low-bypass afterburning turbofan rated at 21,400lb max and 14,400lb military thrust
Weights:	empty 16,535lb, normal takeoff 25,928lb, max 37,478lb
Speed:	max Mach 2.2 at altitude, Mach 1.2 at sea level
Ceiling:	59,000 feet
Range:	interception radius (with external fuel tanks) 435 miles
Armament:	two 30mm DEFA 554 cannon with 125 rounds per gun; two Matra Super 530D and two R550 Magic air-to-air missiles, or four MICA and two Magic AAMs, or up to eight MICA
Crew:	pilot

Mirage 2000C cutaway key

1 Pitot tube
2 Glass fiber radome
3 Flat-plate radar scanner
4 Thomson-CSF RDM multi-role radar unit (initial production aircraft)
5 Cassegrain monopulse planar antenna
6 Thomson-CSF RDI pulse-Doppler radar unit (later production aircraft)
7 Radar altimeter aerial
8 Angle-of-attack probe
9 Front pressure bulkhead
10 Instrument pitot heads
11 Temperature probe
12 Fixed inflight refueling probe
13 Frameless windscreen panel
14 Instrument panel shroud
15 Static ports
16 Rudder pedals
17 Low-voltage formation light strip
18 VHF aerial
19 Nosewheel jack door
20 Hydraulic retraction jack
21 Nose landing gear leg strut
22 Twin nosewheels
23 Towing bracket
24 Torque scissor links
25 Landing/taxiing lamps
26 Nosewheel steering jacks
27 Nose landing gear leg doors
28 Cockpit flooring
29 Centre instrument console
30 Control column
31 Pilot's head-up display (HUD)
32 Canopy arch
33 Cockpit canopy cover
34 Starboard air intake
35 Ejection seat headrest
36 Safety harness
37 Martin-Baker Mk 10 zero-zero ejection seat
38 Engine throttle control and airbrake switch
39 Port side console panel
40 Nosewheel bay
41 Cannon muzzle blast trough
42 Electrical equipment bay
43 Port air intake
44 Intake half-cone center body
45 Air-conditioning system ram air intake
46 Cockpit rear pressure bulkhead
47 Canopy emergency release handle
48 Hydraulic canopy jack
49 Canopy hinge point
50 Starboard intake strake
51 IFF aerial

52 Radio and electronics bay
53 Boundary layer bleed air duct
54 Air-conditioning plant
55 Intake center-body screw jack
56 Cannon muzzle
57 Pressure refueling connection
58 Port intake strake
59 Intake suction relief doors (above and below)
60 DEFA 554 30mm cannon
61 Cannon ammunition box
62 Forward fuselage integral fuel tanks
63 Radio and electronics equipment
64 Fuel system equipment
65 Anti-collision light
66 Air system pre-cooler
67 Air exit louvers
68 Starboard wing integral fuel tank, total internal fuel capacity 1,003 gallons
69 Wing pylon attachment hardpoints
70 Leading-edge slat hydraulic drive motor and control shaft
71 Slat screw jacks
72 Slat guide rails
73 Starboard wing automatic leading-edge slats
74 Matra 550 Magic "dogfight" AAM
75 Missile launch rail
76 Outboard wing pylon
77 Radar warning antenna
78 Starboard navigation light
79 Outboard elevon
80 Elevon ventral hinge fairings
81 Flight control system access panels
82 Elevon hydraulic jacks
83 Engine intake by-pass air spill duct
84 Engine compressor face
85 Hydraulic accumulator
86 Micro turbo auxiliary power unit
87 Main landing gear wheel bay
88 Hydraulic pump
89 Alternator, port and starboard
90 Accessory gearbox
91 Engine transmission unit and drive shaft
92 Machined fuselage main frames
93 SNECMA M53-5 afterburning turbofan
94 Engine igniter unit
95 Electronic engine control unit

96 Bleed air ducting
97 Engine bleed air blow-off valve spill duct
98 Fin root fillet construction
99 Leading-edge ribs
100 Boron/epoxy/ carbon honeycomb sandwich fin skin panels
101 Tail low-voltage formation light strip
102 ECM aerial fairing
103 VOR aerial
104 Dielectric fin tip fairing
105 VHF aerial
106 Tail navigation light
107 Tail radar warning antenna
108 Honeycomb rudder construction
109 Rudder hinge
110 Fin spar attachment joints
111 Rudder hydraulic jack
112 Engine bay thermal lining
113 ECM equipment housing
114 Variable-area afterburner exhaust nozzle
115 Tailpipe sealing flaps
116 Fueldraulic nozzle control jacks
117 Afterburner tailpipe
118 Engine withdrawal rail
119 Wing root extended trailing-edge fillet
120 Ventral brake parachute housing
121 Rear engine mounting main frame
122 Runway emergency arrester hook
123 Port inboard elevon
124 Elevon honeycomb construction
125 Carbon fiber skin panels
126 Elevon hydraulic control jacks
127 Fly-by-wire electronic system command units
128 Outboard elevon
129 Elevon tip construction
130 Port navigation light
131 Radar warning antenna
132 Outboard automatic leading-edge slat
133 Outboard wing pylon attachment hardpoints
134 Machined upper-and lower-wing skin/stringer panels
135 Port wing integral fuel tank
136 Wing rib construction
137 Rear fuselage/ wingroot fairing integral fuel tank
138 Wing spar attachment joints

139 Main spars
140 Landing gear hydraulic retraction jack
141 Main landing gear leg pivot fixing
142 Inboard pylon attachment hardpoints
143 Port airbrakes (open) above and beneath wing
144 Airbrake hydraulic jack
145 Main landing gear leg strut
146 Leading-edge slat hydraulic drive motor
147 Mainwheel leg door
148 Port mainwheel
149 Slat guide rails
150 Screw jacks
151 Auxiliary spar
152 Wing front spar
153 Front spar attachment joint
154 Inboard automatic leading edge slat rib construction
155 4,489-gallon auxiliary fuel tank (fuselage centerline or wing inboard stations)
156 MATRA Super 530 medium-range AAM
157 Missile launch rail
158 Inboard wing pylon

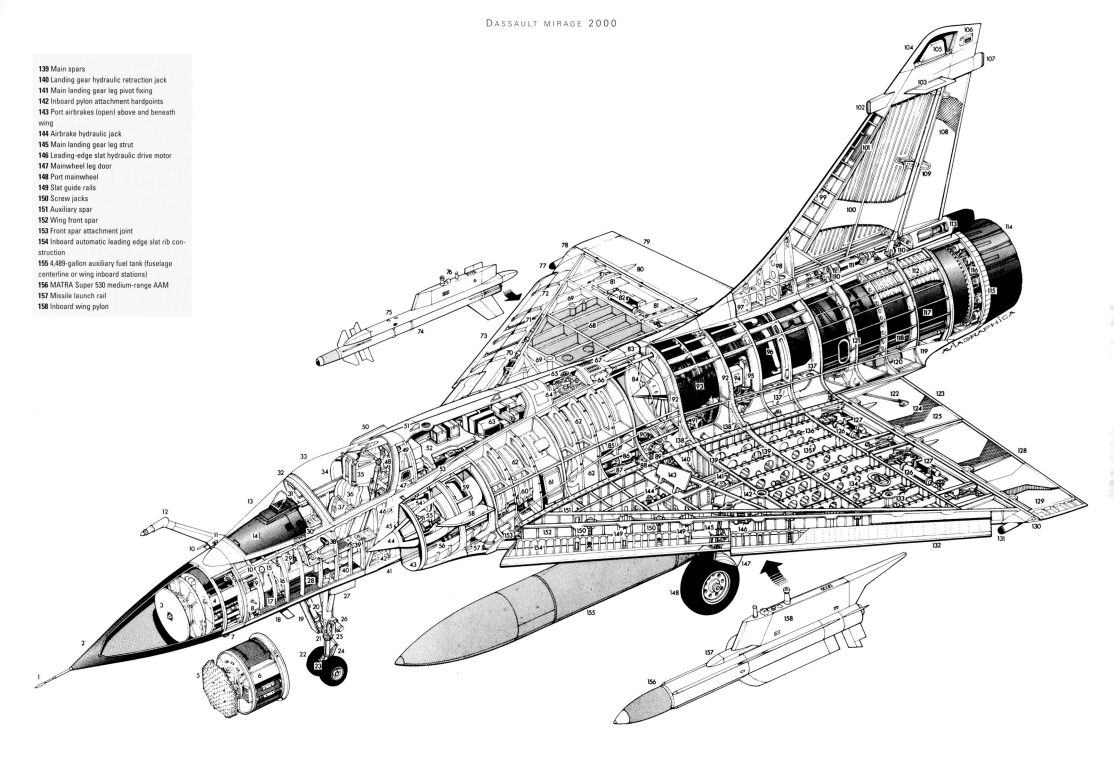

ABOVE: The Mirage 2000N is a two-seat, low-level, high-speed interdiction aircraft, optimized to carry the nuclear-tipped ASMP missile. For night and adverse weather operations, it is fitted with Antilope terrain-following radar.

RIGHT: Two Mirage 2000Es and a two-seater Mirage 2000D of the United Arab Emirates (Abu Dhabi) air force. The huge long range fuel tanks hold almost 450 gallons each. One can be carried under each wing, and a third on the centerline.

OPPOSITE LEFT: Loaded for air combat, this Taiwanese Mirage 2000-5 carries a mix of four MICA medium range and two Magic short range air-to-air missiles, in addition to twin 30mm DEFA 554 cannon. Amraam and Sidewinders are another option.

OPPOSITE RIGHT: Even with three huge external tanks, this *Armée de l'Air* Mirage 2000-5 succeeds in toting five missiles with apparent ease. This apart, the Mirage 2000-5 was the first French fighter to have a "glass" cockpit.

DE HAVILLAND VAMPIRE

LEFT: The second British jet fighter to enter service (in 1946), the de Havilland Vampire was slower, if far more maneuverable, than the twin-engined Gloster Meteor. Armed with rockets, this is the FB 5 close support variant.

The de Havilland Vampire was Britain's second jet fighter designed for service with the Royal Air Force, the first having been the Gloster Meteor. Although it arrived too late to see action in World War II, it was a truly significant design – the first RAF fighter to exceed 500mph, the first jet to cross the Atlantic under its own power, and the first jet to take off from and land on an aircraft carrier. It was one of the most aerobatic jet fighters ever to see service, with outstandingly light and sensitive controls, and noteworthy for its remarkable maneuverability.

Initially known as the Spider Crab, the single-seat D. H. 100 Vampire day fighter was essentially built around the Halford-designed H-1 turbojet, later produced as the Goblin by de Havilland. This had a single-sided centrifugal compressor, an arrangement that, soon after the war, gave way to axial-flow powerplants that were slimmer. A twin-boom configuration was decided upon, the turbojet and the cockpit being mounted in a short central nacelle. Air was drawn from wing root intakes and exhausted between the tail-booms. Thrust losses were minimized by keeping intake ducts and tailpipe as short as possible, and tail surfaces were mounted on booms high above the jet efflux. The front fuselage was of plywood and balsa construction, drawing on de Havilland's wide experience with the Mosquito, the rest of the aircraft being metal.

First flight of an unarmed prototype occurred on September 20, 1943, with Geoffrey de Havilland, Jr, at the controls, followed by two further prototypes, one of which had the definitive armament of four 20mm cannon in the front fuselage. The RAF placed its order on May 13, 1944, and first deliveries of 288 Vampire F Mk 1 production aircraft began the following April. As always intended, the cockpit was pressurized, from the 51st aircraft. The first 41 aircraft had the 2,700lb Goblin 1 turbojet, but this was then replaced by the 3,100lb Goblin 2. The F Mk 3 superseded the F Mk 1, first flying on November 4, 1946, with a redesigned tail and increased interior fuel plus the capability of carrying drop tanks, to meet demands for greater endurance. Some 209 of this version were built in the UK, and 80 similar F Mk 30s in Australia. The main variants that followed were the FB 5 (the most proliferous of all Vampires), FB 6, and FB 9, all optimized as fighter bombers. In addition to well over 1,000 built in the UK for the RAF, several hundred were built for (or license-built by) many other countries, including Australia, Canada, Ceylon, Dominica, Egypt, Finland, France, India, Iraq, Italy, Jordan, Lebanon, Mexico, New Zealand, Norway, Rhodesia, South Africa, Sweden, Switzerland, and Venezuela. Over 3,265 of

all types were built.

Following successful carrier trials in December 1945 with two navalized Vampire F 1s, Britain's Royal Navy ordered 30 Sea Vampire F 20s based on the FB 5, with larger flaps and speed brakes, plus tailhooks on A-frames. They served mainly in a training role to give Fleet Air Arm pilots experience with jet aircraft.

In 1949 a side-by-side two-seat version of the Vampire Mk 5, the D. H. 113, was developed as a company-funded night fighter intended mainly for export. It featured a cockpit from the Mosquito NF Mks 30 and 36. It was designated Vampire NF Mk 10, and 78 were delivered to the RAF, including 15 intended for Egypt but not delivered because of an embargo, as well as 29 subsequently refurbished and sold to India and 14 sold to Italy.

Specifications for de Havilland Vampire F 3

Dimensions:	wingspan 40 feet, length 30 feet 9 inches, height 6 feet 3 inches
Power:	one de Havilland Goblin 1 centrifugal flow turbojet rated at 3,100lb
Weights:	empty 7,134lb, normal takeoff 8,578lb, max 12,170lb
Speed:	max 505mph at 30,000ft, 531mph at sea level
Ceiling:	40,000 feet
Range:	1,145 miles with drop tanks
Armament:	four 20mm Hispano cannon with 150 rounds per gun
Crew:	pilot

Vampire FB.Mk 5 cutaway key

1 Ciné camera port
2 Cockpit fresh air intake
3 Nosewheel leg door
4 Pivoted axle nosewheel suspension
5 Anti-shimmy nosewheel tire
6 Nose undercarriage leg strut
7 Nosewheel door
8 Cannon muzzle blast trough
9 Nosewheel hydraulic jack
10 Nose undercarriage pivot fixing
11 Radio
12 Gun camera
13 Windscreen fluid de-icing reservoir
14 Armored instrument access panel
15 Cockpit front bulkhead
16 Rudder pedals
17 Cockpit floor level
18 Nosewheel housing
19 Instrument panel
20 Reflector gunsight
21 Windscreen panels
22 Side console switch panel
23 Control column
24 Engine throttle
25 Tailplane trim handwheel
26 Undercarriage and flap selector levers
27 Control linkage
28 Cannon barrels beneath cockpit floor
29 Pull-out boarding step
30 Control system cable compensator
31 Emergency hydraulic handpump
32 Pilot's seat
33 Safety harness
34 Sliding canopy rails
35 Cockpit heater
36 Sliding canopy cover
37 Pilot's head and back armor
38 Hydraulic system reservoir
39 Radio equipment bay
40 Ammunition tanks (150 rounds per gun)
41 Plywood/balsa/plywood fuselage skinning
42 Boundary layer splitter
43 Port engine air intake
44 Ventral gun bay (4 x 20mm Hispano cannon)
45 Spent cartridge case and link ejector chute
46 Cannon bay access panel
47 Cockpit heating and pressurising intake
48 Intake ducting
49 Fuselage/front spar attachment joint
50 Fuselage/main spar attachment joint
51 Engine bay fire wall
52 Fuselage fuel tank (total internal system capacity 480 gallons)
53 Fuel filler cap
54 Wooden skin section fabric covering
55 Cockpit air heat exchanger
56 Engine bearer struts
57 de Havilland Goblin DGn 2 centrifugal-flow turbojet
58 Cabin blower
59 Engine accessories
60 Engine bay access panels
61 Starboard wingroot fuel tank
62 Starboard main undercarriage, retracted position
63 Leading-edge fuel tank
64 Starboard drop tank (134.4 gallons)
65 Drop tank pylon
66 Starboard wing fuel tanks
67 Fuel filler cap
68 Gyrosyn compass remote transmitter
69 Starboard navigation light
70 Wingtip fairing
71 Starboard aileron
72 Aileron mass balance weights
73 Trim tab
74 Aileron hinge control
75 Starboard trailing-edge airbrake segment (open)
76 Airbrake hydraulic jack
77 Starboard outer split trailing-edge flap
78 Inboard split trailing-edge flap
79 Engine flame tubes
80 Jet pipe heat shroud
81 Gun heater duct
82 Tailcone framing
83 Jet exhaust nozzle
84 Starboard tail boom
85 Control cable access panels
86 Tailplane bullet fairing
87 Tailplane construction
88 Starboard fin
89 Rudder mass balance
90 Starboard rudder
91 Rudder trim tab
92 Elevator construction
93 Ventral elevator mass balance weights
94 Elevator tab
95 Pitot tube
96 Port fin construction
97 Port rudder
98 Rudder trim tab
99 Tail navigation light
100 Rudder and elevator hinge controls
101 Tail bumper
102 Fin/tailplane attachment joint
103 Tailplane bullet fairing
104 Control cable runs
105 Tailboom frame and stringer construction
106 Radio aerial mast
107 Tailboom skinning
108 Tailboom attachment ring joint
109 Trailing-edge root fillet
110 Port inboard split trailing-edge flap
111 Flap interconnection
112 Hydraulic flap jack
113 False rear spar
114 Flap shroud ribs
115 Port outboard split trailing-edge flap
116 Rotating trailing-edge segment airbrake, open
117 Aileron tab
118 Port aileron construction
119 Aileron mass balance weights
120 Retractable landing/taxiing lamp
121 Wingrib and stringer construction
122 Wingtip fairing
123 Port navigation light
124 Leading-edge nose ribs
125 Fuel filler cap
126 Port wing main fuel tanks
127 Fuel tank interconnection
128 Pylon attachment rib
129 Port 112-Imp gal (509-litre) drop tank
130 Drop tank pylon

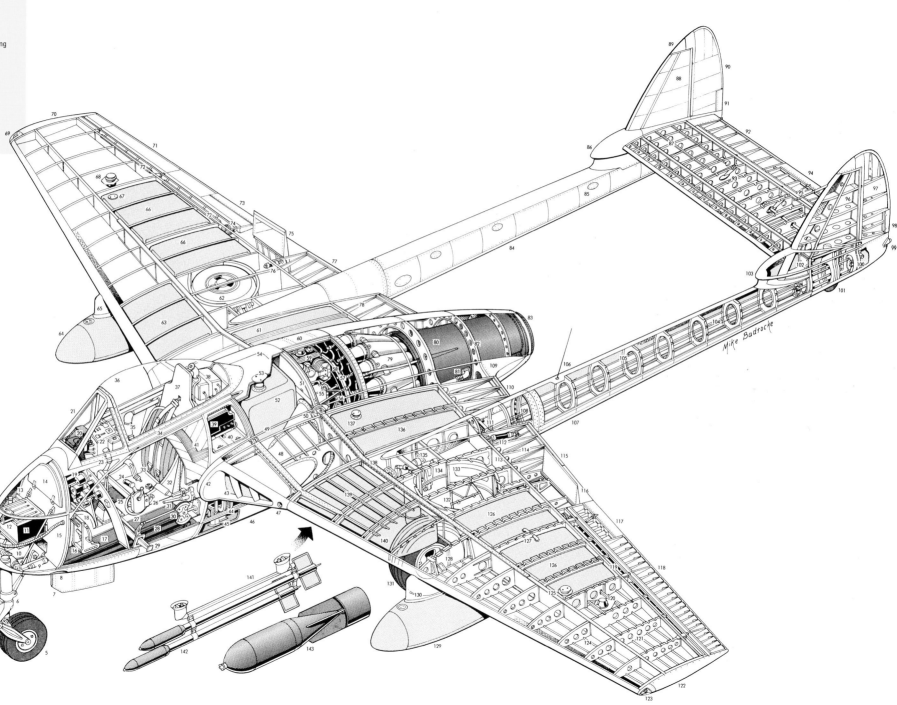

DEWOITINE D 520

Left: The Dewoitine D 520 first flew in October 1938. It was the best French fighter of the early period of World War II, claiming 108 German and Italian aircraft shot down before the Armistice. It was flown by Vichy France, Bulgaria, Italy and Romania later in the war.

Undoubtedly the best French fighter of World War II, the single-seat, single-engined Dewoitine D 520 proved itself markedly more maneuverable than its main opponent, the Messerschmitt Bf 109, although it was well beaten by the German fighter in level speed and low-altitude climb. It was superior to France's main fighter, the Morane-Saulnier M.S. 406, but the French aviation industry had for some years been slow to react to international competition and the growing German threat, in both design and manufacture. The low-wing monoplane D 520, while restoring French fighter design to international standards, was still undergoing unduly protracted gestation at the hands of sluggish industrial progress.

The aircraft had been proposed to meet a June 1936 specification. Two prototypes had been ordered on April 3, 1938, and these flew on October 2, 1938, and January 28, 1939, respectively, joined by a third on May 5 of that year. An initial production order for 200 had been placed on March 14, and a further 510 by July 11. But not one example had come off the production lines when the war began in Europe in September 1939. While deliveries began on January 14, 1940, only 437 had been completed by the time the Armistice was signed by France and Germany just over six months later, on June 22. Delivery schedules were adversely affected by technical problems, including inadequate engine cooling and a poor pneumatic machine gun control system.

The D 520 was designed by Emile Dewoitine in collaboration with Robert Castello and Jaques Henrat. Small but aerodynamically refined, it was of all-metal stressed-skin monocoque construction with a monospar wing. Emphasis on manufacturing economy was achieved by minimizing machine parts and sub-assemblies, and stressing component interchangeability. It had an inline engine, was capable of 320mph, and was armed with a single 20mm cannon and four wing machine guns. In the air, while it was maneuverable and admirable in the dive, performance deficiencies included lack of damping in yaw, oversensitivity to turbulence and abrupt use of the throttle, and a tendency to ground loop.

Although the pilots of l'Armée de l'Air were not familiar with their D 520s they put up as good a fight as possible against German and Italian aircraft with the 403 that had been delivered complete prior to the capitulation. Some reports claimed 147 combat successes for the loss of 85 aircraft and 44 pilots.

With German authorization, production resumed in Vichy France, the first of these D 520s being flown on July 26, 1941. Before and during the German occupation of Vichy France, a further 478 D 520s were built, of which 150 were delivered to Romania and 96 to Bulgaria, with others being used by the *Luftwaffe* for pilot training. Italy's *Regia Aeronautica* acquired a further 72, and exchanged 30 with Germany for captured LeO 451 bombers. The Allies captured some, painted out the German insignia and equipped a *Forces Françaises l'Interieur* unit with them until Spitfires became available on March 1, 1945.

Specifications for Dewoitine D 520

Dimensions: wingspan 33 feet 5.5 inches, length 28 feet 2.6 inches, height 8 feet 5.1 inches

Power: one 935hp Hispano-Suiza HS 12Y45 liquid-cooled vee-12 engine

Weights: empty 4,686lb, normal takeoff 5,909lb (with wing tanks empty), max 6,152lb

Speed: 332mph at 18,000 feet, 264mph at sea level

Ceiling: 33,630 feet

Range: 957 miles with full internal fuel

Armament: one engine-mounted 20mm Hispano-Suiza HS 404 drum-fed cannon with 60 rounds, plus four wing-mounted belt-fed 1934-M39 MAC machine guns with 675 rounds per gun

Crew: pilot

Dewoitine D 520 cutaway key

1 Cannon port
2 Spinner
3 Three-blade Ratier Electric propeller
4 Cannon barrel blast tube
5 Coolant water tank
6 Safety vent
7 Cowling forward frame
8 Auxiliary intake
9 Chin intake
10 Coolant piping
11 Oil cooler intake
12 Intake duct
13 Oil radiator
14 Engine bearer frames
15 Engine accessories
16 Exhaust stubs
17 Hispano-Suiza 12Y45 engine
18 Cowling rear frame
19 Cannon ammunition drum (60 rounds)
20 Oil tank
21 Starboard wing fuel tank
22 Wing skinning
23 Starboard navigation light
24 Starboard aileron
25 Aileron hinge
26 Emergency ring and bead gunsight
27 Fuselage main fuel tank
28 Fuselage main frame upper member
29 Engine bearer upper attachment
30 Bulkhead
31 20mm HS 404 cannon breech
32 Compressor outlet
33 Extinguisher
34 Szydlowski compressor
35 Engine bearer support frame
36 Wing root fairing
37 Starboard mainwheel
38 Port mainwheel well
39 Ventral radiator bath intake
40 Undercarriage retraction mechanism
41 Mainwheel leg pivot
42 Wing machine gun blast tubes
43 Machine-gun ports
44 Mainwheel leg
45 Port mainwheel
46 Mainwheel cover
47 Mainwheel leg door
48 Port wing fuel tank
49 Wing nose ribs
50 Pitot head
51 Port navigation light
52 Wingtip
53 Port aileron frame

54 Aileron hinge
55 Wing rear false spar
56 Wing skinning
57 Wing ribs
58 Two 7.5mm MAC 1934 machine guns
59 Ammunition feed
60 Wing main spar
61 Ammunition boxes (675rpg)
62 Gun hot air
63 Radiator bath
64 Cowling flap inboard profile
65 Radiator outlet flap
66 Port wing flap
67 Retractable radio aerial
68 Wing root fairing
69 Fuselage main frame lower member
70 Wing flap control linkage
71 Rudder pedal bar
72 Instrument panel
73 Command radio receiver
74 Control column grip
75 HF receiver
76 Windscreen
77 OPL RX 39 gunsight
78 Canopy track
79 Pilot's seat
80 Seat adjustment lever
81 Seat mounting frame
82 Tailplane incidence adjustment handwheel
83 Ventral antenna actuation jack
84 Oxygen cylinder
85 Fuselage frame
86 Tailplane incidence cable
87 Oleo reservoirs (2)
88 Sliding canopy (open)
89 Radio equipment (Radio-Industrie 537)
90 Aft canopy fixed glazing
91 Radio relay/lead-in
92 Transmitter antenna (fixed)
93 Dorsal decking
94 Fuselage frames
95 Stringers
96 Equipment/baggage compartment door
97 Compressed air cylinders
98 Elevator control linkage
99 Elevator cables

100 Lift point
101 Rudder cables
102 Fuselage main frame/tailfin spar attachment
103 Tailplane root fairing
104 Fuselage frame
105 Rudder linkage
106 Tailwheel shock absorber
107 Fixed tailwheel
108 Rudder lower hinge
109 Tailplane structure
110 Port elevator frame
111 Rudder tab hinge fairing
112 Rudder tab
113 Elevator control horn
114 Elevator torque tube
115 Tailplane attachment
116 Rudder frame
117 Rudder post
118 Tailfin structure
119 Tailfin front spar
120 Starboard tailplane
121 Tailfin leading-edge
122 Tail navigation light
123 Rudder internal balance
124 Rudder upper hing

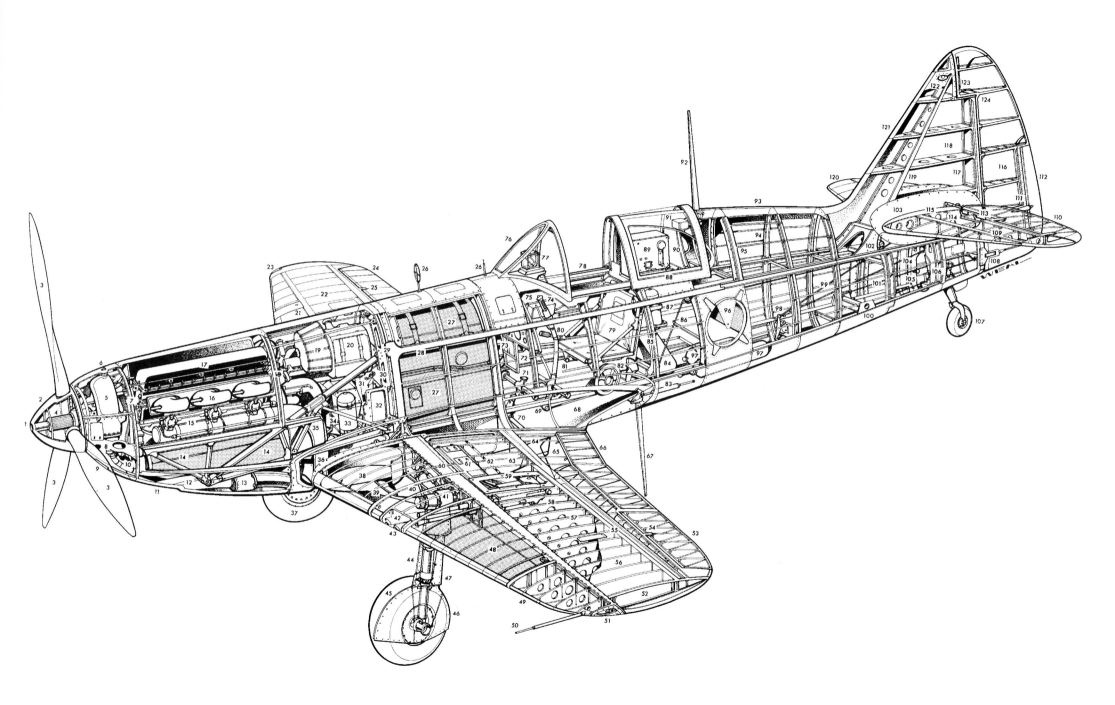

DOUGLAS F3D SKYKNIGHT

LEFT: First flown in 1948, the Douglas F3D Skyknight was the first jet carrier night fighter. Grossly underpowered, it was not a success aboard carriers, and flew mainly from land bases. Seen here is the second XF3D-1 prototype.

In 1946 the U.S. Navy issued the world's first specification for a fighter capable of radar-guided interception at night at 500mph. The result was the F3D Skyknight two-seat, twin-engined, subsonic, carrier-based jet night fighter. It had a simple configuration of a broad fuselage to accommodate the side-by-side two-man crew of pilot and radar operator (and also offering huge fuel capacity), mid-mounted straight wings, two Westinghouse turbojets set low on the fuselage beneath the wings, a conventional tail arrangement, tricycle landing gear, and a stinger-like arrester hook. The wings could be folded straight up for flightdeck parking, there was an adjustable-height wheelskid, and a hydraulically operated air brake was mounted on each side of the fuselage behind the wings. There were no ejection seats. Instead, in an emergency the crew would have to escape feet-first, one at a time, via a ventral chute in the floor behind the flight crew.

A contract for three XF3D-1 prototypes was issued on April 3, 1946, and the first of these flew on March 23, 1948. A production order was placed in June of that year, but it was almost two years before the first of 28 production F3D-1s flew. It was powered by two Westinghouse J34-WE-34 turbojets rated at 3,250lb thrust, and was armed with four 20mm cannon mounted on the underside of the nose. A 1,000lb bomb, or a 150-gallon external fuel tank, could also be carried under each wing. Twelve of the F3D-1s were later modified as F3D-1M missile carriers with four Sparrow air-to-air missiles mounted under the wings.

The first two protypes were fitted with the SCR-720 radar in the nose, but the third prototype and production Skyknights had the planned Westinghouse AN/APQ-35 radar system. This was actually made up of two radars; one would search for and locate fighter-size targets at a range of 20 miles and then pass the data to the other, a targeting radar with a range of two miles, while it carried on searching for other targets. This was an early "track-while scan" radar system which, composed of more than 300 thermionic valves, was time-consuming and difficult to service.

The Skyknight, nicknamed "Willie the Whale" for its less than sleek appearance, was heavy, underpowered, and slow. Because of this, although it was designed as a carrier fighter, not many went to sea, and most were land-based, serving with the U.S. Marine Corps. Production had continued with the F3D-2 (differing primarily from the F3D-1 in having slightly more powerful J34-WE-36 engines, and spoilers rather than ailerons). The first F3D-2 flew on February 14, 1951, and 237 were built for the Marines.

Some were later converted as F3D-2M missile carriers (16 aircraft) and F3D-2Q electronic reconnaissance and countermeasures aircraft (30).

From the spring of 1952 F3D-2 Skynights saw combat in Korea with the Marines. During daylight raids, the Air Force's B-29 Superfortresses were being mauled by North Korean MiG fighters, so their missions were changed to night-time, which for a while reduced losses. But, using ground radar control, the MiGs began to find the B-29s once more, and losses mounted again. Skyknights were drafted in to fly barrier patrols between the MiG bases and the Superfortresses, with some success. On the night of November 2-3, 1952, a MiG-15 became the Skyknight's first victim, the first ever jet-versus-jet night combat victory, with five more successes following, including four MiG-15s. Soon, attacks on the B-29s ceased when Skyknights operated with them.

Shortly after the Korean War, the Skyknight was pulled from service, except for a few that were converted for specific roles, including ten that flew on into the Vietnam War as Marine Corps electronic countermeasures aircraft (by then designated EF-10Bs). The last of these was retired in 1970.

Douglas F3D-2 Skyknight cutaway key

1 Glass-fiber radome
2 AN/APG-26 fire-control radar scanner
3 Scanner mounting framework
4 AN/APS 21 search-radar scanner
5 Scanner tracking mechanism
6 Radar equipment package
7 Modulators
8 AN/APD-35 synchronizer
9 Cannon muzzles
10 Nosewheel door
11 Cannon muzzle blast tubes
12 Front pressure bulkhead
13 Rudder pedals
14 Pilot's instrument panel
15 Control column
16 Instrument panel shroud
17 Mk 20 mod "0" gunsight
18 Pitot head
19 Windscreen wiper
20 Stand-by compass
21 Flat plate armored windscreen panel
22 Radar viewing scope
23 Sliding cockpit entry hatch
24 D/F aerial
25 Headrests
26 Bale-out grab handle
27 Rear bulkhead emergency exit hatch
28 Pilot's rear view mirror
29 Safety harness
30 Radar operator's seat
31 Pilot's seat
32 Circuit breaker panel
33 Engine throttle levers
34 Trim control handwheels
35 Control cable linkages
36 Cockpit pressure floor
37 Forward cannon mountings
38 Nosewheel leg strut
39 Forward retracting nosewheel
40 Hydraulic steering unit
41 Port engine air intake
42 Boundary layer bleed air ducts
43 Cartridge case ejector chutes
44 Ventral escape hatch and hinged slipstream air dam
45 Catapult strop hook
46 20mm cannon (4)
47 Cockpit side console panel
48 Chart case behind seat
49 Rear pressure bulkhead
50 Ammunition feed chutes
51 Ammunition magazines, 200rpg

52 Forward equipment bay
53 Hydraulic system reservoir
54 Fuselage upper longeron
55 Forward fuel tank, capacity 650 gallons
56 Position of "push-in" boarding steps/handgrips on starboard side
57 Fuel system piping
58 Forward tank filler
59 Starboard main undercarriage hydraulic retraction jack
60 Mainwheel bay
61 Wheel door
62 External fuel tank, 150 gallons
63 Tank pylon
64 Spar hinge joint
65 Outer, folding wing panel
66 Starboard board navigation light
67 Aileron mass balance
68 Starboard aileron
69 Outer wing panel, folded position
70 Aileron trim tab
71 Spoiler panel
72 Wing fold hydraulic jack
73 Detachable jury strut
74 External tank tail fins
75 Starboard slotted flap
76 Center fuel tank, capacity 290 gallons
77 Wing spar attachment main bulkheads
78 Close pitched fuselage frames
79 Cable and pipe ducts
80 Rear fuel tank, capacity 410 gallons
81 Tank retaining straps
82 Center and rear tank gravity fillers
83 Starboard airbrake, open
84 Rear fuselage electronic equipment bay
85 Oxygen bottles (2)
86 Tailplane control cables
87 Glass-fiber fin root fillet
88 VHF broadband antenna
89 Fin rib structure
90 Rudder hinge control linkage
91 Two-spar fin torsion box structure
92 Rear fuselage ventilating air intake
93 Starboard tailplane
94 Starboard elevator

95 Fin tip antenna fairing
96 VHF antenna
97 Rudder rib structure
98 Rudder trim tab
99 Elevator hinge control linkage
100 Geared tab
101 Elevator trim tab
102 Port elevator rib structure
103 Elevator horn balance
104 Tailplane two-spar torsion box structure
105 Leading edge ribs
106 Tail navigation and position lights
107 Aft radome
108 Tail warning radar scanner
109 AN/APS28 transmitter/receiver
110 Synchronizer unit
111 Fin spar attachment bulkheads
112 Arrester hook actuator and damper
113 Deck arrester hook
114 Tailwheel hydraulic jack/shock absorber
115 Retractable tailwheel/bumper
116 Port airbrake panel
117 Airbrake housing
118 Airbrake hydraulic jack
119 Hinge point
120 Rear fuselage equipment bay ventral access hatch
121 Exhaust nozzle shroud
122 Port engine exhaust
123 Flap shroud ribs
124 Port spoiler panel
125 Port slotted flap rib structure
126 Aileron trim tab
127 Fixed tab
128 Port aileron
129 Aileron rib structure
130 Wing tip fairing
131 Port navigation light
132 Outer wing panel rib structure
133 Port external fuel tank
134 Tank pylon
135 Front spar hinge joint and locking mechanism
136 Aileron control linkage
137 Wing fold hydraulic jack

Specifications for Douglas F3D-2 Skyknight

Dimensions: wingspan 50 feet, length 45 feet 5 inches, height 16 feet 1 inch

Power: two Westinghouse J34-WE-36A single-spool axial flow turbojets rated at 3,400lb each

Weights: empty 15,107lb, normal takeoff 23,575lb, max 26,731lb

Speed: max 493mph at 35,000 feet

Ceiling: 39,400 feet

Range: 1,146 miles on internal fuel; combat radius 400 miles

Armament: four 20mm M2 cannon with 200 rounds per gun; four Sparrow beam-riding air-to-air missiles on 12 F3D-1M and 16 F3D-2M

Crew: pilot and radar operator

138 Spoiler actuator
139 Flap external hinge and actuating link
140 Main undercarriage hydraulic retraction jack
141 Flap actuating torque shaft
142 Mainwheel leg pivot mounting
143 Breaker strut
144 Shock absorber leg strut
145 Port mainwheel
146 Mainwheel leg door
147 Hinged engine cowling panels
148 Westinghouse J34-WE-136 turbojet engine
149 Engine accessory equipment
150 Oil tank
151 Position of "kick-in" boarding step on starboard side
152 Ventral AN/APN-1 radar altimeter antenna

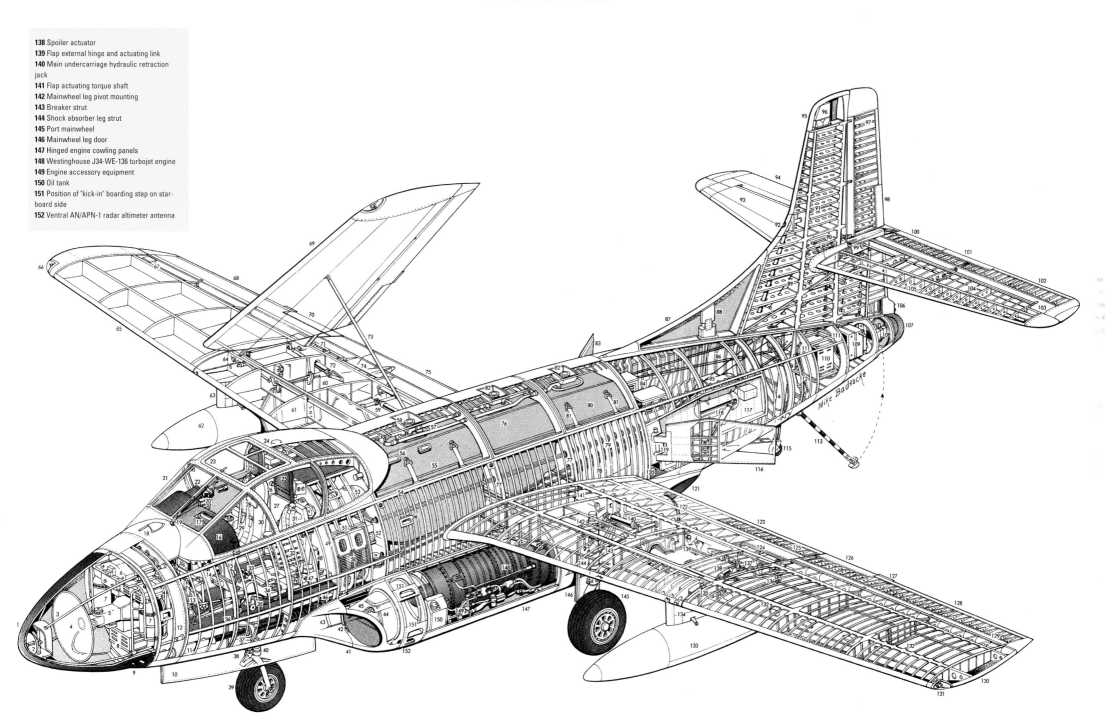

Mike Badrocke

Copyright Mike Badrocke – 2004

OPPOSITE: An early F3D-1 of US Marine squadron VMF 542. Advanced for its day, its Westinghouse APQ-35 radar, which used more than 300 thermionic valves, was a nightmare to keep serviceable. Be that as it may, Skyknights scored several night victories over Korea.

ABOVE: Side by side seating made for a fat fuselage, which gave plenty of space for housing black boxes and fuel. No ejection seats were fitted; in an emergency, the way out was through a ventral chute. The windshield was optically flat.

TOP RIGHT: This is the F3D-2Q Skyknight electronic warfare variant, based on the F3D-2 with slightly more powerful engines. Operated by Marine Squadron VMCJ-3, the type served during the Cuban crisis and in Vietnam, where it was redesignated EF-10B.

RIGHT: Affectionately known as "Willie the Whale," the portly lines are clearly evident on the second prototype, as is the lack of ground clearance. But the engines, which were virtually podded onto the fuselage, gave ease of access for servicing.

DOUGLAS F4D SKYRAY

Following extensive studies into German aerodynamic research at the end of World War II, the U.S. Navy tasked Douglas to design a single-seat, all-weather, general-purpose interceptor that could operate from carriers, fly supersonically, and achieve high rate of climb and good performance at altitude. During 1947-48, a proposal for the Skyray emerged, similar in appearance to a tail-less delta, and two prototypes were ordered on December 16, 1948, under the designation XF-4D-1. It was not a true tail-less delta, but had a broad-chord swept-back wing of unusually low aspect ratio and had no horizontal tail surfaces. The leading edge had automatic slats, while the trailing edge had a much shallower sweep, with elevons.

The design proved challenging for pilots, to say the least. A major problem was that, when decelerating from supersonic to subsonic speeds, a 4.5g pitch-up occurred, which resulted in overstress if the aircraft was already being flown in a high-g turn. Changes had to be made to air intakes and exhaust fairings after early flight-tests featured frequent engine stalls at high speeds above 40,000 feet, and adverse reaction to high-speed turbulence.

The Skyray was designed around the planned Westinghouse J40 engine, but there were major problems with this and it was not ready for the first prototype's flight on January 23, 1951, so both XF4-D1s initially flew with a 5,000lb thrust Allison J35-A-17, and then subsequently with the 7,000lb thrust XJ40-WE-6 engine, and, eventually, with the 11,600lb thrust XJ40-WE-8. Ultimately, with the J40 engine a failure, it was decided in March 1953 to switch to the Pratt & Whitney J57, which necessitated re-engineering of some 80 percent of the Skyray's structures, systems, and installations!

Naturally, these problems caused delays. Nevertheless, the second prototype XF4D-1, powered by an XJ-40-WE-8 engine, set a world absolute speed record of 752.9mph in October 1953. The first production F4D-1 flew on June 5, 1954, and the type went on to set several world time to height records, including one in May 1958 of 2min 36.05sec to 49,212 feet – almost twice as fast as that required by the original specification almost ten years earlier.

Deliveries of F4D-1s to the Navy began on April 16, 1956, and a total of about 420 production types were built before manufacture was terminated in December 1958, when at least 230 were canceled. Skyrays were flown by eleven Navy and six Marine Corps squadrons, both carrier- and land-based units, as well as by three reserve squadrons and specialized units. The first Navy unit to receive F4D-1s was California-based Composite Squadron 3 (VC-3), which carried out the initial service evaluation. VC-3 was later redesignated VFAW-3, and was attached for a time to the Air Defense Command, with which the F4D-1s, while not being involved in combat, carried out missions in support of aerial defense of the continental United States. These aircraft were equipped with special electronics pods on the fuselage centerline pylon, had 300-gallon drop tanks, twelve 2.75-inch unguided rockets in a pack on each of the outer underwing pylons, and a Sidewinder air-to-missile on each of the wing root pylons.

Specifications for Douglas F4D-1 Skyray

Dimensions: wingspan 45 feet 8.25 inches, length 33 feet 6inches, height 12 feet 11 inches

Power: one Pratt & Whitney J57-P-8B twin-spool, axial flow afterburning turbojet rated at 16,000lb max and 10,200lb military thrust

Weights: empty 16,024lb, normal takeoff 22,648lb, max 28,000lb

Speed: max Mach 1.05 at altitude, Mach 0.94 at sea level

Ceiling: 55,000 feet

Range: combat radius 300 miles

Armament: four 20mm Mk 12-0 wing-mounted cannon with 65 rounds per gun; either four 19-shot pods of 2.75 inch FFARs or four AAM-N-9 Sidewinder air-to-air missiles

Crew: pilot

Douglas F4D-Skyray cutaway key

1 Radome
2 Radar scanner dish
3 Scanner tracking mechanism
4 Radome attachment points
5 AN/APQ-50 radar equipment module
6 Radar equipment withdrawal rails
7 Pitot head
8 Windscreen panels
9 Mk II Mod I optical sight
10 Instrument panel shroud
11 Radar azimuth, elevation and range indicator
12 Front pressure bulkhead
13 Rudder pedals
14 Nosewheel door, closed after cycling of undercarriage
15 Door-mounted AN/ARN-21 bearing and range antenna
16 Electrical connectors
17 Nosewhell forks
18 Castoring nosewheel
19 Self-centering snubbers
20 Nosewheel leg door
21 Shock absorber leg strut
22 Cockpit floor level
23 Side console panel
24 Engine throttle lever
25 Control column
26 Radar scope camera
27 Upward-hinging cockpit canopy
28 Rear view mirrors
29 Stand-by compass
30 Canopy open position
31 Flush HF antenna
32 White position light
33 Canopy rear bulkhead
34 Canopy jettison actuator and pneumatic balance strut
35 Ejection seat headrest and face blind firing handle
36 Pilot's Douglas ejection seat, most aircraft retrofitted with Martin-Baker Mk P5 seat
37 Safety harness
38 Ejection seat launch rails
39 Rear pressure bulkhead
40 Boundary layer splitter plate
41 Radio and electronics equipment bay
42 AN/APX-6B IFF antenna
43 AN/ANR-25 UHF homer
44 Port air intake
45 Heat exchanger air intake
46 Venting air intake
47 Intake duct structure
48 Hydraulic reservoirs
49 Boundary layer spill duct
50 Formation light
51 Canopy hinge point
52 Heat exchange exhaust duct
53 Air conditioning equipment bay
54 Venting air louvers
55 Engine control equipment
56 Bifurcated intake duct
57 Front spar root joint
58 Wing root equipment bay
59 Ventral catapult strop hook
60 Fuel filter cap, total internal capacity 639.6 gallons
61 Engine accessory equipment gearbox
62 Forward main engine mounting
63 Port wing root fuel tank
64 Pratt & Whitney J57-P-8 afterburning engine
65 Engine bay sidewall
66 Bleed air supply duct
67 Engine oil tank
68 Compressor bleed spill duct
69 Engine bay firewall
70 Dorsal spine fairing containing fuel and cable ducting
71 Starboard main undercarriage bay
72 Anti-collision light
73 Starboard mainwheel, stowed position
74 Ventral cannon muzzle apertures
75 Recoil springs
76 Ammunition feed chutes
77 Starboard M-12 20mm cannon
78 Wingfold hydraulic jack
79 Starboard automatic leading edge slat, open
80 Slat rails
81 Wingfold hinge joint
82 Elevon hydraulic actuator
83 Starboard outer, folding, wing panel
84 AN/APN-22 antenna
85 Starboard navigation light
86 Elevon trim actuator
87 Outboard elevon
88 Starboard wing folded position
89 Wing fold jury strut
90 Inboard elevon trim actuator
91 Starboard inboard elevon
92 Wing skin paneling
93 Inner corrugated skin doubler
94 Starboard upper airbrake panel, open
95 Formation light
96 Pitch trimmer electric motor and gearbox
97 Rear engine mounting
98 Close pitch fuselage frames
99 Fuel tank access panel
100 Port airbrake panel, upper and lower surfaces, open
101 Airbrake hydraulic jack
102 Pitch trimmer control screw jack
103 Afterburner ducting
104 Wing rear spar and fin spar attachment main frame
105 Cable actuated rudder hinge control
106 Fin rib construction
107 Formation light
108 Remote compass transmitter
109 Servo rudder hydraulic actuator
110 Fin tip aerial fairing
111 AN/ARC-27A UHF antenna
112 Fuel jettison
113 Upper, servo rudder
114 Rudder rib construction
115 Lower, mechanical rudder segment
116 Exhaust shroud
117 Afterburner nozzle control jacks
118 Variable are afterburner nozzle
119 Exhaust nozzle fairing
120 Port wing folded position
121 Port pitch trimmer
122 Pitch trimmer construction
123 Deck arrester hook
124 Retractable tail bumper
125 Wing panel root rib
126 Ammunition magazine, 65 rounds per gun
127 Rear spar
128 Port inboard elevon
129 Elevon rib construction
130 Inboard elevon trim actuator
131 Rear spar hinge joint
132 Elevon control pods
133 Outboard elevon trim actuator
134 Port outboard elevon
135 Elevon horn balance
136 Port navigation light
137 Outer wing panel rib
138 Air portable starter pack

LEFT: The Douglas F4D-1 Skyray was a very exciting aircraft to fly; perhaps a little too much so at times, as attested by the wrinkles plainly evident on the skin. First flown in January 1951, it did not enter service until April 1956.

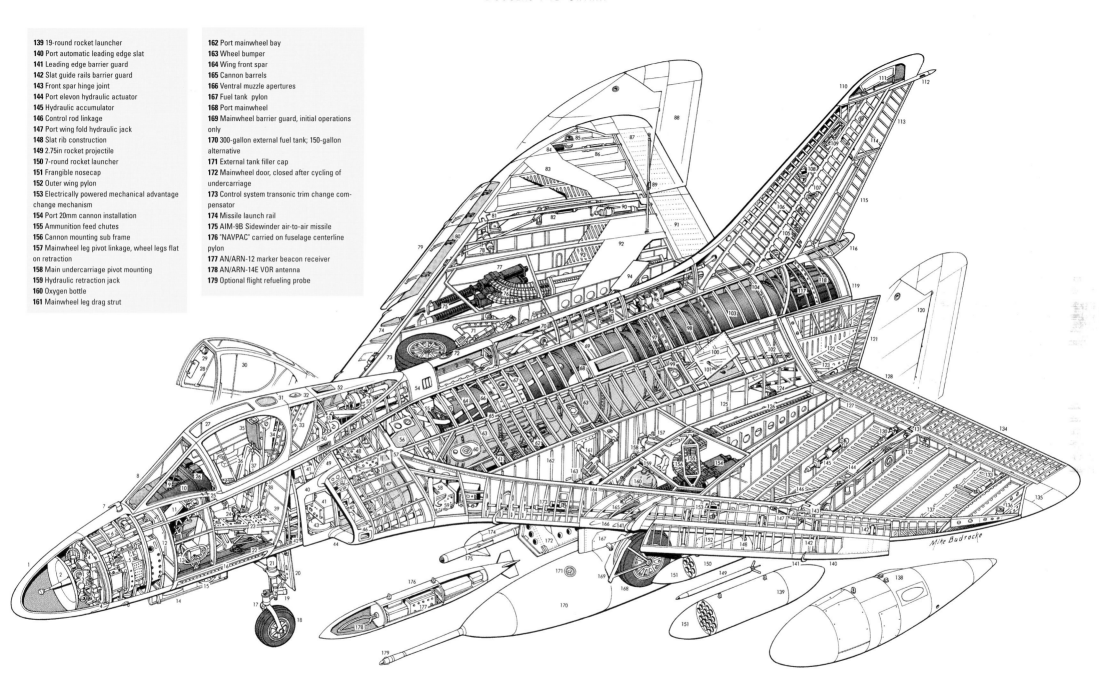

139 19-round rocket launcher
140 Port automatic leading edge slat
141 Leading edge barrier guard
142 Slat guide rails barrier guard
143 Front spar hinge joint
144 Port elevon hydraulic actuator
145 Hydraulic accumulator
146 Control rod linkage
147 Port wing fold hydraulic jack
148 Slat rib construction
149 2.75in rocket projectile
150 7-round rocket launcher
151 Frangible nosecap
152 Outer wing pylon
153 Electrically powered mechanical advantage change mechanism
154 Port 20mm cannon installation
155 Ammunition feed chutes
156 Cannon mounting sub frame
157 Mainwheel leg pivot linkage, wheel legs flat on retraction
158 Main undercarriage pivot mounting
159 Hydraulic retraction jack
160 Oxygen bottle
161 Mainwheel leg drag strut

162 Port mainwheel bay
163 Wheel bumper
164 Wing front spar
165 Cannon barrels
166 Ventral muzzle apertures
167 Fuel tank pylon
168 Port mainwheel
169 Mainwheel barrier guard, initial operations only
170 300-gallon external fuel tank; 150-gallon alternative
171 External tank filler cap
172 Mainwheel door, closed after cycling of undercarriage
173 Control system transonic trim change compensator
174 Missile launch rail
175 AIM-9B Sidewinder air-to-air missile
176 "NAVPAC" carried on fuselage centerline pylon
177 AN/ARN-12 marker beacon receiver
178 AN/ARN-14E VOR antenna
179 Optional flight refueling probe

OPPOSITE: A very unusual shot of a Skyray of VF-101 being "fed to the cat" aboard the British HMS *Ark Royal* during cross-decking operations in 1957. VF-101 was at this time aboard USS *Saratoga*. Steam catapults were fairly new at this time.

OPPOSITE INSET: The unique lines of the Skyray are shown to advantage from this angle. This was the first production aircraft. The "Ford," as it was widely known, could sustain a 70 degree climb angle, which caused problems for air traffic controllers.

LEFT INSET: Compressor stalls often caused flames to come out of the intakes, which was particularly exciting at night, and which may well account for local discoloration seen on this VMF-114 "Ford" aboard *Franklin D Roosevelt* in April 1959.

LEFT: The second prototype XF4D-1 streaks across the Mojave desert in March 1954. Piloted by Jimmy Verdin, this aircraft set an absolute world air speed record in 1953, and five time to altitude records some five years later.

EUROFIGHTER TYPHOON

LEFT: The Eurofighter EF 2000 Typhoon is a quadrinational project shared by Britain, Germany, Italy and Spain. Depicted is the third prototype DA 3, the first to fly with the specially developed Eurojet EJ 200 turbofans.

The Eurofighter is a single-seat, twin-engined, canard delta, bisonic air defense and multi-role fighter whose design was instigated in 1983 by Britain, France, Germany, Italy, and Spain to counter a new generation of agile Soviet combat aircraft, notably the MiG-29 and Su-27, and to keep pace with the United States in fighter technology. A large production run provided the attraction of potential financial economy, although France pulled out of the project in 1985 to concentrate on its indigenous Rafale fighter. The following year the aircraft design and manufacturing consortium Eurofighter Jagdflugzeug GmbH was formed, and later two more consortia were established to produce the EJ 200 engine and the ECR 90 radar and weapon system.

Britain and Italy produced a technology demonstrator called the European Aircraft Programme (EAP) that flew in August 1986, proving such systems as the quadruplex fly-by-wire system and automated wing camber. This had a cranked delta wing, a chin inlet with a lower lip that could be drooped to improve air flow at high performance, and a large vertical tail like that of a Tornado fighter. However, development progress was slow, and it was not until March 27, 1994, that the EF 2000 (named Typhoon in 1998) first flew.

This differs in many ways from the EAP. It has a 53 degree wing sweep, a straight leading edge, tall fin, and all-moving canard foreplanes that are set forward, rather than close-coupled as on Sweden's Gripen. A variety of stealth measures are included, such as shaping that reduces the radar cross-section, and an upward-curved inlet. Significant weight saving results from 70 percent of the surface area (over 40 percent of the structural weight) being composed of carbon reinforced composites.

There are thirteen weapons pylons, four under each wing and five under the fuselage, and a wide variety of short-, medium- and long range air-to-air missiles can be carried as well as attack weapons. There is a 27mm Mauser cannon on all but Britain's RAF aircraft (although reports in 2004 indicated that one would be fitted, without ammunition and unusable, into RAF Eurofighters, as ballast!). Other stores can include laser designator and reconnaissance pods.

The Eurofighter is powered by two Eurojet EJ 200 turbofans, and in the future this will almost certainly be fitted with thrust vectoring nozzles to improve agility and short field performance.

The aircraft has been specifically optimized for beyond visual range combat, with the object of first-shot-first-kill capability, and the close maneuvering dogfight. This requires fast acceleration for maximum energy, and therefore range and maneuverability for the missiles when launched, as well as long range detection and tracking. The radar is the technologically sophisticated multi-mode ECR 90, capable of tracking up to ten targets, supplemented by an infra-red search and track (IRST), and it will have a helmet-mounted sight system for off-boresight missile launch.

It is anticipated that total orders by consortium members will reach about 700 Eurofighters: UK 232 plus an option for 65, Germany 140 air defense and 40 multi-role, Italy 121 plus an option for 9, and Spain 87. Delivery of production aircraft to the air forces of these countries is occurring about now. In addition, export interest has been high, particularly from Australia, Austria, Canada, Greece, Saudi Arabia, and Singapore.

Specifications for Eurofighter EF 2000 Typhoon

Dimensions: wingspan 35 feet 10.75 inches, length 52 feet 4 inches, height 17 feet 4 inches

Power: two Eurojet EJ 200 two-spool afterburning turbofans each rated at 20,250lb max and 13,500lb military thrust

Weights: empty 21,500lb, normal takeoff 34,282lb, max 46,297lb

Speed: max Mach 2+ at altitude, Mach 1.2 at sea level

Ceiling: 60,000 feet

Range: radius of action 1,151 miles

Armament: one 27mm Mauser cannon with 150 rounds (except RAF air-craft), 10 air-to-air missiles (combination of Amraam, Aspide, Meteor, Asraam, Sidewinder)

Crew: pilot

Eurofighter EF 2000 Typhoon cutaway key

1 Glass-fiber reinforced plastic radome, hinged to starboard for access
2 GEC-Marconi Avionics ECR-90 multi-mode pulse-Doppler radar scanner
3 Scanner tracking mechanism
4 Retractable in-flight refueling probe
5 Instrument panel shroud
6 Forward-looking infra-red (FLIR)
7 Radar equipment bay
8 Air data sensor
9 Port canard foreplane
10 Foreplane diffusion-bonded titanium structure
11 Foreplane pivot mounting
12 Hydraulic actuator
13 Rudder pedals
14 Instrument panel with Smiths Industries full-color multi-function head-down-displays (HDD)
15 GEC-Marconi Avionics head-up-display (HUD)
16 Rear view mirrors
17 Upward-hingeing cockpit canopy
18 Pilot's Martin-Baker Mk 16A "zero-zero" ejection seat
19 Control column handgrip, full-authority digital active control technology (ACT) fly-by-wire control system
20 Engine throttle levers, HOTAS controls
21 Side console panel
22 Boarding steps, extended
23 Boundary layer splitter plate
24 Air conditioning pack beneath avionics equipment bay
25 Cockpit rear-sloping pressure bulkhead
26 Cockpit pressurisation valves
27 Canopy latch actuators
28 Canopy rear decking
29 Avionics equipment bay, port and starboard
30 Low-voltage electro-luminescent formation lighting strip
31 Forward fuselage strake
32 Air conditioning system heat exchanger exhaust
33 Intake ramp bleed-air spill duct
34 Port engine air intake
35 Intake lip movable vari-cowl
36 Vari-cowl hydraulic actuators
37 Canopy external release
38 Lower UHF antenna
39 Aft retracting nosewheel

40 Forward fuselage semi-recessed missile carriage
41 Pressure refueling connection
42 Fixed wing inboard leading edge segment
43 Missile launch and approach warning antennae
44 Missile launch and approach warning receivers
45 Leading edge slat drive shaft from central actuating motor
46 Intake ducting
47 Forward fuselage fuel tank, port and starboard
48 Gravity fuel fillers
49 Airbrake hinge mounting
50 Canopy hinge point
51 Center and forward fuselage section of two-seat combat-capable training variant
52 Student pilot's station
53 Instructor's station
54 Dorsal fuel tank
55 Repositioned avionics equipment bays, port and starboard
56 Dorsal airbrake
57 Airbrake hydraulic jack
58 Center fuselage integral fuel tankage
59 Tank access panel
60 Auxiliary Power Unit (APU), cannon bay on starboard side
61 APU exhaust
62 Cannon ammunition magazine
63 Titanium wing panel attachment fittings
64 Main undercarriage wheel bay
65 Carbon-fiber composite (CFC) center fuselage skin paneling
66 Machined wing panel attaching fuselage main frames
67 Anti-collision strobe light
68 TACAN antenna
69 Dorsal spine fairing, air and cable ducting
70 Center section integral fuel tankage
71 Secondary power system (SPS) equipment bay, engine-driven airframe mounted accessory equipment gearboxes
72 Eurojet EJ200 afterburning low-bypass turbofan engine

73 Forward engine mounting
74 Hydraulic reservoirs, port and starboard, dual system
75 Engine bleed-air primary heat exchanger
76 Heat exchanger ram-air intake
77 Starboard wing panel integral fuel tankage
78 Wing tank fire suppressant reticulated foam filling
79 Starboard leading edge slat segments
80 Wing CFC skin panels
81 Starboard wingtip electronic warfare (EW) equipment pod
82 Starboard navigation light
83 GEC-Marconi Avionics towed radar decoy (TRD)
84 Dual TRD housings
85 Starboard outboard elevon
86 HF antenna
87 Upper UHF/IFF antenna
88 Rear position light
89 Fuel jettison
90 Rudder
91 Honeycomb core structure
92 Fin and rudder CFC skin panels
93 Formation lighting strip
94 Fin CFC "sine-wave" spar structure
95 Heat exchanger exhaust shield
96 Fin attachment joints
97 Rear engine mounting
98 Engine bay lining heat shroud
99 Afterburner ducting
100 Tailpipe sealing plates
101 Brake parachute housing
102 Rudder hydraulic actuator
103 Brake parachute door
104 Variable area afterburner nozzles
105 Nozzle hydraulic actuator
106 Runway emergency arrester hook
107 Rear fuselage semi-recessed missile carriage
108 Port CFC inboard elevon
109 Inboard elevon hydraulic actuator
110 Elevon honeycomb core
111 Outboard elevon all-titanium structure
112 Outboard elevon hydraulic actuator
113 Actuator and hinge ventral fairing

114 Outboard pylon mounted chaff/flare launcher
115 Rear ECM/ESM antenna fairing
116 Port wingtip electronic countermeasures/electronic surveillance pod
117 Wing tip formation lighting strip
118 Port navigation light
119 Electronics cooling ram air intake
120 Forward ECM/ESM antenna fairing
121 Outboard missile pylon
122 Intermediate missile pylon
123 Titanium leading edge slat structure
124 Pylon mounting hardpoints
125 Port wing integral fuel tankage
126 Wing panel multi-spar structure
127 Cable conduits
128 Elevon hinge fairing mounted chaff/flare launcher and controller

129 Port mainwheel
130 Mainwheel leg strut
131 Hydraulic retraction jack
132 Undercarriage mounting stub spars
133 Wing root pylon mounting hardpoint
134 Leading edge slat screw jacks and torque shaft
135 Slat guide rails
136 External fuel tank on inboard "wet" pylon
137 Port two-segment leading edge slat, extended
138 Mauser 27mm cannon in starboard wing root
139 Ammunition feed chute

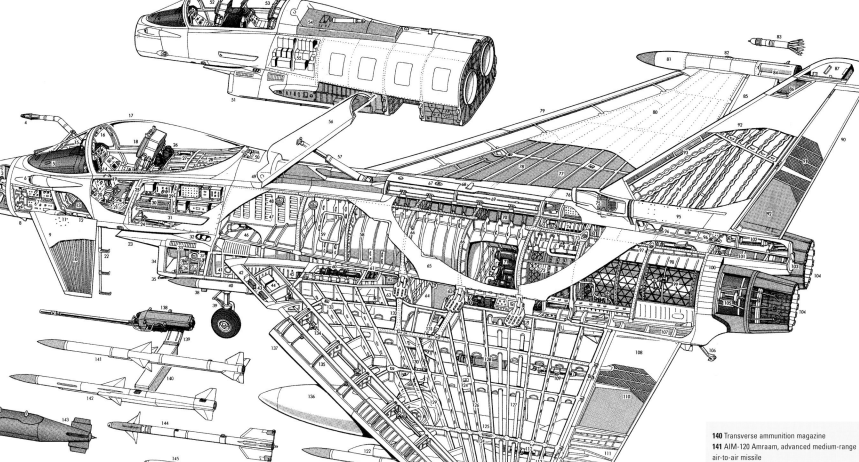

140 Transverse ammunition magazine
141 AIM-120 Amraam, advanced medium-range air-to-air missile
142 BAe/Matra Dynamics Meteor advanced EVR missile
143 BL.755 cluster bomb
144 AIM-9L Sidewinder, short-range air-to-air missile
145 Advanced short-range air-to-air missile Asraam
146 Brimstone air-to-surface anti-armor missile
147 Three-round missile carrier/launcher pylon adapter
148 GBU-24/B Paveway III 2,000lb laser-guided bomb
149 Storm Shadow stand-off precision attack weapon
150 BAe/ Matra Dynamics ALARM, anti-radar missile
151 Type 117, 1,000lb retarded bomb

Copyright Mike Badrocke – 2004

OPPOSITE LEFT: DA 2 and DA 4 in formation in July 1998. Nearest the camera is DA 4, the first two-seater conversion trainer, which will be fully combat-capable. The canard foreplanes are mounted well forward to give a long moment arm for added maneuverability.

OPPOSITE RIGHT: Conceived during the Cold War, the Typhoon was designed to outfly and defeat the latest Russian fighters. As the latter have been widely exported, the threat has not entirely gone away, despite the end of the Cold War.

THIS PAGE: The wingtip pods are: left, the defensive aids subsystem (DASS), and right, towed decoys which confuse and defeat enemy radars and missiles. Drooped slats on the wing leading edges give the impression of a curve.

51

FAIREY FLYCATCHER

It may have looked extremely ungainly, even unattractive, but the Fairey Flycatcher was nonetheless significant in being the first single-seat shipboard fighter of post-World War I concept to enter service, which it did with Britain's Royal Navy in 1923, remaining the Fleet Air Arm's standard and only single-seat fighter until 1932. It served on all the Royal Navy's aircraft carriers during that time, as well as on capital ships, and was also used as both a landplane and floatplane from shore bases. It was also the last type capable of taking off without catapult assistance from small platforms on the gun turrets of capital ships. Furthermore, it was the last fighter that could be used for "slip flights" from carriers: while other aircraft were flying from the main deck above, the Flycatcher could take off from a forward hangar below, along a 60-foot tapered runway, and launching straight over the bows.

In the air, the Flycatcher was an extremely aerobatic fighter, with sensitive handling characteristics, and was very robust. It was the first combat aircraft that was required by Britain's Air Ministry to be capable of diving vertically at full power until it reached terminal velocity.

It was a small, stubby, ugly duckling of an airplane, mainly of wooden construction with fabric skinning. It had a staggered biplane with N-shaped interplane struts. The wings incorporated a camber-changing mechanism. This comprised wide-chord flaps that ran along the entire trailing edges; the outer sections also acted as ailerons. With this mechanism, takeoff and landing runs were shortened and the glide path was steepened. Armament was a pair of .303in Vickers machine guns, and there was provision for four 20lb bombs beneath the center section of the fuselage.

The first prototype Flycatcher flew on November 28, 1922, with a 400hp 14-cylinder Armstrong Siddeley Jaguar II radial engine, with two-bladed wooden propeller, and carried out deck landing trials in February 1923. It was later re-engined with a nine-cylinder Bristol Jupiter IV radial of similar power. The second prototype was flown on May 5, 1923, with a Jaguar II engine, while the third was fitted with an amphibious undercarriage. When fitted with floats or an amphibious undercarriage, the Flycatcher's weight was increased by over 15 percent, which, together with the added drag, adversely affected maneuverability and overall performance. The production model was powered by the Jaguar III or IV engine.

The last of the 206 Flycatchers built (including prototypes) was completed and flown on June 20, 1930. The type was superseded by 1934. A single all-metal fuselage

Flycatcher II was flown on October 4, 1926, but, while it was designed as a potential replacement for the original type, it bore no relationship to the Flycatcher other than design origin, and the sole prototype was written off in a takeoff accident on May 8, 1929.

Specifications for Fairey Flycatcher (landplane version)

Dimensions: wingspan 29 feet, length 23 feet, height 12 feet

Power: one Armstrong Siddeley Jaguar IV 14-cylinder two-row radial air-cooled engine rated at 400hp

Weights: empty 2,038lb, normal takeoff 3,028lb

Speed: max 134mph at sea level, 110mph at 17,000 feet

Ceiling: 19,000 feet

Range: 263 miles

Armament: two .303in belt-fed, synchronized machine guns

Crew: pilot

Fairey Flycatcher cutaway key

1 Steel-tube wingtip
2 Starboard upper aileron-camber flap
3 Aileron control horns
4 Spar bracing struts
5 Control cable pulleys
6 Wing internal bracing
7 Interplane N struts
8 Starboard lower aileron-camber flap
9 Single landing wires
10 Double flying wires
11 Wing fabric covering
12 Spruce leading edge
13 Spinner (not fitted to all aircraft)
14 Starter dog attachment
15 Two-bladed wooden propeller
16 Propeller hub fixing bolts
17 Engine reduction gearbox
18 Armstrong Siddeley Jaguar 14-cylinder two-row radial engine
19 Exhaust pipes
20 Engine mounting bulkhead
21 Fireproof bulkhead
22 Carburetor intake
23 Fuel jettison pipe
24 Throttle control rods
25 Sloping footboards
26 Rudder pedals
27 Front fuselage steel tube construction
28 Fuel tank, capacity 60 gallons
29 Fuel filler cap
30 Wing center section steel tube construction
31 Diagonal bracing wires
32 Aileron cables
33 Aircraft hoisting sling
34 Aldis sight
35 Instrument panel
36 Fuel priming pump
37 Ammunition boxes
38 Ammunition feed chutes
39 Gun mounting
40 One 0.303in (7.7mm) machine gun each side
41 Engine throttle controls
42 Pilot's seat
43 Control column
44 Safety belt
45 Windscreen
46 Sliding cockpit access doors
47 Trailing edge cut-out
48 Headrest
49 Cockpit rear bulkhead
50 Bomb release lever
51 Steel-tube fuselage spool joint

52 Access door
53 Equipment compartment
54 Headrest fairing
55 Dorsal fairing frames
56 Dorsal stringer construction
57 Top longeron
58 Tailplane control cables
59 Elevator cross shaft
60 Fin front fixing
61 Tailplane bracing strut
62 Starboard tailplane
63 Starboard elevator
64 Fin construction
65 Sternpost
66 Rudder construction
67 Steel-tube trailing edge
68 Port elevator
69 Port tailplane construction
70 Elevator push-pull rod
71 Rudder control horn
72 Tailplane incidence control screw jack
73 Tailskid shock absorbers
74 Tailskid
75 Lifting handle
76 Ventral spacers
77 Central frames
78 Ventral stringers
79 Bottom longeron
80 Aileron control horn
81 Port upper aileron-camber flap
82 Top wing rib construction
83 Interplane N struts
84 Aileron connecting cables
85 Port lower aileron-camber flap
86 Steel-tube trailing edge

87 Aileron ribs
88 Steel-tube wing tip
89 Wing tip rib
90 Rear spar
91 Lower aileron control horn
92 Lattice rib construction
93 Interplane strut attachment
94 Front spar
95 Leading-edge ribs
96 Inter-spar compression strut
97 Wing internal bracing
98 Leading-edge stiffeners
99 Spruce leading edge
100 Four 20lb bombs beneath center section
101 Spar root fixing
102 Main undercarriage shock absorber
103 Port mainwheel
104 Tire valve access
105 Brake drum
106 Pivoted axle
107 Hydraulic brake pipe
108 Undercarriage V struts
109 Diagonal bracing wires
110 Axle spreader bar
111 Arresting wire hooks (early aircraft only)
112 Starboard mainwheel

ABOVE: First flown in November 1922, the Fairey Flycatcher was the standard British Fleet Air Arm fighter until 1932. In addition to carrier operations, it could be fitted with floats. The aircraft depicted has just landed on HMS *Furious*.

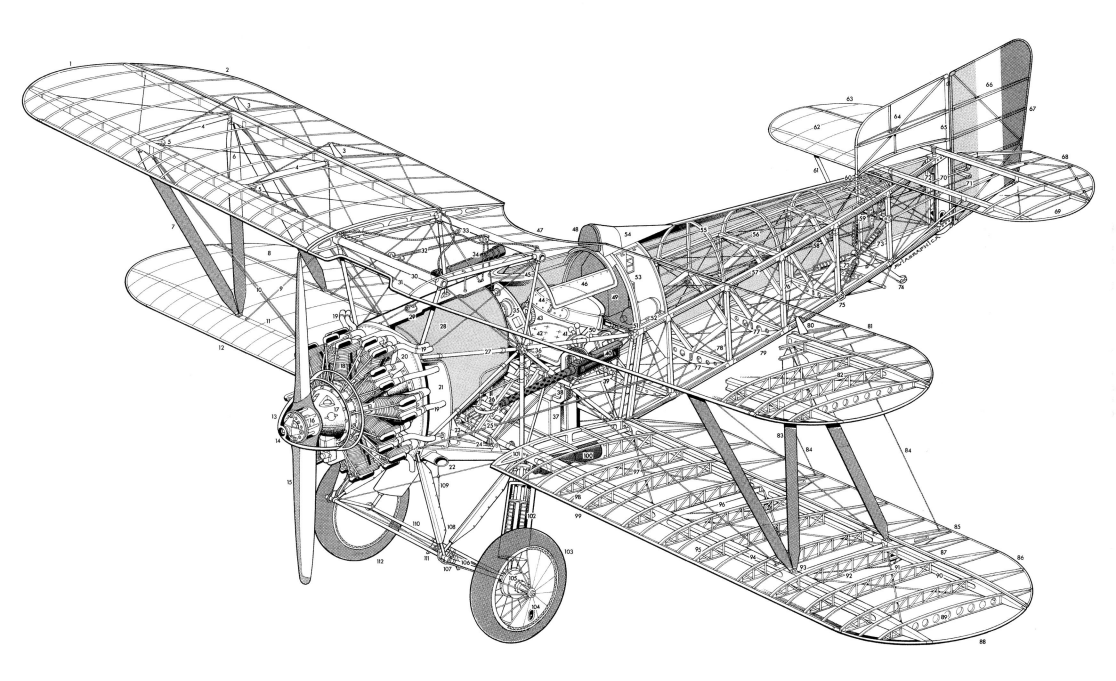

Copyright Mike Badrocke – 2004

FIAT G.50 FRECCIA

LEFT: The Fiat G.50 Freccia was the first Italian all-metal monoplane with a retractable undercarriage to enter service. The pilot was seated high to improve his view, but at the expense of added drag, which reduced performance.

The Fiat G.50 of the late 1930s was the first single-seat monoplane fighter to be built and flown in Italy. While Italian airplane design of the period was excellent, engine development had not kept pace. The cult of the fighter ace had not caught the Italian imagination to the degree that it had with other nations, with the result that fighter development had become comparatively neglected. Moreover, one result of Italy's fighter experience during the Spanish Civil War, in which a dozen pre-production G.50s underwent operational evaluation, was a further reduction in performance. The Republican forces there were flying the better-performing Polikarpov I-16, and the Italian fighters were forced to rely on agility. Thus, maneuver combat, the time-honored dogfight, became all-important in Italian minds, obscuring to a degree the need to develop proper tactics and teamwork. The generally splendid Italian aerobatic pilots failed to realize that standard aerobatic rolls and loops were air display showpieces with little or no relevance to combat.

Influenced by this general mindset, the *Regia Aeronautica* insisted on the best possible forward view for the pilot, and the ability to take deflection shots without the target becoming obscured below the nose. This was achieved by placing the pilot's seat high up in the fuselage, producing a humped-back silhouette, and reducing aerodynamic cleanliness, with adverse effects on performance.

The G.50 Freccia (Arrow) was an all-metal, low-wing monoplane with a retractable undercarriage and a fixed castoring tailwheel. The first of two prototypes built by Fiat's CSAMA subsidiary flew on February 26, 1937, and by July 1939 an initial series of 45 had been built, 12 of these being sent to reinforce the *Aviazione Legionaria* in Spain. Pilots did not like the sliding canopy, which they found difficult to open quickly and interfered with their view, and all but the first few of the next production batch of 191 had open cockpits and, later, a revised vertical tail. Finland ordered 35 of these aircraft in 1939, but delivery was held up by Germany until 1940, when hostilities between Finland and Russia came to a halt.

A modified version, the G.50bis, was flown on September 9, 1940. It had a reprofiled fuselage giving improved pilot view, armor protection and self-sealing tanks, increased internal fuel capacity, a new undercarriage, and extended tailcone. Fiat built 349 G.50bis, and CMASA 97, as well as 100 tandem two-seat G.50B trainers. The G.50V (first flight August 25, 1942) was a single fighter powered by a German-supplied Daimler-Benz DB 601A of 1,175hp, and the single G.50bis-A two-seat shipboard

fighter-bomber, with extended wing, four 12.7mm guns (compared with the G.50's two), and racks for two bombs, flew on October 3, 1942.

The Freccia served in most theaters during World War II, but it suffered against Allied fighters, especially the Hurricane and P-40 Kittyhawk, mainly because of its inferior engine and poor Breda-SAFAT machine guns, which were so heavy that they had to be mounted in the nose rather than the wings. Even against the British RAF Gladiator, a single-seat biplane fighter that had been obsolete when it entered service in 1937, the G.50 achieved little: some 25 percent of Gladiator victories were scored against the Freccia, with the Italian pilots trying to dogfight with the slower but far more maneuverable biplane.

Specifications for Fiat G.50bis Freccia

Dimensions: wingspan 36 feet 0.25 inches, length 25 feet 7 inches, height 9 feet 8.5 inches

Power: one 870hp Fiat A 74 RC 38 14-cylinder two-row radial

Weights: empty 4,579lb, normal takeoff 5,963lb

Speed: max 294mph at 19,690 feet

Ceiling: 28,870 feet

Range: 620 miles

Armament: two 12.7mm Breda-SAFAT belt-fed synchronized machine guns with 150 rounds per gun

Crew: pilot

Fiat G.50bis Freccia cutaway key

1 Pitot static head
2 Starboard navigation light
3 Wing-tip fairing
4 Aileron mass balance weights
5 Starboard fabric-covered aileron
6 Hinge control linkage
7 Aileron tab
8 Control rod linkages
9 Starboard outer wing panel
10 Hamilton-Fiat three-bladed variable-pitch propeller
11 Spinner
12 Propeller hub pitch-change mechanism
13 Engine cooling air intake
14 Cowling nose ring
15 Propeller reduction gearbox
16 Propeller governor
17 Machine gun muzzle blast trough
18 Fiat A.74R.C.38 14-cylinder two-row radial engine
19 Detachable engine cowling panels
20 Carburetor air intake
21 Starboard mainwheel
22 Wheel hub hydraulic brake
23 Exhaust stub
24 Exhaust collector ring
25 Engine accessory equipment compartment
26 Adjustable cowling air flaps
27 Welded tubular steel engine mounting frame
28 Oil tank
29 Machine gun muzzle flash guards
30 Oil filler cap
31 Machine gun barrels
32 Engine bay fireproof bulkhead
33 Outboard flap control linkage
34 Flap fabric covering
35 Starboard outer slotted flap segment
36 Machine gun blister fairings
37 Ammunition feed chute
38 Interrupter gear mechanism
39 Fuel filler caps
40 Forward fuselage fuel tank (total fuel capacity 134.4 gallons/493 gallons including auxiliary tank)
41 Main undercarriage wheel bay
42 Diagonal frame members
43 Center section fuel tank
44 Fuselage access panel
45 Ammunition tank (150rpg)
46 Cartridge case collector box
47 Cartridge case ejector chute
48 Adjustable gun mounting

49 Breda-SAFAT 12.7mm machine guns
50 Armament bay hinged access cover
51 Instrument panel access door
52 Fuselage upper longeron
53 Starboard side hydraulic accumulator
54 Rudder pedal bar
55 Footboards
56 Central flap hydraulic jack
57 Underfloor auxiliary fuel tank
58 Trim control handwheel
59 Control column
60 Engine throttle and propeller control levers
61 Instrument panel
62 Lighting control panel
63 Reflector sight
64 Armored windscreen panel
65 Canopy arch
66 Side transparency panels
67 Hinged cockpit access doors (port and starboard)
68 Door latches
69 Pilot's seat
70 Safety harness
71 Port side console panel
72 Cockpit floor level
73 Adjustable seat mounting
74 ARC 1 radio receiver
75 Starboard side hydraulic pressure accumulator
76 Cockpit rear bulkhead
77 Headrest
78 Turn-over crash pylon
79 Aerial mast
80 Fuselage skin paneling
81 Dorsal section framing
82 Rear fuselage upper longeron
83 Rudder cable linkages
84 Sloping rear fuselage bulkhead
85 Fin spar attachment joints
86 Starboard tailplane
87 Starboard fabric-covered elevator
88 Fin leading edge
89 Tailfin construction
90 Aerial cable
91 Rudder horn balance
92 Fabric-covered rudder

93 Rudder rib construction
94 Tailcone
95 Tail navigation light
96 Port elevator rib construction
97 Tailplane mainspar
98 Tailplane rib construction
99 Elevator hinge control
100 Tailplane spar attachment point
101 Welded tubular steel fin and tailplane support structure
102 Fixed castoring tailwheel
103 Tailwheel shock absorber strut
104 Rear fuselage frame and stringer construction
105 Fuselage lower longeron
106 Elevator push-pull control rod
107 Fire extinguisher bottle
108 Access panels
109 Starter motor pneumatic reservoir
110 Batteries (two)
111 Boarding step
112 Inboard slotted flap segment
113 Trailing edge rib construction
114 Tubular steel wing spar center section construction
115 Aileron control cable quadrant
116 Outer wing panel spar joint
117 Wing panel joint cover strip
118 Double boom rear spar
119 Flap rib construction
120 Outboard slotted flap segment
121 Aileron tab
122 Aileron hinge control
123 Port aileron rib construction
124 Aileron mass balance weights
125 Wing-tip ribs
126 Wing-tip edge member
127 Port navigation light
128 Pitot static head
129 Outer wing panel lattice rib construction
130 Double boom front spar
131 Leading-edge nose ribs
132 Mainwheel leg door
133 Mainwheel door
134 Port mainwheel
135 Mainwheel forks

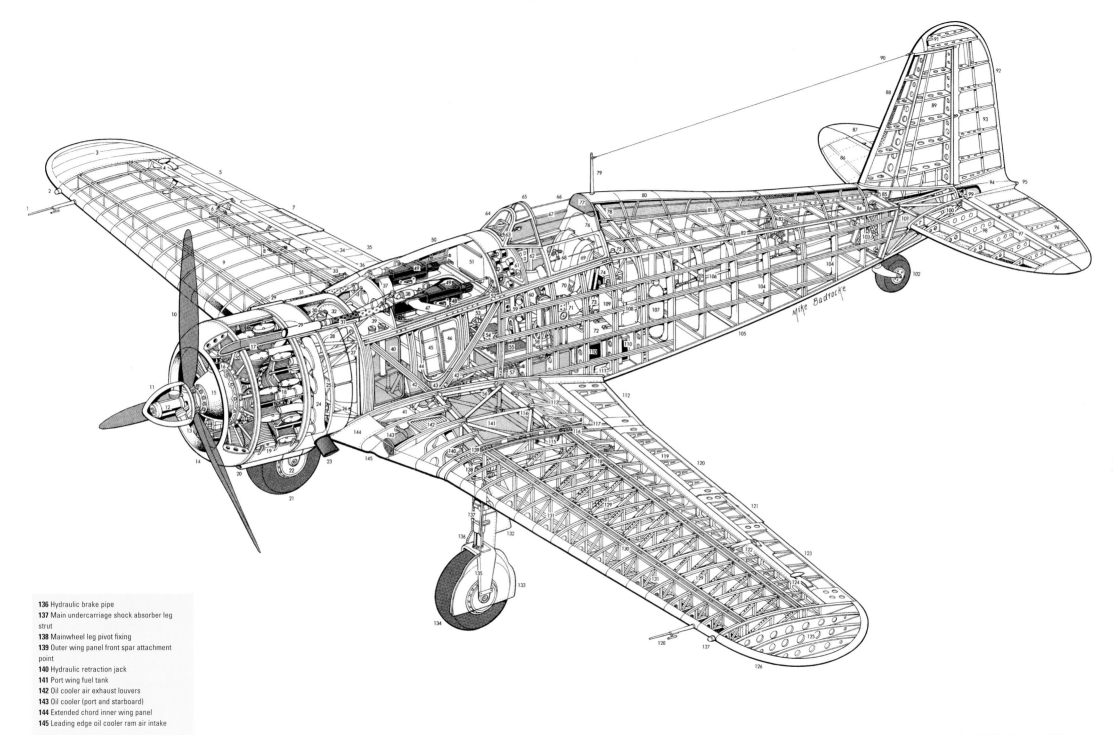

136 Hydraulic brake pipe

137 Main undercarriage shock absorber leg strut

138 Mainwheel leg pivot fixing

139 Outer wing panel front spar attachment point

140 Hydraulic retraction jack

141 Port wing fuel tank

142 Oil cooler air exhaust louvers

143 Oil cooler (port and starboard)

144 Extended chord inner wing panel

145 Leading edge oil cooler ram air intake

Copyright Mike Badrocke – 2004

FOCKE-WULF Fw 190

When Allied fighter pilots first encountered the trim little Focke-Wulf Fw 190 single-seat monoplane over France in 1941 they had a nasty surprise. It represented a small target, possessed superlative control harmony, was both a good dogfighter and excellent gun platform, and in almost all respects was superior to its contemporary, the Spitfire V. It climbed better, rolled much quicker, and was faster in the dive and on the level than the bigger and more sluggish British fighter, generally out-performing it in all departments except turn radius. Roll rate was exceptionally fast, which enabled the German fighter to change direction very quickly, although it was unforgiving if pushed too hard: an irrecoverable high-speed stall and spin was the usual result. Even when the Spitfire IX was introduced and in part redressed the balance, the Fw 190 could outfly it with a roll and dive. The Fw 190A-3 was much lighter and faster than any Allied fighter in service in 1942, and was also much more heavily armed, with two 7.92mm machine guns over the engine and four cannon in the wings.

The Fw 190 prototype first flew on June 1, 1939, and the design was much modified with different engines, redesigned wings, various configurations of armament size and position, leading to a profusion of fighter and fighter-bomber versions (including at least one design with armored leading edges for ramming Allied bombers). The aircraft were produced in great numbers by many factories. Series production commenced with the Fw 190A-1 in September 1940. By the end of the war over 20,000 of all types had been delivered, including the final variant Fw 190D-9 ("Dora 9"), often referred to as the "long-nosed 190," later models of which were redesignated Ta 152 to honor Dipl Ing Kurt Tank, director of Focke-Wulf's design team.

As the Fw 190 was adapted with heavier armament and greater fuel capacity to meet new demands, and in particular to counter the USAAF massed daylight bomber raids, there was an inevitable weight increase, and performance deteriorated. The fighter suffered heavily in the crossfire from the bombers' hundreds of heavy machine guns, which led to wing loading of the A-8, for instance, increasing by over 25 percent compared with that of the A-3. The Fw 190A-8 was fitted with additional armor to protect engine, cockpit, and gun magazines to create the Fw 190A-8/R8 *Sturmbock*, which also had bullet-proof glass added to quarterlights and canopy sides. Performance suffered to the extent that it needed fighter protection against enemy fighters that were escorting the bombers.

Principal production variants were (with various armament arrangements): Fw 190A-1 with 1,600hp BMW 801C-1 engine (102 built); A-2 with BMW 801C-2 engine (426 built); A-3 which standardized on the 1,700hp BMW 801D-2 engine used by all subsequent A-series models, entering service at the end of 1941 (509 built, of which 72 were delivered to Turkey as Fw 190Aa-3s in 1942-43); A-4 which entered service in 1942, having a different radio and being the first to have methanol/water injection, there also being tropical and long-range fighter-bomber variants of this (894 built); the similar A-5 (including a night fighter version with anti-glare panels and shrouded exhausts) with lengthened engine mounting (723 built), some of which were produced in an underground factory in France in 1945, and serving with *l'Armée de l'Air* from 1946; A-6 with revised wing structure (569 built); A-7 with new gunsight and fuselage-mounted machine guns; A-8, the final A-series sub-type that entered service in 1943; and the Fw 190D-9, the final variant, entering service in the fall of 1944.

Left: The Focke-Wulf Fw 190 was Germany's most versatile single-seater of World War II. It was used for everything from air superiority to ground attack. This is an Fw 190F-8/R1 of *Schlachtgeschwader 2*, seen on the Eastern Front in January 1945.

Fw 190A-8 cutaway key

1 Pitot head
2 Starboard navigation light
3 Detachable wingtip
4 Pitot tube heater line
5 Wing lower shell floating rib
6 Aileron hinge points
7 Wing lower shell stringers
8 Leading-edge ribs
9 Front spar
10 Outermost solid rib
11 Wing upper shell stringers
12 Aileron trim tab
13 Aileron structure
14 Aileron activation/control linkage
15 Ammunition box (125rpg)
16 Starboard 20mm MG 151/20E wing cannon (sideways mounted)
17 Ammunition box rear suspension arm
18 Flap structure
19 Wing flap under skinning
20 Flap setting indicator peephole
21 Rear spar
22 Inboard wing construction
23 Undercarriage indicator
24 Wing rib strengthening
25 Ammunition feed chute
26 Static and dynamic air pressure lines
27 Cannon barrel
28 Launch tube bracing struts
29 Launch tube carrier strut
30 Mortar launch tube (auxiliary underwing armament)
31 Launch tube internal guide rails
32 21-cm (WfrGr 21) spin-stabilised Type 42 mortar shell
33 VDM three-bladed adjustable-pitch constant-speed propeller
34 Propeller boss
35 Propeller hub
36 Starboard undercarriage fairing
37 Starboard mainwheel
38 Oil warming chamber
39 Thermostat
40 Cooler armored ring (0.25in/6.5mm)
41 Oil tank drain valve
42 Annular oil tank (14.5 gallons)
43 Oil cooler
44 12-bladed engine cooling fan
45 Hydraulic-electric pitch control unit
46 Primer fuel line
47 Bosch magneto
48 Oil tank armor (0.22in/5.5mm)

49 Supercharger air pressure pipes
50 BMW 801D-2 14-cylinder radial engine
51 Cowling support ring
52 Cowling quick-release fasteners
53 Oil pump
54 Fuel pump (engine rear face)
55 Oil filter (starboard)
56 Wingroot cannon synchronization gear
57 Gun troughs/cowling upper panel attachment
58 Engine mounting ring
59 Cockpit heating pipe
60 Exhaust pipes (cylinders 11-14)
61 MG 131 link and casing discard chute
62 Engine bearer assembly
63 MG 131 ammunition boxes (400rpg)
64 Fuel filter recess housing
65 MG 131 ammunition cooling pipes
66 MG 131 synchronisation gear
67 Ammunition feed chute
68 Twin fuselage 13mm MG 131 machine guns
69 Windscreen mounting frame
70 Emergency power fuse and distributor box
71 Rear hinged gun access panel
72 Engine bearer/bulkhead attachment
73 Control column
74 Transformer
75 Aileron control torsion bar
76 Rudder pedals (EC pedal unit with hydraulic wheelbrake operation)
77 Fuselage/wing spar attachment
78 Adjustable rudder push rod
79 Fuel filler head
80 Cockpit floor support frame
81 Throttle lever
82 Pilot's seat back plate armor (0.31in/8mm)
83 Seat guide rails
84 Side-section back armor (0.19in/5mm)
85 Shoulder armor (0.19in/5mm)
86 Oxygen supply valve
87 Steel frame turnover pylon
88 Windscreen spray pipes
89 Instrument panel shroud
90 1.18in/30mm armored glass quarterlights
91 1.96in/50mm armored glass windscreen
92 Revi 16B reflector gunsight
93 Canopy

94 Aerial attachment
95 Headrest
96 Head armour (0.47in/12mm)
97 Head armor support strut
98 Explosive charge canopy emergency jettison unit
99 Canopy channel side
100 Auxiliary tank: fuel (30.2 gallons) or GM-1 (22.44 gallons)
101 FuG 16ZY transmitter-receiver unit
102 Handhold cover
103 Primer fuel filler cap
104 Autopilot steering unit (PKS 12)
105 FuG 16ZY power transformer
106 Entry step cover plate
107 Two tri-spherical oxygen bottles (starboard fuselage wall)
108 Auxiliary fuel tank filler point
109 FuG 25a transponder unit
110 Autopilot position integration unit
111 FuG 16ZY homer bearing converter
112 Elevator control cables
113 Rudder control DUZ flexible rods
114 Fabric panel (bulkhead 12)
115 Rudder differential unit
116 Aerial lead-in
117 Rear fuselage lift tube
118 Triangular stress frame
119 Tailplane trim unit
120 Tailplane attachment fitting
121 Tailwheel retraction guide tube
122 Retraction cable lower pulley
123 Starboard tailplane
124 Aerial
125 Starboard elevator
126 Elevator trim tab
127 Tailwheel shock strut guide
128 Fin construction
129 Retraction cable under pulley
130 Aerial attachment strut
131 Rudder upper hinge
132 Rudder structure
133 Rudder trim tab
134 Tailwheel retraction mechanism access panel
135 Rudder attachment/actuation fittings

Specifications for Focke-Wulf Fw 190A-8

Dimensions:	wingspan 34 feet 5.5 inches, length 29 feet 4.25 inches, height 12 feet 11.5 inches
Power:	one 1,700hp BMW 801D-2 two-row 14-cylinder radial (with methanol/water injection giving 2,100hp)
Weights:	empty 7,650lb, normal takeoff 9,656lb, max 10,803lb
Speed:	speed 408mph at 20,670 feet, 355mph at sea level
Ceiling:	37,400 feet
Range:	643 miles
Armament:	four 20mm MG 151 cannon (two in wing roots and two in the wing), two 13mm MG 131 machine guns in upper cowling
Crew:	pilot

136 Rear navigation light
137 Extension spring
138 Elevator trim tab
139 Port elevator structure
140 Tailplane construction
141 Semi-retracting tailwheel
142 Forked wheel housing
143 Drag yoke
144 Tailwheel shock strut
145 Tailwheel locking linkage
146 Elevator actuation lever linkage
147 Angled frame spar
148 Elevator differential bellcrank
149 FuG 25a ventral antenna
150 Master compass sensing unit
151 FuG 16ZY fixed loop homing antenna
152 Radio compartment access hatch
153 Single tri-spherical oxygen bottle (port fuselage wall)
154 Retractable entry step
155 Wingroot fairing
156 Fuselage rear fuel tank (77.4 gallons)
157 Fuselage/rear spar attachment
158 Fuselage forward fuel tank (61.2 gallons)
159 Port wingroot cannon ammunition box (250
rpg)
160 Ammunition feed chute
161 Port wingroot MG 151/20E cannon
162 Link and casing discard chute
163 Cannon rear mount support bracket
164 Upper and lower wing shell stringers
165 Rear spar
166 Spar construction
167 Flap position indicator scale and peephole
168 Flap actuating electric motor
169 Port 20mm MG 151/20E wing cannon (sideways mounted)
170 Aileron transverse linkage
171 Ammunition box (125rpg)
172 Ammunition box rear suspension arm
173 Aileron control linkage
174 Aileron control unit
175 Aileron trim tab
176 Port aileron structure
177 Port navigation light
178 Outboard wing stringers
179 Detachable wingtip
180 A-8/R1 variant underwing gun pack (in place
of outboard cannon)
181 Link and casing discard chute
182 Twin unsynchronized 20mm MG 151/20E
cannon
183 Light metal fairing (gondola)
184 Ammunition feed chutes
185 Ammunition boxes (125 rpg)
186 Carrier frame restraining cord
187 Ammunition box rear suspension arms
188 Leading-edge skinning
189 Ammunition feed chute
190 Ammunition warming pipe
191 Aileron bellcrank
192 Mainwheel strut mounting assembly
193 EC-oleo shock strut
194 Mainwheel leg fairing
195 Scissors unit

196 Mainwheel fairing
197 Axle housing
198 Port mainwheel
199 Brake lines
200 Cannon barrel
201 FuG 16ZY Morane antenna
202 Radius rods
203 Rotating drive unit
204 Mainwheel retraction electric motor
housing
205 Undercarriage indicator
206 Sealed air jack
207 BSK 16 gun camera
208 Retraction locking hooks
209 Undercarriage locking unit
210 Armament collimation tube

211 Camera wiring conduits
212 Wheel well
213 Cannon barrel blast tube
214 Wheel cover actuation strut
215 Ammunition hot air
216 Port inboard wheel cover
217 Wingroot cannon barrel
218 ETC 501 carrier unit
219 ETC 501 bomb rack
220 SC 500 bomb (500kg/1,102lb)

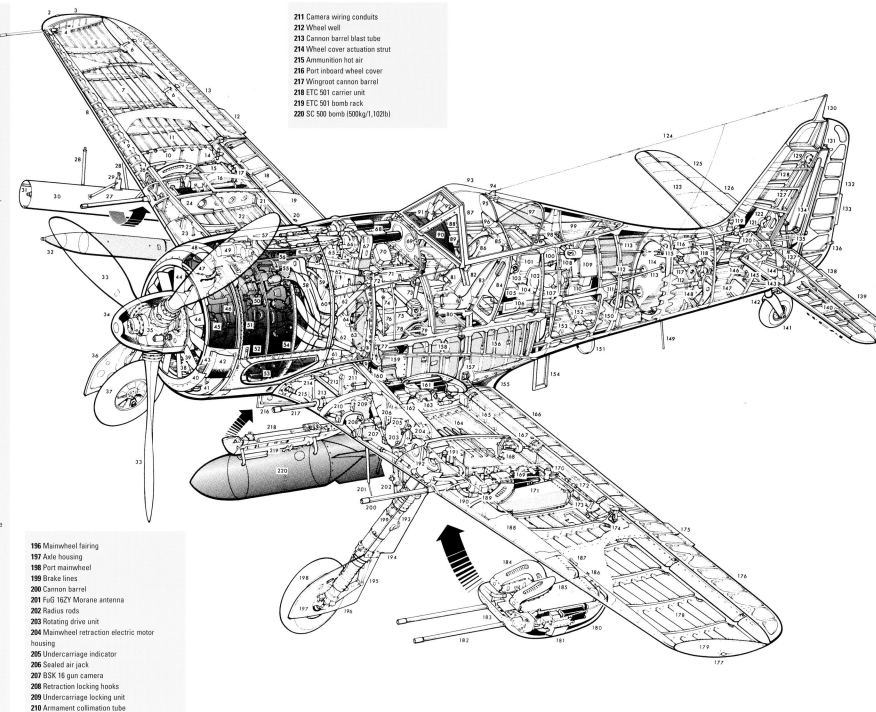

ABOVE LEFT: With power cart connected and the pilot's parachute on the port tailplane, this Fw 190A-3 stands ready to scramble at short notice, probably some time in 1942. The one-piece sliding canopy provided a good all-round view.

ABOVE: A pre-series Fw 190A-0 runs up its engine. It was designed as a rough and tough cavalry horse to supplement the thoroughbred but more delicate Bf 109 in *Jagdwaffe* service. Early versions were more than a match for contemporary Spitfires.

LEFT: Mechanics swarm all over this pre-series Fw 190A-0. First flown in June 1939, it had a delay in service entry of more than two years because of problems with engine and cockpit overheating, cowlings that blew off at high speeds, and structural weakness.

RIGHT: Mistel combinations consisted of war-weary bombers loaded with high explosives and controlled in the air by fighters mounted above them. It was not very successful. This Mistel consists of a Ju 88 controlled by an Fw 190.

GENERAL DYNAMICS F-16 FIGHTING FALCON

LEFT: The General Dynamics (now Lockheed) F-16A Fighting Falcon was one of the most versatile aircraft of its era. This Edwards-based F-16 of the 6512th Test and Evaluation Squadron is seen carrying a Norwegian Penguin anti-shipping missile.

The single-seat, single-engined, supersonic jet air superiority and multi-role fighter F-16 evolved during the 1970s following the design's success in the US Air Force Light Weight Fighter (LWF) competition for a small, relatively inexpensive aircraft and after it had met more stringent requirements for a more powerful (and heavier and more expensive) Air Combat Fighter (ACF). Production of further developed aircraft began in 1978, and the USAF formally accepted the first in August 1978. The F-16 was formally named Fighting Falcon in July 1980 and the first squadron declared operational shortly after. Two versions were ordered, the single-seat F-16A fighter and the two-seat F-16B trainer.

The F-16 is stressed to pull 9g and is unusual in that the pilot's seat is angled back to help counter the high-g effects on him. While these types were identical in size, the trainer had a shorter range due to the extra seat taking up fuel capacity. Some 272 F-16A/B versions were converted to F-16ADF (air defense fighter) standard with upgrades from 1986 for the dedicated fighter role of Air National Guard units.

June 1984 saw the first flight of the improved F-16C and D, which have improved radar and engines and are capable of flying precision day or night attack missions plus beyond visual range (BVR) interceptions. Some F-16Cs feature the LANTIRN pod system as fitted to the F-15E Strike Eagle for the strike role.

The U.S. Navy ordered F-16Ns for dissimilar aircraft ("aggressor") training. They were built with less capable mission equipment and radar and didn't feature any armaments although AIM-9 Sidewinder acquisition rounds were fitted. This led to a "hot machine" but the resulting fatigue problems from constant high-g maneuvers was a contribution to their withdrawal after just seven years.

The F-16 Fighting Falcon (also known in USAF service as "Electric Jet" or "Viper") has, through various versions, been developed into a truly multi-mission warplane. It is integrally armed with a single M61 multi-barreled 20mm cannon. A single hardpoint in the centerline under the fuselage is normally used for a drop tank or electrnic warfare pod. A further two points either side of the air intake are used for targeting devices such as the LANTIRN pods. Built into the wingtips are missile rails for AIM-9 Sidewinder, AIM-7 Sparrow or AIM-120 Amraam air-to-air missiles. Under the wings are three hardpoints on each side. Pylons can be fixed to these to carry a range of bombs, drop tanks, missiles and rockets, and these can range from four 2,000lb Mk.84 bombs to twelve 500lb Mk.82 bombs.

These could also be Paveway LGB, AGM-130 or the new JDAM air-to-ground missiles in the form of AGM-85 Mavericks or AGM-88 HARM anti-radiation munitions carried especially by F-16CJs that operate in the suppression of enemy air defenses (SEAD) role. A range of GBU submunitions can also be carried as can additional drop tanks or ECM pods.

Some 250 F-16s were deployed to the Middle East for Operation Desert Storm in 1991. Although the F-15 Eagle accounted for nearly all Iraqi aircraft shot down, the F-16s demonstrated their dual-role capability, being heavily used in strike and interdiction, destroying radar sites, tanks and trucks, rather than as fighters. The multi-role fighter has also seen action more recently in Bosnia, Afghanistan, and again in Iraq in 2003-4.

With well over 4,000 F-16s having been built for more than twenty countries, and with demand continuing, production is expected to continue beyond 2010.

Specifications for General Dynamics F-16C

Dimensions: wingspan 31 feet, length 49 feet 3 inches, height 16 feet 8.5 inches

Power: one General Electric F110-GE-100 two-spool afterburning turbofan rated at 28,982lb max and 17,260lb military thrust

Weights: empty 19,020lb, normal takeoff 28,500lb, max 42,300lb

Speed: max Mach 2+ at altitude, Mach 1.2 at sea level

Ceiling: 50,000+ feet

Range: operational radius 490 miles with four air-to-air missiles and one external fuel tank

Armament: one 20mm M61A1 six-barrel rotary cannon with 511 rounds, six AIM-9 Sidewinder, AIM-120 Amraam, R550 Magic 2, MICA, or Python 3 air-to-air missiles, or a combination

Crew: pilot

F-16C Block 50/52 cutaway key

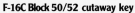

1 Pitot head/air data probe
2 Glass-fiber radome
3 Lightning conducting strips
4 Planar radar scanner
5 Radome hinge point, opens to starboard
6 Scanner tracking mechanism
7 ILS glideslope antenna
8 Radar mounting bulkhead
9 Incidence vane, port and starboard
10 IFF antenna
11 GBU-12B laser-guided bomb
12 AN/APG-68 digital pulse-Doppler, multi-mode radar equipment bay
13 Forward oblique radar warning antennas, port and starboard
14 Front pressure bulkhead
15 Static ports
16 Fuselage forebody strake fairing
17 Forward avionics equipment bay
18 Canopy jettison charge
19 Instrument panel shroud
20 Instrument panel, multi-function CRT head-down displays
21 Sidestick controller, fly-by-wire control system
22 Video recorder
23 GEC wide-angle head-up display
24 CBU-52/58/71 submunition dispenser
25 LAU-3A 19-round rocket launcher
26 2.75in (68mm) FFAR
27 CBU-87/89 Gator submunition dispenser
28 Starboard intake flank (No. 5R) stores pylon adaptor
29 LANTIRN (FLIR) targeting pod
30 One-piece frameless cockpit canopy
31 Ejection seat headrest
32 McDonnell Douglas ACES II zero-zero ejection seat
33 Side console panel
34 Canopy frame fairing
35 Canopy external emergency release
36 Engine throttle lever incorporating HOTAS (hands-on throttle-and-stick) radar controls
37 Canopy jettison handle
38 Cockpit section frame structure
39 Boundary layer splitter plate
40 Fixed-geometry engine air intake
41 Nosewheel, aft retracting
42 LANTIRN (FLIR/TFR) navigation pod
43 Port intake flank (No. 5L) stores pylon adaptor
44 Port position light
45 Intake duct framing

46 Intake ducting
47 Gun gas suppression muzzle aperture
48 Aft avionics equipment bay
49 Cockpit rear pressure bulkhead
50 Canopy hinge point
51 Ejection seat launch rails
52 Canopy rotary actuator
53 Conditioned air delivery duct
54 Canopy sealing frame
55 Canopy aft glazing
56 600-gallon external fuel tank
57 Garrett hydrazine turbine emergency power unit (EPU)
58 Hydrazine fuel tank
59 Fuel tank bay access panel
60 Forward fuselage bag-type fuel tank, total internal capacity 6972lb (3162kg)
61 Fuselage upper longeron
62 Conditioned air ducting
63 Cannon barrels
64 Forebody frame construction
65 Air system ground connection
66 Ventral air conditioning system equipment bay
67 Centerline 300-gallon fuel tank
68 Mainwheel door hydraulic actuator
69 Mainwheel door
70 Hydraulic system ground connectors
71 Gun bay ventral gas vent
72 GE M61A1 Vulcan 20mm rotary cannon
73 Ammunition feed chute
74 Hydraulic gun drive motor
75 Port hydraulic reservoir
76 Center fuselage integral fuel tank
77 Leading-edge flap drive hydraulic motor
78 Ammunition drum with 511 rounds
79 Upper position light/refuelling floodlight
80 TACAN antenna
81 Hydraulic accumulator
82 Starboard hydraulic reservoir
83 Leading-edge flap drive shaft
84 Inboard, No. 6 stores station 4,500lb (2041kg) capacity
85 Pylon attachment hardpoint
86 Leading-edge flap drive shaft and rotary actuators

87 No. 7 stores hardpoint, capacity 3,500lb (1588kg)
88 Starboard forward radar warning antenna
89 Missile launch rails
90 AIM-120 Amraam medium-range AAMs
91 MXU-648 baggage pod, carriage of essential ground equipment and personal effects for off-base deployment
92 Starboard leading-edge maneuver flap, down position
93 Outboard, No. 8 stores station, capacity 700lb (318kg)
94 Wingtip, No. 9 stores station, capacity 425lb (193kg)
95 Wingtip Amraam
96 Starboard navigation light
97 Fixed portion of trailing edge
98 Static dischargers
99 Starboard flaperon
100 Starboard wing integral fuel tank
101 Fuel system piping
102 Fuel pump
103 Starboard wingroot attachment fishplates
104 Fuel tank access panels
105 Universal air refuelling receptacle (UARSSI), open
106 Engine intake centrebody fairing
107 Airframe mounted accessory equipment gearbox
108 Jet fuel starter
109 Machined wing attachment bulkheads
110 Engine fuel management equipment
111 Pressure refuelling receptacle ventral adaptor
112 Pratt & Whitney F100-PW-229 afterburning turbofan engine
113 VHF/IFF antenna
114 Starboard flaperon hydraulic actuator
115 Fuel tank tail fins
116 Sidebody fairing integral fuel tank
117 Position light
118 Cooling air ram air intake
119 Finroot fairing
120 Forward engine support link
121 Rear fuselage integral fuel tank
122 Thermally insulated tank inner skin
123 Tank access panels

124 Radar warning system power amplifier
125 Finroot attachment fittings
126 Flight control system hydraulic accumulators
127 Multi-spar fin torsion box structure
128 Starboard all-moving tailplane (tailplane panels interchangeable)
129 General Electric F110-GE-129 alternative powerplant
130 Fin leading-edge honeycomb core
131 Dynamic pressure probe
132 Carbon-fiber fin skin paneling
133 VHF comms antenna (AM/FM)
134 Fintip antenna fairing
135 Anti-collision light
136 Threat warning antennas
137 Static dischargers
138 Rudder honeycomb core structure
139 Rudder hydraulic actuator
140 ECM antenna fairing
141 Tail navigation light
142 Variable-area afterburner nozzle
143 Afterburner nozzle flaps
144 Nozzle sealing fairing
145 Afterburner nozzle fueldraulic actuators (5)
146 Port split trailing-edge airbrake panel, open, upper and lower surfaces
147 Airbrake actuating linkage
148 Port all-moving tailplane
149 Static dischargers
150 Graphite-epoxy tailplane skin panels
151 Leading-edge honeycomb construction
152 Corrugated aluminum sub-structure
153 Tailplane pivot mounting
154 Tailplane hydraulic actuator
155 Fuel jettison chamber, port and starboard
156 Afterburner ducting

157 Rear fuselage machined bulkheads
158 Port navigation light
159 AN/ALE-40(VO-4) chaff/flare launcher, port and starboard
160 Main engine thrust mounting, port and starboard
161 Sidebody fairing frame structure
162 Runway arrester hook
163 Composite ventral fin, port and starboard
164 Port flaperon hydraulic actuator
165 Flaperon hinges
166 Port flaperon, lowered
167 External fuel tank tail fairing
168 Flaperon honeycomb core structure
169 Fixed portion of trailing edge
170 Static dischargers
171 Port navigation light
172 Wingtip, No. 1 stores station, capacity 425lb (193kg)
173 Port wingtip Amraam
174 AGM-88 HARM (High-speed Anti-Radiation Missile}

175 Mk 84 low-drag 2,000lb (907kg) HE bomb
176 Mk 83 Snakeye retarded bomb
177 AIM-9L Sidewinder air-to-air missile
178 Missile launch rails
179 No. 2 stores station, capacity 700lb (318kg)
180 No. 3 stores station, capacity 3,500lb (1588kg)
181 Port forward radar warning antenna
182 Mk 82 500lb (227kg) HE bombs
183 Triple ejector rack
184 Intermediate wing pylon
185 Leading-edge maneuver flap honeycomb core structure

186 Flap drive shaft and rotary actuators
187 Multi-spar wing torsion box structure
188 Port wing integral fuel tankage
189 No. 4 stores station hardpoint, capacity 4,500lb (2041kg)
190 Wing panel root attachment fishplates
191 Undercarriage leg mounted landing light
192 Articulated retraction/drag link
193 Main undercarriage leg strut
194 Shock absorber strut
195 Port leading-edge maneuver flap, down position

196 Inboard wing pylon
197 Port mainwheel, forward retracting
198 Fuel filler caps
199 Port 370-gallon external tank
200 Centerline, No. 5 stores pylon, capacity 2,200lb (998kg)
201 AN/ALQ-184(V)-2 (short) ECM pod
202 AGM-65 Maverick air-to-surface missiles
203 LAU-88 triple missile carrier/launcher

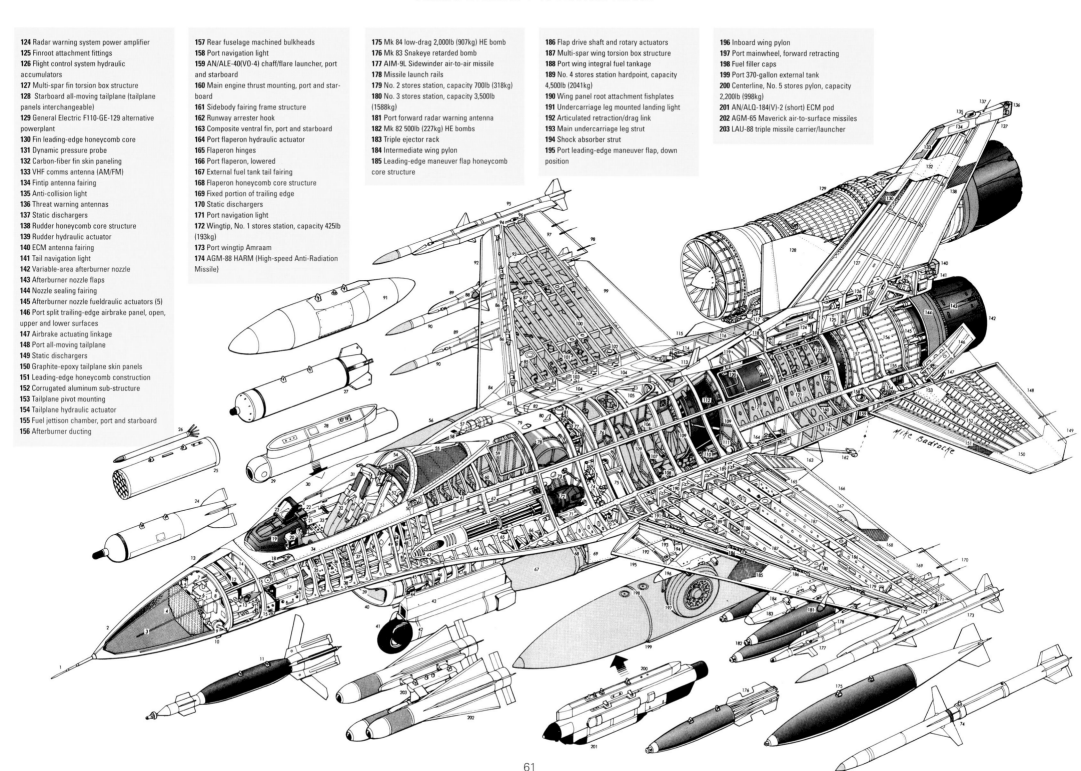

Mike Badrocke

OPPOSITE: Many weaponry and systems proving trials are carried out over the Nevada ranges near "Fightertown," as Nellis AFB is known, by the 474th Tactical Fighter Wing. This aircraft has what appears to be a countermeasures pod under the port wing.

OPPOSITE: INSET: "Fighting Falcon" is not a name much used by F-16 pilots. Rather, it is known as the Viper, or, in recognition of its fly-by-wire system, as the Electric Jet. The superb view from the cockpit is clearly apparent from this angle.

BELOW: Designed as a close air combat fighter without compromise to offset the agile Soviet MiGs, the Fighting Falcon was first deployed to USAFE based at Hahn in Germany in 1982-83, with the 50th Tactical Fighter Wing.

INSET: The F-16 has been continually updated since its first flight back in January 1974. This is a Block 50 F-16C of the 6512th Test and Evaluation Squadron based at Edwards, seen carrying a variety of external stores in 1994.

OPPOSITE: Aircraft of the five launch customers, seen in the mid-1980s. The nearest belongs to the Netherlands air force; next to it is a USAFE machine. In the lead is a Belgian aircraft, with Danish and Norwegian F-16s beyond it.

THIS PAGE: Experiments with decoupled flight modes were made using the AFTI (Advanced Fighter Technology Integration) F-16, the external signs of which are movable ventral fins. It was however judged too difficult for the average squadron jock to handle.

LEFT INSET: Although designed as an affordable light fighter, and small by modern standards, the F-16 is still significantly larger than the World War II P-51D Mustang. But one thing they share in common is the clear view bubble canopy.

RIGHT INSET: The Fighting Falcon has been exported to twenty-one nations to date, where its reliability and versatility are widely appreciated. Banking steeply over the Ardennes, this is a Belgian Air Force machine.

GLOSTER JAVELIN

In 1947 Britain's Air Ministry issued Specification F.4/48 for a two-seat, twin-engined all-weather interceptor fighter to counter the threat of a nuclear attack by high altitude bombers. Both de Havilland and Gloster submitted proposals, and both were contracted to build prototypes on April 13, 1949. The de Havilland project was the DH 110, which lost out in this competition but the company went on to develop their design further, it eventually becoming the two-seat, twin-engined, swept-wing jet fighter that entered service with the Royal Navy as the Sea Vixen. Gloster's proposal, the P.280, became the Javelin, the Royal Air Force's first delta-winged fighter, and its first missile-armed jet interceptor.

Gloster took advantage of research carried out into Germany's delta-wing research, and after the first prototype, designated GA.5, had flown (on November 26, 1951) with a triangular wing, the company reworked the design to produce a wing that was kinked at the mid-point of its leading edge, reducing the angle of sweep on the outboard section and giving a longer chord at the wing tip. This modification, which remained for all subsequent Javelins, improved stability at high subsonic speeds and added to the maneuverability of this huge fighter, the emphasis of which was on endurance and high altitude performance, rather than supersonic speed. The basic design also had an enormous broad-chord fin topped by a T-tail, and the fuselage was very large, containing two widely spaced turbojet engines.

So that it could fly and fight at night and in all weather conditions the Javelin was fitted with radio and radar equipment that was sophisticated for the period, some of it from the United States. The radar scanner was mounted in the nose. It was able to locate a target up to twenty miles away, presenting this information onto the radar operator's screens, and subsequently via a "collimeter" onto an angled piece of glass in front of the pilot's main reflector gunsight. The radar operator told the pilot how to steer to intercept the enemy, and the pilot then flew manually in a curve of pursuit until he could attack with guns or rockets. Later versions of the Javelin introduced the Firestreak heat-homing missiles, but the same interception procedure was followed.

Early versions of the Javelin had a metal hood with small portholes, it being considered that this semi-darkness would improve readability of the radar displays. However, later marks of the interceptor had a clear Perspex canopy for the navigator, it being decided that an extra pair of eyes to watch the sky would be a benefit during air combat.

Several prototypes were built and flown, each with modifications for different purposes (ranging from more powerful engines, armament trials with four 30mm Aden cannon armament, more pointed radome, air-to-air refueling capability, external drop tanks, and powered ailerons to clear Perspex canopy for the radar operator). There also seemed to be endless modifications to production aircraft, such that there were no fewer than eight fighter variants to enter service, with many aircraft undergoing post-production modifications.

The first RAF squadron to receive Javelins did so on February 24, 1956, and the type was finally withdrawn from service in 1968. Production ceased in 1960, with a total of 385 of all variants having been built.

Specifications for Gloster Javelin FAW 8

Dimensions: wingspan 52 feet, length 56 feet 3 inches, height 16 feet

Power: two Armstrong Siddeley Sapphire ASSa 7R Mk 205/206 single-spool, axial-flow afterburning turbojets each rated at 12,300lb max and 11,000 military thrust

Weights: empty 28,000lb, loaded 37,410lb, max 46,090lb

Speed: max 701mph at sea level, 620mph at 37,000 feet

Ceiling: over 50,000 feet

Range: 930 miles

Armament: two wing-mounted 30mm Aden cannon and four Firestreak infrared-homing air-to-air missiles

Crew: pilot and radar operator

LEFT: The Gloster Javelin, two of which are seen here with a highly modified Canberra, had a troubled development. First flown in November 1951, it went through nine different variants in a production run of just 385 aircraft.

Javelin FAW.Mk 9R cutaway key

1 Detachable flight refueling probe, used for overseas deployment
2 Glass-fiber radome
3 AI.Mk 22 radar scanner dish (American AN/APQ-43)
4 Scanner tracking mechanism
5 Radar transmitter/ receiver
6 Radar mounting bulkhead
7 Instrument venturi
8 Aft-retracting nosewheel
9 Mudguard
10 Torque scissor links
11 Lower IFF antenna
12 Nose equipment bay access door
13 Additional (long-range) oxygen bottles
14 Radar modulator
15 Upper IFF antenna
16 Front pressure bulkhead
17 Rudder pedals
18 Standard oxygen bottle stowage, port and starboard
19 Side console panel
20 Engine throttle levers
21 Control column
22 Pilot's instrument panel
23 Instrument panel shroud
24 Windscreen rain dispersal air duct
25 Starboard engine intake
26 Windscreen panels
27 Pilot's gyro gunsight
28 Rearward-sliding cockpit canopy
29 Ejection seat faceblind firing handle
30 Pilot's Martin-Baker Mk 4 ejection seat
31 Seat mounting rails
32 Port engine air intake
33 Intake lip bleed air de-icing
34 Intake duct framing
35 Rebecca homing antenna
36 Radar altimeter transmitting antenna
37 Missile cooling system heat exchanger
38 Cold air unit and compressor
39 Port intake duct
40 Radar operator's instrument console
41 Radar indicator
42 Fixed canopy centre section
43 Missile cooling system air bottles
44 Radar operator's rearward-sliding canopy
45 Radar operator's Martin-Baker ejection seat
46 Cockpit pressure shell framing
47 Missile control system equipment
48 Engine compressor intake
49 IPN engine starter fuel tank
50 Central equipment bay

51 Engine-driven gearbox with generators and hydraulic pumps
52 Cabin air system heat exchanger
53 Flight control rods
54 Gee antenna
55 Canopy tail fairing with heat exchanger outlet duct
56 Wing spar attachment fuselage main frame
57 Starboard main undercarriage wheel bay
58 Gun heating system air reservoirs
59 Starboard leading edge fuel tanks Nos 1, 2 and 3. Total internal capacity 1,140 gallons
60 120-gallon external pylon tanks
61 Starboard wing pylons
62 Pylon aerodynamic fairings
63 Cannon muzzle blast fairings with frangible caps
64 Cannon barrel blast tubes
65 30-mm ADEN cannon, four carried for Far Eastern deployment, two only for European operations
66 Link collector boxes
67 Gun camera
68 Aileron control rod and pitch stabiliser
69 Aileron servodyne
70 Vortex generators, three rows
71 Starboard pitot head
72 Starboard navigation light
73 Formation light
74 Starboard aileron
75 Aileron spar
76 Fixed portion of trailing edge
77 Starboard airbrake, upper and lower surfaces
78 Airbrake hydraulic jack (2)
79 Flap hydraulic jack (2)
80 Ventral flap panel
81 Ammunition magazines, 100 rounds per gun
82 Rear fuel tanks, Nos 4 and 5
83 Engine exhaust, zone-3, cooling air intake
84 Artificial feel simulator pressure heads
85 Starboard engine bay
86 Fuselage center keel structure
87 Rudder feel simulator
88 Port Armstrong Siddeley Sapphire Sa.7R turbojet with 12 percent limited reheat
89 Engine bay firewall

90 Turbine section
91 Central fuel system collector tanks
92 Engine exhaust duct
93 Fin-mounted bulkhead
94 Fin spar attachment joint
95 Servomotor
96 Rudder servodyne
97 Fin rib structure
98 Leading-edge ribs and control runs
99 Hydraulic accumulators
100 Tailplane hydraulic power control unit
101 Tailplane operating beam
102 Fixed tailplane centre section
103 Tailplane spar bearing
104 Tubular tailplane spar
105 Starboard trimming tailplane
106 Starboard elevator
107 UHF antenna
108 Tail navigation light
109 Tail warning radar antenna
110 Elevator operating linkage
111 Port elevator rib structure
112 Tailplane single spar and rib structure
113 Rudder rib structure
114 Afterburner nozzles
115 Detachable fuselage tail section, engine removal
116 Afterburner duct
117 Tail section joint frame
118 Wing rear spar attachment joint
119 Port flap housing
120 Flap hydraulic jacks
121 Airbrake hydraulic jacks
122 Semi-span rear spar
123 Port airbrake panel, upper and lower surfaces
124 Fixed trailing-edge rib structure
125 Cartridge case ejection chutes
126 Port aileron
127 Aileron rib structure
128 Aileron servodyne
129 Formation light
130 Wingtip member structure
131 Port navigation light
132 Port pitot head
133 Outer wing panel rib structure
134 Wing main spar

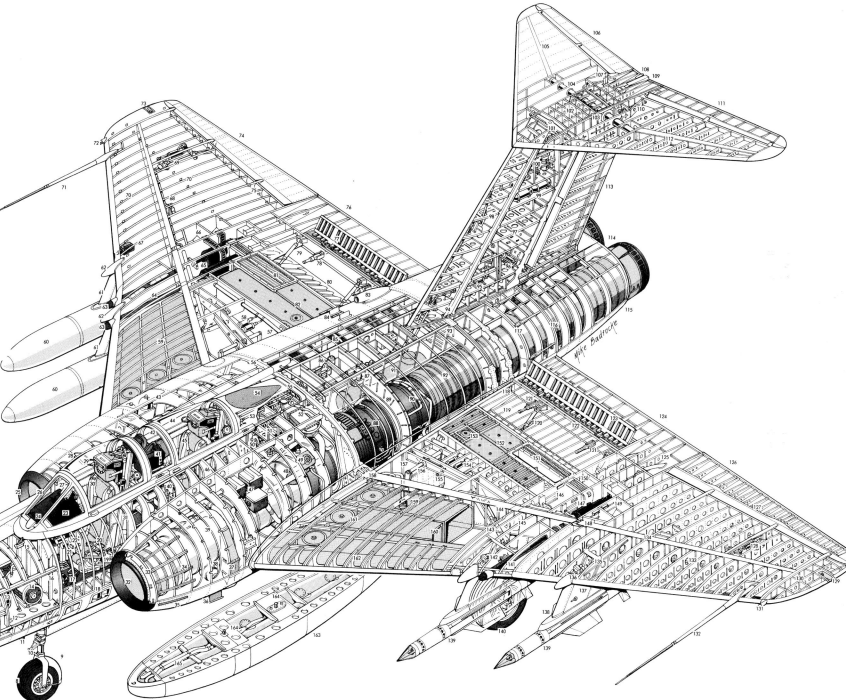

Mike Badrocke

LEFT: A twin-engined two-seater, the Javelin was designed as a night and all-weather interceptor. Unusually, it combined a delta wing with a high-set T-tail. Here, three F(AW) Mk 9s, the final variant, are led by an F(AW) Mk 7, all carrying "bosom" tanks.

ABOVE: The pen-nib fairing between the jet pipes, plus the absence of pitot sensors on the fin, appear to indicate that these are F(AW) Mk 1 Javelins. Armament consisted of four 30mm Aden cannon.

OPPOSITE INSET: The weapon fit of Javelins from the F(AW) Mk 7 onwards was the Firestreak heat homing air-to-air missile, which entered service in August 1958. By this time, Javelins had an all-flying tail. Note vortex generators outboard on the wing.

OPPOSITE: The Javelin was never a sleek airplane; nor was it ever any more than transonic. Given a thinner wing, it could have been much better, and the "bosom" tanks and cockpit outline didn't help. This is an F(AW) Mk 7 of Britain's RAF No 33 Squadron.

GLOSTER METEOR

The single-seat, twin-engined, subsonic Meteor jet day fighter was Britain's first jet fighter and the only British jet to see service during World War II. Having been designed to Specification F.9/40, Gloster Aircraft's experimental aircraft, the E.28/39, was an eminently straightforward barrel-like machine powered by an engine designed by Frank Whittle, pioneer of jet propulsion. The E.28/39 first flew on May 15, 1941, powered by one 860lb thrust Power Jets (Whittle) centrifugal-flow turbojet.

The evolved first prototype Meteor (the fifth prototype airframe) first flew on March 5, 1943, with two de Havilland H.1 turbojets, while the first airframe flew on July 24, 1943. Twenty pre-series aircraft powered by Rolls-Royce Welland 1,700lb thrust turbojets were delivered as Meteor Is, and the first of these flew on January 12, 1944. Sixteen Meteor F.Is equipped one flight of RAF 616 Squadron on July 12, 1944.

The Meteor was surprisingly large, with generous wing area, carrying the engines on the wings, away from the fuselage. It had a nosewheel tricycle undercarriage, and the cockpit was located well ahead of the wing leading edge, giving excellent pilot view. The overall configuration, however, made the early marks poor performers, but proved beneficial in the long run because, taking advantage of engine development by Rolls-Royce, the Meteor became a multi-role aircraft with outstanding speed, acceleration, and climb.

The Meteor's initial interception missions were flown against German V-I flying bombs, the first all-jet encounters in history. The first major production model was the Meteor F.III, fifteen with the Welland engines, but the other 195 with 2,000lb thrust Derwent I engines. The Meteor F.III also had a stronger airframe, additional fuel capacity, sliding canopy, and, on the final fifteen, longer engine nacelles. These fighters were sent to the European mainland from February 1945 to try to combat the Me 262, the most revolutionary fighter of the war. Although they did not engage in air combat with manned enemy aircraft, Meteors destroyed several German aircraft on the ground. One fault was that, in a dive, the Meteor reached its critical Mach number of 0.74 very quickly, and this resulted in uncontrollable buffeting. To contain the speed to acceptable limits, dive brakes were fitted.

The Meteor F.IV was fitted with Derwent 5 engines of 3,500lb thrust each, with lengthened nacelles on the wings, which were reduced in span and area to improve speed and rate of roll. This mark set world speed records of 606mph in 1945, and 616mph the following year.

The final dedicated fighter version was the F.8. It had Derwent 8 engines, a strengthened airframe, the small wings of the F.IV, lengthened fuselage, revised tail surfaces, new cockpit canopy, and an ejection seat. The first prototype of this mark flew on October 12, 1948, and deliveries to the RAF began at the end of 1949. A total of 1,183 were built for the RAF and for export.

The Royal Australian Air Force received 93 ex-RAF Meteor F.8s, these becoming the only twin-engined day jet fighters in combat in the Korean War of 1951-53. While it had a thrust to weight ratio approaching that of the MiG-15, its draggy airframe reduced performance and the F.8 was outclassed by the Russian-built fighter. Meteors were also in service with both Egypt and Israel in the Suez conflict of late 1956.

LEFT: The Gloster Meteor was the first British jet fighter to enter service, in 1944. In the early models, performance was not markedly better than conventional fighters, but the potential for improvement was quickly realized. This is the F. Mk III.

Specifications for Gloster Meteor F.8

Dimensions: wingspan 37 feet 2 inches, length 44 feet 7 inches, height 13 feet

Power: two Rolls-Royce Derwent 8 centrifugal-flow turbojets each rated at 3,600lb thrust

Weights: empty 10,684lb, normal takeoff 15,700lb, max 19,100lb

Speed: max 598mph at 10,000ft

Ceiling: 44,000 feet

Range: 600 miles

Armament: four nose-mounted 20mm Hispano Mk 5

Crew: pilot

Meteor F.Mk III cutaway key

1 Starboard detachable wingtip
2 Starboard navigation light
3 Starboard recognition light
4 Starboard aileron
5 Aileron balance tab
6 Aileron mass balance weights
7 Aileron control coupling
8 Aileron torque shaft
9 Chain sprocket
10 Cross-over control runs
11 Front spar
12 Rear spar
13 Aileron (inboard) mass balance
14 Nacelle detachable tail section
15 Jet pipe exhaust
16 Internal stabilising struts
17 Rear spar 'spectacle' frame
18 Fire extinguisher spray ring
19 Main engine mounting frame
20 Engine access panel(s)
21 Nacelle nose structure
22 Intake internal leading-edge shroud
23 Starboard engine intake
24 Windscreen de-icing spray tube
25 Reflector gunsight
26 Cellular glass bulletproof windscreen
27 Aft-sliding cockpit canopy
28 Demolition incendiary (cockpit starboard wall)
29 RPM indicators (left and right of gunsight)
30 Pilot's seat
31 Forward fuselage top deflector skin
32 Gun wobble button
33 Control column grip
34 Main instrument panel
35 Nosewheel armored bulkhead
36 Nose release catches (10)
37 Nosewheel jack bulkhead
38 Nose ballast weight location
39 Nosewheel mounting frames
40 Radius rod (link and jack omitted)
41 Nosewheel pivot bearings
42 Shimmy-damper/ self-centring strut
43 Gun camera
44 Camera access
45 Aperture
46 Nose cone
47 Cabin cold-air intake
48 Nosewheel leg door
49 Picketing rings
50 Tension shock absorber

51 Pivot bracket
52 Mudguard
53 Torque strut
54 Doorhoop
55 Wheel fork
56 Retractable nosewheel
57 Nosewheel doors
58 Port cannon trough fairings
59 Nosewheel cover
60 Intermediate diaphragm
61 Blast tubes
62 Gun front mount rails
63 Pilot's seat pan
64 Emergency crowbar
65 Canopy de-misting silica gel cylinder
66 Bulletproof glass rear view cut-outs
67 Canopy track
68 Sea bulkhead
69 Entry step
70 Link ejection chutes
71 Case ejection chutes
72 20-mm Hispano Mk III cannon
73 Belt feed mechanism
74 Ammunition feed necks
75 Ammunition tanks
76 Aft glazing (magazine bay top door)
77 Leading ramp
78 Front spar bulkhead
79 Oxygen bottles (2)
80 Front spar carry-through
81 Tank bearer frames
82 Rear spar carry-through
83 Self-sealing (twin compartment) main fuel tank, capacity 198 gallons in each half
84 Fuel connector pipe
85 Return pipe
86 Drain pipes
87 Fuel filler caps
88 Tank doors (2)
89 T.R.1143 aerial mast
90 Rear spar bulkhead (plywood face)
91 Aerial support frame
92 R.3121 (or B.C.966M IFF installation
93 Tab control cables
94 Amplifier
95 Fire extinguisher bottles (2)

96 Elevator torque shaft
97 T.R.1143 transmitter/ receiver radio installation
98 Pneumatic system filler
99 Pneumatic system (compressed) air cylinders
100 Tab cable fairlead
101 Elevator control cable
102 Top longeron
103 Fuselage frame
104 IFF aerial
105 DR compass master unit
106 Rudder cables
107 Starboard lower longeron
108 Cable access panels (port and starboard)
109 Tail section joint
110 Rudder linkage
111 Tail ballast weight location
112 Fin spar/fuselage frame
113 Rudder tab control
114 Fin structure
115 Torpedo fairing
116 Tailplane spar/upper fin attachment plates
117 Upper fin section
118 Starboard tailplane
119 Elevator horn and mass balance
120 Starboard elevator
121 Rudder horn and mass balance
122 Rudder upper hinge
123 Rudder frame
124 Fixed tab
125 Rear fairing
126 Tail navigation light
127 Elevator torque shaft
128 Elevator trim tab
129 Elevator frame
130 Elevator horn and mass balance
131 Tailplane structure
132 Rudder combined balance trim tab
133 Rudder lower section
134 Elevator push-rod linkage
135 Rudder internal/ lower mass balance weight
136 Emergency landing tailskid
137 Tail section riveted joint
138 Port lower longeron
139 Fuselage stressed skin
140 Wingroot fairing

141 Inboard split flap
142 Airbrake (upper and lower surfaces)
143 Flap indicator transmitter
144 Rear spar
145 Inter-coupler cables (airbrake/airbrake and flap/flap)
146 Port mainwheel well
147 Roof rib station
148 Front diaphragm
149 Undercarriage beam
150 Undercarriage retraction jack
151 Undercarriage sidestay/downlock
152 Front spar
153 Nose ribs
154 Aileron control runs
155 Mainwheel door inner section
156 Ventral tank transfer pipe
157 Tank rear fairing
158 Filler stack pipes
159 Ventral tank attachment strap access doors
160 Anti-surge baffles
161 Fixed ventral fuel tank, capacity 126 gallons
162 Air pressure inlet
163 Tank front fairing

164 Port mainwheel
165 Starboard engine intake
166 Intake internal leading edge shroud
167 Auxiliary gearbox drives (vacuum pump/generator)
168 Nacelle nose structure
169 Starter motor
170 Oil tank
171 Rolls-Royce W.2B/23C Derwent I
172 Main engine mounting frame
173 Combustion chambers
174 Rear spar spectacle frame
175 Jet pipe thermo-coupling
176 Nacelle aft frames
177 Nacelle detachable tail section
178 Jet pipe suspension link
179 Jet pipe exhaust
180 Gap fairing tail section
181 Rear-spar outer wing fixing
182 Outer wing rib No. 1
183 Engine end rib
184 Engine mounting/ removal trunnion
185 Gap fairing nose section
186 Front-spar outer wing fixing

187 Nose ribs
188 Intermediate riblets
189 Wing ribs
190 Aileron drive chain sprocket
191 Aileron torque shaft
192 Retractable landing lamp
193 Port aileron
194 Aileron balance tab
195 Rear spar
196 Front spar
197 Pitot head
198 Port navigation light
199 Outer wing rib No. 10/wingtip attachment
200 Port recognition light

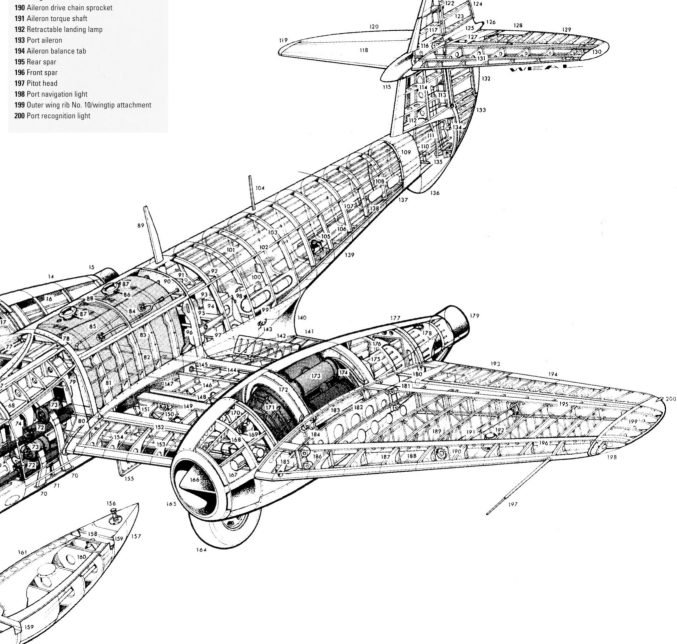

OPPOSITE INSET: The Meteor F. Mk IV was powered by two Rolls-Royce Derwent 5 turbojets in lengthened nacelles, and had a reduced wingspan. Much faster than the Mk III, in 1946 the Mk F. IV was twice used to set new absolute world air speed records.

OPPOSITE: The definitive Meteor day fighter was the F. Mk VIII; elements of two auxiliary squadrons, Nos 600 and 615, are seen here. In all the fighter served with eleven air arms, and was operated by Australia in Korea, where it was outclassed by the MiG-15.

LEFT: Meteor F. Mk IIIs of No 56 Squadron pose for the camera after World War II. Similar in layout to the German Me 262, it had two main advantages: the forward cockpit position was far superior, and it was fitted with airbrakes to control diving speed.

INSET: The two-seater Meteor conversion trainer was adapted by Armstrong Whitworth as a makeshift night fighter, with AI 21 radar in the nose, and with the cannon moved to the wings outboard of the engines. This is the NF. 14, the final Meteor variant.

GRUMMAN F4F-4 WILDCAT

LEFT: The Grumman F4F Wildcat was tough and hard-hitting. It held the ring for the U.S. Navy against the far more maneuverable Zero for the first nine months of the Pacific War.

The Grumman F4F Wildcat, the only U.S. Navy fighter to serve throughout all of World War II, was first designed as a biplane in 1935. Designated the XF4FA, this version soon showed that it could not compete with monoplane fighters and an alternate design was ordered in 1936. This was the XF4F-2, a mid-wing, all-metal monoplane with landing gear that retracted into the fuselage. In flight tests, it proved to be 10mph faster than its competitor, the F2A-1 Buffalo, which had earlier shown the F4F biplane design as obsolete. Though the F2A won the fly-off tests in 1938, modifications to the Wildcat were pushed ahead and a new prototype, the XF4F-3, with increased wingspan, altered tail design and a more powerful engine, showed such promise that initial orders were placed for it in 1939. Other models followed, including F4F-4 and -7, and versions ordered by Britain and France (the aircraft for the latter not being delivered because of France's surrender, and being instead transferred to Britain).

The first Wildcats to be delivered to U.S. Navy squadrons went to VF-4 and VF-7 at NAS Norfolk, assigned to the carriers *Ranger* and *Wasp*, respectively. By the end of 1941, the Navy and Marine Corps had received 248 of the stubby little fighters. These suffered their first combat losses at the Marine air stations at Ewa, Hawaii, and Wake Island on December 7, 1941, during Japanese attacks, but soon avenged themselves against raiding bombers at Wake before being overcome by the vastly superior numbers of the attacking force. This was not the F4F's first taste of combat. As Martlets in Britain's Royal Navy they had already seen action against the *Luftwaffe* off the British coast, the type's first air combat victory occurring on December 25, 1940, when a Junkers Ju 88 was shot down over Scapa Flow.

The F4F-4, introduced in 1941, had six rather than the previous Wildcat's four heavy machine guns, self-sealing fuel tanks, a bullet-proof windshield, and 139lb of armor protection. It also added a new feature to the Wildcat: folding wings. Though manually operated, this alteration added to the aircraft's utility, particularly on the small flight decks of escort carriers where Wildcats soon appeared as teammates to another Grumman product, the TBF Avenger, as part of the anti-submarine warfare effort in the Atlantic. Wildcats participated in the important Pacific theater sea battles of Coral Sea and Midway and served with the Marines at Guadalcanal. They also made up the Navy's fighter force during the North African landings in November 1942.

The Wildcat was generally inferior in performance to Japan's Zero – in speed, climb rate, acceleration, and turn radius. But it could absorb far more damage than the Zero, and was therefore more difficult to shoot down, and in fact its rate of roll was better at speeds above 250mph. While inferior in performance in certain respects to many of the fighters met in combat, Wildcats, because of their rugged construction and the well trained men who flew them, maintained a victory-to-loss ratio of nearly seven to one, even though they were the only carrier-based fighters operated by the Navy during the first half of the war in the Pacific.

In April 1942, Eastern Aircraft assumed Wildcat production to allow Grumman to concentrate on the F6F. Eastern's versions were designated FM-1s and FM-2s, and, in British service, as Wildcat Vs and VIs. The FM-2 was recognized by its taller stabilizer.

Specifications for Grumman F4F-4 Wildcat

Dimensions: wingspan 38 feet, length 29 feet, height 11 feet 4 inches

Power: one Pratt & Whitney R-1830-86 14-cylinder Twin Wasp radial engine rated at 1,200hp

Weights: empty 5,895lb, normal takeoff 7,975lb, max 8,762lb

Speed: max 320mph at 18,800 feet, 275mph at sea level

Ceiling: 34,000 feet

Range: 770 miles

Armament: six 0.50in wing-mounted Browning M2 machine guns with 240 rounds per gun, plus two 100lb bombs

Crew: pilot

F4F-4 Wildcat cutaway key

1 Starboard navigation light
2 Wingtip
3 Starboard formation light
4 Rear spar
5 Aileron construction
6 Fixed aileron tab
7 All riveted wing construction
8 Lateral stiffeners
9 Forward canted main spar
10 "Crimped" leading-edge ribs
11 Solid web forward ribs
12 Starboard outer gun blast tube
13 Carburetor air duct
14 Intake
15 Curtiss three-bladed, constant-speed propeller
16 Propeller cuffs
17 Propeller hub
18 Engine front face
19 Pressure baffle
20 Forward cowling ring
21 Cooler intake
22 Cooler air duct
23 Pratt & Whitney R-1830-86 radial engine
24 Rear cowling ring/flap support
25 Controllable cowling flaps
26 Downdraft ram air duct
27 Engine mounting ring
28 Anti-detonant regulator unit
29 Cartridge starter
30 Generator
31 Intercooler
32 Engine accessories
33 Bearer assembly welded cluster joint
34 Main beam
35 Lower cowl flap
36 Exhaust stub
37 Starboard mainwheel
38 Undercarriage fairing
39 Lower drag link
40 Hydraulic brake
41 Port mainwheel
42 Detachable hub cover
43 Low-pressure tire
44 Axle forging
45 Upper drag link
46 Oleo shock strut
47 Ventral fairing
48 Wheel well
49 Pivot point
50 Landing light
51 Main forging

52 Compression link
53 Gun camera port
54 Counter balance
55 Anti-detonant tank
56 Retraction sprocket
57 Gear box
58 Stainless steel firewall
59 Engine bearers
60 Actuation chain (undercarriage)
61 Engine oil tank
62 Oil filler
63 Hoisting sling installation
64 Bullet resistant windscreen
65 Reflector gunsight
66 Panoramic rear-view mirror
67 Wing fold position
68 Adjustable headrest
69 Shoulder harness
70 Canopy track sill
71 Pilot's adjustable seat
72 Instrument panel shroud
73 Undercarriage manual crank
74 Control column
75 Rudder pedals
76 Fuselage/front spar attachment
77 Main fuel filler cap
78 Seat harness attachment
79 Back armor
80 Oxygen cylinder
81 Reserve fuel filler cap
82 Alternative transmitter/receiver (ABA or IFF) installation
83 Battery
84 IFF and ABA dynamotor units
85 Wing flap vacuum tank
86 Handhold
87 Turnover bar
88 Rearward-sliding Plexiglas canopy
89 Streamlined aerial mast
90 Mast support
91 One-man Mk IA life-raft stowage
92 Upper longeron
93 Toolkit
94 Aerial lead-in
95 Elevator and rudder control runs
96 "L"-section fuselage frames
97 IFF aerial

98 Dorsal lights
99 Whip aerial
100 Wing-fold jury strut
101 Fin fairing
102 Access panel
103 Tailwheel strut extension arm
104 Rudder trim tab control flexible shaft
105 Tailplane rib profile
106 Starboard tailplane
107 Static balance
108 Elevator hinge (self-aligning)
109 Fin construction
110 Rudder upper hinge
111 Aerial
112 Insulator
113 Aerial mast
114 Rudder post
115 Rudder construction
116 Aluminum alloy leading-edge
117 Rudder trim tab
118 Elevator torque tube
119 Port elevator
120 Elevator trim tab
121 Elevator hinge (self-aligning)
122 Arresting hook (extended)
123 Tailplane spar
124 Rear navigation light
125 Towing lug
126 Rudder torque tube support
127 Elevator control linkage
128 Rudder control cable
129 Arresting hook spring
130 Tailwheel shock strut
131 Rear fuselage frame/bulkhead
132 Forged castor fairing
133 Tailwheel
134 Tailwheel centering springs
135 Alclad flush-riveted stressed skin
136 Lifting tube
137 Remote compass transmitter
138 Tailwheel lock cable
139 Arresting hook cable
140 "Z"-section fuselage stringers
141 ZB relay box
142 Transmitter
143 Elevator and rudder tab controls
144 Antenna relay unit

145 Radio junction box
146 Receiver unit and adapter
147 Inertia switch
148 Radio equipment support rack
149 Entry foothold
150 Reserve fuel tank, capacity 27 gallons
151 Fuselage/rear spar attachment
152 Wing hinge line
153 Main (underfloor) fuel tank, capacity 117 gallons
154 Stub wing end rib and fairing
155 Inboard gun blast tubes
156 Plexiglas observation panel
157 Ventral antenna
158 Outboard gun port
159 ZB antenna
160 Fixed D/F loop

161 Two 0.50in (12.7mm) Browning M2 machine guns
162 Outboard gun access/loading panels
163 ABA antenna
164 Flap profile
165 Outboard 0.50in (12.7mm) Browning M2 machine gun
166 Aileron control linkage
167 Aileron trim tab
168 Port aileron
169 Aileron hinges (self-aligning)
170 Port formation light
171 Port navigation light
172 Wing skinning
173 Bomb rack (optional)
174 Fragmentation bomb
175 Pitot head

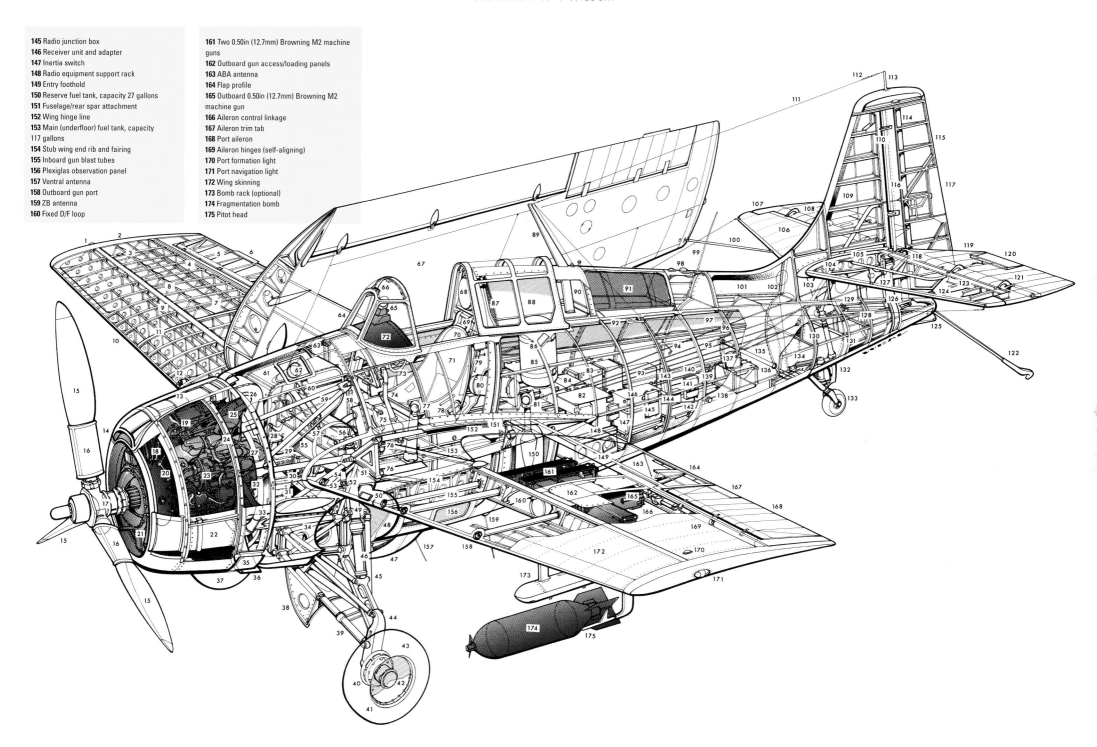

OPPOSITE: The tall fin and the vertical aerial show that this example of the Grumman F4F Wildcat is actually a Mk VI. F4Fs served with Britain's Fleet Air Arm throughout World War II, where they were mostly known as Martlets.

OPPOSITE INSET: The high seat position and the down-sloped cowling gave a good view over the nose for deflection shooting. The lack of wing folding and only two machine guns in each wing show that this is the F4F-3 Wildcat.

LEFT: A Martlet I lines up ready for a carrier takeoff (its arrester hook is up!). The type opened its account on Christmas Day 1940, when two land-based Martlets shot down a Junkers Ju 88 over the Fleet anchorage at Scapa Flow.

INSET: Martlets from the Mk II onwards had wing folding, as seen here, which enabled them to fit on the lifts of British carriers, which in turn allowed them to be deployed aboard. They could also operate from small escort carriers.

RIGHT: Grumman F4F-4 Wildcats played a major part in the great carrier battles of Coral Sea and Midway, the latter a turning point in the war. The markings shown here were in use between July and September 1943.

OPPOSITE: The red spot in the center of the white star indicates an early war picture, as this was deleted from about mid-1942. The narrow track main gear retracting into the fuselage is a typically Grumman concept.

OPPOSITE TOP: Probably a prewar picture of an F4F-2 Wildcat. It was not pretty; it was not an outstanding performer, but it was tough and survivable, with a hefty punch. Not for nothing did Grumman become known as "The Ironworks"!

OPPOSITE BOTTOM: April 1941, and a British Fleet Air Arm pilot prepares to take off for his first flight in a Martlet I. FAA Martlets and Wildcats saw action throughout the war, their final victims three German Bf 109s over Norway in March 1945.

GRUMMAN F6F HELLCAT

Left: In appearance, the Grumman F6F Hellcat was basically a scaled-up Wildcat. Dimensions apart, the main external difference was a low, rather than a mid-set wing, into which the main gears retracted.

The Hellcat vies with the Spitfire for the accolade of being the greatest fighter of World War II, and certainly can have few equals in terms of combat successes – more than 6,000 enemy aircraft shot down, 4,947 by U.S. Navy carrier squadrons, 209 by land-based Marine Corps units, and the remainder by Allied Hellcat units. In just one day, June 19,1944, in what became known as "The Great Marianas Turkey Shoot," it is credited with shooting down no fewer than 243 Japanese carrier aircraft of a total of 328 destroyed, compared with just 28 U.S. Navy losses from all causes.

While it was not the fastest shipboard fighter of the war, nor the most agile, both of these characteristics trailed behind the design aims of its makers, Grumman, who would not permit them to compromise structural strength, armor protection and firepower in their plans for a primarily air superiority fighter capable of seeking our the enemy so that he could be engaged in combat. Grumman's speed of design to manufacture to service entry was also truly astonishing. Two prototypes were ordered on June 30, 1941, and less than a year later the first was being flight-tested. Within fourteen weeks, on October 3, 1942, the first production aircraft, the F6F-3, was flown. Navy squadrons began to equip with Hellcats from January 1943. Their operational debut occurred on August 31, and by the end of that year fifteen squadrons were flying the type, and no fewer than 2,555 F6Fs had been delivered. When production terminated in November 1945, some 12,275 Hellcats had been built.

Grumman had been contracted to supply a successor to the company's F4F Corsair, which had served well in the early stages of the war, but was proving to be outclassed by the faster, better-turning Zero. While the Corsair remained in production (built as the FM-1 and British-serving Martlet V by General Motors), the F6F took the Pacific by storm and was much more than a developed F4F. In attaining more speed, greater climb, better maneuverability, good protection, increased endurance and more ammunition, its empty weight almost doubled that of the Corsair. Unusual features were its 334sq ft of square-tipped, low-set wings, which had a distinct kink, and its rearward-retracting landing gear.

Protection of the pilot and vital parts of the forward fuselage, such as around the oil system, was afforded by 212lb of armor plating. Its Pratt & Whitney R-2800-10 Double Wasp 18-cylinder radial engine was adopted to maximize acceleration in level flight by giving the angle of attack for minimum drag. Originally, the Double Wasp

provided 2,000hp, but in 1944 water injection was added to boost emergency rating to 2,200hp in the R-2800-10W, which became standard.

While the Hellcat could not maneuver with its Japanese opponents, it was faster and could out-dive them. Furthermore, it possessed more firepower and could absorb more punishment. It was stable in flight, although was apt to display marked changes in directional and lateral trim with alterations in speed and power.

The F6F-5, first flown on April 4, 1944, standardized progressive improvements made to the F6F-3. The F6F-3N and F6F-5N were night fighters with APS-6 radar on a wing pod; the F6F-5K was a drone, and the F6F-5P a photo-reconnaissance version.

Britain's Fleet Air Arm received 930 F6F-5s from July 1943, originally naming them Gannets but later Hellcat IIs; these were initially used to cover anti-shipping strikes in European waters, and from late 1944 operated throughout the Far East.

Specifications for Grumman F6F-3 Hellcat

Dimensions:	wingspan 42 feet 10 inches, length 33 feet 4 inches, height 14 feet 5 inches
Power:	one Pratt & Whitney R-2800-10W 18-cylinder Double Wasp radial rated at 2,200hp
Weights:	empty 9,042lb, normal takeoff 12,186, max takeoff 13,221lb
Speed:	max 376mph at 22,800 feet, 324mph at sea level feet
Ceiling:	37,500 feet
Range:	1,085 miles
Armament:	six 0.50in wing-mounted Browning M2 machine guns with 400 rounds per gun
Crew:	pilot

F6F-5 Hellcat cutaway key

1 Radio mast
2 Rudder balance
3 Rudder upper hinge
4 Aluminum alloy fin ribs
5 Rudder post
6 Rudder structure
7 Rudder trim tab
8 Rudder middle hinge
9 Diagonal stiffeners
10 Aluminum alloy elevator trim tab
11 Fabric-covered (and taped) elevator surfaces
12 Elevator balance
13 Flush-riveted leading-edge strip
14 Arrester hook (extended)
15 Tailplane ribs
16 Tail navigation (running) light
17 Rudder lower hinge
18 Arrester hook (stowed)
19 Fin main spar lower cut-out
20 Tailplane end rib
21 Fin forward spar
22 Fuselage/finroot fairing
23 Port elevator
24 Aluminum alloy-skinned tailplane
25 Section light
26 Fuselage aft frame
27 Control access
28 Bulkhead
29 Tailwheel hydraulic shock-absorber
30 Tailwheel centring mechanism
31 Tailwheel steel mounting arm
32 Rearward-retracting tailwheel (hard rubber tyre)
33 Fairing
34 Steel plate door fairing
35 Tricing sling support tube
36 Hydraulic actuating cylinder
37 Flanged ring fuselage frames
38 Control cable runs
39 Fuselage longerons
40 Relay box
41 Dorsal rod antenna
42 Dorsal recognition light
43 Radio aerial
44 Radio mast
45 Aerial lead-in
46 Dorsal frame stiffeners
47 Junction box
48 Radio equipment (upper rack)
49 Radio shelf
50 Control cable runs
51 Transverse brace
52 Remote radio compass
53 Ventral recognition lights (three)
54 Ventral rod antenna
55 Destructor device
56 Accumulator
57 Radio equipment (lower rack)
58 Entry hand/footholds
59 Engine water injection tank
60 Canopy track
61 Water filler neck
62 Rear-view window
63 Rearward-sliding cockpit canopy (open)
64 Headrest
65 Pilot's head/shoulder armor
66 Canopy sill (reinforced)
67 Fire extinguisher
68 Oxygen bottle (port fuselage wall)
69 Water tank mounting
70 Underfloor self-sealing fuel tank (60 gallons)
71 Armored bulkhead
72 Starboard console
73 Pilot's seat
74 Hydraulic handpump
75 Fuel filler cap and neck
76 Rudder pedals
77 Central console
78 Control column
79 Chart board (horizontal stowage)
80 Instrument panel
81 Panel coaming
82 Reflector gunsight
83 Rear-view mirror
84 Armored glass windshield
85 Deflection plate (pilot forward protection)
86 Main bulkhead (armor-plated upper section with hoisting sling attachments port and starboard)
87 Aluminum alloy aileron trim tab
88 Fabric-covered (and taped) aileron surfaces
89 Flush-riveted outer wing skin
90 Aluminum alloy sheet wingtip (riveted to wing outer rib)
91 Port navigation (running) light
92 Formed leading-edge (approach/landing light and camera gun inboard)
93 Fixed cowling panel
94 Armor plate (oil tank forward protection)
95 Oil tank (19 gallons)
96 Welded engine mount fittings
97 Fuselage forward bulkhead
98 Aileron control linkage
99 Engine accessories bay
100 Engine mounting frame (hydraulic fluid reservoir attached to port frames)
101 Controllable cooling gills
102 Cowling ring (removable servicing/ access panels)
103 Pratt & Whitney R-2800-10W twin-row radial air-cooled engine
104 Nose ring profile
105 Reduction gear housing
106 Three-bladed Hamilton Standard Hydromatic controllable-pitch propeller
107 Propeller hub
108 Engine oil cooler (center) and supercharger intercooler
109 Oil cooler deflection plate under-protection
110 Oil cooler duct
111 Intercooler intake duct
112 Mainwheel fairing
113 Port mainwheel
114 Auxiliary tank support/attachment arms
115 Cooler outlet and fairing
116 Exhaust cluster
117 Supercharger housing
118 Exhaust outlet scoop
119 Wing front spar web
120 Wing front spar/fuselage attachment bolts
121 Undercarriage mounting/pivot point on front spar
122 Inter-spar self-sealing fuel tanks (port and starboard: 87.5 gallons each)
123 Wing rear spar/fuselage attachment bolts
124 Structural end rib
125 Slotted wing flap profile
126 Wing flap center-section
127 Wing fold line
128 Starboard wheel well (doubler-plate reinforced edges)
129 Gun bay
130 Removable diagonal brace strut
131 Three 0.5in (12.7mm) Colt Browning machine guns
132 Auxiliary tank aft support

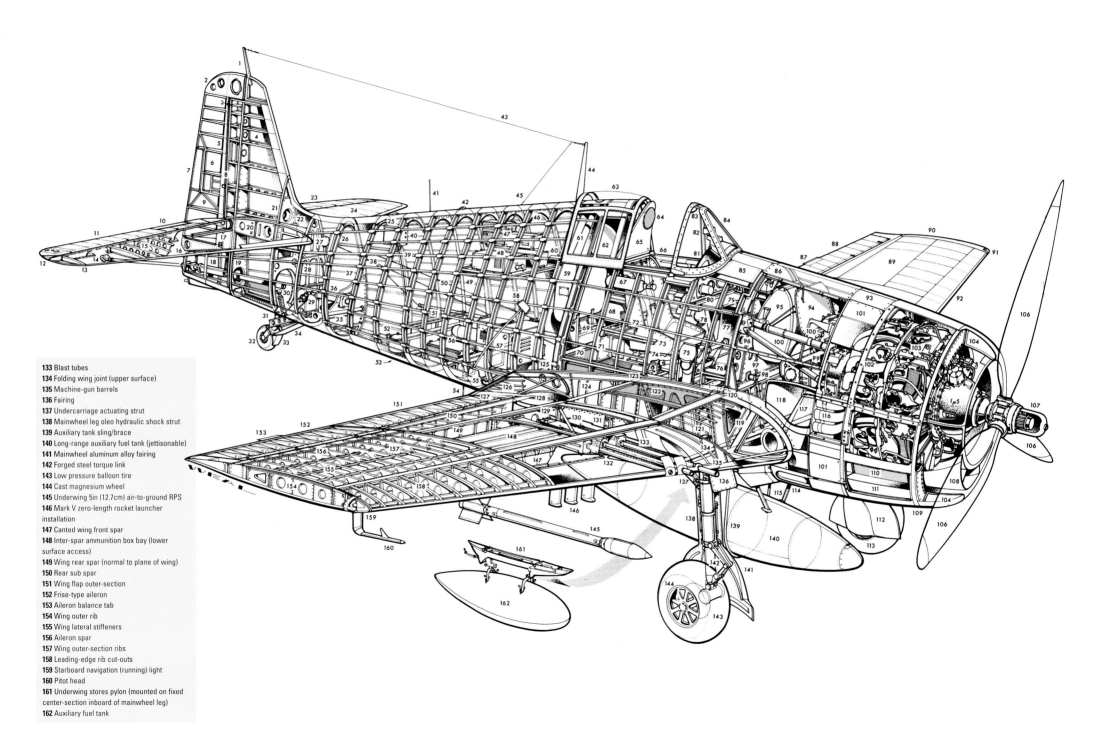

133 Blast tubes
134 Folding wing joint (upper surface)
135 Machine-gun barrels
136 Fairing
137 Undercarriage actuating strut
138 Mainwheel leg oleo hydraulic shock strut
139 Auxiliary tank sling/brace
140 Long-range auxiliary fuel tank (jettisonable)
141 Mainwheel aluminum alloy fairing
142 Forged steel torque link
143 Low pressure balloon tire
144 Cast magnesium wheel
145 Underwing 5in (12.7cm) air-to-ground RPS
146 Mark V zero-length rocket launcher
installation
147 Canted wing front spar
148 Inter-spar ammunition box bay (lower
surface access)
149 Wing rear spar (normal to plane of wing)
150 Rear sub spar
151 Wing flap outer-section
152 Frise-type aileron
153 Aileron balance tab
154 Wing outer rib
155 Wing lateral stiffeners
156 Aileron spar
157 Wing outer-section ribs
158 Leading-edge rib cut-outs
159 Starboard navigation (running) light
160 Pitot head
161 Underwing stores pylon (mounted on fixed
center-section inboard of mainwheel leg)
162 Auxiliary fuel tank

RIGHT: Hellcat carrier trials. Its viceless handling, ability to outfly the Japanese Zero, and rugged construction made it ideal for carrier operations. As 23-victory Hellcat ace Gene Valencia commented: "If they could cook, I'd marry one!"

OPPOSITE: F6F-3 Hellcats line up for launch, showing the huge Pratt & Whitney R-2800 Double Wasp radial engine rated at 2,200hp. Radial engines, although creating more drag than inlines, were far less susceptible to battle damage.

OPPOSITE INSET BOTTOM: The F6F-3 made its operational debut in August 1943 with an attack on Marcus Island. In all, more than 4,000 of this variant were built. This is a VF-12 aircraft, pictured at about the time of the Great Marianas Turkey Shoot.

OPPOSITE INSET TOP: Taken aboard USS *Lexington*, this picture shows a recently landed F6F-3 in 1944, being pushed forward as the pilot walks away. At about double the weight of the Wildcat, it takes an awful lot of manpower.

Opposite inset: A fine study of a rugged F6F-3, one of 252 delivered as Hellcat Is to Britain's Royal Navy under Lend-Lease. From July 1943 these covered anti-shipping strikes off Norway. Late the following year these RN Hellcats were deployed to the Pacific, but most of the air combat was over by then.

Opposite: In February 1945, a Hellcat comes to grief aboard USS *Lexington*. Having missed the arrester wires, it hit the barrier, rupturing the drop tank. The pilot, Ensign Ardon R. Ives, makes his precarious escape along the wing.

Above: The British Fleet Air Arm also used Hellcats. The example shown is in Pacific Fleet markings, adopted to avoid "own goals." It has just "boltered," having missed the arrester wires, as is shown by the deployed tail hook.

Left: The F6F-5 entered service in 1944, in which the inner 0.50-inch machine guns were replaced by 20mm cannon. Clearly visible here is the negative thrust line of the Twin Wasp engine, adopted to maximize acceleration in level flight.

GRUMMAN F9F PANTHER

The single-seat, single-engined F9F Panther became a mainstay of U.S. Navy and Marine forces in the Korean War, being the first carrier jet fighter to see combat when it began operations in Korea on July 3, 1950, and the first to shoot down a MiG-15. Mainly used for ground attack and interdiction, Panthers nevertheless scored a further five victories against the small, deadly MiG, for one loss, and additionally, on their first mission, accounted for at least two other Russian-designed fighters, Yak-9s.

The F9F series began when development was initiated on the large, four-jet XF9F-1 night fighter with radar in the nose and a two-man crew seated in tandem. But before design work was completed, the XF9F-1 was dropped and the project shifted to the single-seat, single-jet XF9F-2 day fighter without radar. The imported Rolls-Royce Nene jet engines of the two XF9F-2 prototypes were replaced in production F9F-2s by Pratt & Whitney-built J42 Nenes in the aft fuselage, with the jet pipe ending under the tail. The new fighter had a straight wing, with a leading edge flap to give variable camber, trailing edge flaps inboard and hydraulically powered ailerons outboard. The horizontal tail was set high on a large triangular fin. Permanently attached tip-mounted external fuel tanks were the most obvious change added to all Panthers early in the program.

In the XF9F-3 and production F9F-3s, an Allison J33 replaced the Nene. Only engine installation details differed between the -2 and -3 Panthers. While the first aircraft to see squadron service were the -3s, which VF-51 received in May 1949, the Nene-powered -2 became the sole production version following early deliveries. An increased thrust version of the Allison J33 led to the -4 with a longer fuselage and increased-area vertical tail. The same airframe with the P&W-produced J48 version of the Rolls-Royce Tay engine became the F9F-5. For servicing, the Panther came apart like a Meccano set, with access to the engine, for example, being achieved by unbolting the rear fuselage and wheeling it clear on a dolly.

The -5s joined the -2s as the major production versions. Photo versions, the Navy-modified -2P and Grumman-built -5P, also served in carrier air groups of the early 1950s. A total of 1,385 Panthers were delivered to the Navy, whose aircraft were midnight blue, whereas Marine Panthers were gray. On one occasion a gray Marine Panther was fitted with a dark blue Navy tail, to become "The Blue-tailed Fly." Conversely, a Navy Panther received a gray tail to become "Vice Versa"! The last Marine combat squadrons to use Panthers kept their -5s until late 1957, and a few drone F9F-5KDs remained to be redesignated DF-9Fs in 1962.

As the -4 and -5 Panthers replaced the -2s in carrier squadrons, the -2s took over advanced training, drone/drone control, reserve squadron and other duties, followed in turn by the -4s and -5s as they were replaced by their swept-wing successors, the F9F-6, -7 and -8 Cougars. The -6 retained the fuselage and tail assembly of the Panther, but had a thinner wing embodying 35 degrees of sweepback; the -7 was virtually identical but had an Allison J33-A-16 in place of the -6's J48-P-6A engine, and the final fighter Cougar had an upgraded and more powerful J48-P-8A engine, marginally lengthened fuselage, enlarged wing area (some 40 percent greater than the original Panther's) and increased internal fuel.

LEFT: First flown in November 1947, the F8F was named Panther, thus perpetuating Grumman's line of "cats." Armed with four 20mm cannon, the Panther flew extensively in the Korean War, in which it destroyed six MiG-15s in air combat, for one loss.

F9F-8 (F-9J) Cougar cutaway key

1 Flight refueling probe
2 Deck barricade deflector
3 Cannon muzzles
4 Gun ranging radar antenna (AN/APG-30A)
5 D/F loop aerial
6 D/F transmitter/ receiver
7 Battery
8 Voltage regulators
9 Cannon barrels
10 UHF homing adapter antenna
11 Antenna housing
12 Cannon recoil spring
13 M3 20mm cannon (four)
14 Nose cone withdrawal rail
15 Inboard gun ammunition tanks (190rpg)
16 Ammunition feed chutes
17 Outboard gun ammunition tanks (190rpg)
18 Armored cockpit front pressure bulkhead
19 Nose undercarriage leg strut
20 Shimmy damper
21 Nosewheel
22 Torque scissor links
23 Nosewheel doors
24 VHF aerial on starboard nosewheel door
25 Alternators
26 Nosewheel bay
27 Cockpit floor level
28 Rudder pedals
29 Ejection seat footrests
30 Control column
31 Instrument panel
32 Instrument panel shroud
33 Bullet proof windscreen
34 Radar gunsight (Aero 5D-1)
35 Starboard side console panel
36 Pilot's ejection seat
37 Engine throttle control
38 Retractable boarding step
39 Perforated ventral airbrake (port and starboard)
40 Airbrake hydraulic jack
41 Kick-in boarding steps
42 Boundary layer splitter plate
43 Port air intake
44 Cockpit port side console panel
45 Pressurisation and air conditioning valves
46 Cockpit rear pressure bulkhead
47 Safety harness
48 Face-blind firing handle
49 Sliding canopy rail
50 Cockpit canopy cover
51 Ejection seat launch rails
52 Pilot's back armor

53 Canopy external latch
54 Oxygen bottle
55 Equipment bay access door
56 Forward fuselage fuel tank
57 Fuselage frame and stringer construction
58 Main longeron
59 Canopy aft glazing
60 Sliding canopy jack
61 Wing-fold spar hinge joint
62 Wing-fold hydraulic jack
63 Fuel filler cap
64 Starboard wing fence
65 Wing main fuel tanks (total internal capacity 1,063 gallons)
66 Leading edge integral fuel tank
67 Starboard navigation light
68 Wing tip fairing
69 Starboard wing folded position
70 Fixed portion of trailing edge
71 Lateral control spoilers divided lengthwise between 'flaperons' (forward) and 'flaperettes' (aft)
72 Starboard flap
73 Spoiler hinge control links
74 Spoiler hydraulic jack
75 Rear spar hinge joint
76 Fuselage skin plating
77 Wing spar/fuselage main frame
78 Fuel system piping
79 Fuel filler caps
80 Fuselage rear fuel tank
81 Control cable ducts
82 Rear spar/fuselage main frame
83 Engine accessory compartment
84 Compressor intake screen
85 Supplementary air intake doors (open)
86 Pratt & Whitney J48-P-8A centrifugal-flow turbojet
87 Rear fuselage break point (engine removal)
88 Engine mounting main frame
89 Engine flame cans
90 Secondary air intake door open
91 Fireproof bulkhead
92 Jet pipe heat shroud
93 Water injection tank
94 Water filler cap

95 Fuselage/fin root frame construction
96 Fin attachment joint
97 Tailfin construction
98 Starboard tailplane
99 Starboard elevator
100 Fin tip VHF aerial
101 Rudder construction
102 Rudder mass balance
103 Fin/tailplane fairing
104 Tail navigation lights
105 Lower rudder segment trim tab
106 Elevator trim tab
107 Port elevator
108 Elevator horn balance
109 Port tailplane construction
110 Tailplane hinge joint
111 Tailplane trim jack
112 Exhaust nozzle shroud
113 Jet exhaust nozzle
114 Sting-type deck arrester hook
115 Retractable tail bumper
116 Wing root trailing edge fillet
117 Arrester hook damper and retraction jack
118 Rear fuselage framing
119 Jet pipe
120 Intake duct aft fairing
121 Port Fowler flap
122 Spoiler hydraulic jack
123 Rear spar
124 Wing rib construction
125 Lateral control spoilers "flaperons" (forward) and "flaperettes" (aft)
126 Trim tab electric actuator
127 Electrically operated trim tab (port only)
128 Fuel jettison vent
129 Port wing tip fairing
130 Fuel vent valve
131 Port navigation light
132 Fuel venting ram air intake
133 Port wing main fuel tanks
134 Main spar
135 Cambered leading-edge ribs
136 Leading edge integral fuel tank
137 Wing ordnance pylon (four)
138 Missile launch rail
139 AIM-9B Sidewinder air-to-air missile

Specifications for Grumman F9F-5 Panther

Dimensions: wingspan 38 feet over tip tanks, length 39 feet 1.5 inches, height 12 feet 3.5 inches

Power: one Pratt & Whitney J48-P-6A centrifugal-flow turbojet rated at 7,00lb thrust with water injection

Weights: empty 10,178lb, normal takeoff 17,818lb, max 19,261lb

Speed: max 614mph at sea level, 579mph at 25,000 feet

Ceiling: 42,800 feet

Range: 1,300 miles with tip tanks

Armament: four nose-mounted 20mm M2 cannon with 190 rounds per gun, two 1,000lb bombs or six 5in rockets

Crew: pilot

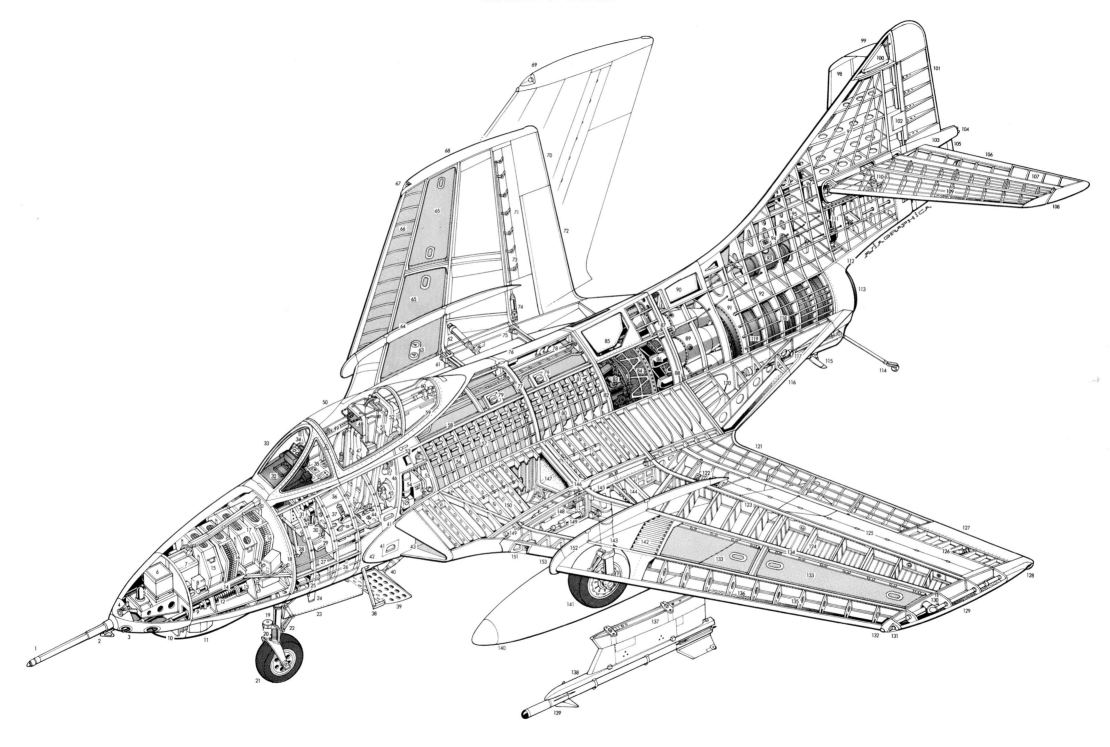

OPPOSITE: The excellent handling of the Panther led to its selection by the US Navy Blue Angels aerobatic team, an F8F-2 of which is seen here demonstrating its hydraulic wing folding as it taxies in after a display.

TOP LEFT: Fixed wingtip tanks were a feature of all Panthers, but for safety reasons the need to land at minimum weight, especially on carriers, was paramount. Here an F8F-2 is shown jettisoning fuel from both tanks at once.

LEFT: Midnight blue U.S. Navy Panthers practice a formation takeoff (USMC Panthers had a gray paint job). On one occasion in Korea, a damaged Marine Corps Panther was fitted with a Navy rear end to become the Blue-tailed Fly.

ABOVE: Modified with 30 degree swept wings and tail surfaces, the Panther became the F8F-8 Cougar. Seen here is the F8F-8B, armed with four early Sidewinders and carrying low drag drop tanks, which supplanted the wingtip tanks of the Panther.

GRUMMAN F-14 TOMCAT

LEFT: First flown in December 1970, the Grumman F-14 Tomcat was destined to be the first and only variable sweep wing carrier fighter to enter service, and more sadly, the last of Grumman's "cat" series of fighters.

In the 1960s, the U.S. Navy was under pressure to field a navalized version of the F-111 swing-wing fighter being developed for the Air Force, but that version was doomed to failure since it was not only too heavy, lacked maneuverability, had engine problems, and was inferior in performance to the Navy's F-4 Phantom, but also could not land on aircraft carriers! The Navy and Grumman, meanwhile, had been working on an advanced carrier fighter, which evolved into the two-seat, twin-engined, bisonic F-14A Tomcat all-weather jet carrier interceptor fighter, and the prototype first flew in December 1970. The type entered service in October 1972, becoming the first variable-geometry shipboard aircraft to do so.

The Tomcat is a high performance, variable-geometry fighter which can sweep its wings back to 68 degrees for high supersonic speed yet can achieve a relatively slow approach to the carrier with them swept to just 10 degrees. When on the deck, the wings can be further swept to 75 degrees to enable this large fighter to maneuver more easily.

The F-14A was initially powered by two Pratt & Whitney TF30-P-412A turbofans that had proved troublesome on the F-111, and it was planned to substitute this with the General Electric F101, but rising costs prohibited this, endangering even the entire F-14 program until finance was raised by an order from Iran. Eventually, in April 1987, production commenced of the F-14A(Plus), later redesignated F-14B, with the General Electric F110-GE-400 powerplant. Some 70 F-14Bs were produced.

The definitive Tomcat version, the F-14D was first flown in March 1990, featuring 60 percent new avionics, including the latest Hughes APG-71 radar and "glass cockpit." A total of 55 F-14Ds were produced, some of them entirely new, others rebuilds.

The heart of the Tomcat fighter's combat capability is the successful combination of the Hughes AWG-9 weapon control system and the AIM-54 Phoenix air-to-air missile. Often working in conjunction with the E-2C Hawkeye to monitor airspace well forward of the fleet (some 300 to 400 miles), the Tomcat's radar can detect enemy intruders 133 miles away, while the Phoenix can carry out a beyond visual range (BVR) attack on a confirmed hostile aircraft, or cruise missile, at a range over 90 miles. The Tomcat can carry six Phoenix missiles, all of which can be fired and controlled by the system at the same time.

In more recent years new roles for the Tomcat have seen it carrying air-to-ground ordnance in the form of free-fall and laser-guided bombs, and joint direct attack muni-

tions (JDAMs) for which a LANTIRN pod can be fitted. Another role is reconnaissance, for which a number have been fitted with the Tactical Air Reconnaissance Pod System (TARPS). The Tomcat is also equipped with a Fast Tactical Imagery (FTI) system that enables it to transmit and receive targeting/reconnaissance imagery rather than needing to return to the carrier before images can be seen. In operational use the Tomcat is more likely to carry a mixture of long, medium and short range air-to-air missiles, including AIM-7 Sparrows and AIM-9 Sidewinders.

The first time the Tomcat fired in anger was in August 1981 when two threatening Libyan Su-22 "Fitters" were engaged – the first of several encounters. The Navy fighters have also seen operations over Iraq where they were used as bombers and also shot down a Mi-8 "Hip" helicopter. The U.S. Navy plans to continue operating the F-14 Tomcat until 2007, by which time it will have been replaced by the F/A-18E and F Super Hornet.

Specifications for Grumman F-14D Tomcat

Dimensions: wingspan 64 feet 1.5 inches at min sweep, 38 feet 2.5 inches
at max sweep, length 61 feet 11 inches, height 16 feet

Power: two General Electric F110-GE-400 two-spool afterburning turbofans each rated at 27,080lb max and 16,610lb military thrust

Weights: empty 41,780lb, normal takeoff 61,200lb, max 70,000lb

Speed: max Mach 2.34 at altitude with four AIM-120 Amraam, limited to Mach 1.88 with full external stores, Mach 1.2 at sea level

Ceiling: 53,000 feet

Range: tactical radius 510 miles

Armament: one 20mm M61A-1 six barrel rotary cannon with 675 rounds, four AIM-120 Amraam and four AIM-9 Sidewinder air-to-air missiles (early models carrying up to six AIM-54 Phoenix long range AAMs)

Crew: pilot and weapons systems officer

F-14D Tomcat cutaway key

1 Pitot head
2 Glass-fiber radome
3 IFF aerial array
4 AN/APG-71 flat plate radar scanner
5 Scanner tracking mechanism
6 Infra-red search and track sensor (IRST) and television camera housing
7 Cannon port
8 Weapons system avionics equipment bay
9 Angle of attack transmitter
10 ADF aerial
11 Flight refueling probe
12 Pilot's head-up display
13 Instrument panel shroud
14 Temperature probe
15 Rudder pedals
16 Control column
17 Electro-luminescent formation lighting strip
18 Nosewheel doors
19 Catapult strop link
20 Twin nosewheels, forward-retracting
21 Boarding ladder, extended
22 M61A1 Vulcan cannon
23 Ammunition drum
24 Pull-out steps
25 Pitot static head
26 Engine throttle levers
27 Pilot's Martin-Baker Mk 14 Navy Aircrew Common Ejection Seat (NACES)
28 Upward-hinged cockpit canopy cover
29 Naval flight officer's instrument console
30 Kick-in step
31 Tactical information display hand controller
32 NFO's ejection seat
33 Rear avionics equipment bay
34 Air data computer
35 Electrical system relays
36 Fuselage missile pallet
37 AIM-54A Phoenix air-to-air missile
38 Port engine air intake
39 Port navigation light
40 Variable-area intake control ramps
41 Intake ramp hydraulic actuators
42 Air conditioning pack
43 Forward fuselage fuel tanks
44 Canopy hinge point
45 UHF/TACAN aerial
46 Starboard navigation light
47 Mainwheel stowed position
48 Starboard intake duct spill door

49 Dorsal control and cable duct
50 Central flap and slat drive hydraulic motor
51 Emergency hydraulic generator
52 Intake by-pass door
53 Electron-beam welded titanium wing pivot box
54 Port wing pivot bearing
55 Pivot box beam integral fuel tank
56 UHF datalink/IFF aerial
57 Honeycomb skin panels
58 Wing glove stiffeners
59 Starboard wing pivot bearing
60 Flap and slat drive shaft and gearbox
61 Starboard leading-edge slat
62 Wing panel fully forward position
63 Navigation light
64 Wingtip formation light
65 Roll control spoilers
66 Outboard manoeuvre flaps
67 Inboard high-lift flap
68 Flap sealing vane
69 Mainwheel leg hinge fitting
70 Variable wing-sweep screw jack
71 Wing glove sealing plates
72 Wing glove pneumatic seal
73 Starboard wing fully swept position
74 Starboard all-moving tailplane
75 Fin-tip aerial fairing
76 Tail navigation light
77 Starboard rudder
78 Rudder hydraulic actuator
79 Variable-area afterburner nozzle control jack
80 Dorsal airbrake (split ventral surfaces)
81 Chaff/flare dispensers
82 Fuel jettison
83 ECM antenna
84 Aluminum honeycomb fin skin panels
85 Anti-collision light
86 Formation lighting strip
87 ECM aerial
88 Port rudder
89 Variable-area afterburner nozzle
90 Port all-moving tailplane
91 Tailplane boron-fiber skin panels
92 Tailplane pivot bearing

93 Afterburner ducting
94 Tailplane hydraulic actuator
95 Ventral fin
96 Formation lighting strip
97 Hydraulic equipment bay
98 Hydraulic reservoir
99 General Electric F110-GE-400 afterburning turbofan engine
100 Rear fuselage fuel tank bays
101 Flight control system linkages
102 Engine bleed air ducting
103 Port wing-sweep crew jack
104 Inboard high-lift flap hydraulic jack
105 Flap hinge links
106 Flap honeycomb construction
107 Port wing fully swept position
108 Port maneuver flaps
109 Wingtip formation light
110 Navigation light
111 Port leading-edge slat
112 Slat guide rails
113 Wing integral fuel tank
114 Machined wing rib construction
115 Main undercarriage leg strut
116 Port mainwheel, forward-retracting
117 Wing glove mounted AIM-54A air-to-air missile
118 AIM-9L Sidewinder air-to-air missile
119 Wing glove pylon
120 Mainwheel door
121 External fuel tank
122 GBU-12D/B Paveway II, 500lb (227kg) laser-guided bomb
123 Mk 82 Snakeye, 500-lb (227-kg) retarded bomb
124 Phoenix pallet weapons adapter
125 GBU-24A/B Paveway III, 2,000lb (907kg) laser-guided bomb
126 AN/AAQ-14 LANTIRN navigation and targeting pod, carried on starboard glove pylon
127 GBU-16 Paveway II, 1,000lb (454kg) laser-guided bomb
128 Mk 83 AIR, 1,000lb (454kg) retarded bomb
129 Mk 83 AIR inflated ballute
130 Mk 7 submunition dispenser

131 LAU-97, 4-round rocket launcher
132 5in (127mm) Zuni FFAR (Folding-Fin Air Rocket)
133 TARPS reconnaissance pod, carried in centerline tunnel
134 ALQ-167 counter-measures pod, carried on forward fuselage Phoenix pallet station

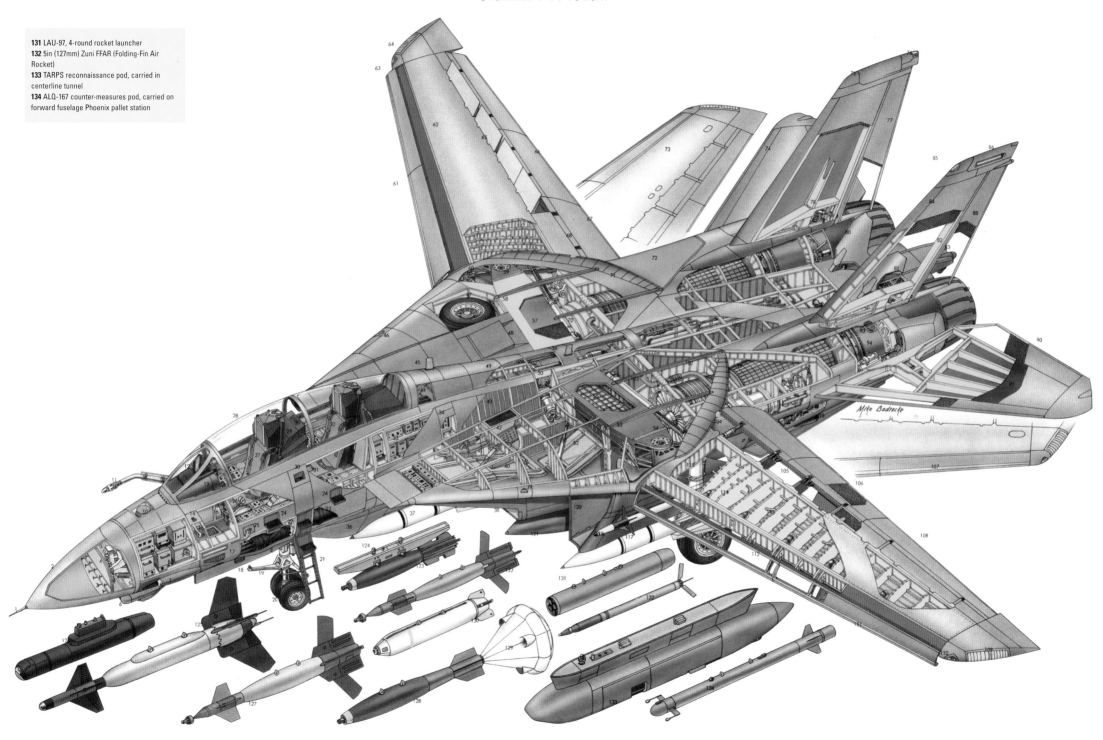

LEFT: A Tomcat arrives back on board during exercise Distant Drum. Maximum wing sweep reduced approach and landing speeds to acceptable levels. It also improved loiter time on station by an appreciable amount.

OPPOSITE LEFT INSET: The disruptive splinter (German WW2-style) camouflage of this VF-32 Tomcat appears to indicate that it has recently taken part in the AIMVAL/ACEVAL exercise at Nellis AFB in 1977.

ABOVE: Armed with a mix of AIM-54 Phoenix and AIM-9 Sidewinders, this Tomcat of VF-84 Jolly Rogers lines up on the deck of USS *Theodore Roosevelt* during Operation Provide Comfort in 1991.

OPPOSITE: A VF-84 Jolly Rogers F-14A Tomcat seen on patrol. Although designed as a dedicated air defense interceptor, the Tomcat has since been adapted to carry air-to-surface munitions.

INSET LEFT: A Tomcat makes an emergency landing on USS *Kittyhawk* in 1984, having missed the arrester wires and hit the barrier. In US naval aviation, carrier landings tend to be debriefed even before the mission.

LEFT: This VF-32 Swordsmen Tomcat goes to full afterburner just prior to catapult launch from the USS *Dwight D. Eisenhower* in June 1994. The up-engined F-14APlus and F-14D can launch on military power only.

HAWKER HUNTER

LEFT: **First flown in July 1951, the Hawker Hunter has long been considered a classic fighter. This is an FGA Mk 6, powered by a Rolls-Royce Avon, serving with the RAF's No 229 Operational Conversion Unit at Chivenor.**

The single-seat, single-engined Hawker Hunter was the truly classic day fighter of the 1950s, and the first genuinely transonic aircraft to serve with Britain's Royal Air Force. With shapely contours, but extremely robust, it stayed in first-line RAF service for almost two decades, and flew with at least twenty air arms around the world.

The Hunter's 40-degree swept wings were mounted mid-set into the fuselage, which had a dorsal spine (containing control runs to rudder and elevators) extending back into a swept-back fin on which, about one-third of the way up, was mounted the horizontal tail. The cockpit canopy, set well ahead of the wings for good pilot view, was faired into the forward end of the dorsal spine. The main armament was four 30mm Aden cannon, which were fitted in the form of a pack that also contained the 100 rounds of ammunition for each cannon. This pack could be replaced easily to give quick turnaround. On the Hunter F Mk 6 up to 3,600lb of other ordnance, such as bombs and rockets, could also be carried.

Although the Hunter first flew in prototype form on July 21, 1951, it was not until three years later that the initial F Mk 1 models entered RAF service, this long gestation period resulting from a variety of teething problems. While the tough and agile aircraft, whose handling was superb, eventually earned a reputation as "a pilot's airplane," the design did have a basic shortcoming that could not be resolved: it was chronically short of fuel tankage and therefore endurance. Even some experienced pilots ran out of fuel and had to eject or belly-land. This problem was to a degree mitigated on later marks, F Mk 4 onward, by an increase in internal fuel capacity and the provision of drop tanks beneath the wings.

The F Mk 1 also suffered from the early Avon engines surging during gun firing, and the imposition of speed limits adversely affected this version's performance as a fighter. The problem was not experienced with the Sapphire-powered F Mk 2, and nor with later marks fitted with improved Avon engines.

By the time production ceased in 1959, there had been 1,972 Hunters built, including trainers and some that were manufactured under license in the Netherlands and Belgium. Almost a third were later refurbished and converted for a variety of roles for the RAF and many export customers. The other roles included fighter ground attack (as FGA Mk 9s), and reconnaissance (as FR Mk 10s).

The Hunter first saw combat with India in the Indo-Pakistan War of 1965, and during further hostilities between these countries in 1971. It was larger, more pow-

erful, faster and accelerated better than the Pakistani-flown Sabres, and with four 30mm Aden cannon packed a much heavier punch. However, it bled off speed faster in a hard turn. Some 22 Pakistani Sabres carried Sidewinder air-to-air missiles, making the Indian Air Force fighter pilots treat all F-86Fs with great respect. The IAF claimed at least ten missile-armed F-86 Sabres and a supersonic MiG-19 during the two conflicts. Hunters also fought against Israeli aircraft in the Arab-Israeli wars of 1966, 1967, and 1973.

Specifications for Hawker Hunter F Mk 6

Dimensions: wingspan 33 feet 8 inches, length 45 feet 10.5 inches, height 13 feet 2 inches

Power: one Rolls-Royce Avon 203 axial-flow turbojet rated at 10,000lb military thrust

Weights: empty 14,122lb, normal takeoff 17,750lb, max 23,800lb

Speed: max 714mph, Mach 0.938, at sea level, 627mph, Mach 0.95, at 36,000 feet

Ceiling: 51,500 feet

Range: operational radius 318 miles

Armament: four 30mm Aden revolver cannon under the nose, with 100 rounds per gun, up to 3,600lb of bombs and rockets

Crew: pilot

Hunter FGA.Mk 9 cutaway key

1 Radome
2 Radar scanner dish
3 Ram air intake
4 Camera port
5 Radar ranging equipment
6 Camera access panel
7 Gun camera
8 Ground pressurisation connection
9 Nosewheel door
10 Oxygen bottles
11 IFF aerial
12 Electronics equipment
13 Nosewheel bay
14 De-icing fluid tank
15 Pressurisation control valves
16 Cockpit front bulkhead
17 Nose landing gear leg
18 Nosewheel forks
19 Forward retracting nosewheel
20 Nosewheel leg door
21 Cannon muzzle port
22 Gun blast cascade deflectors
23 Rudder pedals
24 Bullet proof windscreen
25 Cockpit canopy framing
26 Reflector gunsight
27 Instrument panel shroud
28 Control column
29 Cockpit section fuselage frames
30 Rearward sliding cockpit canopy cover
31 Pilot's starboard side console
32 Martin Baker Mk 3H ejector seat
33 Throttle control
34 Pilot's port side console
35 Cannon barrel tubes
36 Pneumatic system airbottles
37 Cockpit canopy emergency release
38 Cockpit rear pressure bulkhead
39 Air conditioning valve
40 Ejector seat headrest
41 Firing handle
42 Air louvers
43 Ammunition tanks
44 Ammunition link collector box
45 Cartridge case ejectors
46 Batteries
47 Port air inlet
48 Boundary layer splitter plate
49 Inlet lip construction
50 Radio and electronics equipment bay
51 Sliding canopy rail
52 Air conditioning supply pipes
53 Control rod linkages
54 Communications aerial
55 Fuselage double frame bulkhead
56 Boundary layer air outlet

57 Secondary air inlet door spring loaded
58 Inlet duct construction
59 Forward fuselage fuel tank
60 Starboard inlet duct
61 Starboard wing fuel tank
62 276-gallon drop tank
63 Inboard pylon mounting
64 Leading edge dog tooth
65 120-gallon drop tank
66 Outboard pylon mounting
67 Wing fence
68 Leading edge extension
69 Starboard navigation light
70 Starboard wingtip
71 Whip aerial
72 Fairey hydraulic aileron booster jack
73 Starboard aileron
74 Aileron control rod linkage
75 Flap cut out section for drop tank clearance
76 Starboard flap construction
77 Flap hydraulic jack
78 Flap synchronising jack
79 Starboard main landing gear mounting
80 Retraction jack
81 Starboard landing gear bay
82 Dorsal spine fairing
83 Main wing attachment frames
84 Main spar attachment joint
85 Engine starter fuel tank
86 Air conditioning system
87 Engine inlet compressor face
88 Air conditioning pre-cooler
89 Cooling air outlet louvres
90 Rear spar attachment
91 Aileron control rods
92 Front engine mountings
93 Rolls Royce Avon 207 engine
94 Bleed air duct
95 Engine bay cooling flush air Intake
96 Rear engine mounting
97 Rear fuselage joint ring
98 Joint ring attachment bolts
99 Tailplane control rods
100 Fuel piping from rear tank
101 Rear fuselage fuel tank
102 Fuel collector tank
103 Jetpipe mounting rail
104 Fin root fairing
105 Hydraulic accumulator
106 Tailplane trim jack

107 Fairey hydraulic elevator booster
108 Tailplane mounting pivot
109 Rudder hinge control rods
110 Starboard tailplane
111 Starboard elevator
112 Tailfin construction
113 Fin tip aerial fairing
114 Rudder construction
115 Rudder trim tab
116 Trim tab control jack
117 Tailplane anti buffet fairing
118 Tail navigation light
119 Brake parachute housing
120 Tailpipe fairing
121 Port elevator construction
122 Tailplane construction
123 Detachable tailcone
124 Tailplane spar mounting frames
125 Jetpipe
126 Jetpipe access doors
127 Rear fuselage frame and stringer construction
128 Airbrake jack housing
129 Airbrake retracted position
130 Airbrake operating jack
131 Airbrake open position
132 Engine bearing cool air outlet
133 Wing root trailing edge fillet
134 Flap housing construction
135 Port main landing gear bay
136 Main wheel door
137 Port main landing gear retraction jack
138 Main landing gear leg pivot mounting
139 Flap synchronising jack
140 Hydraulic flap jack
141 Port flap
142 Rear spar
143 Aileron control rods
144 Aileron trim tab
145 Port aileron construction
146 Fairey hydraulic aileron booster
147 Wing tip construction
148 Port navigation light
149 Pitot tube
150 3in (7.62cm) rocket projectiles
151 Leading edge extension ribs
152 Wing rib construction
153 Main spar
154 Dowty main landing gear leg
155 Shock absorber torque links

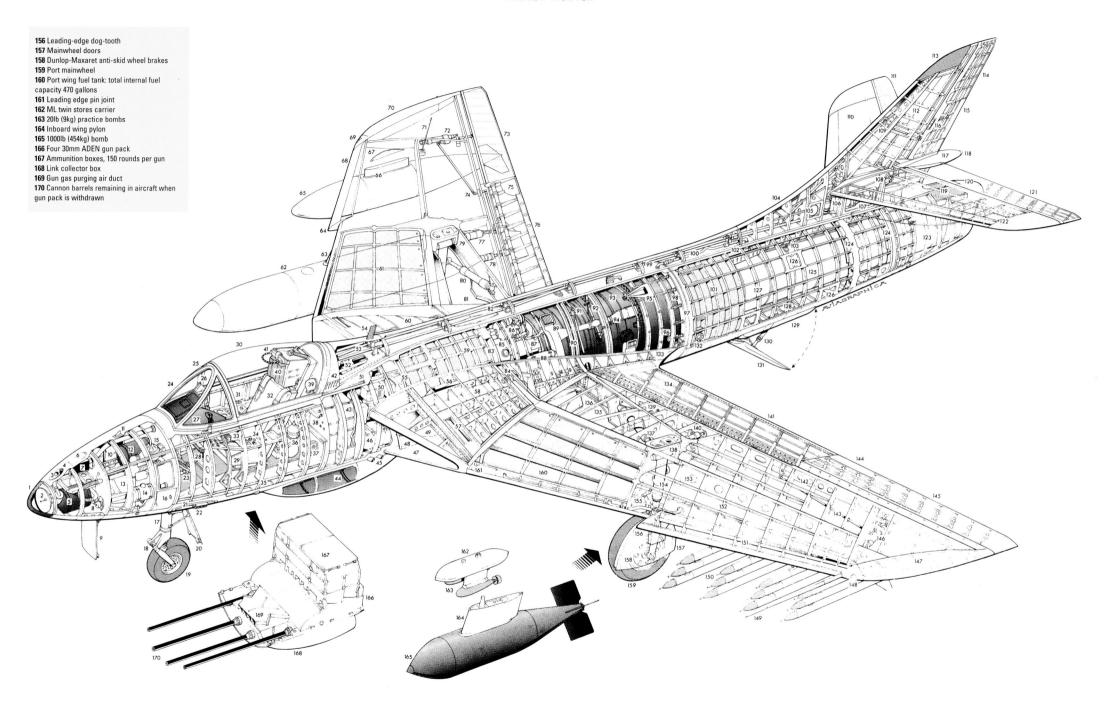

156 Leading-edge dog-tooth
157 Mainwheel doors
158 Dunlop-Maxaret anti-skid wheel brakes
159 Port mainwheel
160 Port wing fuel tank: total internal fuel capacity 470 gallons
161 Leading edge pin joint
162 ML twin stores carrier
163 20lb (9kg) practice bombs
164 Inboard wing pylon
165 1000lb (454kg) bomb
166 Four 30mm ADEN gun pack
167 Ammunition boxes, 150 rounds per gun
168 Link collector box
169 Gun gas purging air duct
170 Cannon barrels remaining in aircraft when gun pack is withdrawn

OPPOSITE INSET: Although never carrier-compatible, a number of Hunters served with the British Fleet Air Arm as trainers. The aircraft shown was built as a Mk 4, served with an RAF reserve squadron, and was then converted to a GA 11 weapons trainer for the FAA.

OPPOSITE: New and rebuilt Hunters were widely exported, to a total of eighteen countries as diverse as Saudi Arabia and Switzerland. They saw action with the RAF over Suez in 1956, with India in 1967 and 1971, and with Iraq and Jordan in 1967.

LEFT: The sleek and beautiful Hunter, which briefly held the world absolute air speed record in 1953, served with the RAF between 1956 and 1971, first as an air defense fighter; later in the ground attack role.

ABOVE: The Hunter Mk 6, seen here with unguided rockets underwing. Its clean lines are spoiled only by the "Sabrinas," collection tanks for shell cases, and the ventral speed brake, which looks like (and was) an afterthought.

HAWKER HURRICANE

LEFT: Unfairly over-shadowed by the Spitfire during the Battle of Britain, Hawker Hurricane squadrons made up two thirds of the RAF fighters in the battle, and accounted for two thirds of *Luftwaffe* casualties.

The Hawker Hurricane built a tremendous reputation early in World War II, bearing the brunt of the defense of France and Britain in 1940. The single-seat, single-engined fighter was a Sidney Camm low-wing monoplane design that was rooted in the mid-1930s. Early models featured a simple tubular-metal cross-braced construction fabric-covered from aft of the cockpit, which was enclosed and set high enough to give the fighter its recognizable hump-backed appearance and the pilot a reasonable view over the nose. The wings were also fabric-covered originally, but this was changed to a light alloy skinning early on. The main wheels were inward-retracting beneath the wings. The fighter's eight cannon were housed in the wings.

The first fighter of monoplane construction to enter service with the RAF, the Hurricane was also the RAF's first combat aircraft capable of exceeding 300mph. It was initiated as a private venture, and was first flown on November 6, 1935. An initial production contract for 600 was placed on July 20, 1936, and the first production example flew on October 12 the following year. This had a Rolls-Royce Merlin II engine driving a fixed-pitched two-bladed propeller. On January 24, 1939, flight-testing began with a Merlin III engine and a constant-speed three-bladed propeller, and this combination became the standard for the Hurricane I. The fabric skin was replaced by metal stressed-skin, and aircraft embodying this change were delivered from September 29, just twenty-six days after the outbreak of war in Europe. The following month Hurricanes were in combat in France.

The Hurricane was quick to prove itself a "pilot's airplane," with good control harmony at all speeds, and, although becoming tail-heavy in a dive, pleasing aerobatically. It was a good gun platform, and did not suffer the wing-flexing when firing in maneuvering flight that dogged its contemporary, the Spitfire. However, when it met its *Luftwaffe* equivalent, the Messerschmitt Bf 109, it was found to be inferior in most performance respects. Nevertheless, the Hurricane did enjoy a decided advantage over the 109 in low-altitude maneuverability and in turning circle at all altitudes. Also, its rugged structure was able to absorb greater battle damage than its enemy counterpart and remain airborne.

Combat experience in France and in the Battle of Britain emphasized previously identified areas for improving the Hurricane's performance and gun-power, and pilot armor. In September 1940 the Hurricane IIA entered service, powered by the uprated Merlin XX engine. Then came the Hurricane IIB armed with twelve wing-mounted Browning machine guns, delivered from late 1940, and during 1941 the IIC with four 20mm Hispano-Suiza cannon in the wings.

The enemy didn't stand still, however, and improved versions of the Bf 109 represented increased danger for the Hurricane, which was superseded in the air-to-air role in UK-based squadrons during 1942, although it continued to serve as a ground attack fighter. Further versions were developed, including the IID for the dedicated anti-armor role, equipped with two 40mm cannon and two 0.303in guns. Hurricanes had already served as night fighters from 1940, and adaptation of shore-based versions for naval use had begun in 1941, leading to the various models called Sea Hurricanes. Some had tailhooks for conventional carrier operation, while others were launched by catapult from CAM (Catapult Aircraft Merchantman) ships, with the pilots having to ditch and wait for rescue if they couldn't reach land.

Well over a dozen air arms flew Hurricanes, and there were over 14,500 of all models produced in all.

Specifications for Hawker Hurricane I

Dimensions:	wingspan 40 feet, length 31 feet 5 inches, height 12 feet 11.5 inches
Power:	one Rolls-Royce Merlin II V-12 liquid cooled engine rated at 1,050hp
Weights:	empty 5,085lb, normal takeoff 6,661lb
Speed:	max 316mph at 17,750 feet
Ceiling:	35,600 feet
Range:	425 miles
Armament:	eight 0.303in wing-mounted Colt-Browning machine guns with 300 rounds per gun
Crew:	pilot

Hurricane Mk I cutaway key

1 Starboard navigation light
2 Wingtip fairing
3 Fabric-covered aileron
4 Aluminum alloy wing skin panelling
5 Aileron hinge control
6 Starboard outer wing panel
7 Inboard torsion box heavy-gauge skin panel
8 Starboard landing lamp
9 Rotol three-bladed propeller
10 Spinner
11 Propeller hub pitch change mechanism
12 Spinner back plate
13 Propeller reduction gearbox
14 Cowling fairing
15 Starboard machine-gun muzzles
16 Upper engine cowling
17 Coolant pipes
18 Rolls-Royce Merlin III 12-cylinder liquid-cooled Vee engine
19 Exhaust stubs
20 Engine-driven generator
21 Forward engine mounting
22 Ignition control unit
23 Engine bearer struts
24 Lower engine cowlings
25 Starboard mainwheel
26 Manual-type inertia starter
27 Hydraulic pumps
28 Carburetor air intake
29 Cooling air scoop
30 Rear engine mounting
31 Single-stage supercharger
32 Port magneto
33 Coolant system header tank
34 External bead sight
35 Coolant filler cap
36 Starboard wing gun bay
37 Ammunition magazines
38 Starboard Browning 0.303in (7.7mm) machine guns (4)
39 Fuel filler cap
40 Engine bay canted bulkhead
41 Rear engine mounting struts
42 Pneumatic system air bottle (gun firing)
43 Wing spar centre-section carry-through
44 Lower longeron/wing spar joint
45 Rudder pedals
46 Pilot's foot boards
47 Control column linkage
48 Fuselage (reserve) fuel tank, capacity 33.6 gallons
49 Fuel tank bulkhead
50 Control column hand grip
51 Instrument panel
52 Reflector gunsight
53 Starboard split trailing-edge flap
54 Bulletproof windscreen panel
55 Canopy internal handle
56 Rear view mirror
57 Sliding cockpit canopy cover
58 Plexiglass canopy panels
59 Canopy framework
60 Canopy external handle
61 Starboard side "break-out" emergency exit panel
62 Safety harness
63 Seat height adjustment lever
64 Oxygen supply cock
65 Engine throttle lever
66 Elevator trim tab control handwheel
67 Oil pipes to radiator
68 Radiator flap control lever
69 Cockpit section tubular fuselage framework
70 Coolant system piping
71 Pilot's oxygen cylinder
72 Boarding step
73 Seat back armour
74 Pilot's seat
75 Armored headrest
76 Turn-over crash pylon struts
77 Canopy rear fairing construction
78 Sliding canopy rail
79 Battery
80 TR 9D radio transmitter/receiver
81 Radio shelf
82 Downward identification light
83 Flare launch tube
84 Handgrip
85 Plywood skin panel
86 Dorsal fairing stringers
87 Upper identification light
88 Aerial mast
89 Aerial lead-in
90 Wooden dorsal section formers
91 Fuselage upper longeron
92 Rear fuselage fabric covering
93 Aluminum alloy tailplane leading edge
94 Starboard fabric-covered tailplane
95 Fabric-covered elevator
96 Aluminum alloy fin leading edge
97 Forward fin mounting post
98 Tailplane spar attachment joint
99 Elevator hinge control
100 Fin rib construction
101 Tailfin fabric covering
102 Diagonal bracing strut
103 Stern post
104 Rudder mass balance weight
105 Aileron cable
106 Rear aerial mast
107 Fabric-covered rudder
108 Aluminum alloy rudder framework
109 Tail navigation light
110 Rudder tab
111 Elevator trim tab
112 Port elevator rib construction
113 Elevator horn balance
114 Port tailplane rib construction
115 Diagonal spar bracing struts
116 Rudder control horn
117 Tail control access panel
118 Ventral tailwheel fairing
119 Fixed, castoring tailwheel
120 Dowty shock absorber tailwheel strut
121 Ventral fin framework
122 Lifting bar socket
123 Aluminum alloy lateral formers
124 Tail control cables
125 Rear fuselage tubular framework
126 Diagonal wire bracing
127 Lateral stringers
128 Fuselage lower longeron
129 Pull-out boarding step
130 Wing root trailing-edge fillet
131 Ventral access hatch
132 Walkway
133 Flap hydraulic jack
134 Inner wing panel rear spar
135 Outer wing panel spar attachment joint
136 Gun heater air duct
137 Wing panel joint cover strip
138 Flap shroud ribs
139 Port split trailing-edge flap
140 Aluminum alloy aileron rib construction
141 Port fabric-covered aileron

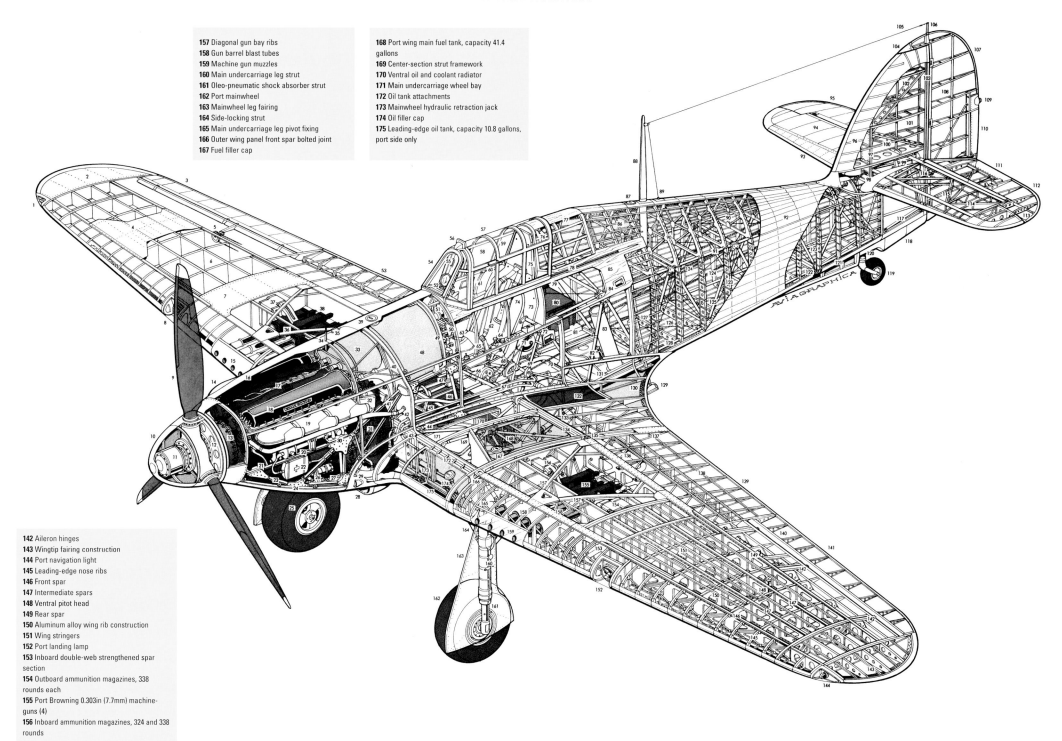

157 Diagonal gun bay ribs
158 Gun barrel blast tubes
159 Machine gun muzzles
160 Main undercarriage leg strut
161 Oleo-pneumatic shock absorber strut
162 Port mainwheel
163 Mainwheel leg fairing
164 Side-locking strut
165 Main undercarriage leg pivot fixing
166 Outer wing panel front spar bolted joint
167 Fuel filler cap

168 Port wing main fuel tank, capacity 41.4 gallons
169 Center-section strut framework
170 Ventral oil and coolant radiator
171 Main undercarriage wheel bay
172 Oil tank attachments
173 Mainwheel hydraulic retraction jack
174 Oil filler cap
175 Leading-edge oil tank, capacity 10.8 gallons, port side only

142 Aileron hinges
143 Wingtip fairing construction
144 Port navigation light
145 Leading-edge nose ribs
146 Front spar
147 Intermediate spars
148 Ventral pitot head
149 Rear spar
150 Aluminum alloy wing rib construction
151 Wing stringers
152 Port landing lamp
153 Inboard double-web strengthened spar section
154 Outboard ammunition magazines, 338 rounds each
155 Port Browning 0.303in (7.7mm) machine-guns (4)
156 Inboard ammunition magazines, 324 and 338 rounds

LEFT: A carefully posed picture of cannon-armed Hurricane IICs of No 87 Squadron. This variant entered service in June 1941, by which time the Hurricane was being phased out in favor of the Spitfire.

RIGHT: Sergeant Jim "Ginger" Lacey in the cockpit of his No 501 Squadron Hurricane during the Battle of Britain. At the end of October 1940, he had claimed 23 victories, five in France, and including 13 Bf 109s over England.

BELOW: The giveaway on this picture of a Hurricane IIC is the "tin" glare shield between the engine exhaust and the pilot's eyeline. Hurricane IICs were increasingly used for night interdiction over enemy territory.

A propaganda photograph of pilots of No 504 Squadron supposedly running to their Hurricane fighters, despite the parachutes banging into the backs of their legs. These are early Hurricane Mk 1s, with two-bladed fixed-pitch propellers.

OPPOSITE INSET BELOW: The sole remaining flying Hurricane of the Battle of Britain Memorial Flight comes in to land. What the fighter lacked in perform-ance, it made up for in survivability, described by a leading ace as "a collection of non-essential parts."

OPPOSITE: As 1940 drew to a close, several Hurricane squadrons convert-ed to night fighting, among them the black-painted No 87 Squadron shown here. But without effective guidance from the ground, they achieved little.

OPPOSITE INSET TOP: A Hurricane IIB prepares to take off from Vaenga airstrip, near Murmansk, piloted by a Russian gener-al. In all, nearly 3,000 Hurricanes were supplied to the Soviet Union, almost a fifth of total Hurricane production.

LEFT: Amazingly, Hurricanes were exported before the war. Among the recipients was the Yugoslav air force, as seen here. This virtually ensured that the *Luftwaffe* knew plenty about the Hurricane even before they encoun-tered it in combat.

HAWKER TEMPEST (and SEA FURY)

LEFT: Developed from the Typhoon, the Tempest V was the most potent Allied fighter of the late war period at low and medium levels. With a cropped wing similar to that of the Spitfire, its greatest weakness was its Napier Sabre engine.

The Hawker Tempest evolved from the troubled Typhoon and, through a process of incremental design, became progressively more different internally and externally, so that as the Tempest V it became the RAF's top-performance piston-engined fighter at the close of World War II, and in fact one of the best medium and low level fighters of the conflict.

The Typhoon had a thick wing, with a thickness/chord ratio varying from 19.5 percent at the root to 10 percent at the tip, the greatest thickness being at 30 percent chord. This caused "compressibility" – local airflow exceeding the speed of sound – leading to poor performance and occasional erratic flight behavior at high speeds. While the Typhoon was being produced, Hawker's designer, Sidney Camm, set about creating a thinner wing in September 1941, and came up with a new laminar-flow wing with a root thickness five inches less and an elliptical planform resembling that of a Spitfire. There was less fuel capacity in the new wing, and to make up for and even increase this the forward fuselage was lengthened by 21 inches, the engine being moved forward, and tail surfaces were made larger to compensate for the extra length. With other refinements, there were so many refinements to what emerged as Typhoon II, ordered in November 1941, that the fighter was renamed Tempest.

Because of the urgency to provide the RAF with the new fighter, the Tempest V was ordered into production ahead of earlier versions that were under development and tests. It had a Typhoon-type Sabre IIA engine of 2,180hp, with the 2,200hp Sabre IIB and 2,260hp being fitted in later production batches. Armament consisted of four new short-barrel Hispano V cannon that were 25lb lighter than those fitted in the Typhoon, and also had a 15 percent faster rate of fire.

The Tempest V entered service in April 1944 and set about destroying 638 of the 1,771 flying bombs shot down by the RAF during that summer. The type's first combat victories against German aircraft were achieved on June 8, 1944 – three Messerschmitt Bf 109Gs north of Rouen. The Tempest's speed (432mph at 18,400 feet) and hitting power enabled it to take on the best of the 1944-45 German fighters, even the Me 262. But the latter flew fast and low to make it impossible for Allied radar screens to pick them up. A technique called "rat-catching" was evolved whereby a brace of Tempests would be sent to known Me 262 bases to hit the German jets as they landed. Limited successes were won, but the dense flak that screened every German airfield made these forays very dangerous and unprofitable. Overall, Tempests destroyed 240 enemy aircraft in the air and on the ground, including seven Me 262 and three Ar 234 jet-powered aircraft, but suffered high losses, mostly to flak and engine failure.

A total of 1,149 Sabre-engined Tempests were ordered. Of these, the final 300 were to be Tempest VIs with 2,340hp Sabre VA engines, but only 142 were completed and these did not see wartime operational service, and were withdrawn by 1949. The Tempest II, which was to be the RAF's last single-seat, single-piston-engined fighter to enter production, was intended to be used against the Japanese, but again did not see service during the war. Of 452 built, about 300 were delivered post-war.

Tempest IIs were additionally flown by India and Pakistan, while New Zealand flew Tempest Vs.

Early in 1943 Hawker began design work on a smaller and lighter version of the Tempest II, and this evolved as the Fury land-based fighter for the RAF, and the navalized version, the Sea Fury shipboard interceptor for the Fleet Air Arm. The main differences between the Fury/Sea Fury and the Tempest were that the former had radial engines in place of the Tempest's horizontal-H with pronounced chin inlet, and a reduction in both span and wing area, achieved essentially by eliminating the original wing center section. This structural change improved rate of roll, but increased turning radius, while the application of wing-folding and adding a tailhook to the Sea Fury also increased weight.

Some 200 Furies were ordered by the RAF, but the contract was cancelled at the end of World War II, while Sea Furies entered service with the Royal Navy in 1947, with 50 F Mk 10s and 615 FB Mk 11s having been built by the time production ceased in 1950. Some of these went to the Australoan and Canadian navies, while reconditioned Sea Furies were sold to Burma and Cuba, and some versions served with the Netherlands (license-built), Iraq and Pakistan.

Hawker Sea Fury cutaway key

1 Spinner
2 Rotol five-bladed constant-speed propeller of 12ft 9in (3.89m) diameter
3 Propeller hub pitch change mechanism
4 Spinner backplate
5 Engine cowling ring
6 Cooling air intake
7 Propeller reduction gear casing
8 Detachable engine cowlings
9 Bristol Centaurus Mk 18 18-cylinder two-row radial sleeve valve engine
10 Exhaust stubs
11 Carburetor intake ducting
12 Starboard British Hispano Mk 5 20mm cannon
13 Recoil springs
14 Cannon muzzles
15 60lb (27.22kg) ground attack rocket projectiles
16 Zero-length rocket launcher rails
17 Wing folding jack
18 Wing fold latching mechanism
19 Starboard outer wing panel
20 Starboard navigation light
21 Wing tip fairing
22 Starboard aileron
23 Aileron hinge control
24 Push-button control rod
25 Aileron spring tab
26 Retractable landing/taxiing lamp
27 Ammunition box (290 rounds port and starboard)
28 Starboard wing folded position
29 Outer split trailing edge flap
30 Ammunition feed drum blister fairings
31 Cannon breeches
32 Oil tank (14 Imp gal/63.65 litre capacity)
33 Engine cartridge starter
34 Engine bearer struts
35 Hydraulic reservoir
36 Accessory drive gearbox
37 Engine cooling air outlet
38 Wing front spar attachment joint
39 Fireproof engine compartment bulkhead
40 Fuselage double frame
41 Main fuel tank (116.4 gallons)
42 Fuel tank vent
43 Filler cap
44 Fuselage top longeron
45 Rudder pedals
46 Auxiliary fuselage fuel tank (36 gallons)
47 Fuselage bottom longeron
48 Rear wing spar attachment joint
49 Oxygen bottle
50 Control column
51 Instrument panel
52 Bullet proof windscreen
53 Mk 4B reflector sight
54 Windscreen framing
55 Pilot's starboard side console
56 Pilot's seat
57 Engine throttle and propeller controls
58 Radio equipment
59 Port side console
60 Seat back armor plate
61 Safety harness
62 Headrest
63 Armored headrest support
64 Sliding cockpit canopy cover
65 Canopy rails
66 Tailplane control rod
67 Rear fuselage joint frame
68 Whip aerial
69 Fuselage skin plating
70 Elevator push-pull control rod
71 Tailplane attachment joint frame
72 Fin root fillet
73 Starboard tailplane
74 Starboard elevator
75 Tailfin construction
76 Curved fin leading edge
77 Sternpost
78 Rudder construction
79 Mass balance weight
80 Rudder tab
81 Deck arrester hook
82 Elevator trim tab
83 Port elevator
84 Tailplane construction
85 Tailplane spar joints
86 Rudder hinge control
87 Tail navigation light
88 Arresting hook attachment link
89 Tailwheel hydraulic retraction jack
90 Tailwheel
91 Tailwheel doors
92 Rear fuselage double bulkhead
93 Tailwheel bay
94 Tailwheel bay bulkhead
95 Fuselage frame and stringer construction
96 Rudder push-pull control rod
97 Remote compass transmitter
98 Ventral aerial
99 Handgrip
100 Radio transmitter/receiver
101 Trailing edge wing root fillet
102 Retractable "stirrup-type" step

Specifications for Hawker Tempest V

Dimensions: wingspan 41 feet, length 33 feet 8 inches, height 16 feet 1 inch

Power: one Napier Sabre IIB 24-cylinder horizontal-H liquid-cooled engine rated at 2,400hp

Weights: empty 9,250lb, normal takeoff 11,400lb, max 13,640lb

Speed: max 435mph at 17,000 feet, 392mph at sea level

Ceiling: 34,800 feet

Range: 740 miles

Armament: four 20mm wing-mounted Hispano-Suiza V cannon with 150 rounds per gun, two 1,000lb bombs or eight 3in rockets

Crew: pilot

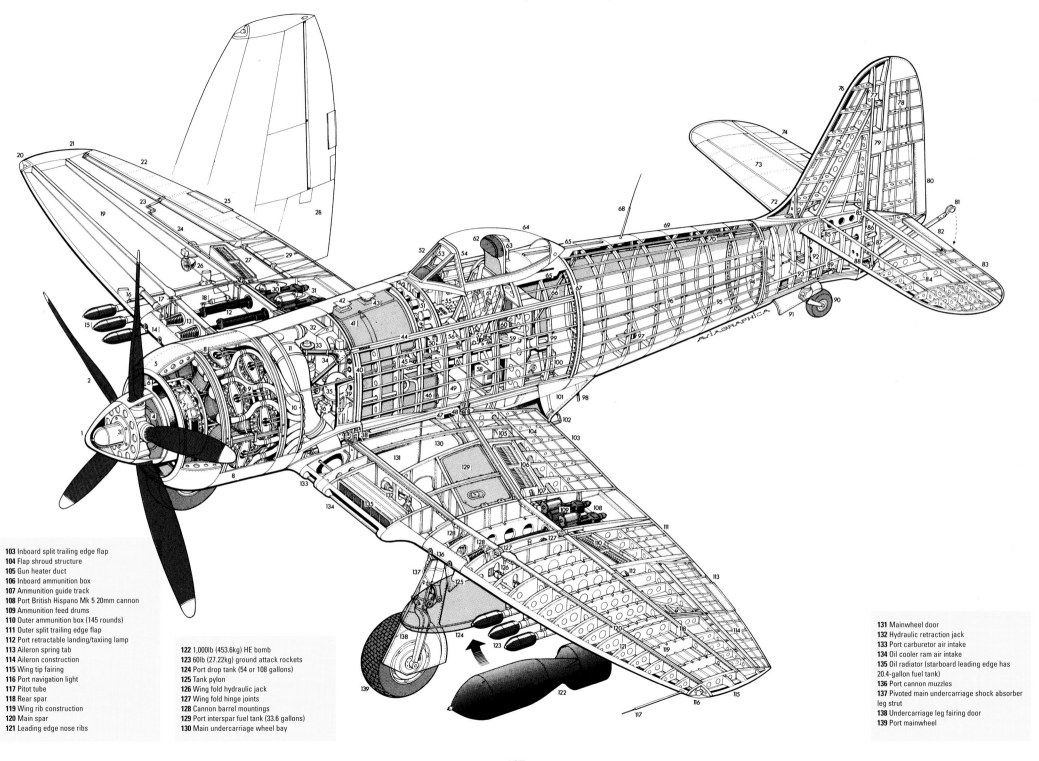

103 Inboard split trailing edge flap
104 Flap shroud structure
105 Gun heater duct
106 Inboard ammunition box
107 Ammunition guide track
108 Port British Hispano Mk 5 20mm cannon
109 Ammunition feed drums
110 Outer ammunition box (145 rounds)
111 Outer split trailing edge flap
112 Port retractable landing/taxiing lamp
113 Aileron spring tab
114 Aileron construction
115 Wing tip fairing
116 Port navigation light
117 Pitot tube
118 Rear spar
119 Wing rib construction
120 Main spar
121 Leading edge nose ribs

122 1,000lb (453.6kg) HE bomb
123 60lb (27.22kg) ground attack rockets
124 Port drop tank (54 or 108 gallons)
125 Tank pylon
126 Wing fold hydraulic jack
127 Wing fold hinge joints
128 Cannon barrel mountings
129 Port interspar fuel tank (33.6 gallons)
130 Main undercarriage wheel bay

131 Mainwheel door
132 Hydraulic retraction jack
133 Port carburetor air intake
134 Oil cooler ram air intake
135 Oil radiator (starboard leading edge has 20.4-gallon fuel tank)
136 Port cannon muzzles
137 Pivoted main undercarriage shock absorber leg strut
138 Undercarriage leg fairing door
139 Port mainwheel

OPPOSITE INSET: Hawker Tempest Vs of No 501 Squadron. Discounting the aggressive chin intake, its lines were astonishingly slender. In all, Tempest pilots claimed 240 enemy aircraft destroyed, ten of them jets, for twenty-three air combat losses.

OPPOSITE: Fastest of the defending fighters, not excluding the jet Meteor, the Tempest V was used against the Doodlebug threat, shooting down 638 out of 1,771 V-1s (36 percent) between June 13 and September 5, 1944.

ABOVE: Hoicked up level to align the four 20mm Hispano cannon correctly with the sight, this Tempest V carries four unguided rockets under each wing. However, its main value was as an air superiority fighter at medium altitudes.

RIGHT: This photograph of a Tempest V carrying invasion stripes has been heavily retouched (presumably for security reasons). The type served with twelve RAF squadrons in all. A total of 800 were built before production ended in August 1945.

HAWKER TYPHOON

The Hawker Typhoon, the heaviest and most powerful single-seat, single-engined warplane planned at the time of its inception in the late 1930s, was originally designed by Sidney Camm as a high-altitude interceptor for Britain's RAF. Ordered into production while it was still dogged by engine and rear fuselage problems, its maneuverability and high altitude performance were poor. In service as a fighter, its success rate was low against German counterparts, only one pilot reaching double figures – Johnny Baldwin, who claimed fifteen victories, all except two being Messerschmitt Bf 109Gs and Fw 190As. By contrast it was ultimately developed into a superb ground attack machine that in a single day in 1944 knocked out no fewer than 175 German tanks in France's Falaise Gap during the Allies' liberation of Europe.

The Typhoon was certainly big, rugged, and fast – it being the first RAF aircraft capable of exceeding 400mph. It featured the traditional Hawker tubular metal structure for the front and middle fuselage, while the rear fuselage was of metal monocoque construction, with fabric-covered rudder. The thick wings were slightly cranked, and the main undercarriage legs were located at the crank. Cockpit access on early models was via a folding roof hatch, car-door fashion, but this afforded unacceptable rearward view and was amended to a sliding bubble canopy on late-production machines. There was a massive chin radiator beneath the nose.

The main problems centered around the complex, untried – and, in early service, unreliable – Napier Sabre engine that had 24 cylinders arranged in an H-form. These problems almost led to cancellation of the entire project. The first of two Typhoon prototypes was flown on February 24, 1940, and the production aircraft flew in May the following year with the 2,100hp Sabre I engine. The Typhoon could be fitted with either twelve 0.303in machine guns or four 20mm cannon, and 105 aircraft were built with machine guns, since cannon feed mechanisms were in short supply. However, cannon armament and the 2,180hp Sabre IIA became standardized, although the 2,200hp Sabre IIB and 2,260hp Sabre IIC progressively replaced the IIA in Typhoons, which entered squadron service from September 1941.

The Typhoon's poor rate of climb and altitude performance meant that it was restricted to the low and medium altitude role where in 1942 its sheer speed enabled it to counter the German Fw 190A, which was at that time making low-level hit-and-run raids and outclassing the Spitfire V. Furthermore, by the time the Tempest, which evolved from the Typhoon, entered service in 1944, the latter was being switched to close air support and tank-busting. For this it was originally equipped with a pair of 250lb bombs, but this was increased to two 1,000lb bombs or eight 60lb rockets. The Typhoon had found its forté, and hundreds of them performed round-the-clock operations from rough forward strips.

A total of 3,315 Typhoons were delivered (having been built by Gloster Aircraft), the last reaching RAF squadrons in November 1945, by when it had been largely replaced by the Tempest. Sixty Typhoons were fitted with oblique and vertical cameras as FR Mk Ibs, and one was tested as a night fighter with AI Mk IV radar. Aside from Britain's RAF, Typhoons saw service with Australia, Canada and New Zealand.

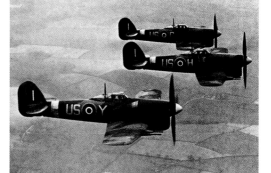

LEFT: Hawker Typhoon IBs of No 56 Squadron in April 1943. The type was first flown in February 1940, but engine problems delayed its service entry until September of the following year. Even then, structural problems with the tail were encountered.

Specifications for Hawker Typhoon IB

Dimensions: wingspan 41 feet 7 inches, length 31 feet 10 inches, height 14 feet 10 inches

Power: one Napier Sabre IIA 24-cylinder horizontal-H liquid-cooled engine rated at 2,180hp

Weights: empty 8,690lb, normal takeoff 11,780lb, max 13,250lb

Speed: max 412mph at 19,000 feet, 374mph at 5,500 feet

Ceiling: 34,000 feet

Range: 690 miles

Armament: four 20mm wing-mounted Hispano-Suiza cannon with 140 rounds per gun, two 1,000lb bombs or eight 3in rockets

Crew: pilot

Typhoon Mk IB cutaway key

1 Starboard navigation light
2 Starboard aileron
3 Fixed trim tab
4 Aileron hinge control
5 Landing lamp
6 Ammunition boxes
7 Starboard Hispano Mk II 20mm cannon
8 Split trailing-edge flaps
9 Starboard main fuel tank, capacity 48 gallons
10 Self-sealing leading-edge fuel tank, capacity 42 gallons
11 Cannon barrel fairings
12 Rocket launcher rails
13 60lb (27kg) ground attack rockets
14 Main undercarriage leg fairing
15 Starboard mainwheel
16 de Havilland four-bladed propeller
17 Air intake
18 Propeller pitch change mechanism
19 Spinner
20 Armored spinner backplate
21 Coolant tank, capacity 8.7 gallons
22 Supercharger ram air intake
23 Oil radiator
24 Coolant radiator
25 Radiator shutter
26 Engine mounting block
27 Tubular steel engine support framework
28 Exhaust stubs
29 Napier Sabre II, 24-cylinder flat H engine
30 Engine cowlings
31 Cartridge starter
32 Engine compartment fireproof bulkhead
33 Oxygen bottle
34 Gun heating air duct
35 Hydraulic reservoir
36 Footboards
37 Rudder pedals
38 Oil tank, capacity 21.6 gallons
39 Oil tank filler cap
40 Instrument panel
41 Bullet-proof windscreen
42 Reflector sight
43 Control column handgrip
44 Engine throttle controls
45 Trim handwheels
46 Emergency hydraulic hand pump
47 Forward fuselage steel tube construction
48 Pilot's seat
49 Safety harness
50 Back and head armor plate
51 Pneumatic system air bottle
52 Rearward-sliding canopy cover
53 Aft fuselage joint
54 Canopy rails
55 Radio transmitter/ receiver
56 Fuselage double frame
57 Whip aerial
58 Fuselage skinning
59 Starboard tailplane
60 Starboard elevator
61 Elevator trim tab
62 Fin leading edge
63 Fin construction
64 Rudder sternpost
65 Fabric-covered rudder construction
66 Rudder trim tab
67 Tail navigation light
68 Elevator trim tab
69 Port tailplane construction
70 Tailplane spar attachments
71 Tailwheel hydraulic jack
72 Forward-retracting tailwheel
73 Dowty oleo-pneumatic tailwheel strut
74 Tailplane spar fixing double bulkhead
75 Tailplane attachment joint strap
76 External strengthening fishplates
77 Elevator mass balance
78 Elevator cross shaft
79 Cable guides
80 Tailplane control cables
81 Rear fuselage frame and stringer construction
82 Wing root fillet
83 Spar root pin joints
84 Undercarriage door hydraulic jack
85 Mainwheel door
86 Main undercarriage bay
87 Rear spar
88 Port main fuel tank, capacity 48 gallons
89 Flap shroud construction
90 Port split trailing-edge flaps
91 Flap hydraulic jack
92 Port gun bays
93 Port Hispano Mk II 20mm cannon
94 Ammunition feed drum
95 Ammunition boxes, 140 rounds per gun
96 Gun heater air ducts
97 Port aileron
98 Fixed aileron tab
99 Wingtip construction
100 Port navigation light
101 Wing rib construction
102 Wing stringers
103 Front spar
104 Leading-edge nose ribs
105 Gun camera
106 Camera port
107 Landing lamp
108 1,000-lb (454-kg) bomb
109 Long-range tank, capacity 108 gallons
110 Underwing stores pylon
111 Cannon barrel fairings
112 Recoil spring
113 Leading-edge construction
114 Main undercarriage leg
115 Undercarriage leg fairing door
116 Oleo-pneumatic shock absorber strut
117 Port mainwheel
118 Undercarriage locking mechanism
119 Mainwheel hydraulic jack
120 Wing spar inboard girder construction
121 Port leading-edge fuel tank, capacity 42 gallons

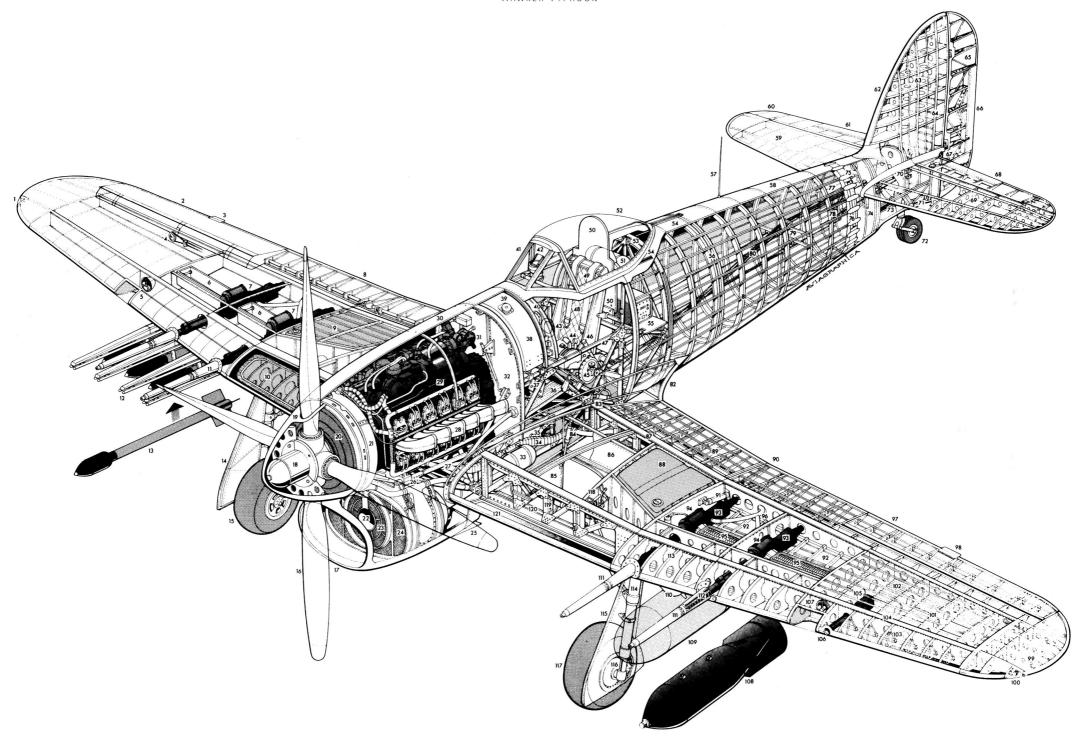

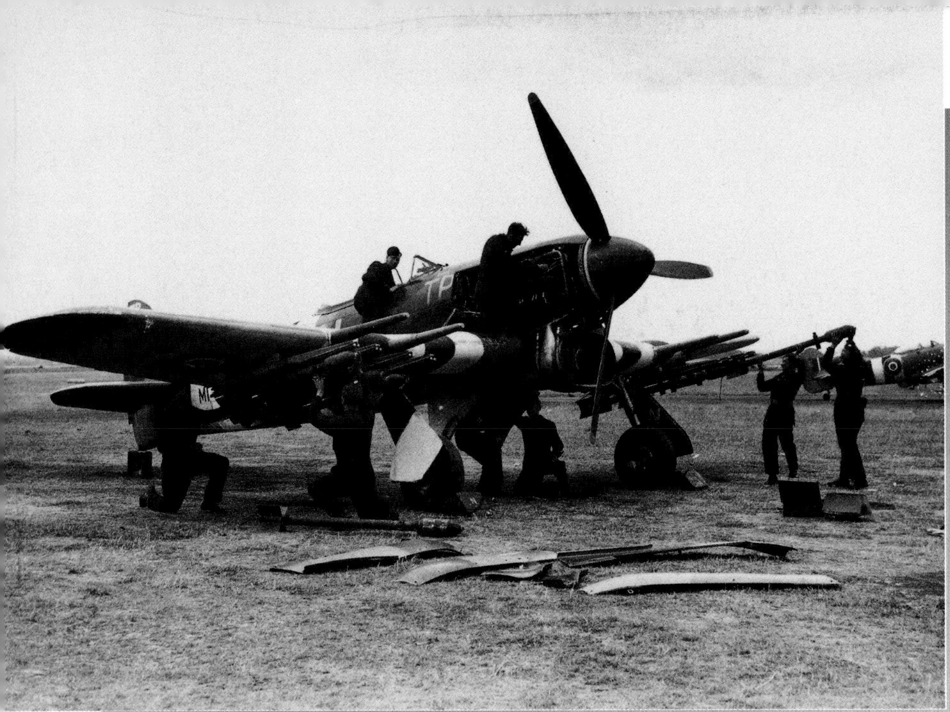

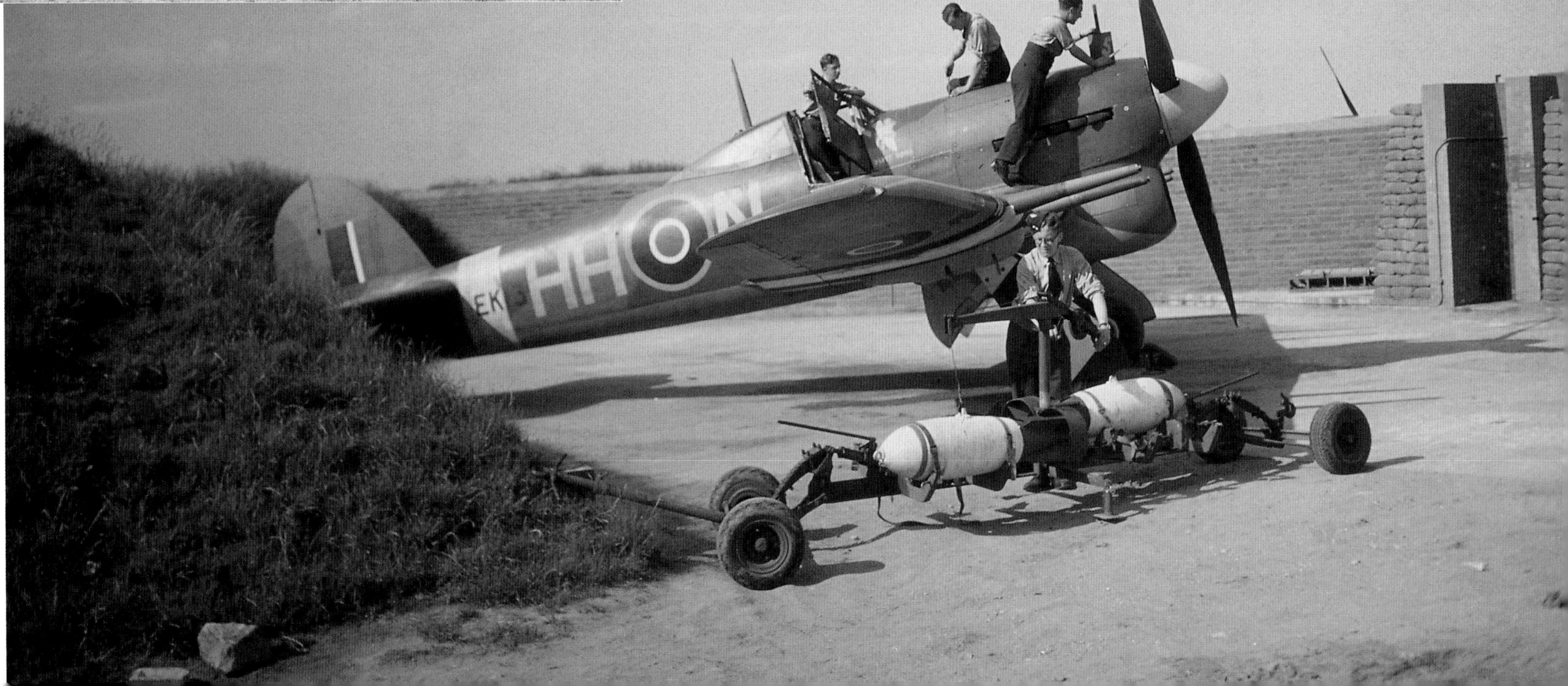
HH

OPPOSITE: **Although fast at low level, the Typhoon's altitude performance, rate of climb and maneuverability were all disappointing. However, it became an admirable ground attack fighter, able to carry two 1,000 pound bombs.**

OPPOSITE INSET: **Much of the Typhoon's reputation rests on its prowess as a tank buster. For this, the preferred weapon was the 60 pound rocket, eight of which were carried underwing and seen here being loaded on a No 198 Squadron aircraft shortly after D-Day.**

LEFT INSET: **Originally intended as a replacement for the Hurricane, the Typhoon had a thick wing that easily accommodated four 20mm Hispano cannon with 140 rounds each. In fact, the first production models carried twelve .303 inch Browning machine guns.**

LEFT: **Underwing carriage of eight rocket projectiles and their launch rails was drag-inducing, as was the folding framed canopy on this early model. Later variants featured sliding bubble canopies for good all-round vision.**

HEINKEL He 280

LEFT: The Heinkel He 280 has two claims to fame. It was the first fighter to fly on turbojet power alone, on March 30, 1941, and the first fighter to be designed to have an ejector seat from the outset. It failed to enter service.

The world's first turbojet-powered combat aircraft, the Heinkel He 280 was also the first twin-jet, the first jet to be other than a research aircraft, the first fighter designed from the outset with a pilot ejection seat, and was notable for the first recorded use of the ejection seat to save the pilot.

The Heinkel 280 was a single-seat, twin-engined, subsonic jet fighter. Two engines were needed because early jets afforded limited thrust. Development of the planned engines – Heinkel-Hirth HeS 8A centrifugal-flow turbojets – lagged behind that of the airframe, as was common. Therefore, the first prototype, the He 280 V1, took to the air for the first time on September 22, 1940, but as an unpowered glider, towed to altitude by an He 111. Over the next few months there were a further forty unpowered flights. The second prototype, V2 fitted with similar engines, first flew on March 30, 1941. It was not until June 5, 1942, that the third prototype, V3, first flew, with similar engines output-boosted to 1,100lb thrust. There were five further airframes built, the fifth of which, the V5, was selected as the pre-series prototype for the He 280A. This became the first airframe to be armed, with three 20mm MG 151 cannon. The planned He 280B would have had six cannon, as well as a 1,102lb bomb load.

The Heinkel 280 had a complete straight wing leading edge, but the trailing edge followed a curve outboard. Engine nacelles were fitted beneath the wings so that they could be accessed easily, and the tailplane was unusual in that it was mounted on a stub fin above the rear fuselage, clear of the engine exhausts. The tailplane had a full-span elevator and twin fins and rudders. The undercarriage was a tricycle arrangement.

In early 1942 Heinkel arranged a mock dogfight with an Fw 190, which was easily bested by the He 280. However, there were problems with the HeS 8 engine, which was not delivering the power predicted. Heinkel considered alternative powerplants, the axial-flow Junkers Jumo 004B which powered the rival Messerschmitt Me 262, and BMW 003 turbojets. The V2 prototype was re-engined with the Jumo and flew on March 16, 1943. It proved faster than the Me 262, climbed better and had a higher ceiling. But it was relatively undergunned, had less endurance, and experienced tail flutter.

Nevertheless, there were plans to power the V4, V5 and V6 prototypes with the BMW 003, and to build the fighter as the He 280B, with the Jumo engine initially and then with the BMW 003. But while contractual negotiations were under way for 300 fighters, on March 27, 1943,

Heinkel were instructed to abandon all further work on the He 280, and the type never entered service. The V1 prototype was fitted with four Argus As 014 pulse jets, but this crashed on January 13, 1943, after it had been towed into the air by two Bf 110s, and before the As 014s were lit; the test pilot, unable to jettison the towline, ejected.

Prototypes V4, V5 and V6 were not completed, and V7 and V8 were used for aerodynamic research by the German Research Unit for Gliding. V8 was fitted with Jumo 004Bs engines, and this aircraft flew on July 19, 1943.

Specifications for Heinkel He 280A

Dimensions: wingspan 40 feet 0.25 inches, length 34 feet 1.5 inches, height 10 feet 1.5 inches

Power: two Heinkel-Hirth HeS 8A centrifugal-flow turbojets each rated at1,653lb military thrust

Weights: empty 6,735lb, normal takeoff 9,482lb

Speed: max 559mph at 19,685 feet, 541mph at sea level

Ceiling: 37,732 feet

Range: 603 miles

Armament: three nose-mounted 20mm Mauser MG 151 cannon

Crew: pilot

Heinkel He 280 V5 (He 280A-1) cutaway key

1 Nose cone
2 Nose undercarriage pivot fixing
3 Leg compression strut for retraction
4 Torque scissors links
5 Nosewheel forks
6 Nosewheel (aft retracting)
7 Shock absorber leg strut
8 Nosewheel leg door
9 Retraction/breaker strut
10 Hydraulic retraction jack
11 Cannon muzzle ports
12 Cannon barrels
13 Nose undercarriage wheel bay
14 Nose compartment frame construction
15 Nosewheel doors
16 Battery
17 Ammunition magazine
18 Ammunition feed chutes
19 Cannon recoil spring housings
20 Cannon mountings
21 MG 151 20mm cannon (three)
22 Electrical relay panel
23 Cockpit bulkhead
24 Cannon electrical firing control units
25 Fuel filler cap
26 Rudder pedals
27 Footboard
28 Forward fuel tank
29 Retractable boarding step
30 Cockpit floor level
31 Trim control handwheels
32 Control column
33 Instrument panel
34 Instrument panel shroud
35 Armored glass windscreen panel
36 Starboard engine nacelle
37 Revi reflector sight
38 Radio controls
39 Engine throttle levers
40 Compressed-air ejection seat
41 Ejection seat rails
42 Safety harness
43 Headrest
44 Sliding cockpit canopy
45 Starboard outer wing panel
46 Leading-edge skinning
47 Starboard navigation light
48 Wing-tip fairing
49 Starboard aileron
50 Aileron tabs
51 Aileron control linkages
52 Outboard flap segment

53 Headrest fairing
54 Fuel filler cap
55 Mainwheel bay (wheel stowed vertically)
56 Wing spar center-section carry-through
57 Sliding canopy rail
58 Rear main fuel tank
59 Radio equipment bay
60 Starboard side access door
61 Aerial mast
62 Fuselage skin plating
63 Aerial cable
64 Starboard tailfin
65 Rudder mass balance
66 Starboard rudder
67 One-piece elevator
68 Elevator mass balance
69 One-piece variable-incidence trimming tailplane
70 Trimming tailplane pivot fixing
71 Elevator hinge control
72 Taiplane rib construction
73 Tail navigation light
74 Port fin rib construction
75 Fin-tip fairing
76 Rudder rib construction
77 Ground-adjustable rudder tab
78 Rudder hinge control
79 Lower mass balance
80 Tailskid
81 Rudder control cable quadrant
82 Tailplane incidence control lever
83 Control push rods and cables
84 Rear fuselage frame and stringer construction
85 Master compass
86 Step
87 Ventral aerial
88 Wing-root fillet
89 Port plain flap inboard segment
90 Flap interconnecting torque shaft
91 Nozzle fairing
92 Engine exhaust nozzle
93 Port outboard plain flap segment
94 Aileron rib construction
95 Aileron tabs
96 Port aileron

97 Wing-tip fairing
98 Port navigation light
99 Leading-edge nose ribs
100 Outer wing panel rib construction
101 Jet pipe
102 Engine mounting ribs
103 Wing spars
104 Main undercarriage leg pivot fixing
105 Hydraulic retraction jack
106 Mainwheel bay doors
107 Forward main engine housing
108 Rear engine mounting
109 Heinkel-Hirth HeS 8A turbojet
110 Pitot mast
111 Port mainwheel
112 Levered-suspension axle beam
113 Axle pivoting link for vertical stowage
114 Cowling bulkhead
115 Engine accessory equipment
116 Generator
117 Accessory equipment gearbox
118 Ventral oil tank
119 Compressor air intake
120 Cooling air intake by-pass duct
121 Detachable cowling nose section
122 Engine air intake

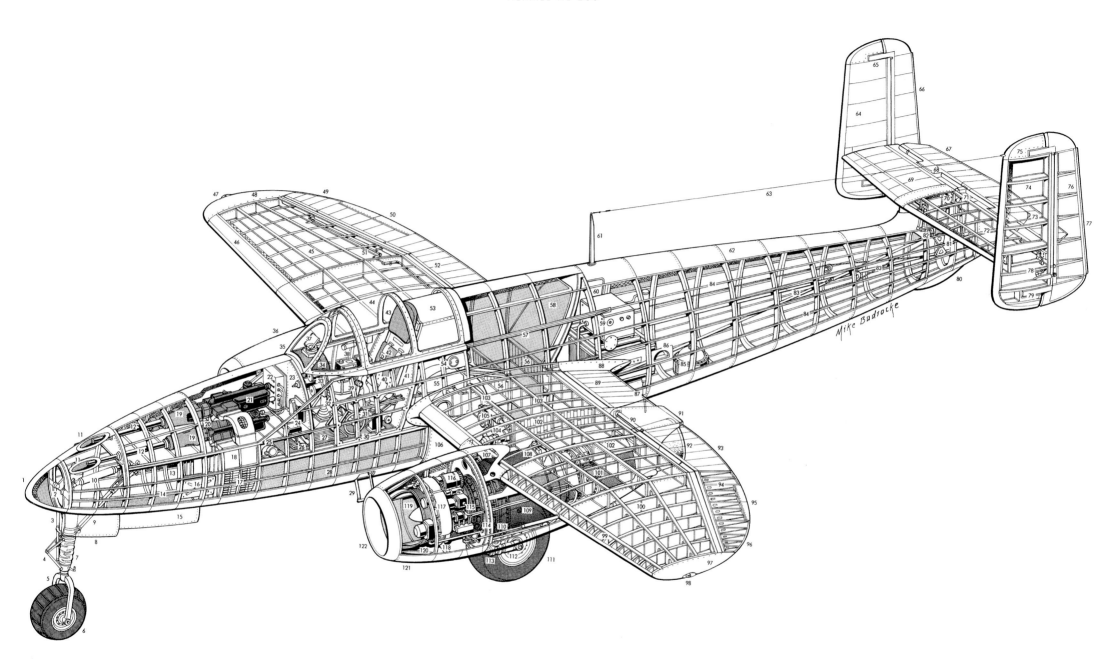

LOCKHEED F-104 STARFIGHTER

LEFT: Fighter pilots returning from Korea clamored for ever more performance. Lockheed responded by wrapping the smallest possible airframe around the largest available engine, to produce the F-104A Starfighter.

Since the very start of air combat, the advantage most to be sought was altitude. When in Korea American F-86 pilots found that the Russian-built MiG-15 had a significantly better high-altitude performance, they clamored for a fighter that could out-fly it. The result, first flown as the XF-104 on February 7, 1954, was the Lockheed F-104 Starfighter single-seat, single-engined bisonic jet day fighter that represented a radical advance in the state of the art. It was the first fighter capable of sustained speeds in excess of Mach 2, and the first aircraft to hold world speed and altitude records simultaneously. Few aircraft have had greater impact on fighter technology, and it was to become one of the most controversial warplanes ever manufactured in quantity. Originally intended as purely an air superiority day fighter, it was later completely restressed to meet new strength requirements, with the F-104C introducing equipment for ground attack and the F-104G (see below) carrying comprehensive radar, an inertial navigation system and other changes for the whole spectrum of tactical missions.

The design was optimized for high performance: the smallest possible airframe wrapped around the largest possible engine, the new and unproven General Electric J79. With an extremely sleek fuselage and straight wings that were tiny and incredibly thin (just 4.2 inches at the root), and a high-set T-tail, the Starfighter was promptly dubbed "the missile with a man in it"!

While handling was very precise, it was totally unforgiving of pilot error. High wing loading (115lb/sq.ft) meant that turn capability was exceptionally high. To a certain extent this was offset by having a leading edge that could hinge down as a slat, and trailing edge flaps having boundary layer control using engine bleed air. There were hydraulically boosted powered ailerons outboard. The wings, with 10 degrees of anhedral, had no carry-through structure, but were bolted to the fuselage mainframes. On top of the fin the tailplane was a high-set, single-piece, all-moving slab, and this meant that a downward-ejecting seat had to be fitted, which was blamed for many pilot losses.

The F-104A, the initial production model with the J79-GE-3B engine and armed with a 20mm rotary cannon and two Sidewinder air-to-air missiles, was accepted by the U.S. Air Force in December 1958, and 153 were built. Ten of these were later supplied to Pakistan and 24 to Taiwan (22 of these being transferred to Jordan). Some of the original USAF machines were re-engined with the uprated J79-GE-19. Between September 1958 and June 1959, some 77 F-104Cs followed the 104A into USAF service as single-seat

tactical strike fighters with provision for bombs or missiles on the wing and fuselage, and a detachable flight-refueling probe. While the USAF deactivated its F-104As in 1969, the F-104C remained in service until July 1975.

The F-104 was regarded as a superb flying machine, but not successful as a fighter: it could not turn tightly, and its radar and avionics were out of synch with its performance. This was borne out by poor performance in combat in Southeast Asia and for Pakistan in the Indo-Pakistan wars of 1965 and 1971.

But it was as a low-level bomb truck with (mainly) European air forces that the Starfighter finally made its mark. Although not adopted by the United States, the 104G, dubbed Super Starfighter, became the subject of an unprecedented global manufacturing program. Canada, Japan, Germany, Italy, the Netherlands and Belgium produced more than 2,000 between 1961 and 1966, and 245 of the later Lockheed/Aeritalia F-104S interception version with Sparrow missiles were also built in Italy (including 40 for Turkey).

Specifications for Lockheed F-104A Starfighter

Dimensions:	wingspan 21 feet 11 inches, length 54 feet 9 inches, height 13 feet 6 inches
Power:	one General Electric J79-GE-3B single-spool, axial-flow after burning turbojet rated at 14,800lb max and 9,600lb military thrust
Weights:	empty 13,384lb, normal takeoff 22,614lb, max 25,840lb
Speed:	max over Mach 2.2 at altitude, over Mach 1 at sea level
Ceiling:	64,795 feet
Range:	730 miles with external tanks
Armament:	one 20mm M61-A six barrel Vulcan rotary cannon with 725 rounds, two or four AIM-9 Sidewinder air-to-air missiles, later two AIM-7 Sparrow or Aspide AAMs with two Sidewinders
Crew:	pilot

F-104S Starfighter cutaway key

1 Pitot tube
2 Radome
3 Radar scanner dish
4 R21G/H multi-mode radar equipment
5 Radome withdrawal rails
6 Communications aerial
7 Cockpit front bulkhead
8 Infra-red sight
9 Windscreen panels
10 Reflector gunsight
11 Instrument panel shroud
12 Rudder pedals
13 Control column
14 Nose section frame construction
15 Control cable runs
16 Pilot's side console panel
17 Throttle control
18 Safety harness
19 Martin-Baker IQ-7A ejection seat
20 Face blind seat firing handle
21 Cockpit canopy cover
22 Canopy bracing struts
23 Seat rail support box
24 Angle of attack probe
25 Cockpit rear bulkhead
26 Temperature probe
27 Nosewheel doors
28 Taxiing lamp
29 Nosewheel leg strut
30 Nosewheel
31 Steering linkage
32 AIM-7 Sparrow avionics (replacing M61 gun installation of strike model)
33 Inertial platform
34 Avionics compartment
35 Avionics compartment shroud cover
36 Cockpit aft glazing
37 Ram air turbine
38 Emergency generator
39 Avionics compartment access cover
40 Fuselage frame construction
41 Pressure bulkhead
42 Ammunition compartment auxiliary fuel tank 121.8 gallons
43 Fuel feed pipes
44 Flush-fitting UHF aerial panel
45 Anti-collision light
46 Starboard intake
47 Engine bleed air supply to air-conditioning
48 Gravity fuel fillers
49 Fuselage main fuel tanks (total internal capacity 895.2 gallons

50 Pressure refueling adaptor
51 Intake shock cone centre body
52 De-iced intake lip
53 Port intake
54 Shock cone boundary layer bleed
55 Boundary layer bleed air duct
56 Auxiliary intake
57 Hinged auxiliary intake door
58 Navigation light
59 Leading-edge flap jack
60 Intake trunking
61 Fuselage main longeron
62 Wingroot attaching members
63 Intake flank fuel tanks
64 Wing-mounting fuselage mainframes
65 Control cable runs
66 Electrical junction box
67 Dorsal spine fairing
68 Starboard inboard pylon
69 Leading-edge flap (lowered)
70 AIM-7 Sparrow AAM
71 Missile launch rail
72 Starboard outer pylon
73 Tip tank vane
74 Tip tank latching unit
75 Starboard wingtip tank
76 Fuel filler caps
77 Starboard aileron
78 Aileron power control jacks
79 Power control servo valves
80 Fuel lines to auxiliary tanks
81 Flap blowing duct
82 Starboard blown flap (lowered)
83 Engine intake compressor face
84 Intake spill flaps
85 Aileron torque shaft
86 Hydraulic reservoir
87 Air-conditioning bleed air supply pipe
88 General Electric J79-GE-19 turbojet
89 Engine withdrawal rail
90 Starboard airbrake (open)
91 Fin root fillet
92 Elevator servo controls
93 Elevator/all-moving tailplane hydraulic jacks
94 Push-pull control rods

95 Tailfin construction
96 Fin tip fairing
97 Tailplane rocking control arm
98 Starboard tailplane
99 One-piece tailplane construction
100 Tailplane spar
101 Tailplane spar central pivot
102 Fin trailing-edge construction
103 Rudder construction
104 Rudder power control jacks
105 Rudder servo valves
106 Exhaust duct
107 Fully-variable afterburner exhaust nozzle
108 Fin attachment joints
109 Fin-carrying mainframes
110 Afterburner duct
111 Nozzle control jacks
112 Steel and titanium aft fuselage construction
113 Rear navigation lights
114 Aft fuselage attachment joint
115 Brake parachute housing
116 Port airbrake (open)
117 Airbrake scissor links
118 Fuselage strake (both sides)
119 Emergency runway arrester hook
120 Airbrake jack
121 Air exit louvres
122 Primary heat exchanger
123 Wingroot trailing-edge fillet
124 Flap hydraulic jack
125 Flap blowing slot
126 Port blown flap (lowered)
127 Aileron servo valves
128 Aileron power control jacks
129 Port aileron
130 Tip tank fins
131 Port navigation light
132 Port wingtip fuel tan, 339.6 gallons capacity
133 Fuel filler caps
134 Outboard pylon mounting rib
135 Wing multi-spar construction
136 Inboard pylon mounting rib
137 Main undercarriage leg door
138 Shock absorber strut
139 Swivel axle control rods

140 Port mainwheel
141 Leading-edge flap (lowered)
142 Leading-edge flap rib construction
143 Port outboard pylon
144 Missile launch rail
145 Port AIM-7 Sparrow AAM
146 Mk 82 500lb (227kg) bomb
147 Mk 83 1,000lb (454kg) bomb
148 Bomb mounting shackles
149 Auxiliary fuel tank (195.6 gallons capacity)
150 Port inboard wing pylon
151 Pylon attachments
152 LAU-3A 2.75in (70mm) FFAR pod (19 rockets)
153 AIM-9 Sidewinder AAM
154 Missile launch rail
155 Fuselage stores pylon adaptor

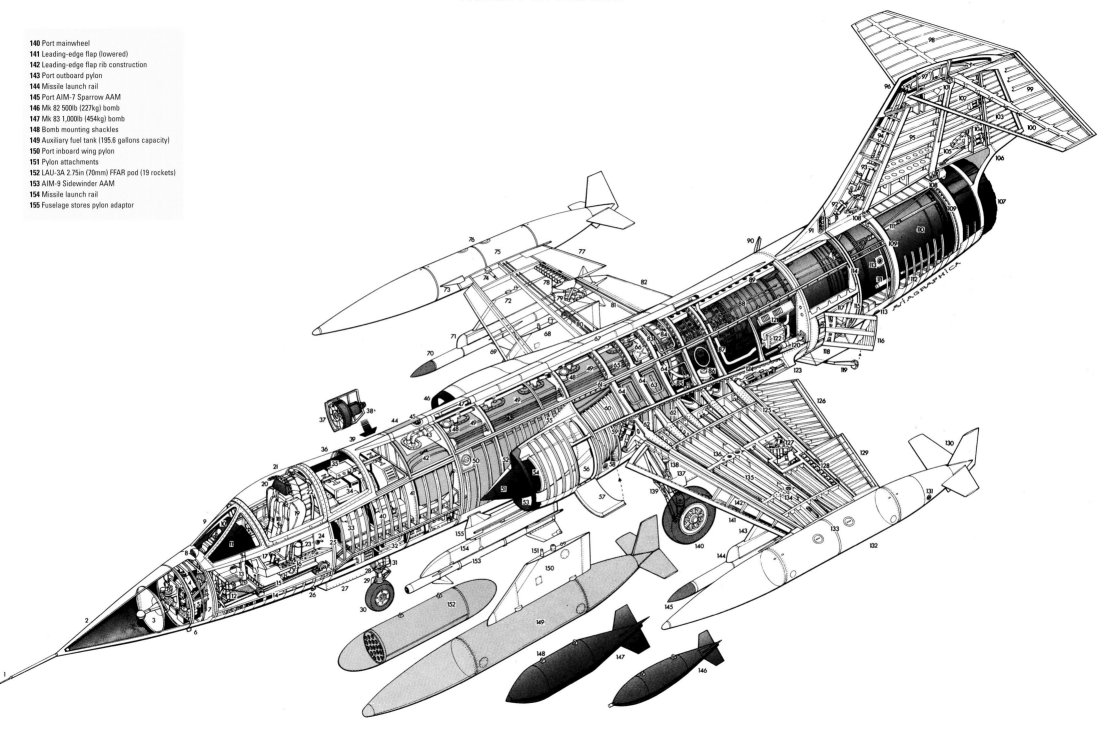

RIGHT: A turkey in maneuver combat due to its high wing loading, the Starfighter was developed into the F-104G tactical aircraft. Notorious for its high accident rate with the *Luftwaffe*, it was nevertheless operated successfully by other nations, notably Denmark.

RIGHT BELOW: A formation of Royal Canadian Air Force (now Canadian Defense Force) CF-104s. Although the Starfighter was a very precise handling aircraft with a fast rate of roll, at high speeds its rate of turn was derisory.

OPPOSITE: Canada became a major user of the CF-104 Starfighter, although the air-to-air role was ignored. This spectacularly painted CF-104 is obviously heading for a "Tiger Meet," almost certainly somewhere in Europe.

LOCKHEED P-38 LIGHTNING

LEFT: First flown in January 1939, the Lockheed P-38 Lightning was designed as a high altitude interceptor, but in the European theater was first used as a long range escort, then in the attack role.

The P-38 Lightning, designed in the late 1930s to meet a tough specification for a high altitude interceptor, emerged with a radical twin-boom configuration that had the cockpit in a central nacelle, and clocked up a number of "firsts." It was the first single-seat fighter of twin-boom arrangement to see service. It was the first squadron fighter fitted with turbo-superchargers, and the first aircraft to encounter the compressibility problem. It was the first fighter with a nosewheel undercarriage, and the first (from the P-38J) to have power-boosted controls. It was also the only twin-engined, single-seat fighter powered by piston engines to go into large-scale production and extensive service in World War II.

To achieve high altitude performance, American aircraft and engine designers came up with turbo-supercharging. Air from the intake was ducted to the rather large turbo-supercharger, the turbine of which was driven by very hot exhaust gases ducted from the engine. The intake air, having been compressed in the turbo-supercharger, was then ducted back to the engine aspiration system.

Turbo-superchargers were large and heavy, however, and primarily to house them Lockheed selected a twin-boom arrangement with a turbo-supercharger behind each engine and a radiator astern of both. There were twin fins and rudders, and cannon and machine gun armament was fitted into the nose of the central nacelle ahead of the pilot. An odd feature for a fighter was a yoke control column rather than a stick.

It was not surprising that the P-38 was large and heavy. It was fast, but its twin engines, large span, and high wing loading (almost twice that of contemporary fighters) rendered it not very agile, even though combat flaps were fitted to later models to increase usable lift during heavy maneuvering.

The prototype Lighting, XP-38, first flew on January 27, 1939, and the first operational version, the P-38D with armor protection for the pilot and self-sealing tanks, was delivered to the U.S. Army Air Corps from August 1941. By August 1945, when production ended, 9,923 of all types had been delivered.

The Lightning's combat debut came against the *Luftwaffe* over Tunisia in 1942, where it was often forced to fly at medium or low levels, well below its best altitude, and it was outmatched by the Messerschmitt Bf 109G and Focke-Wulf Fw 190A, especially in the turn. It was also used in the bomber escort role in Europe from 1943. Here, its long range was of advantage, but again it was outmaneuvered by German fighters, and by September 1944 it

was withdrawn from that role, and was widely used for strafing and close air support instead.

However, the P-38 became the most successful American fighter in China and the Pacific, largely supplanting the P-40 Warhawk from mid-1943. Its exceptional range made it ideal for the long-distance missions during the island-hopping campaign, while its speed and altitude performance gave it a distinct edge over most Japanese fighters it encountered. Its high wing loading meant that it was unable to turn with them but, by staying high and choosing their moment, Lightning pilots were able to succeed against their better-turning adversaries by using dive and zoom tactics. One spectacular and unusual success came on April 18, 1943, when eighteen P-38s were ordered to intercept two Mitsubishi G4M "Betty" bombers that were carrying the great Japanese Navy Commander Admiral Yamamoto and his entourage, escorted by Zero fighters, en route from Rabaul to Ballale. Two of the Lightnings fought their way through the desperate Zero attacks to shoot down the bombers, rejoin their comrades, and return to base at Henderson Field on Guadalcanal.

Specifications for Lockheed P-38L Lightning

Dimensions: wingspan 52 feet, length 37 feet 10 inches, height 12 feet 10 inches

Power: two Allison V-1710-111/113 turbo-supercharged liquid-cooled V-12 engines each rated at 1,600lb

Weights: empty 14,100lb, normal takeoff 17,500lb, max 21,600lb

Speed: max 414mph at 25,000 feet, 360mph at 5,000 feet

Ceiling: 40,000 feet

Range: 2,260 miles

Armament: one 20mm Hispano AN-M-2C cannon with 150 rounds, four 0.50in Browning M2 machine guns with 500 rounds per gun, all nose-mounted, provision for bombs and rockets under wing

Crew: pilot

P-38 Lightning cutaway key

1 Starboard navigation light
2 Wingtip trailing edge strake
3 Landing light (underwing)
4 Starboard aileron
5 Aileron control rod/quadrant
6 Wing outer spar
7 Aileron tab drum
8 Aileron tab control pulleys
9 Aileron tab control rod
10 Aileron trim tab
11 Fixed tab
12 Tab cable access
13 Flap extension/retraction cables
14 Control pulleys
15 Flap outer carriage
16 Fowler-type flap (extended)
17 Control access panel
18 Wing spar transition
19 Outer section leading-edge fuel tanks (P-38J-5 and subsequent) capacity 55.2 gallonseach
20 Engine bearer/bulkhead upper attachment
21 Firewall
22 Triangulated tubular engine bearer supports
23 Polished mirror surface panel (undercarriage visual check)
24 Cantilever engine bearer
25 Intake fairing
26 Accessories cooling intake
27 Oil radiator (outer sections) and intercooler (center section) tripleintake
28 Spinner
29 Curtiss-Electric three blade (left) handed propeller
30 Four machine gun barrels
31 Cannon barrel
32 Camera-gun aperture
33 Nose spar
34 Bulkhead
35 Machine gun blast tubes
36 Four 0.5in (12.7mm) machine guns
37 Cannon flexible hose hydraulic charger
38 Chatellerault-feed cannon magazine (150 rounds)
39 Machine gun firing solenoid
40 Cannon ammunition feed chute
41 Nose armament cowling clips
42 Case ejection chute (port lower machine gun)
43 Ammunition box and feed chute (port lower machine gun)
44 Case ejection chute (port upper machine gun)
45 Ammunition box and feed chute (port upper machine gun)
46 Radio antenna
47 Ejection chute exit (shrouded when item 52 attached)
48 Nosewheel door
49 Nosewheel shimmy damper assembly and reservoir
50 Torque links
51 Towing eye
52 Type M10 triple-tube 4.5-in (11.4-cm) rocket-launcher

53 Rearward-retracting nosewheel
54 Alloy spokes cover plate
55 Fork
56 Rocket-launcher forward attachment (to 63)
57 Nosewheel lower drag struts
58 Nosewheel oleo leg
59 Nosewheel pin access
60 Side struts and fulcrum
61 Actuating cylinder
62 Upper drag strut
63 Rocket-launcher forward attachment bracket
64 Rudder pedal assembly
65 Engine controls quadrant
66 Instrument panel
67 Spectacle grip cantilevered control wheel
68 Non-reflective shroud
69 Lynn-3 reflector sight mounting
70 Optically-flat bullet-proof windscreen
71 External rear-view mirror
72 Armored headrest
73 Rearward-hinged canopy
74 Pilot's armored seat back
75 Canopy bracing
76 Downward-winding side windows
77 Wing root fillets
78 Nosewheel well
79 Port reserve fuel tank, capacity 60 gallons
80 Fuel filler cap
81 Main (double I-beam) spar
82 Fuel filler cap
83 Flap inner carriage
84 Port main fuel tank, capacity 90 gallons
85 Flap control access
86 Flap structure
87 Entry ladder release
88 Flap drive motor
89 Fuel surge tank and main hydraulic reservoir in aft nacelle
90 Radio equipment compartment
91 Turnover support pylon
92 Flap control access
93 Aerial attachment
94 Starboard inner flap
95 Flap push-pull rod
96 Starboard main fuel tank, capacity as 84
97 Main spar
98 Engine control runs
99 Starboard reserve fuel tank, capacity as 79
100 Starboard oil tank
101 Cooling louvres
102 Cabin heater intake
103 Turbo-supercharger cooling intakes
104 Turbine cooling duct
105 Exhaust turbine
106 Supercharger housing

107 Wingroot/boom fillet
108 Coolant/radiator return pipe (left and right)
109 Exhaust waste gate outlet
110 Access panel
111 Boom Joint (Station 265)
112 Radiator/coolant supply pipe
113 Mainwheel well
114 Mainwheel doors
115 Radiator intake
116 Starboard outer radiator fairing
117 Radiator grille
118 Engine coolant radiator assembly
119 Exit flap
120 Tool and baggage compartment
121 Boom structure
122 D/R master compass housing
123 Boom/tail attachment joint (Station 393)
124 Starboard lower fin
125 Tail bumper skid shoe
126 Elevator control pulley
127 Rudder stop
128 Elevator control horn
129 Fixed tip
130 Radio aerials
131 Tail surface control pulleys
132 Aerodynamic mass balance
133 Aerial attachments
134 Starboard rudder
135 Tab control rod and drum
136 Rudder trim tab
137 Elevator abbreviated torque tube
138 Tailplane stressed skin
139 Elevator pin hinges (eight off)
140 Elevator
141 Upper and lower mass balances
142 Elevator trim tab
143 Tailplane structure
144 Stiffeners
145 Port fin structure
146 Elevator pulley access
147 Rudder tab drum access
148 Tail running light (port)
149 Aerodynamic mass balance
150 Rudder framework
151 Rudder trim tab
152 Fixed tip structure
153 Tail surfaces/boom (quatrefoil bulkhead) attachment flanges
154 Rudder lower section
155 Tail bumper skid shoe
156 Elevator pulley access
157 Port lower fin
158 Elevator, rudder, and table cables
159 Battery compartment
160 Radiator exit flap

161 Engine coolant radiator assembly
162 Radiator housing
163 Radiator/coolant supply pipe
164 Radiator intake
165 Coolant/radiator return pipe
166 Oxygen cylinder
167 Port inner radiator fairing
168 Flare tube (port and starboard booms)
169 Mainwheel doors
170 Mainwheel well
171 Exhaust waste gate outlet
172 Turbine cooling duct
173 Exhaust turbine
174 Supercharger assembly

175 Supercharger/ intercooler duct
176 Carburetor intake duct
177 Carburetor air intake
178 Abbreviated rear spar
179 Flap outer section
180 Tab cable access
181 Fixed tab
182 Aileron trim tab
183 Aileron full-span piano-wire hinge
184 Underwing pitot attachment
185 Raked web stiffener (outboard of rear spar)
186 Aileron structure
187 Outer wing pressed sheet ribs
188 Aileron counterweight
189 Junction box
190 Port navigation lights
191 Port wingtip structure
192 Leading-edge ribs

193 Pitot head
194 Wing leading-edge skin join (fabric-covered piano-wire hinge)
195 Wing outer section I-beam box spar
196 Leading-edge stringers (no fuel tanks in early P-38Js)
197 Wing inner surface corrugation
198 Spar single/double I-beam box spar transition
199 Mainwheel leg doors
200 Rearward-retracting mainwheel
201 Mainwheel oleo leg
202 Alloy spoked hub
203 Cantilever axle
204 Torque links

205 Hydraulic brake cable
206 Drag strut
207 Side strut
208 Drag links
209 Fulcrum
210 Actuating cylinder
211 Multi-bolt outer wing fixings
212 Turbo-supercharger cooling intakes
213 Cabin heater intake
214 Cooling louvers
215 Carburetor duct
216 Outer section wing fillet
217 Insulated exhaust shroud duct
218 Intercooler/ carburetor duct
219 Supercharger/intercooler duct
220 Outlet
221 Oil radiator shutter
222 Intercooler
223 Exhausts

224 Allison V-1710-89/91 twelve-cylinder Vee engine
225 Magnetos/distributors
226 Intake fairing
227 Header feed pipes
228 Port outer oil radiator
229 Spark-plug and magneto cooling intake
230 Coolant header tank
231 Propeller hub
232 Oil radiator (outer sections) and intercooler (center section triple intake

233 Curtiss-Electric three-blade (right) handed propeller
234 Inner section underwing stores including
235 Jettisonable auxiliary fuel tank, or
236 Smoke generator, or
237 1,000lb (454kg) bomb

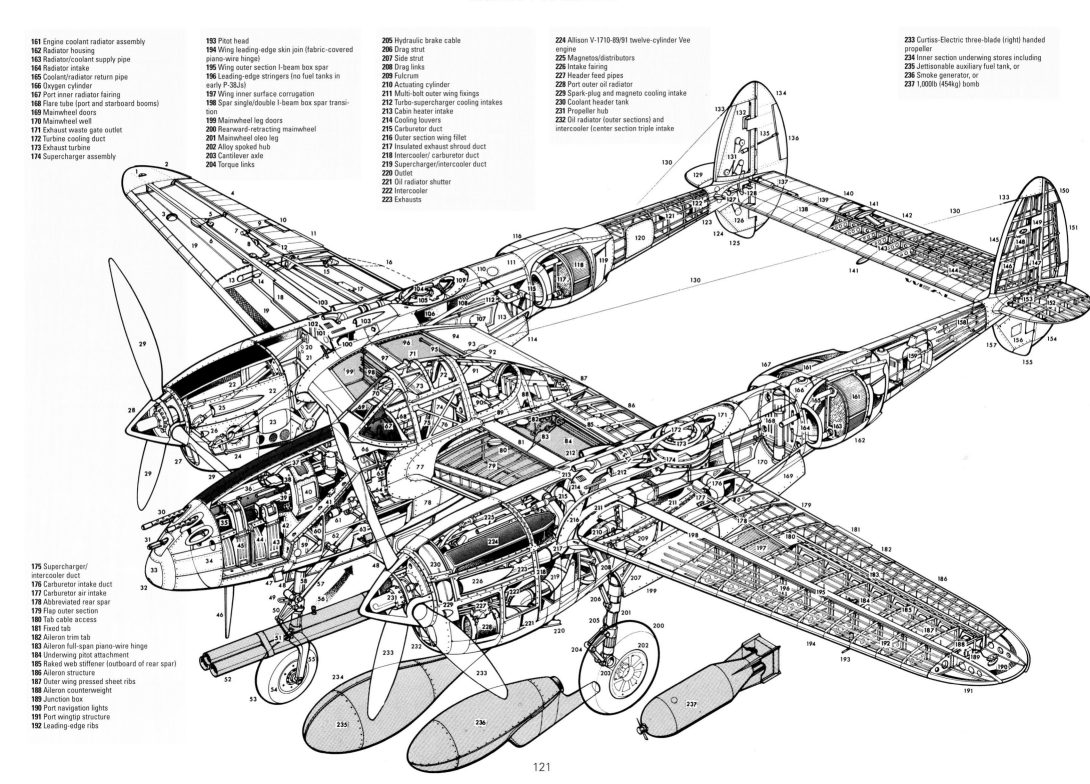

OPPOSITE: To meet the high altitude requirement, the Allison V-1710 engines needed bulky turbochargers, which could be housed only in the fuselage. In the twin-engined Lightning, these could be placed only in booms behind each engine.

LEFT INSET: A very early Lightning, clearly showing the central nacelle housing the cockpit and the guns, typically one cannon and four heavy machine guns. Another Lightning oddity was the use of a yoke control column.

LEFT: As a fighter, the greatest successes by Lightnings were in the Pacific, where the type's altitude performance was exploited to the full, its pilots using dive and zoom tactics against the Japanese aircraft.

LOCKHEED P-80 SHOOTING STAR

LEFT: The Lockheed P-80 Shooting Star was the first American jet fighter to enter service, in February 1945. The P-80 gave sterling service in Korea. These are P-80Cs of the 94th Hat in the Ring fighter squadron.

The Lockheed P-80 became the first operational jet fighter to enter service with the U.S. Army Air Force in February 1945, and, having been redesignated F-80 and being sent to war in Korea, scored the first jet-versus-jet victory when one shot down a MiG-15 in November 1950.

The Shooting Star single-seat, single-engined subsonic jet fighter evolved from the XP-80, designed from June 23, 1943, around a 2,460lb thrust Whittle-derived de Havilland H-1B turbojet engine. Its first flight occurred on January 8, 1944. During flight test it achieved 502mph at 20,480 feet. However, when the H-1B engine did not become available, the design had to be extensively reworked around the General Electric I-40 (later called the Allison J33) turbojet of 3,850lb thrust, leading to a larger and heavier aircraft. Two additional prototypes were built, as XP-80As, which flew on June 10 and August 1, 1944. Thirteen similar service test YP-80s followed, and the initial production version, the P-80A, was ordered on April 4, 1944. These entered service in February 1945, and four were rushed to Europe but did not engage in air combat there.

The P-80A was exceptionally clean aerodynamically. It had a straight, low-mounted wing, the wing section being of an untried laminar flow type, which was successful. Control surfaces were hydraulically boosted, there were airbrakes mounted on the fuselage, and the aft fuselage was detachable. The engine was located amidships in the fuselage. The undercarriage was of tricycle type.

The first order was for 1,000 aircraft, with a supplementary contract in the following year for a further 2,500, but after the Allies' victory in the Pacific the initial contract was reduced to 917 P-80As and the supplementary contract was cancelled altogether.

The initial 345 P-80As were fitted with the General Electric J33-GE-11 engine of 3,50lb thrust. They were armed with six 0.50in guns. The next 218 aircraft had 4,000lb thrust J33-A-17 engines. These aircraft were followed by 240 delivered as P-80Bs, which had upgraded engines, equipment and armament, and a thinner wing. The final production variant was the P-80C, redesignated F-80C, of which the first 238 (including 50 delivered to the U.S. Marine Corps as To-1s) were powered by the J33-A-23 engines of 4,600lb thrust. It also had improved fuel controls and an ejection seat. A total of 798 of this model were built during 1948-49, while 254 A and B models were converted to similar standards.

It was the F-80C that was sent into combat during the Korean War. The giant Boeing B-29s, which had initially been bombing the North in relative safety, were proving vulnerable to the small, maneuverable MiG-15. The Shooting Stars were pressed into service as escorts for the bombers but found themselves outperformed by the little MiGs, and the escorting F-80s were unable to give the B-29s adequate protection. Despite achieving 37 air combat victories, including six MiG-15s, with the famous first jet-versus-jet victory occurring on November 8, 1950, the generally outclassed F-80 spent most of the war in the close support role until being withdrawn from first-line squadrons within eight months of the end of the Korean conflict.

After the war, the Shooting Star served with the USAF Air National Guard until March 1961. A T-33A trainer variant proved extremely popular, almost 7,000 of them being built for service with more than 20 countries. Some F-80Cs were subsequently supplied to a number of Latin American air arms.

Specifications for Lockheed P-80C Shooting Star

Dimensions: wingspan 38 feet 10.5 inches, length 34 feet 6 inches, height 11 feet 4 inches

Power: one Allison J35-A-35 centrifugal-flow turbojet rated at 5,400lb military thrust

Weights: empty 8,240lb, normal takeoff 12,650lb, max 16,856lb

Speed: max 580mph at sea level

Ceiling: 39,500 feet

Range: 716 miles

Armament: six 0.50in Browning M-2 machine guns with 300 rounds per gun, eight 5in unguided rockets, or two 1,000lb bombs, or six napalm tanks

Crew: pilot

F-80C Shooting Star cutaway key

1 Nose antenna fairing
2 D/F loop aerial
3 Machine gun muzzles
4 Oxygen tank
5 Nose compartment access panel
6 Port and starboard ammunition boxes, 300 rounds per gun
7 0.5in (12.7mm) machine guns
8 Spent cartridge case and link ejector chutes
9 Landing and taxiing lamps
10 Nosewheel leg torque scissors
11 Nosewheel
12 Steering linkage
13 Nosewheel doors
14 Retraction strut
15 Radio and electrical equipment bay
16 External canopy-release handle
17 Cockpit front bulkhead
18 Windscreen heater duct
19 Bulletproof windscreen panel
20 Reflector gunsight
21 Instrument panel shroud
22 Instrument panel
23 Rudder pedals
24 Cockpit floor level
25 Nosewheel bay
26 Intake lip fairing
27 Port air intake
28 Boundary layer bleed air duct
29 Intake ducting
30 Boundary layer air exit louvres
31 Engine throttle control
32 Safety harness
33 Pilot's ejection seat
34 Cockpit rear bulkhead
35 Starboard side console panel
36 Sliding cockpit canopy cover
37 Ejection seat headrest
38 Canopy aft decking
39 D/F sense antenna
40 Starboard wing fuel tanks
41 Fuel filler caps
42 Leading-edge tank
43 Fletcher-type tip tank, capacity 265 gallons
44 Tip tank, capacity 165 gallons
45 Tip tank filler cap
46 Starboard navigation light
47 Aileron balance weights
48 Starboard aileron
49 Aileron hinge control
50 Trailing-edge fuel tank
51 Starboard split trailing-edge flap
52 Flap control links
53 Fuselage fuel tank, total internal capacity 657 gallons
54 Fuselage main longeron
55 Center fuselage frames
56 Intake trunking
57 Main undercarriage wheel well
58 Wing spar attachment joints
59 Pneumatic reservoir
60 Hydraulic accumulator
61 Control access panel
62 Spring-loaded intake pressure relief doors
63 Allison J33-A-23 centrifugal-flow turbojet engine
64 Rear fuselage break point
65 Rear fuselage attachment bolts (three)
66 Elevator control rods
67 Jet pipe bracing cable
68 Fin-root fillet
69 Elevator control link
70 Starboard tailplane
71 Starboard elevator
72 Fin construction
73 Pitot tube
74 Fintip communications antenna fairing
75 Rudder mass balance
76 Rudder construction
77 Fixed tab
78 Elevator and rudder hinge control
79 Tail navigation light
80 Jet pipe nozzle
81 Elevator tabs
82 Port elevator construction
83 Elevator mass balance
84 Tailplane construction
85 Fin/tailplane attachment joints
86 Tailplane fillet fairing
87 Jet pipe mounting rail
88 Rear fuselage frame and stringer construction
89 Gyrosyn radio compass flux valve
90 Fuselage skin plating
91 Jet pipe support frame
92 Trailing-edge wingroot fillet
93 Flap drive motor
94 Port split trailing-edge flap
95 Flap shroud ribs
96 Trailing-edge fuel tank bay
97 Rear spar
98 Trailing-edge ribs
99 Port aileron tab
100 Aileron hinge control
101 Upper-skin panel aileron hinge line
102 Aileron construction
103 Wingtip fairing construction
104 Tip tank
105 Port navigation light
106 Tip tank mounting and jettison control
107 Detachable lower wing skin panels
108 Port wing fuel tank bays
109 Inter tank bay ribs
110 Front spar
111 Corrugated leading-edge inner skin
112 Port stores pylon
113 1,000lb (454kg) HE bomb
114 5in (127mm) HVAR ground attack rockets (10 rockets maximum load)
115 HVAR mountings
116 Port mainwheel
117 Mainwheel doors
118 Wheel brake pad
119 Main undercarriage leg strut
120 Retraction jack
121 Upper skin panel wing stringers
122 Wingroot leading-edge extension
123 Port ventral airbrake

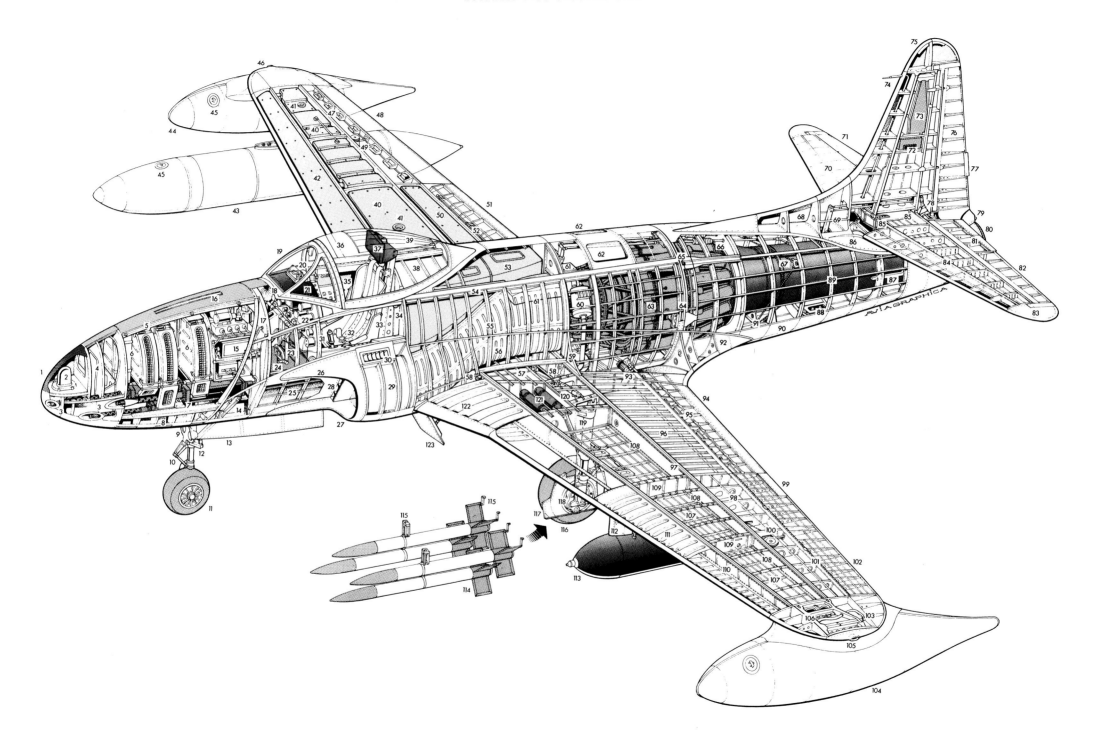

LOCKHEED MARTIN F/A-22 RAPTOR

LEFT: The Lockheed Martin F-22A Raptor was the winner of the USAF Advanced Tactical Fighter competition launched in September 1985. Seen here is one of the two YF-22 prototypes, which first flew in September 1990.

The F/A-22 Raptor is the result of a co-operative arrangement between Lockheed Martin and Boeing to design, develop and build a new generation tactical fighter. It is a single-seat, twin-engined, bisonic air superiority fighter that will replace the F-15 Eagle, and will become operational from late 2005. It combines stealth design with the supersonic, highly maneuverable, dual-engine, long-range requirements of an air-to-air fighter, and it also will have an inherent air-to-ground capability. The F/A-22 has first-look, first-shot, first-kill capability. Its stealth characteristics enable it to penetrate sophisticated integrated radar as well as concentrated SAM (surface-to-air missile) threats. To achieve this the F-22 is capable of supersonic cruise, has an agile capability enhanced with thrust vectoring, and is equipped with advanced integrated avionics.

Weapons are carried internally to enable supersonic cruise to be maintained without afterburner, and also for stealth reasons. The F/A-22 features three weapons bays – one on each side of the intake ducts to accommodate AIM-120 Amraam/AIM-9 Sidewinder air-to-air missiles – while a further large ventral weapons bay permits carriage of additional AAMs and/or air-to-ground ordnance, such as the GBU-32 JDAM. It is anticipated therefore that the F-22 will be able to operate in advance of other forces to detect and destroy enemy fighters so as to gain air dominance, as well as attacking principal targets.

One of the stealthy characteristics of the design is that all fuel is carried internally, which has resulted in a large aircraft. All surfaces are angled carefully to deflect incoming radar impulses away from the emitter, and other stealth measures have been employed.

The Raptor's wing is a rhomboidal planform, with 42 degree sweepback on the leading edge and 17 degree sweepback on the trailing edge. The leading edge is slatted, whereas the trailing edge has all-moving ailerons outboard and flaperons inboard. The airframe is built of titanium, aluminum, composites, steel, and other materials. Titanium and both thermoset and thermoplastic composites comprise the largest percentage of materials, 30 and 26 percent, respectively. There are large twin fins, and rudders are outward-canted and are also used as airbrakes. The balanced design of the F/A-22 incorporates performance (supercruise, maneuver advantage, acceleration), reliability, maintainability and supportability (high readiness, self-sufficiency, reduced support), survivability (low observability), integrated avionics, optimum payload, and affordability (low life-cycle cost, reduced deployability costs).

The prototype YF-22 was first flown on September 29, 1990, and, following a competitive flyoff against the rival Northrop YF-23, was announced winner of the Air Force's Advanced Tactical Aircraft (ATF) program in April 1991. Construction began of eleven pre-production aircraft, later reduced to nine on cancellation of a pair of F-22B two-seat trainers. Initial figures showed a requirement for 750 F-22s but by 1997 this had been reduced to 339 at a cost of $187 million each.

The F-22 was named Raptor on April 9, 1997, when the first Engineering/Manufacturing/Development (EMD) aircraft was rolled out. This aircraft first flew on September 7 of that year. The F-22 designation has also since been amended to reflect the additional ground attack role. F/A-22s are currently undergoing flight tests at Edwards Air Force Base, California. It is anticipated that the F/A-22 will enter service in 2005, replacing the F-15C. Tyndall Air Force Base, Florida, is currently being prepared for its new arrival.

Specifications for F/A-22A Raptor

Dimensions: wingspan 44 feet 6 inches, length 62 feet 1 inch, height 16 feet 8 inches

Power: two Pratt & Whitney F119-PW-100 twin-spool axial-flow afterburning turbofans each rated at 35,000lb maximum thrust (military thrust classified), with pitch-vectoring (vectored thrust) nozzles

Weights: empty 31,607lb, normal takeoff classified, max 55,000lb

Speed: max Mach 2.0 at altitude, Mach 1.21 at sea level, supercruise Mach 1.8

Ceiling: over 50,000 feet

Range: 2,000 miles

Armament: one 20mm M61A-2 six-barrel cannon with 460 rounds, six AIM-120C Amraam and two AIM-9T Sidewinder air-to-air missiles in internal bays, plus other weapons carried externally

Crew: pilot

Lockheed Martin F-22A Raptor cutaway key

1 Composite radome
2 Northrop-Grumman/Texas Instruments AN/APG-77 multi-mode radar scanner
3 Canted radome mounting bulkhead
4 Pitot head
5 Air-data sensor system receivers, four positions
6 Radar equipment bay
7 Missile launch detector windows
8 Cockpit front pressure bulkhead
9 Forward fuselage machined aluminum alloy sidewall panel
10 Underfloor avionics equipment bays
11 Avionics equipment modules, downward hinging for access
12 Electro-luminescent formation lighting strip
13 Composite fuselage chine skin paneling
14 Rudder pedals
15 Instrument console housing six multi-function full-color LCD displays
16 GEC-Marconi Avionics head-up display (HUD)
17 Upward-hinging cockpit canopy
18 McDonnell Douglas ACES II (modified) ejection seat
19 Starboard side console panel with sidestick controller for digital fly-by-wire flight control system
20 Port side control panel with engine throttles
21 Off-base ladder stowage
22 Cockpit sloping rear pressure bulkhead
23 Electrical power equipment bay
24 Battery bay
25 Nosewheel doors
26 Landing and taxiing lights
27 Forward retracting nosewheel
28 Torque scissor links
29 Port engine intake
30 Titanium intake frame
31 Intake bleed-air spill duct
32 Inlet bleed-air door/spoiler panel
33 Bleed-air door hydraulic actuator
34 Data-link support antenna, microwave landing system (MLS) antenna beneath intake
35 Air-cooled flight critical equipment cooling air intake in boundary layer diverter duct, blower for ground operations
36 Boundary layer diverter spill duct
37 On-board oxygen generating system (OBOGS)
38 No. 1 fuselage fuel tank
39 Canopy hinge point
40 Canopy actuator, electrically powered
41 Starboard engine air intake
42 Intake spill and boundary layer bleed air ducts
43 Lateral avionics equipment bay
44 Missile launch detector window
45 Data-link antenna
46 ACFC cooling air exhaust ducts
47 Forward fuselage production joint
48 Composite intake duct
49 Canopy emergency jettison control
50 Lateral missile bay doors
51 Missile launch rail
52 Launch rail trapeze arm
53 Hydraulic rail actuator
54 Environmental control system equipment bay
55 Fuselage main longeron
56 Ventral missile bay
57 L-band antenna
58 No. 2 integral fuselage fuel tank
59 Machined fuselage main frame, typical
60 Illuminated flight refueling receptacle, open
61 Airframe-mounted auxiliary equipment gearbox, shaft-driven from engines
62 Intake overpressure spill doors
63 Global positioning system (GPS) antenna
64 Ammunition feed chute, 48-round ventral fuselage transverse magazine
65 M61AZ six-barrel lightweight rotary cannon
66 Cannon barrels
67 Cannon muzzle aperture beneath flip-up door
68 Wing root EW antenna
69 Communication/Identification (CNI) UHF antenna
70 CNI band 2 antenna
71 600-gallon external tanks
72 Starboard leading edge flap, lowered
73 Flap drive shaft and rotary actuators
74 ILS localiser antenna
75 Carbon-fiber composite wing skin panel
76 Starboard navigation light, above and below
77 Wing tip EW antenna
78 Starboard aileron
79 Formation lighting strip
80 Aileron hudraulic actuator
81 Starboard flaperon, downward position
82 Starboard wing integral fuel tank
83 Power system inverter, port and starboard
84 Starboard mainwheel, stowed position
85 Fuselage sidebody integral fuel tank
86 Hydraulic equipment bay
87 Fuel/air and fuel/oil heat exchangers
88 Fuel transfer piping
89 No. 3 fuselage integral fuel tank with onboard inert gas generating system (OBIGS)
90 Engine bleed-air primary heat exchanger
91 Engine compressor intake
92 Port hydraulic reservoir
93 Hydraulic accumulator
94 Port sidebody integral fuel tankage
95 Pratt & Whitney F119-PW-100 afterburning turbofan engine
96 Engine bay machined frames
97 Central fireproof keel unit
98 Stored energy system (SES) reservoirs, engine relighting
99 Engine bay thermal lining
100 Fin root attachment joints
101 Composite fin leading edge and skin panel
102 Multi-spar all-composite fin structure
103 Starboard composite rudder
104 Starboard tailplane
105 "Cats-eye" control surface interface, all positions
106 CNI VHF antenna
107 Rudder hydraulic actuator
108 Rudder lower fairing
109 Engine exhaust nozzle sealing plates
110 Two-dimensional convergent-divergent thrust-vectoring afterburner nozzle
111 CNI Band 2 antenna
112 Runway emergency arrester hook housing
113 Fin leading edge CNI VHF antenna
114 Formation lighting strip
115 Port rudder
116 Airbrake via differential rudder deflection
117 TaIplane pivot mounting
118 Port rear CNI Band 2 antenna
119 Port all-moving tailplane
120 Tailplane all-composite structure
121 Carbon-fiber skin panels with honeycomb core

122 Composite tailplane spar
123 Tailplane hydraulic actuator
124 Port flaperon
125 Flaperon hydraulic actuator
126 Wing rear spar, titanium
127 All-composite flaperon construction
128 Aileron hydraulic actuator
129 Formation lighting strip
130 Port all-composite aileron
131 Band 3 EW antenna
132 Port navigation light, above and below
133 Port leading edge flap
134 Port ILS localiser antenna
135 Wing pylons can carry ferry tanks and AIM-
120 missiles in transport configuration or twin
AIM-120 missiles on dedicated launcher
136 Composite leading edge flap structure
137 Leading edge flap drive shaft and rotary
actuators
138 Titanium front spar
139 Pylon attachment hardpoints
140 Titanium pylon mounting ribs
141 Port wing integral fuel tank
142 Multi-spar wing structure
143 Carbon-fiber composite sine-wave spars
144 Wing root attachment fittings
145 Port mainwheel bay
146 APU exhaust
147 Allied Signal Auxiliary Power Unit (APU)
148 APU intake
149 Main undercarriage leg pivot mounting
150 Hydraulic retraction jack
151 Mainwheel leg strut
152 Port CNI UHF antenna
153 Port CNI Band 2 antenna
154 Port mainwheel
155 Leading edge flap drive motor

156 Port Band 3 and 4 EW antenna
157 Ventral missile bay doors, open
158 AIM-120 Amraam medium-range air-to-air
missiles, four in ventral bay (six AIM-120C compressed Amraam alternative)
159 AIM-9M Sidewinder close-range air-to-air
missile
160 AIM-9X advanced Sidewinder
161 GBU-30 JDAM 1,000lb joint direct attack
munition

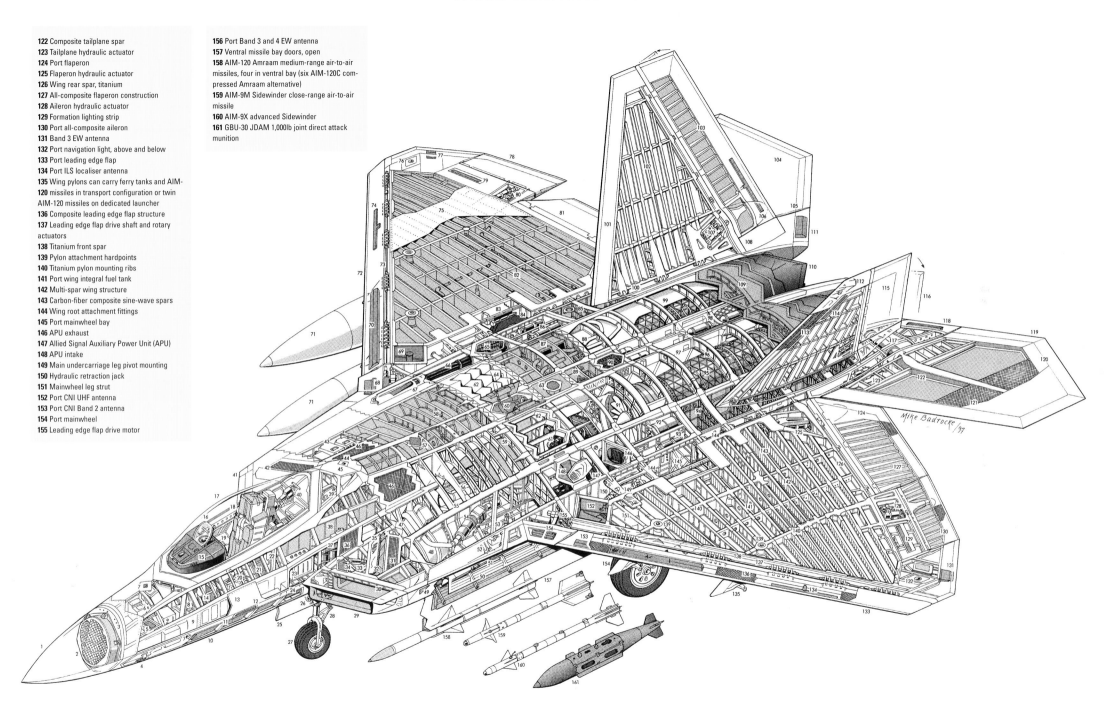

Mike Badrocke/97

OPPOSITE INSET: Trapezoidal intakes, a diamond-shaped front fuselage cross-section, and outward canted tail surfaces are stealth features of the YF-22, designed to deflect emissions from hostile radars away at an angle.

OPPOSITE: The first preproduction F-22A Raptor in flight. The intakes can be seen to be raked back at an angle, while the fins and rudders are canted both forward and back by carefully calculated angles.

LEFT: Contrails stream from the wingtips as this YF-22 reefs into a hard turn. It was designed to outfly and outfight all present and future adversary aircraft for many years to come.

ABOVE: Added maneuverability is conferred by pitch-only vectoring engine nozzles. Maximum speed is Mach 2, but the Raptor is designed to supercruise – to sustain high supersonic speeds without using afterburning.

RIGHT: The weapon of choice for the Raptor is the AIM-120 Amraam, seen here during launch trials in 1990, with Sidewinder backup. As a stealth measure, these are carried in, and launched from, internal weapons bays.

OPPOSITE FAR RIGHT: Despite having a large volume of internal fuel, the Raptor will still rely on flight refueling for many missions. The red structure at the rear of the hooked-up aircraft is an anti-spin parachute.

McDONNELL F-101 VOODOO

LEFT: The McDonnell F-101 Voodoo was initially designed as a long range escort fighter for Strategic Air Command, but it soon became obvious that this was an impossibility. In consequence, the F-101A became a bomb truck.

The F-101 Voodoo was a huge aircraft for its class, evolving from the McDonnell XF-88 of 1948 as a deep penetration fighter escort for bombers of the U.S. Air Force's Strategic Air Command (SAC). Unfortunately, at that time fast, high-altitude jet bombers were coming along that made escort fighters unnecessary, even if they could keep up over vast distances. When the Voodoo emerged as the single-seat F-101A, the first flying on September 29, 1954, observers were amazed that it had two very powerful J57 turbojet engines, which enabled it to fly with enormous fuel loads in its fuselage that was almost seventy feet long. It was armed with four 20mm cannon. And the Voodoo was certainly no slouch: one set a world speed record of 1,207mph on December 12, 1957, while a reconnaissance version, RF-101, completed a round trip Los Angeles-New York-Los Angeles in a record time of 6 hours 46 minutes.

The Pratt & Whitney J57 engines were at the time the most powerful available. They were fed by sharp-lipped wing root inlets and had variable nozzles side by side, set low, with the fuselage carried well past and above them. The fin sloped back and the tail was high-set. The Voodoo's wings were moderately swept, and the increased chord inboard gave a cranked trailing edge, permitting large flaps to be fitted.

In U.S. service, the F-101A Voodoo went to Tactical Air Command (TAC) as an attack aircraft, joining squadrons from May 1957. A total of 77 F-101As were completed, the single-seat Voodoos being restressed for low-altitude tactical operations.

Production continued with the C model with strengthened wing structure. This first flew on August 21, 1957. There were 47 F-101Cs built, the last delivered on June 27, 1958, but 166 tactical reconnaissance RF-101Cs were delivered, similar to earlier RF-101As but with the C's wing structure. Some 61 F-101As and Cs were modified to RF-101G and H tactical reconnaissance aircraft.

Design development of the F-101B two-seat all-weather interceptor began in 1955. In essence this was a new tandem two-seat forward fuselage grafted onto the standard F-101A airframe, although it did have more powerful J57 engines. A Hughes MG-13 fire-control system and radar took the place of the gun armament, tied in with the F-101B's four AIM-4 Falcon air-to-air missiles, two carried internally and two externally on the rotary weapons bay door. Later, these were supplemented by two nuclear-tipped AIR-2A Genie unguided rockets carried underwing. Inflight-refueling equipment was installed.

The Voodoo was the world's first supersonic photo-reconnaissance aircraft, and it was used for low-altitude photo coverage of missile sites during the 1962 Cuban Missile Crisis, and during the Vietnam War in the late 1960s.

There were 401 F-101Bs and 79 F-101Fs, the latter with dual controls and combat capability. Some F-101Bs were modified as TF-101B trainers with dual controls but less combat. The Royal Canadian Air Force received 56 of the F-101Bs between July 1961 and May 1962, and a further ten F-101Fs. Many were later exchanged for later upgraded former USAF F-101Bs, and a further ten F-101Fs.

Two-seat Voodoos stayed in USAF first-line service until spring 1971, then soldiered on in the Air National Guard until 1983. The RCAF kept its Voodoos in first-line service until 1985.

Specifications for McDonnell F-101B Voodoo

Dimensions: wingspan 39 feet 8.4 inches, length 67 feet 5 inches, height 18 feet

Power: two Pratt & Whitney J57-P-55 two-spool, axial-flow afterburning turbojets each rated at 16,900lb max and 10,700lb military thrust

Weights: empty 28,492lb, normal takeoff 45,461lb, max 51,724lb

Speed: max Mach 1.63, 1,094mph at 35,500 feet

Ceiling: 51,000 feet

Range: combat radius 852 miles

Armament: four AIM Falcon air-to-air missiles and two AIR-2A Genie unguided nuclear rockets

Crew: pilot and radar/weapons officer

F-101C cutaway key

1 Radome
2 Scanner dish
3 Radar tracking mechanism
4 Radar mounting bulkhead
5 Refueling probe doors
6 Radar modulating units
7 Refueling probe hydraulic jack
8 Flight refueling probe, extended
9 Forward avionics equipment bay, radar and weapons system equipment
10 Nose compartment access panels
11 Angle of attack transducer
12 Pitot head
13 Nosewheel doors
14 Emergency brake reservoir
15 Cannon muzzles
16 Cockpit pressure floor
17 Cockpit air-conditioning ducting
18 Front pressure bulkhead
19 Rudder pedals
20 Control column
21 Instrument panel
22 Instrument panel shroud
23 K-19 (Mk 7) gunsight
24 Armored glass windscreen panel
25 MA-7 flight indicator radar scope
26 Canopy cover
27 Canopy mounted flush aerial
28 Headrest
29 Safety harness
30 Canopy external release
31 Pilot's ejection seat
32 Throttle levers
33 Side console panel
34 Cockpit pressurisation valve
35 Cannon barrel seals
36 Nose undercarriage pivot fixing
37 Cannon barrel fairings
38 Nose undercarriage leg strut
39 Landing and taxiing lamps
40 Twin nosewheels
41 Torque scissor links
42 Ventral AW aerial
43 Cannon barrels
44 Control rod runs
45 Anti-g valve
46 Rear pressure bulkhead
47 Canopy hydraulic jack
48 Canopy aft fairing
49 Rear avionics equipment bay, navigation and communications systems
50 Canopy hinge
51 Ammunition access door

52 Ammunition magazine, 375 rounds per gun
53 Feed chutes
54 M39 20mm cannon (single cannon on starboard side, fourth weapon replaced by transponder equipment)
55 Heat exchanger flush air intake
56 Circuit breaker panel
57 Air-conditioning plant
58 Autopilot rate gyros
59 Control linkages
60 Hydraulic accumulators
61 Boundary layer splitter plate
62 Port engine air intake
63 Intake duct framing
64 Port hydraulic system reservoir
65 Boundary layer bleed air spill duct
66 Wing spar attachment main bulkhead
67 Forward fuselage fuel tanks; total system capacity 2,146 gallons
68 Fuel filler cap, pressure refueling connector on starboard side
69 Fuel system piping
70 Anti-collision light
71 Starboard wing panel
72 Wing fence
73 Starboard navigation light
74 Fixed portion of trailing edge
75 Starboard aileron
76 Aileron mass-balance weights
77 Aileron hydraulic actuator
78 Main undercarriage pivot fixing
79 Starboard split trailing-edge flap
80 Boom type refuelling receptacle, open
81 Wing spar and engine mounting main bulkheads
82 Centre fuselage fuel tank
83 Fuel vent piping
84 Fuselage upper access panels
85 Fuselage top longeron
86 Aft fuselage fuel tanks
87 Control cable duct
88 Fuel filler cap
89 Finroot fillet
90 Tailcone joint frame
91 Artificial feel system bellows
92 Starboard airbrake, open

93 Tailfin construction
94 Remote compass transmitter
95 Artificial feel system ram air intake
96 VHF aerial
97 Starboard tailplane construction
98 Fintip fairing
99 Tail navigation lights
100 Rudder mass-balance
101 Tailplane sealing plate
102 Tailplane pivot fixing
103 Port all-moving tailplane
104 Rudder construction
105 Tailplane hydraulic actuator
106 Rudder hydraulic actuator
107 Fuel jettison, port and starboard
108 Parachute door
109 Brake parachute housing
110 Parachute release mechanism
111 Tailboom construction
112 Control system linkages
113 Tailplane autopilot controller
114 Port airbrake housing
115 Airbrake hydraulic jack
116 Port airbrake, open
117 Tailcone heat shield
118 Engine exhaust nozzle
119 Variable-area afterburner nozzle
120 Nozzle control jacks
121 Nozzle shroud
122 Engine bay ventral access panels
123 Afterburner duct
124 Afterburner fuel spray manifold
125 Rear engine mounting frame
126 Port Pratt & Whitney J57-P-13 afterburning turbojet
127 Bleed air spill duct
128 Compressor bleed air spill duct
129 Flap position transmitter
130 Flap hydraulic jack
131 Flap shroud ribs
132 Port split trailing-edge flap
133 Plain undercarriage pivot fixing
134 Aileron hydraulic actuator
135 Port aileron construction
136 Mass-balance weight
137 Fixed portion of trailing edge

138 Wingtip fairing
139 Port navigation light
140 Main spar
141 Lower wing skin/stringer panel
142 Port wing fence
143 Detachable leading-edge access panel
144 Mainwheel doors
145 Port mainwheel
146 Main undercarriage leg strut
147 Hydraulic retraction jack
148 Front spar
149 Wing ribs
150 Aileron control rod linkage
151 Autopilot controller
152 Engine starter/generator
153 Main undercarriage wheel bay
154 Engine oil tank, 5.5 gallons
155 Forward engine mounting
156 Compressor intake
157 Hydraulic pumps
158 Oil cooler
159 Intake conical centre-body
160 Intake duct main frame
161 Wing spar attachment joints
162 Ventral fuel tank 450 gallons
163 Mk 84 2,000lb (907kg) low-drag HE bomb
164 Mk 7 1-megaton free-fall nuclear weapon

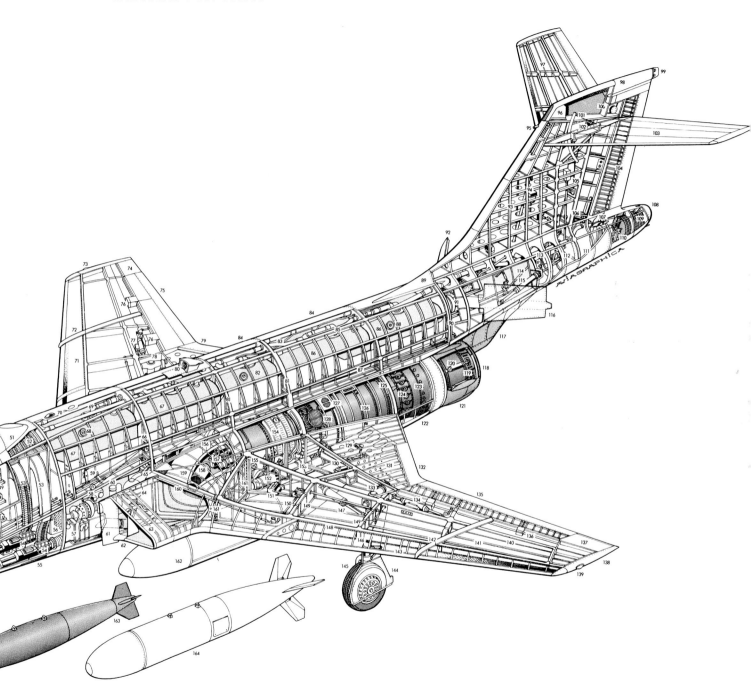

OPPOSITE: First flown in 1957, the F-101B as seen here was a two-seat all-weather interceptor, a role to which it was suited by virtue of its great range and endurance. Armament consisted of four AIM-4 Falcons and two AIR-2 Genie nuclear rockets.

OPPOSITE INSET: The Royal Canadian Air Force was the only non-US user of the Voodoo interceptor, as the CF-101B, with various classified items removed, and no provision for Genie. These remained in service until early 1985.

LEFT: Three USAF F-101Bs overfly New York at low level. Front line service in the USAF ended in the spring of 1971, but the type was operated by Air National Guard units until 1982. Many were converted to the reconnaissance mission.

ABOVE: Streaming its braking parachute, an F-101A Voodoo comes to a halt. This single-seat fighter variant was armed with four 20mm cannon. Small-winged like the Lockheed F-104 Starfighter, it was a turkey in a turning fight.

McDONNELL DOUGLAS F-4 PHANTOM

LEFT: The McDonnell Douglas F-4 Phantom II was arguably the most versatile aircraft of its generation. This is the definitive Air Force fighter variant, the F-4E with an internal 20mm Vulcan cannon, and slatted wing leading edges.

When it was designed in the late 1950s, what was then called the F4H-11 Phantom II was by a wide margin the most potent fighter in the world, with outstanding all-round flight performance (resulting in twenty-one world records). It was originally designed as a naval fighter by McDonnell in 1954 and ordered as the F3H-G, but this had changed to F-4 with the revised designation system prior to the first flight on May 27, 1958. The Navy initially ordered the F-4A and was joined by the Marine Corps in operating the F-4B with increased power and then RF-4B reconnaissance model. The Phantom's increasing reputation stirred the Air Force whose orders for the F-4C/RF-4C eventually topped 1,000. These were similar to the F-4B/RF-4B but incorporated a different radar and other avionics systems. A number of F-4Cs were modified to EF-4C and fitted with electronic warfare equipment to enable them to detect and identify enemy surface-to-air missile sites and attack them with anti-radiation missiles. This role was referred to as the Wild Weasel.

They were followed by the F-4D and F-4E for the Air Force. The F-4D was based on the F-4C, the main difference being a new radar. The F-4E was fitted with a 20mm cannon and for space reasons a new solid state radar with a smaller scanner. The original F-4G was built in small numbers for the Navy for trials using a data-link for interception control.

The F-4J was ordered for the Navy and Marine Corps, featuring more powerful engines and increased fuel, and therefore strengthened main undercarriage and larger wheels. Drooped ailerons managed to reduce approach speeds, while a new bombing system facilitated the release of nuclear weapons at any altitude.

The F-4N was a rebuilt Navy F-4B, additionally incorporating a number of small equipment changes. The F-4S was a rebuilt Navy and Marine Corps F-4J in a program that ran on from the F-4N. Some strengthening of the airframe and undercarriage was undertaken, and automatic maneuvering slats were fitted to the wing. Smokeless engines were also fitted.

The first Phantoms involved in the Vietnam War were Navy F-4Bs of VF-142 and VF-143 operating from USS *Constellation* in August 1964. The first air-to-air "kill" took place in April 1965 when F-4Bs from VF-96 from USS *Ranger* bounced some Chinese MiG-17s near Hainan Island. A MiG was shot down by an F-4B Phantom which subsequently mysteriously disappeared. Marine Corps F-4Bs were first deployed in April 1965, together with Air Force F-4Cs. By the end of the war a total of 525 Air Force

and 72 Marine Phantoms had been lost.

The last major American user of the Phantom was the Air Force with the F-4G, rebuilt from F-4Es. They were used in the Wild Weasel role, some twenty-four being deployed in Operation Desert Storm in 1991. The last was retired in 1996 when they were replaced by the F-16. Stored Phantoms have been providing a source for remote controlled drones, designated QF-4 Phantoms.

In a variety of configurations, with different engines and weapons fits, and for varying roles, the Phantom joined at least a dozen non-U.S. air services, and many are still operational. In the fighter role alone, it has achieved over 280 combat successes (with mainly U.S. and Israeli users).

Specifications for McDonnell Douglas F-4E Phantom II

Dimensions:	wingspan 38 feet 4 inches, length 63 feet, height 16 feet 3 inches
Power:	two General Electric J79-GE-17 two-spool, axial-flow afterburning turbojets each rated at 17,900lb max and 10,900lb military thrust
Weights:	empty 29,535lb, normal takeoff 45,750lb, max 61,795lb
Speed:	max Mach 2.04 at 40,000 feet, Mach 1.10 at sea level
Ceiling:	55,000 feet
Range:	combat radius 500 miles
Armament:	one six-barrel M61A-1 cannon with 639 rounds, (typically) four AIM-7 Sparrow and four AIM-9 Sidewinder air-to-air missiles interchangeable with Skyflash and Shafrir, plus wide range of air-to-surface ordnance
Crew:	pilot and weapons systems officer

RF-4C Phantom II cutaway key

1 Pitot head
2 Radome
3 Radar scanner dish
4 Radar dish tracking mechanism
5 Texas Instruments AN/APQ-99 forward-looking radar unit
6 Nose compartment construction
7 No. 1 camera station
8 KS-87 forward oblique camera
9 Forward radar warning antennas, port and starboard
10 Camera bay access hatches
11 Ventral camera aperture
12 KA-57 low-altitude panoramic camera
13 Lateral camera aperture (alternative KS-87 installation)
14 No. 2 camera station
15 ADF sense aerial
16 Windscreen rain dispersal air duct
17 Camera viewfinder periscope
18 Nose undercarriage emergency air bottles
19 Recording unit
20 No. 3 camera station
21 KA-91 high-altitude panoramic camera
22 Air-conditioning ram air intake
23 Landing/taxiing lamp (2)
24 Lower UHF/VHF aerial
25 Nosewheel leg door
26 Torque scissor links
27 Twin nosewheels, aft retracting
28 Nosewheel steering mechanism
29 AN/AVQ-26 "Pave Tack" laser designator pod
30 Swiveling optical package
31 Fuselage centerline pylon adaptor
32 Sideways-looking radar antenna (SLAR)
33 Electro-luminescent formation lighting strip
34 Canopy emergency release handle
35 Air-conditioning plant, port and starboard
36 Cockpit floor level
37 Front pressure bulkhead
38 Rudder pedals
39 Control column
40 Instrument panel
41 Radar display
42 Instrument panel shroud
43 LA-313A optical viewfinder
44 Windscreen panels
45 Forward cockpit canopy cover
46 Face blind seat firing handle
47 Pilot's Martin-Baker Mk.H7 ejection seat
48 External canopy latches
49 Engine throttle levers
50 Side console panel
51 Intake boundary layer splitter plate
52 APQ-102R/T SLAR equipment
53 AAS-18A infra-red reconnaissance package
54 Intake front ramp
55 Port engine air intake
56 Intake ramp bleed air holes
57 Rear canopy external latches
58 Rear instrument console
59 Canopy centre arch
60 Starboard engine air intake
61 Starboard external fuel tank, capacity 369.6 gallons
62 Rear view mirrors
63 Rear cockpit canopy cover
64 Navigator/Sensor Operator's Martin-Baker ejection seat
65 Intake ramp bleed air spill louvres
66 Avionics equipment racks
67 Rear pressure bulkhead
68 Liquid oxygen converter
69 Variable intake ramp jack
70 Intake rear ramp door
71 Fuselage centerline external fuel tank, capacity 600 gallons
72 Position of pressure refuelling connection on starboard side
73 ASQ-90B data annotation system equipment
74 Cockpit voice recorder
75 Pneumatic system air bottle
76 Bleed air ducting
77 Fuselage No. 1 fuel cell, capacity 214.8 gallons
78 Intake duct framing
79 Boundary layer spill duct
80 Control cable runs
81 Aft avionics equipment bay
82 IFF aerial
83 Upper fuselage light
84 Fuselage No. 2 fuel cell, capacity 184.8 gallons
85 Center fuselage frame construction
86 Electro-luminescent formation lighting strip
87 Engine intake center-body fairing
88 Intake duct rotary spill valve
89 Wing spar attachment fuselage main frames
90 Control cable ducting
91 In-flight refueling receptacle, open
92 Starboard main undercarriage leg pivot fixing
93 Starboard wing integral fuel tank, capacity 314.4 gallons
94 Wing pylon mounting
95 Boundary layer control air duct
96 Leading-edge flap hydraulic actuator
97 Inboard leading-edge flap segment, down position
98 Leading-edge dog-tooth
99 Outboard wing panel attachment joint
100 Boundary layer control air ducting
101 Hydraulic flap actuator
102 Outboard leading-edge flap
103 Starboard navigation light
104 Electro-luminescent formation light
105 Rearward identification light
106 Starboard dihedral outboard wing panel
107 Wing fuel tank vent pipe
108 Starboard drooping aileron, down position
109 Aileron flutter damper
110 Starboard spoilers, open
111 Spoiler hydraulic actuators
112 Fuel jettison and vent valves
113 Aileron hydraulic actuator
114 Starboard ventral airbrake panel
115 Starboard blown flap, down position
116 TACAN aerial
117 Fuel system piping
118 No. 3 fuselage fuel cell, capacity 146.4 gallons
119 Engine intake compressor face
120 General Electric J79 GE-15 afterburning turbojet engine
121 Ventral engine accessory equipment gearbox
122 Wing rear spar attachment joint
123 Engine and afterburner control equipment
124 Emergency ram air turbine
125 Ram air turbine housing
126 Turbine doors, open
127 Turbine actuating link
128 Port engine bay frame construction
129 No. 4 fuselage fuel cell, capacity 200.4 gallons

130 Jet pipe heat shroud
131 No. 5 fuselage fuel cell, capacity 180 gallons
132 Fuel feed and vent system piping
133 LORAN aerial
134 Dorsal access panels
135 Fuel pumps
136 No. 6 fuselage fuel cell, capacity 212.4 gallons
137 Photographic flare dispenser, port and starboard
138 Flare compartment doors, open
139 Ram air intake, tailcone venting
140 Tailcone attachment bulkhead
141 Three-spar fin torsion box construction
142 Fin rib construction
143 Electro-luminescent formation lighting strip
144 HF aerial panel
145 Anti-collision light
146 Stabilator feel system pressure head
147 Fin leading edge
148 Fin tip aerial fairing
149 Upper UHF/VHF aerial
150 Tail navigation light
151 Rudder horn balance
152 Rudder
153 Honeycomb trailing-edge panels
154 Fuselage fuel cell jettison pipe
155 Rear radar warning antennas
156 Tailcone/brake parachute hinged door
157 Brake parachute housing
158 Honeycomb trailing-edge panel
159 Port all-moving tailplane/stabilator
160 Stabilator mass balance weight
161 Stabilator multi-spar construction
162 Pivot sealing plate
163 All-moving tailplane hinge mounting
164 Rudder hydraulic actuator
165 Tailplane hydraulic actuator
166 Heat-resistant tailcone skinning
167 Arrester hook, lowered
168 Arrester hook stowage
169 Stabilator feel system balance mechanism
170 Artificial feel system pneumatic bellows
171 Arrester hook jack and shock absorber
172 Variable-area afterburner exhaust nozzle
173 Engine bay cooling exit louvres
174 Afterburner duct
175 Exhaust nozzle actuators

176 Hinged engine cowling panels
177 Port blown flap, down position
178 Boundary layer control air blowing slot
179 Lateral autopilot servo
180 Airbrake jack
181 Flap hydraulic jack
182 Rear spar
183 Port spoiler hydraulic jack
184 Aileron hydraulic actuator
185 Aileron flutter damper
186 Port spoiler housing
187 Aileron rib construction
188 Port drooping aileron, down position
189 Wing fuel tank jettison pipe
190 Honeycomb trailing-edge panels
191 Port dihedral outer wing panel
192 Fixed portion of trailing edge
193 Rearward identification light
194 Electro-luminescent formation light
195 Port navigation light
196 Outboard leading-edge flap, lowered
197 Boundary layer control air blowing slot
198 Leading-edge flap actuator
199 Outer wing panel multi-spar construction
200 Outer wing panel attachment joint
201 Leading-edge dog-tooth
202 Port mainwheel
203 Mainwheel multi-plate disc brake
204 Mainwheel leg door
205 Outboard wing pylon
206 Inner wing panel outboard leading-edge

flap, down position
207 Leading-edge flap rib construction
208 Wing pylon mounting
209 Main undercarriage leg pivot fixing
210 Hydraulic retraction jack
211 Undercarriage uplock
212 Port ventral airbrake panel, open
213 Main undercarriage wheel bay
214 Hydraulic reservoir
215 Hydraulic system accumulator
216 Port wing integral fuel tank, capacity 314.4 gallons

217 Two-spar torsion box fuel tank construction
218 Wing skin support posts
219 Leading-edge boundary layer control air duct
220 Bleed air blowing slot
221 Outboard flap actuator
222 Inboard leading-edge flap, lowered
223 Hydraulic flap actuator
224 Inboard wing pylon
225 AN/ALQ-101 ECM pod
226 Port external fuel tank, capacity 369.6 gallons

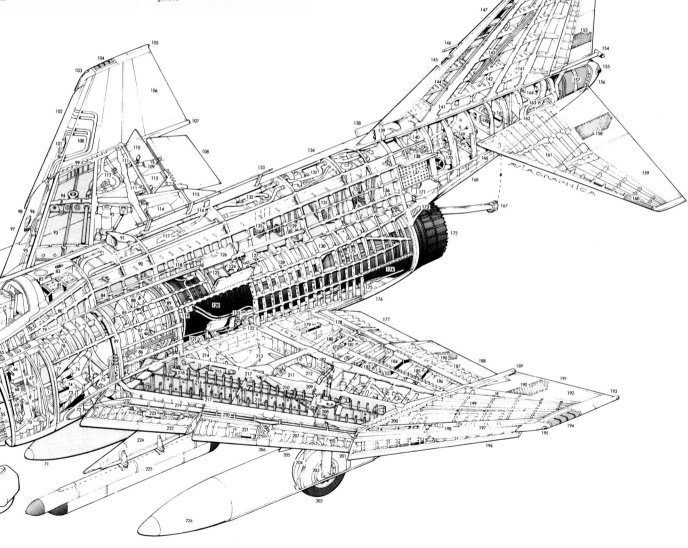

OPPOSITE: Phantoms taxi out for takeoff in Exercise Team Spirit in 1985. The outboard wing panels were cranked up at 12 degrees to improve stability, while the stabilizers were canted sharply down to avoid wing wash at high alpha.

BELOW: F-4Es of the 4th Tactical Fighter Wing based at Seymour Johnson depart on a practice air-to-air mission. Both carry underwing drop tanks to extend range and endurance.

RIGHT: This USAF F-4E carries a full complement of missiles: four medium range semi-active radar homing Sparrows, and four short range AIM-9 Sidewinders. Phantoms have scored at least 282 air combat victories in various conflicts.

ABOVE: F-4E Phantom IIs in what is for them close formation. Air superiority, interception, air-to-ground, defense suppression, reconnaissance – the Phantom could do it all. It was the backbone of the U.S. Air Force, Navy and Marine Corps for many years.

LEFT: British Phantoms were powered by Rolls-Royce Spey turbofans. This example carries a full air-to-air load of four Skyflash medium range and four Sidewinder short range AAMs, plus five BL-755 cluster bomb units (CBUs).

OPPOSITE INSET: The F-4 Phantom started life as a carrier air defense interceptor before being adapted for other missions. This is an F-4N of VF 151. The F-4N was essentially a rebuilt and greatly upgraded F-4B.

OPPOSITE The Phantom has served with a dozen nations in all. This picture shows an Imperial Iranian Air Force F-4E taking off from Shiraz, way back in 1977 when the Iranians were still numbered among the "good guys."

McDONNELL DOUGLAS F-15 EAGLE

LEFT: A McDonnell Douglas F-15C Eagle of the 27th Fighter Squadron, 1st Fighter Wing, seen over Iraq. This was the first unit to become operational on the type, at Langley AFB in late 1976.

In the late 1960s the U.S. Air Force perceived a requirement for an air superiority fighter that could outfight several new combat aircraft unveiled by the Russians in 1967. McDonnell Douglas's proposal was selected from three competitive designs and construction of twenty prototypes commenced. The first made its maiden flight on July 27, 1972, and the first production F-15A was delivered in November 1974.

The USAF specification called for a long range fighter with a powerful radar, good acceleration and a max speed of Mach 2+. The result is USAF's current twin-engined, bisonic all-weather air superiority fighter with secondary attack capability, which has been in service now for about thirty years. With a high engine power to weight ratio, it is a large aircraft capable of pulling over 5g. And it sure has teeth: armament comprises one fixed M61A-1 20mm six-barrel cannon for close up, while various air-to-air missiles are carried under the wing and fuselage. Initially these were four AIM-9L/M Sidewinder and four AIM-7F/M Sparrows but these have given way to the AIM-120 Amraam more recently. Additional fuel can be carried in drop tanks, while air-to-air refueling can enable combat air patrols (CAP) to be flown for lengthy periods; in fact, they are limited more by crew fatigue than aircraft performance.

The initial model was the F-15A of which 355 were produced for the USAF. Many of these have been retired and replaced by 409 F-15Cs that entered service in 1979. These featured additional fuel and a greater maximum take off weight (MTOW). Upgrades have enabled the F-15 to take advantage of weapon improvements and the fitting of the latest electronic warfare (EW) packages. A number of two-seat versions (B and D) were also built. Such was the performance of the F-15 that one of the YF-15B prototypes was modified to demonstrate that the type was capable of carrying a variety of bombs and being operated in the strike role. This led to the F-15E Strike Eagle, a two-seat interdictor with more powerful engines permitting a take-off weight of 81,000lb.

The F-15A and latterly the F-15C have for years been at the forefront of the USAF fighter force, with squadrons based in Germany and the UK as well as on mainland USA. They have seen extensive operations in the Middle East. During Operation Desert Storm in 1991 they displayed their impressive combat capability, with F-15C fighters accounting for 34 of the Air Force's 37 air-to-air victories over Iraqi aircraft. Once that war ended they were involved in Operation Southern Watch to patrol the UN-sanctioned no-fly zone in southern Iraq and Operation Provide Comfort over northern Iraq. Subsequently, they have operated in support of NATO in Bosnia followed by operations in Afghanistan and most recently in the second Gulf War in Iraq.

The Eagle also seen service with Israel and Saudi Arabia, and also Japan, the latter aircraft having been license-built by Mitsubishi as the F-15J. Total combat successes for the Eagle exceed 100 for no losses.

F-15As have now been transferred to the Air National Guard, while the remaining F-15Cs will continue to be operated until replaced by the F/A-22 Raptor from 2005.

Specifications for McDonnell Douglas F-15C Eagle

Dimensions: wingspan 42 feet 9.5 inches, length 63 feet 9 inches, height 18 feet 5.5 inches

Power: two Pratt & Whitney F100-PW-220 two-spool, axial-flow, afterburning turbofans each rated at 23,770lb max and 14,590lb military thrust

Weights: empty 28,600lb, normal takeoff 44,500lb, max 68,000lb

Speed: max Mach 2.5 at 40,000 feet, Mach 1.2 at sea level

Ceiling: 65,000 feet (combat)

Range: combat radius 740 miles

Armament: one M61A-1 20mm multi-barrel internal gun with 675 rounds, plus four AIM-9L/M Sidewinder and four AIM-7F/M Sparrow air-to-air missiles, or combination of AIM-9L/M, AIM-7F/M and AIM-120 Amraam missiles

Crew: pilot

F-15E Eagle cutaway key

1 Glass-fiber radome
2 Hughes AN/APG-70 I-band pulse-Doppler radar scanner
3 Radar mounting bulkhead
4 ADF sense antenna
5 Avionics equipment bay, port and starboard
6 UHF antenna
7 Pitot head
8 AGM-130 TV-guided air-to-surface weapon
9 TACAN antenna
10 Formation lighting strip
11 Incidence probe
12 Rudder pedals
13 Instrument panel shroud
14 Pilot's head-up display
15 Frameless windscreen panel
16 B61 tactical nuclear weapon
17 AIM-7F Sparrow air-to-air missile
18 LANTIRN navigation pod, mounted beneath starboard intake
19 FLIR aperture
20 Terrain-following radar
21 Upward-hinging cockpit canopy
22 Pilot's ACES II ejection seat
23 Side console panel
24 Engine throttle levers
25 Boarding steps
26 Extended boarding ladder
27 Forward-retracting nosewheel
28 Landing/taxiing lights
29 Nosewheel leg shock absorber strut
30 Underfloor control runs
31 Flying controls duplicated in rear cockpit
32 Radar hand controller
33 Weapons Systems Officer's ACES II ejection seat
34 Canopy hinge point
35 Cockpit air-conditioning pack
36 Port variable capture area "nodding" air intake
37 Boundary layer spill air louvers
38 Nodding intake hydraulic actuator
39 Variable-area intake ramp doors
40 Intake ramp hydraulic actuator
41 Boom-type flight refueling receptacle, open
42 Air supply duct to conditioning system
43 Ammunition magazine, 512 rounds
44 Forward fuselage fuel tanks
45 Ammunition feed chute
46 Engine intake ducting
47 Center fuselage fuel tanks
48 Fuel tank bay access panel
49 Airbrake hydraulic jack
50 Dorsal airbrake honeycomb construction
51 Upper UHF antenna
52 Starboard intake by-pass air spill duct
53 M61A-1 Vulcan 20mm cannon

54 Anti-collision light
55 Starboard wing pylon carrying GBU-10, AIM-7M and AIM-120
56 Pylon mounting hardpoint
57 Starboard wing integral fuel tank, fire suppressant foam filled
58 Leading edge flush HF antenna panels
59 Ventral view showing carriage of 12 Mk 82 500lb (22-kg) bombs
60 610-gallon external fuel tanks (3)
61 LANTIRN navigation and targeting pods
62 Wing pylon mounted AIM-9M and AIM-120 air-to-air missiles
63 Forward ECM transmitting antenna
64 Starboard navigation light
65 Wingtip formation light
66 Fuel jettison
67 Starboard aileron
68 Starboard plain flap
69 Trailing-edge fuel tank
70 Engine bay cooling intake bleed air louvres
71 Compressor intake
72 Central airframe-mounted engine accessory equipment gearbox
73 Machined main fuselage/wing spar attachment bulkheads
74 Pratt & Whitney F100-PW-229 afterburning turbofan engines
75 Engine bleed air cross-ducting
76 Forward engine mounting
77 Main engine mounting "spectacle" beam
78 Afterburner ducting
79 Rear fuselage/engine bay diffusion-bonded all-titanium structure
80 Tailplane hydraulic actuator
81 Starboard fin
82 Fintip ECM antenna
83 Anti-collision light
84 Starboard rudder
85 Starboard all-moving tailplane
86 Aft ECM transmitting antenna
87 Variable area afterburner nozzle
88 Nozzle actuating linkage
89 Nozzle shroud panels
90 Fueldraulic afterburner nozzle actuators
91 Two-spar fin torsion box structure
92 Boron-fiber fin skin panelling
93 Radar warning antenna
94 Port rear ECM antenna
95 White strobe light

96 Port rudder honeycomb core construction
97 Tailplane pivot mounting
98 Port aft ECM transmitting antenna
99 Port all-moving tailplane
100 Boron-fiber tailplane skin panelling
101 Machined tailplane trunion mounting fitting
102 Leading edge dog-tooth
103 Runway emergency arrester hook, lowered
104 Formation lighting strip
105 Engine bleed air primary heat exchangers, port and starboard
106 Port trailing-edge fuel tank bay
107 Flap hydraulic jack
108 Port plain flap
109 Aileron hydraulic actuator
110 Port aileron honeycomb core construction
111 Fuel jettison
112 Port formation light
113 Port navigation light
114 Forward ECM transmitting antenna
115 Engine bleed air primary heat exchanger air intake and exhaust ducts
116 GBU-28 "Deep-Throat" laser-guided bomb
117 GBU-12 laser-guided bombs
118 CFT pylons
119 Port conformal fuel tank (CFT)
120 AXQ-14 datalink pod
121 Mk 84 2,000lb (90-kg) HE bomb
122 GBU-24 laser-guided bomb
123 Outer wing panel dry bay
124 Port wing integral fuel tankage
125 Multi-spar wing panel structure
126 Port pylon hardpoint
127 Wing stores pylon
128 Missile launch rails
129 AIM-120 AMRAAM
130 AIM-9M Sidewinder air-to-air missile
131 Leading-edge flush HF antenna
132 Stores management system equipment
133 CBU-87 sub-munition dispensers
134 Port LANTIRN targeting pod
135 Centreline external tank
136 AGM-65 Maverick air-to-surface missiles
137 Triple missile carrier/launch rail
138 GBU-15 electro-optical guided glide bomb

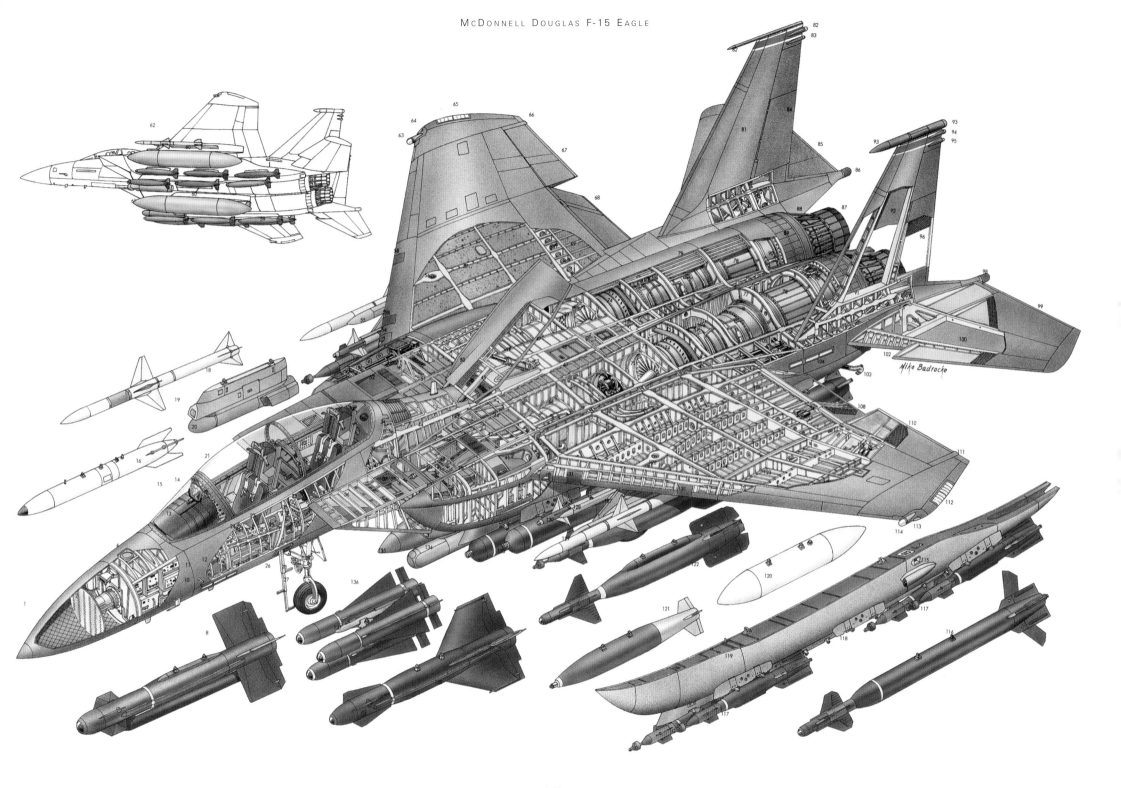

OPPOSITE: Designed as the ultimate air combat fighter, the Eagle has lived up to its promise, with more than a hundred air combat victories for no losses. From this angle the conformal fuel tanks, introduced to extend endurance, are clearly visible.

OPPOSITE INSET: Although still very potent, the Eagle is now well past its 32nd birthday. Its design took no account of stealth, and little can be done to reduce its radar signature, which by modern standards is on the large side.

LEFT: The final Eagle variant is the F-15E interdictor. Beefed up from the fighter variant, to give a massive all-up weight of 81,000 pounds, there is little external difference apart from the two-seater cockpit and the paint job.

BELOW: A near-perfect formation of F-15Cs of the 18th Tactical Fighter Wing based at Okinawa in the Pacific. The world-wide deployment of Eagles was the visible sign of American resolve through the dark days of the Cold War.

OPPOSITE INSET: Unlike its McDonnell Douglas Phantom predecessor, the F-15C did not carry its Sparrows semi-submerged, but on the edges of the conformal fuel tanks (CFTs). The huge centerline fuel tank extends the range for long distance deployments.

LEFT: Reefing into a hard turn, an F-15 streams contrails from its wingtips. Despite its size, and it is a heavyweight among fighters, it is remarkably agile, as many opponents have found to their cost.

RIGHT: An unusual view of a weatherworn F-15C. Clearly visible are the intake duct bleed air louvers and the intake bypass air spill ducts.

BELOW: Noses high, two Japanese Air Self-Defense Force F-15s make a formation landing. A unique feature of the Eagle is the "nodding" intake, seen here in the down position, which is used to smooth the airflow into the engine at high angles of attack.

McDONNELL DOUGLAS F/A-18 HORNET

Left: The McDonnell Douglas F/A-18 Hornet was the first aircraft designed to be equally good as a fighter or attacking surface targets. This is an F/A-18C of VFA-131 Wildcats, flying from the carrier *Eisenhower*.

The McDonnell Douglas F/A-18 Hornet is a development of the Northrop YF-17 design that was the losing contender (to the F-16) for the USAF Light Weight Fighter (LWF) in the early 1970s. The U.S. Navy decided in 1974 to commence their own search for a multi-mission lightweight fighter – the VFAX competition – to replace the A-7 Corsair. Following much redesign, what emerged as the F-18 Hornet was first flown as a prototype in November 1978, with production aircraft being delivered from May 1980.

It was originally intended to develop two separate versions – the F-18 fighter and A-18 attack aircraft, but it was decided to combine both roles in one aircraft, which was ordered to replace the Navy's A-7 and the Marines' F-4 Phantoms. The initial production aircraft for the Navy were the F/A-18A single-seat strike aircraft and the F/A-18B two-seat trainer, which is combat capable. In 1986 production commenced on the F/A-18C single-seat version with improved avionics and also the F/A-18D two-seat model, and these ultimately replaced the A-4 Skyhawks, F-4s, A-7s and A-6 Intruders serving the Navy and/or Marines.

The Hornet is a truly multi-missions aircraft. It is armed with just a single 20mm M61 cannon in the nose. However, it also has seven hardpoints for pylons that can carry an assortment of drop-tanks, equipment and ordnance. In addition, the wing tips have an integral rail for AIM-9 Sidewinder air-to-air missiles. The outer pylons could take additional missiles. These could be more AIM-9s, or AIM-7 Sparrows or their replacement, the AIM-120 Amraams. Alternatively, these pylons can be used to carry FLIR or other pods/sensors. For the offensive role, weapons carried here could be AGM-64 Harpoon/SLAM/SMAM-ER or AGM-65 Maverick. The centerline is normally used for a drop-tank but can also be used for air-to-ground weapons, as can the two inner hardpoints under the wing. Ordnance on the inner pylons can include Mk-80 series, LGB or JDAM bombs, AGM-88 HARM anti-radiation or AGM-154 JSOW missiles.

The Hornet flew its first combat missions during Operation Prairie Fire in March 1986 when it neutralized Libyan SAM sites with AGM-88 HARM missiles. During Desert Storm in 1991 some 190 Navy and Marine Corps F/A-18 Hornets flew over 10,000 sorties on a variety of roles. During one, four fully bombed-up F/A-18Cs were 35 miles from a target when they were warned by a Hawkeye that a pair of Iraqi MiG-21s had maneuvered to intercept them. The Hornet wing men switched from attack to the air-to-air role, acquired and dispatched the targets with three missiles, then switched back to the attack role, and suc-

cessfully engaged their ground targets before returning to their carrier, USS *Saratoga*, without further incident.

The F/A-18A/B/C/D versions, including the Night Attack Hornet, will serve for many years to come. The Hornet has been a winner in export markets, too, with overseas customers including Australia, Canada, Finland, Kuwait, Malaysia, Spain, and Switzerland.

In the meantime, a larger, more powerful version, the F/A-18E/F Super Hornet has been developed, incorporating various stealth measures and a projected active array radar. It has been in service since 1999, with initial operational capability having been achieved in 2001. The Navy expects to receive at least 548 Super Hornets, and maybe as many as 1,000 depending on progress with the multi-national Joint Strike Fighter currently under development.

Specifications for McDonnell Douglas F/A-18C Hornet

Dimensions: wingspan 37 feet 6 inches, length 56 feet, height 15 feet 3.5 inches

Power: two General Electric F404-GE-402 two-spool, axial-flow afterburning turbofans each rated at 17,700lb max and 10,860lb military thrust

Weights: empty 23,000lb, normal takeoff 36,970lb, max 56,000lb

Speed: Mach 1.7 at altitude, Mach 1.01 at sea level

Ceiling: 50,000+ feet

Range: operational radius over 460 miles

Armament: one M61A-1 20mm multi-barrel cannon with 570 rounds, plus combination of AIM-9 Sidewinder, AIM-7 Sparrow, AIM-120 Amraam air-to-air missiles plus air-to-surface missiles and bombs

Crew: pilot

F/A-18D Hornet cutaway key

1 Glass-fiber radome, hinged to starboard
2 Planar radar array radar scanner
3 Scanner tracking mechanism
4 Cannon port and gun gas purging intakes
5 Radar module withdrawal rails
6 Hughes AN/APG-73 radar equipment module
7 Formation lighting strip
8 Forward radar warning antennas
9 UHF/IFF antenna
10 Pitot head, port and starboard
11 Incidence transmitter
12 Canopy emergency release
13 Ammunition drum, 570 rounds
14 M61A1 Vulcan 20mm rotary cannon
15 Retractable inflight-refueling probe
16 Single piece wrap-round windscreen
17 Pilot's Kaiser AN/AVQ-28 raster HUD
18 Instrument panel with multi-function colour CRT displays
19 Control column
20 Rudder pedals
21 Ammunition loading chute
22 Ground power socket
23 Nose undercarriage wheel bay
24 Catapult strop link
25 Twin nosewheels, forward-retracting
26 Retractable boarding ladder
27 Nosewheel hydraulic jack
28 Nosewheel leg-mounted deck signaling and taxi lights
29 Forward avionics equipment bays, port and starboard
30 Engine throttle levers
31 Pilot's Martin-Baker SJU-6/A ejection seat
32 Rear cockpit rudder pedals (dual flight control system interchangeable with radar and weapons controllers)
33 Rear instrument console with multi-function CRT displays
34 Single-piece upward-opening cockpit canopy
35 AWW-7/9 datalink pod for Walleye missile, fuselage centerline pylon-mounted
36 AGM-62 Walleye II ER/DL air-to-surface missile, starboard outboard pylon only
37 Naval flight officer's helmet with GEC-Marconi Avionics Cats Eyes night-vision goggles
38 Naval flight officer's SJU-5/A ejection seat
39 Sidestick radar and weapons controllers, replacing dual flight-control system
40 Liquid oxygen converter
41 Ventral radar warning antenna

42 Rear avionics equipment bays, port and starboard
43 Cockpit rear pressure bulkhead
44 Canopy actuator
45 Starboard navigation light
46 Tailfin aerodynamic load-alleviating strake
47 Upper radar warning antennas
48 Forward fuselage bag-type fuel cell
49 Radar/avionics equipment liquid cooling units
50 Fuselage centerline pylon
51 Boundary layer splitter plate
52 Port navigation light
53 Fixed-geometry engine air intake
54 Cooling air spill louvers
55 Cabin air conditioning system equipment
56 Leading-edge flap drive motor
57 Boundary layer spill duct
58 Air conditioning system heat exchanger exhaust
59 Center fuselage fuel cells
60 Wing panel root attachment joints
61 Central Garrett GTC36-200 auxiliary power unit (APU)
62 Airframe-mounted engine accessory equipment gearbox, port and starboard
63 Engine bleed air ducting to conditioning system
64 Fuel tank bay access panels
65 Upper UHF/IFF/datalink antenna
66 Starboard wingroot joint
67 Starboard wing integral fuel tank
68 Stores pylons
69 Mk 83 1,000lb (454kg) LDGP bomb
70 Leading-edge flap
71 Starboard secondary navigation light
72 Wingtip missile launch rail
73 AIM-9L Sidewinder air-to-air missile
74 Outer wing panel, folded position
75 Drooping aileron
76 Aileron hydraulic actuator
77 Wing-fold hydraulic rotary actuator
78 Drooping flap vane
79 Starboard slotted flap, operates as flaperon at low speeds
80 Flap hydraulic actuator

81 Hydraulic reservoirs
82 Reinforced fin-root attachment joint
83 Multi-spar fin structure
84 Fuel jettison pipe
85 Graphite/epoxy tail unit skin panels with glass-fibre tip fairings
86 Tail position light
87 AN/ALR-67 receiving antenna
88 AN/ALQ-165 low-band transmitting antenna
89 Fuel jettison
90 Starboard all-moving tailplane
91 Starboard rudder
92 Radar warning system power amplifier
93 Rudder hydraulic actuator
94 Airbrake panel, open
95 Airbrake hydraulic jack
96 Fin formation lighting strip
97 Fuel venting air intake
98 Anti-collision beacon, port and starboard
99 Port rudder
100 Port AN/ALQ-165 antenna
101 AN-ALQ-67 receiving antenna
102 AN/ALQ-165 high-band transmitting antenna
103 Variable-area afterburner nozzles
104 Nozzle actuators
105 Afterburner duct
106 Port all-moving tailplane
107 Tailplane bonded honeycomb core structure
108 Deck arrester hook
109 Tailplane pivot mounting
110 Tailplane hydraulic actuator
111 Full-authority digital engine controller (FADEC)
112 General Electric F404-GE-400 afterburning turbofan engine
113 Rear fuselage formation lighting strip
114 Engine fuel control units
115 Fuselage side mounted AIM-7 Sparrow air-to-air missile
116 Port slotted flap
117 Control surface bonded honeycomb core structure
118 Wing-fold rotary hydraulic actuator and hinge joint
119 Port aileron hydraulic actuator

120 Port drooping aileron
121 Wingtip AIM-9L Sidewinder air-to-air missile
122 Port leading-edge flap
123 Mk 82SE Snakeye 500lb (227kg) retarded bomb
124 Mk 82 500lb (227kg) LDGP bombs
125 Twin stores carrier
126 Port wing stores pylons
127 Pylon mounting hardpoints
128 Multi-spar wing panel structure
129 Port wing integral fuel tank
130 Leading-edge flap-shaft driven rotary actuator
131 Port mainwheel
132 Levered suspension main undercarriage leg strut
133 Shock absorber strut
134 Ventral AN/ALE-39 chaff/flare launcher
135 330-gallon external fuel tank
136 Strike camera housing
137 AN/ASQ-173 laser spot tracker/strike camera (LST/SCAM) pod
138 Fuselage starboard side LST/SCAM pylon adaptor
139 Port side FLIR pod adaptor
140 AN/AAS-38 forward-looking infra-red (FLIR) pod
141 CBU-89/89B Gator sub-munition dispenser

142 GBU-12 D/B Paveway II 500lb (227kg) LGB
143 LAU-10A Zuni four-round rocket launcher
144 5in (127mm) FFAR
145 AGM-88 HARM anti-radar missile
146 AGM-65A Maverick air-to-ground anti-armor missile
147 AGM-84 SLAM air-to-surface missile
148 Advanced tactical airborne reconnaissance system (ATARS) unit, interchangeable with gun pack/ammunition magazine (F/A-18D(RC))
149 Sensor viewing apertures
150 Infra-red linescanner
151 Low- and/or medium-altitude electro-optical scanner

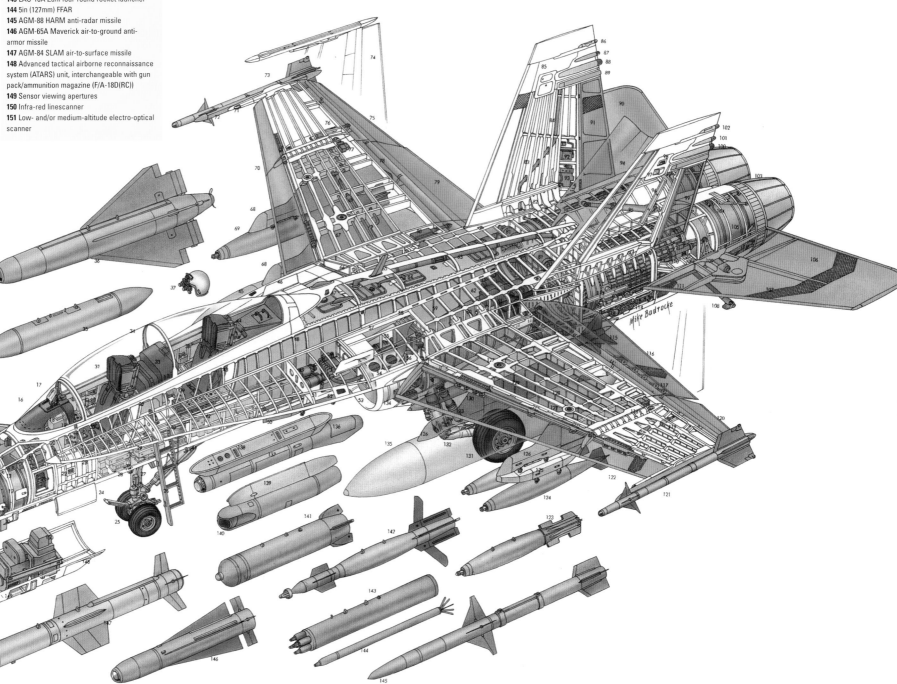

RIGHT: The F/A-18E/F Super Hornet, which entered service with VFA-122 in 1999, is not only rather larger and heavier than its progenitor, but has certain stealth features, such as the intakes to its F414-GE-400 turbofans, as seen here.

OPPOSITE LEFT: Posing for the camera in a vertical climb, the letters NJ on the fin of this two-seater F/A-18D denote that it belongs to VFA-125 Rough Raiders, the US Navy fleet readiness squadron based on the Pacific Coast.

OPPOSITE RIGHT: Although the Hornet is a true multi-role bird, squadrons tend to specialize depending on whether their pilots have shown most aptitude for air combat or surface attack. This F/A-18C of VFA-147 Argonauts undergoes maintenance on USS Carl Vinson.

BELOW: Even Admirals fly! Vice Admiral Timothy J. Keating arrives aboard USS *Nimitz* in this F/A-18F of VFA-41 Black Aces during "Iraqi Freedom." Keating was at the time the commander of the USN Fifth Fleet.

RIGHT INSET: Four F/A-18A Hornets from Test and Evaluation Squadron VX-4 are seen on USS *Constellation* in 1982, with underwing tanks but no weapons. The huge leading edge extensions are very apparent from this angle.

OPPOSITE: Decoy flares are a standard defense against heat-seeking missiles as this F/A-18C Hornet of VFA-94 Mighty Shrikes demonstrates. Only one AIM-9 Sidewinder is carried on the wingtip of this aircraft.

OPPOSITE INSET: While AIM-7 Sparrows and AIM-9 Sidewinders were the original missiles of choice for the Hornet, other weapons have been tested. Seen here is the Asraam, carried by a two-seater Australian F/A-18B.

MESSERSCHMITT Bf 109

LEFT: With flaps down and leading edge slots extended, this beautifully restored Messerschmitt Bf 109G-14 comes in to land. Overweight and tricky to handle, it had to be flown onto the ground with the engine at full throttle.

First flown in August 1935, the Bf 109 made its combat debut in Spain, and became the main German fighter of World War II, being employed on every front to which the *Luftwaffe* was committed. Totaling about 35,000 of all types, and flown by about a dozen air arms, it was built in greater numbers than any other combat airplane before or since. It was progressively up-gunned and up-engined, but the extra weight adversely affected its handling qualities, which had never been particularly benign. Losses in takeoff and landing accidents were high. This apart, it was an extraordinarily durable warplane and virtually all the high-scoring *Luftwaffe* aces flew it at one time or another.

Designed by Willy Messerschmitt and Robert Lusser, the Bf 109 was proposed by the Bayerische Flugzeugwerke (hence the Bf) to meet the 1934 *Luftfahrtministerium* requirement for a monoplane fighter to replace the He 51 and Ar 68 biplanes. To achieve good performance, the designers set out to build the smallest and lightest air-frame that could be wrapped around the most powerful engine then under development. Including features that had been used individually on other aircraft, they created the first single-seat fighter to combine with the low-wing cantilever monoplane configuration a flush-riveted, all-metal, stressed-skin monocoque structure, a retractable undercarriage and an enclosed cockpit. It also had a combination of automatic leading-edge slots and slotted trailing-edge flaps, radical for its time and compensating for a relatively high wing loading compared with its contemporary fighters. It was angular, with squared-off wingtips and a rectangular braced tailplane. The cockpit was enclosed in a heavy metal-framed canopy that was side-hinged, an enduring feature of the fighter being relatively poor pilot visibility.

As the Bf 109 evolved into numerous models and sub-types, its good points included its small size and low cross-section, high acceleration, fast climb and dive, excellent maneuverability, and the fact that it could be produced cheaply and rapidly. Drawbacks included narrow landing gear, severe swing on takeoff and landing, poor lateral control at high speeds and the fact that the automatic wing-slats tended to open in tight turns or in the slip-stream of an intended victim, interfering with precision gun tracking in combat.

Following early versions – relatively low-powered Bf 109B (the first series production type), C and D – came the 109E (called "Emil") which was in great quantity by the time war broke out in Europe in 1939. Until 1941 this was the *Luftwaffe*'s most important fighter, capable of defeating the many and varied fighters it met in combat, with the single exception of Britain's Spitfire (which it greatly outnumbered). The 109E (delivered in many sub-types) was fitted with the 1,100hp Daimler-Benz DB 601A engine

(replacing the earlier, less powerful Jumo) featuring fuel injection, which allowed it to perform negative-g maneuvers without loss of power. Armament comprised two wing-mounted MG FF Oerlikon cannon and two nose-mounted synchronized Rheinmetall Borsig MG 17 machine guns, which had more hitting power than that fitted on earlier types.

Bf 109F had a more powerful engine, sleeker nose, redesigned wing with rounded tips, shallower underwing radiators, improved aileron surfaces and plain flaps, and was generally considered the best flying machine of the type, becoming operational in 1941.

However, the Bf 109G ("Gustav") became the dominant version from 1942, making up 70 percent of the total 109s received by the *Luftwaffe*. But weight had grown and the type was not as good in the air as the lighter E and F, demanding persistent pilot attention, requiring constant high-power settings, and having even worse takeoff and landing characteristics. A few extended-span, high-altitude H models were built, but from October 1944 the standard production series was the K, with clear-view "Galland-hood" (also featured on some late G models), revised wooden tail, and minor structural changes.

After the war, Czech and Spanish derivatives were built, the final airplane flying in 1956, some 21 years after the first of the classic 109 was produced.

Specifications for Messerschmitt Bf 109G-6

Dimensions:	wingspan 32 feet 6.5 inches, length 29 feet 7 inches, height 11 feet 2 inches
Power:	one Daimler-Benz DB 605A liquid-cooled V-12 engine rated at 1,475hp, with water methanol injection
Weights:	empty 5,952lb, normal takeoff 6,944lb
Speed:	max 387mph at 22,965 feet, 338mph at sea level
Ceiling:	38,550 feet
Range:	450 miles
Armament:	one 30mm Rheinmetall Borsig MK 108 cannon firing through the spinner, two 20mm Mauser MG 151 cannon underwing, and two Rheinmetall Borsig 13mm MG 131 synchronized machine guns above the engine
Crew:	pilot

Bf 109E-4 cutaway key

1 Hollow propeller hub
2 Spinner
3 Three-bladed VDM variable-pitch propeller
4 Propeller pitch-change mechanism
5 Spinner back plate
6 Glycol coolant header tank
7 Glycol filler cap
8 Cowling fastener
9 Chin intake
10 Coolant pipe fairing
11 Exhaust forward fairing
12 Additional (long-range) oil tank
13 Daimler-Benz DB 601A engine
14 Supplementary intakes
15 Fuselage machine gun troughs
16 Anti-vibration engine mounting pads
17 Exhaust ejector stubs
18 Coolant pipes (to underwing radiators)
19 Oil cooler intake
20 Coolant radiator
21 Radiator outlet flap
22 Cowling frame
23 Engine mounting support strut
24 Spent cartridge collector compartment
25 Ammunition boxes (starboard loading)
26 Engine supercharger
27 Supercharger air intake fairing
28 Forged magnesium alloy cantilever engine mounting
29 Engine mounting/forward bulkhead attachment
30 Ammunition feed chutes
31 Engine accessories
32 Two fuselage-mounted MG17 machine guns
33 Blast tube muzzles
34 Wing skinning
35 Starboard cannon access
36 20mm MG FF wing cannon
37 Leading-edge automatic slot
38 Slot tracks
39 Slot actuating linkage
40 Wing main spar
41 Intermediate rib station
42 Wing end rib
43 Starboard navigation light
44 Aileron outer hinge
45 Aileron metal trim tab
46 Starboard aileron
47 Aileron/flap link connection
48 Combined control linkage
49 Starboard flap frame
50 Cannon ammunition drum access
51 Fuselage machine-gun cooling slots
52 Gun mounting frame
53 Firewall/bulkhead
54 Instrument panel near face (fabric covered)
55 Oil dipstick cover
56 Control column
57 Oil filler cap (tank omitted for clarity)
58 Rudder pedal assembly
59 Aircraft identity data plate (external)
60 Mainspar center-section carry-through
61 Underfloor control linkage
62 Oxygen regulator
63 Harness adjustment lever
64 Engine priming pump
65 Circuit breaker panel
66 Hood catch
67 Starboard-hinged cockpit canopy
68 Revi gunsight (offset to starboard)
69 Windscreen panel frame
70 Canopy section frame
71 Pilot's head armor
72 Pilot's back armor
73 Seat harness
74 Pilot's seat
75 Seat adjustment lever
76 Tailplane incidence handwheel
77 Cockpit floor diaphragm
78 Landing flaps control hand wheel
79 Seat support frame
80 Contoured ("L" shape) fuel tank
81 Tailplane incidence cables
82 Fuselage frame
83 Rudder cable
84 Oxygen cylinders
85 Fuel filler/overspill pipes
86 Baggage compartment
87 Entry handhold (spring-loaded)
88 Canopy fixed aft section
89 Aerial mast
90 Aerial
91 Fuel filler cap
92 Fuel vent line
93 Radio pack support brackets
94 Anti-vibration bungee supports
95 FuG VII transmitter/ receiver radio pack
96 Aerial lead-in
97 Tailplane incidence cable pulley
98 Rudder control cable
99 Monocoque fuselage structure
100 Radio access/first-aid kit panel
101 Elevator control cables
102 Fuselage frame
103 Lifting tube
104 Tailfin root fillet
105 Tailplane incidence gauge (external)
106 Tailplane support strut
107 Starboard tailplane
108 Elevator outer hinge
109 Elevator balance
110 Starboard elevator
111 Tailfin structure
112 Aerial stub
113 Rudder balance
114 Rudder upper hinge
115 Rudder frame
116 Rudder trim tab
117 Tail navigation light
118 Port elevator frame
119 Elevator balance
120 Rudder control quadrant
121 Tailplane structure
122 Elevator torque tube sleeve
123 Tailplane end rib attachment
124 Fuselage end post
125 Elevator control rod
126 Port tailplane support strut
127 Non-retractable tailwheel
128 Tailwheel leg
129 Elevator control cable rod link
130 Tail wheel leg shock-absorber
131 Rudder control cable
132 Fuselage stringer
133 Accumulator
134 Fuselage half ventral join
135 Electrical leads
136 Fuselage panel
137 Radio pack lower support frames
138 Entry foothold (spring loaded)
139 Wingroot fillet
140 Flap profile
141 Port flap frame
142 Port aileron frame
143 Aileron trim tab

144 Rear spar
145 Port wingtip
146 Port navigation light
147 Wing main spar outer section
148 Solid ribs
149 Leading-edge automatic slot
150 Rib cut-outs
151 Control link access plate
152 Wing rib stations
153 Port wing 20mm MG FF cannon installation
154 Ammunition drum access panel
155 Inboard rib cut-outs
156 Flap visual position indicator
157 Control access panel
158 Main spar/fuselage attachment fairing
159 Wing control surface cable pulleys

160 Port mainwheel well
161 Wheel well (zipped) fabric shield
162 20mm MG FF wing cannon
163 Wing front spar
164 Undercarriage leg tunnel rib cut-outs
165 Undercarriage lock mechanism
166 Wing/fuselage end rib
167 Undercarriage actuating cylinder
168 Mainwheel leg/fuselage attachment bracket
169 Leg pivot point
170 Mainwheel oleo leg
171 Mainwheel leg door
172 Brake lines
173 Torque links
174 Mainwheel hub

175 Axle
176 Port main wheel
177 Mainwheel half-door
178 Ventral ETC center-line stores pylon, possible loads include:
179 Early-type (wooden) drop tank
180 79.2-gallon (Junkers) metal drop tank
181 551lb (250kg) HE bomb, or
182 551lb (250kg) SAP bomb

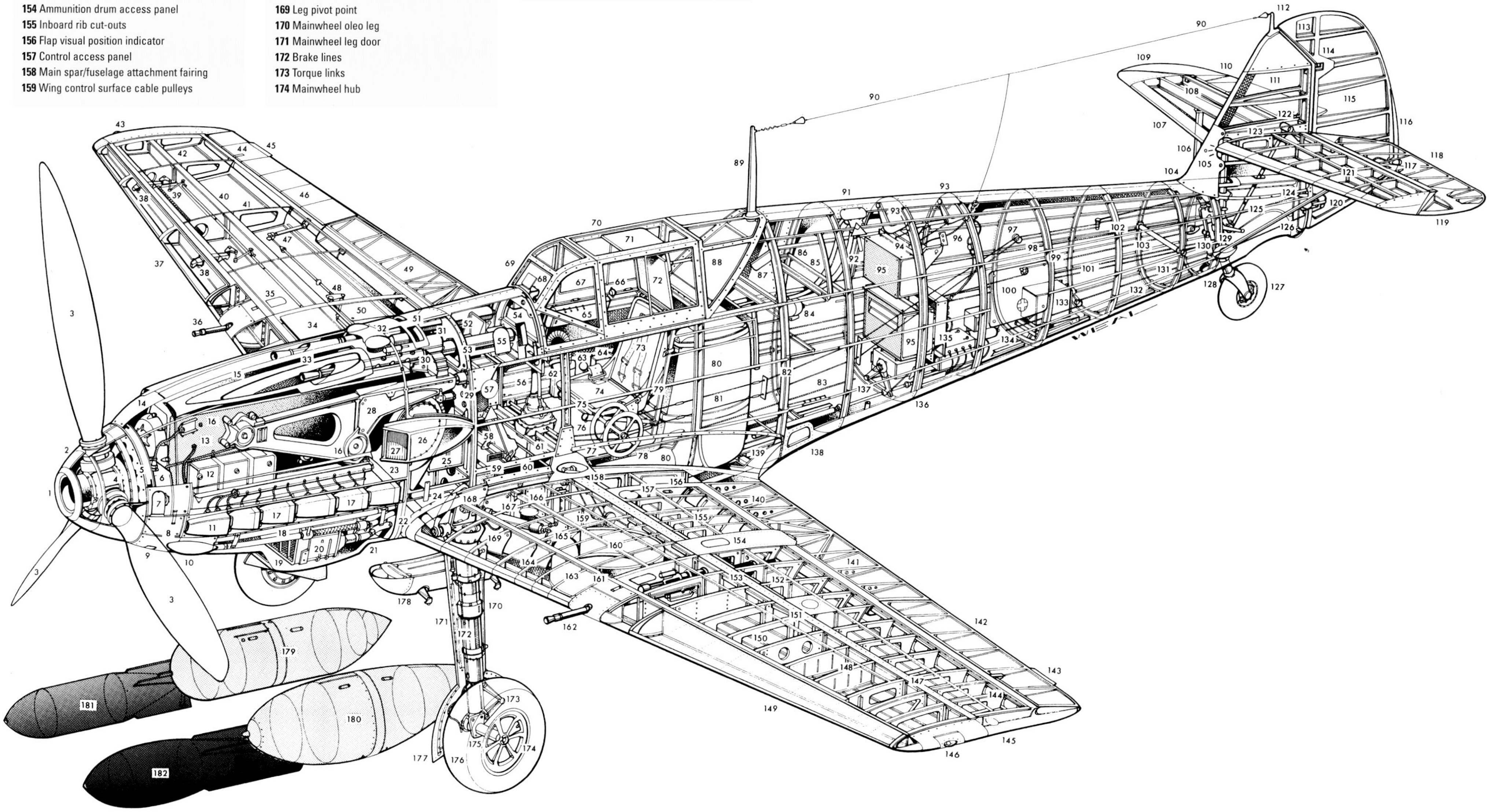

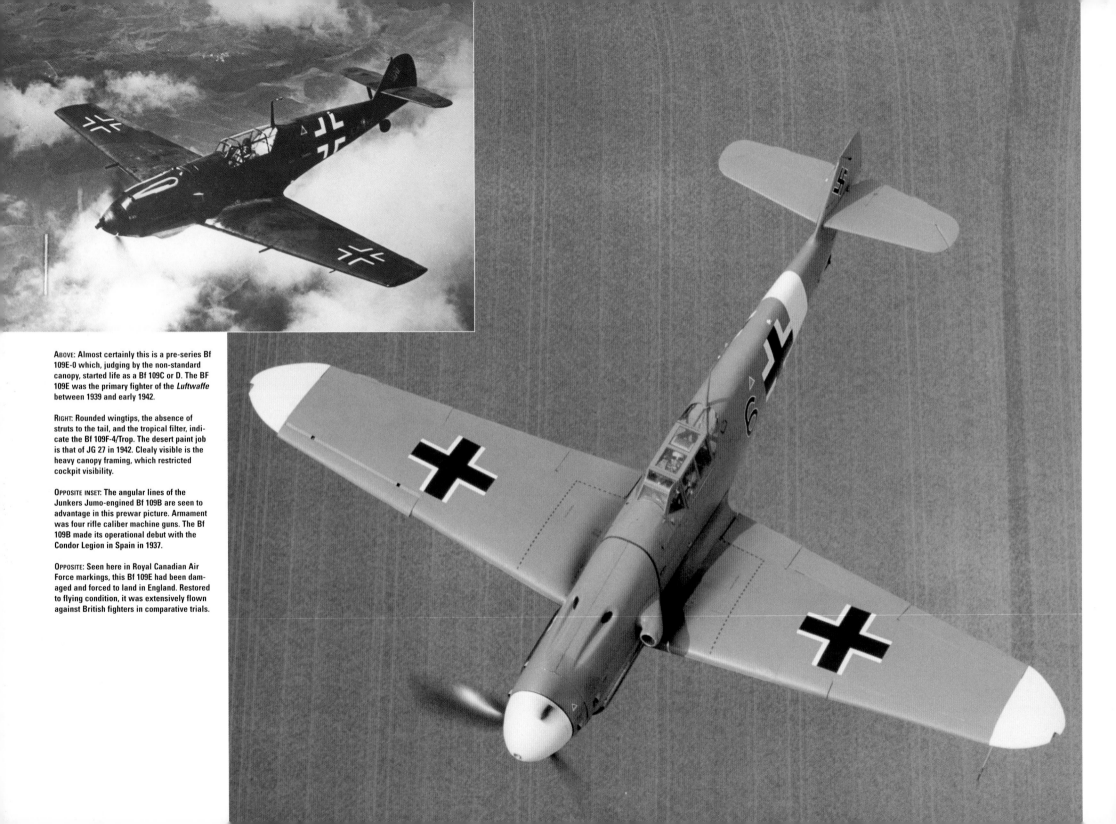

ABOVE: Almost certainly this is a pre-series Bf 109E-0 which, judging by the non-standard canopy, started life as a Bf 109C or D. The BF 109E was the primary fighter of the *Luftwaffe* between 1939 and early 1942.

RIGHT: Rounded wingtips, the absence of struts to the tail, and the tropical filter, indicate the Bf 109F-4/Trop. The desert paint job is that of JG 27 in 1942. Clearly visible is the heavy canopy framing, which restricted cockpit visibility.

OPPOSITE INSET: The angular lines of the Junkers Jumo-engined Bf 109B are seen to advantage in this prewar picture. Armament was four rifle caliber machine guns. The Bf 109B made its operational debut with the Condor Legion in Spain in 1937.

OPPOSITE: Seen here in Royal Canadian Air Force markings, this Bf 109E had been damaged and forced to land in England. Restored to flying condition, it was extensively flown against British fighters in comparative trials.

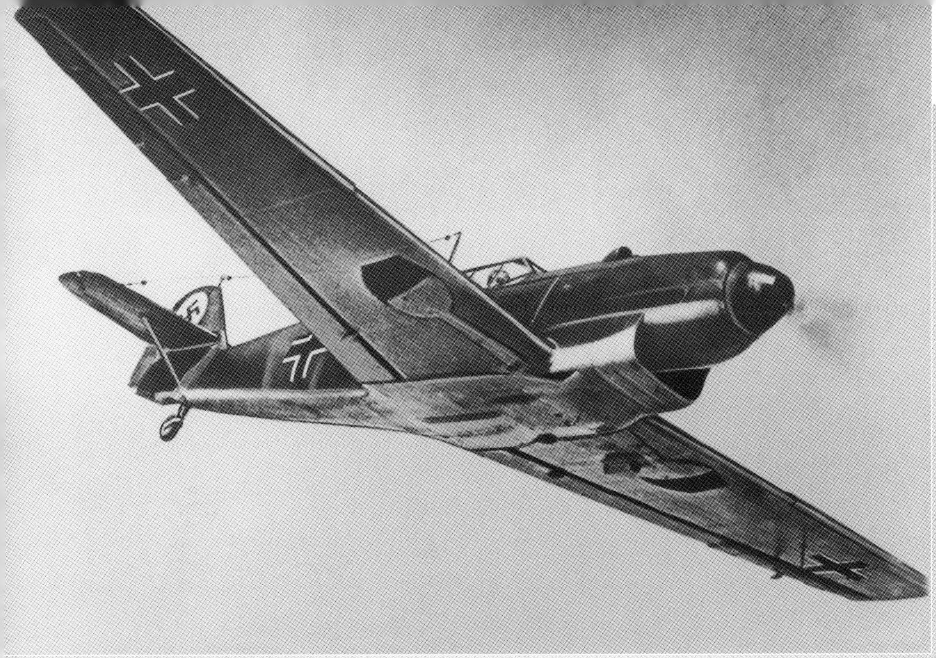

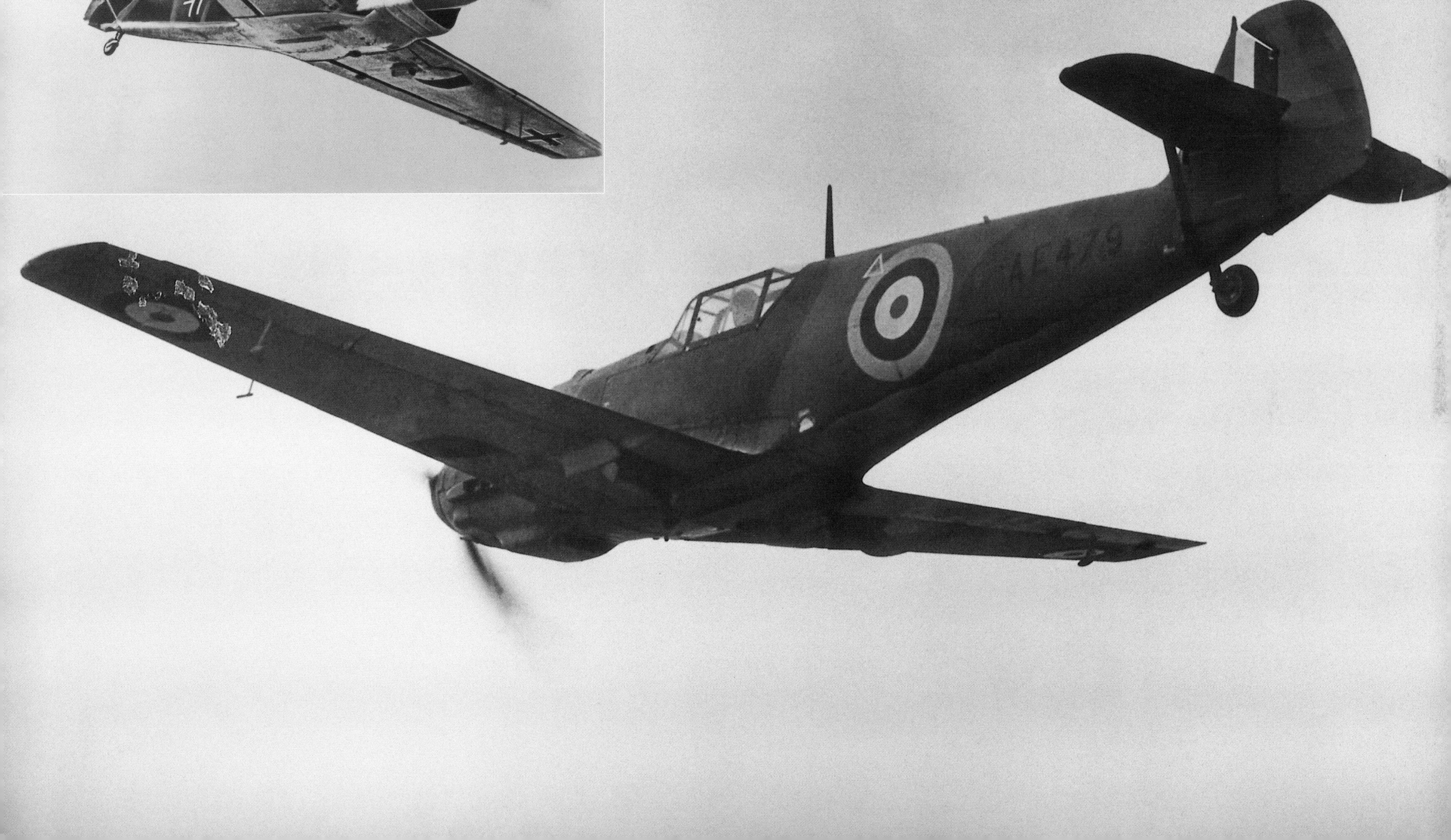
AE479

RIGHT INSET: The rather flimsy narrow track main gear of the Bf 109 gave rise to many landing accidents, and not a few on takeoff. Like most fighters of its era, forward view when taxiing varied between poor and non-existent.

BELOW: Exacerbated by the ever-present blowing sand, and hampered by the lack of facilities, servicing in the desert was far from easy. This is a Bf 109E-4/Trop of I/JG 27, seen late in 1941.

OPPOSITE: Somewhere in France; sometime in 1940, the *Jagdwaffe* standard flies in front of a Bf 109E of JG 53, resplendent in the new "overwater" camouflage scheme adopted by fighter units of *Luftflotte 3*, which had the longest Channel crossing.

OPPOSITE INSET: Luftwaffe ground crewmen in Russia, in the summer of 1942, strain to push this Bf 109G of *JG 54 Grunherz*, some with their hands inside the open slots. Just why is unclear, since the engine is already completely opened up for inspection.

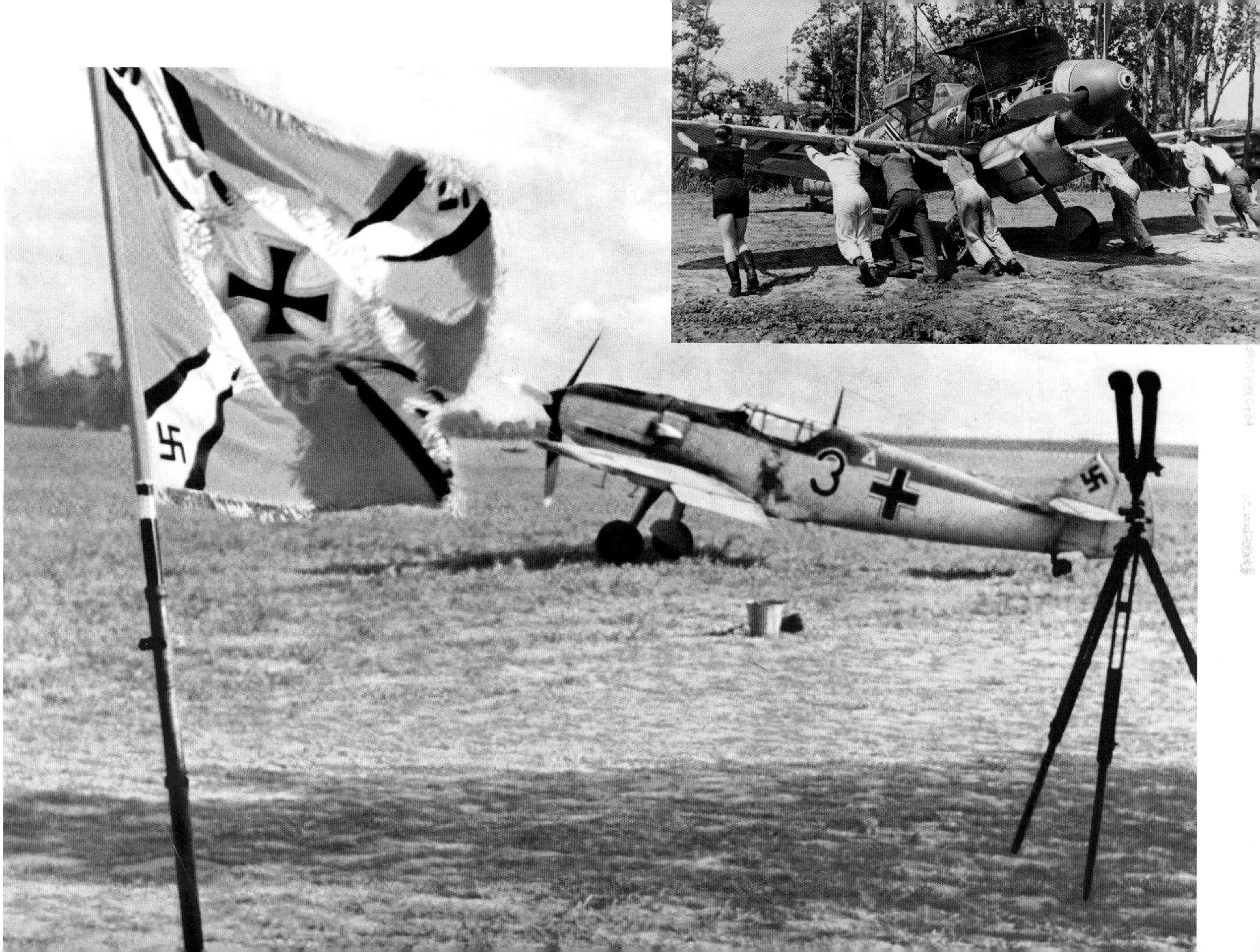

MESSERSCHMITT Bf 110

LEFT: What can only be described as a fashion for long range heavy fighters led to the Messerschmitt Bf 110 in the 1930s. Deficient in performance and maneuverability, it was no match for contemporary single-seaters.

The concept of long-range strategic fighters saw several twin-engined designs emerge during the 1930s, of which the elegant Bf 110, Göring's favorite fighter, was the best. It was cast in the destroyer (*Zerstörer*) role, intended to carve through the enemy fighters as it escorted the German bombers deep into enemy heartlands. While it was successful early in World War II against obsolescent fighters in the Poland campaign, and during the *Blitzkrieg* operations through the European Low Countries and France, it was heavy and relatively unmaneuverable, and in daylight it was outclassed by modern single-seat, single-engined fighters, such as the Spitfire and Hurricane, as its poor showing in the Battle of Britain was to highlight.

In the summer of 1940, in the skies of Southern England it was faced with determined (even desperate) foe flying good fighter aircraft backed up by an efficient ground control system. Losses among *Zerstörergeschwadern* soon forced the Germans to provide Bf 109 escorts for the escort! When attacked, the Bf 110 units adopted the defensive circle, in which the tail of the preceding airplane was covered by the one behind it. While this was difficult for its opponents to crack, it was hardly offensive either. By the end of the year the type was withdrawn from the Channel coast.

But when fitted out with airborne radar and especially when used as a night fighter, the Bf 110 did achieve some success. However, it was increasingly loaded with equipment such that it ended up with barely enough performance to catch the Allies' bombers over Europe.

The Bf 110 was a monoplane with angular wings set low in a long fuselage that housed the pilot and radar operator forward and a rear-facing radio operator who manned a single swiveling machine gun in the tail. Main armament comprised (on the 110C) two Oerlikon MGFF cannon and four 7.9mm machine guns in the nose. The wings had automatic leading edges outboard of the twin engines, and ailerons and slotted flaps in the trailing edges. The taiplane was positioned at the top of the empennage, and had endplate fins and rudders. The main undercarriage folded up into the engine nacelles. Although directional control on takeoff was poor, handling in the air was considered good, and pilots liked the airplane. The basic design proved flexible enough to permit variations in engines and application of equipment well beyond that which the designers had planned.

A total of 6,050 Bf 110s of all versions were built. The prototype first flew on May 12, 1936, the type entered service in early 1939, and production ceased in December 1941, with the type due to be replaced by Bf 210 two-seat fighters with dive-bombing capability. When production of the Bf 210 was stopped in 1942, the Bf 110's production lines reopened in February of that year until March 1945.

By then, the Bf 110 had also been developed as a fast bomber, ground attack aircraft, long-range reconnaissance fighter, and night fighter, with the Bf 110G-4 being the final variant. Various engine fits, radars and weapons had been fitted, including (on the Bf 110F-4/U1) a pair of upward-firing 30mm cannon in a "*schräge Musik*" installation, and on the Bf 110G-2/R3 21cm mortars to destroy U.S. Army Air Force bombers.

Specifications for Messerschmitt Bf 110G-4

Dimensions:	wingspan 53 feet 4 inches, length 39 feet 7.25 inches, height 13 feet 8.5 inches
Power:	two 1,475hp Daimler-Benz DB 605B-1 liquid-cooled V-12 engines with water methanol injection, each rated at 1,475hp
Weights:	empty 11,230lb, normal takeoff 20,701lb, max 21,799lb
Speed:	max 342mph at 22,965 feet, 311 mph at sea level
Ceiling:	26,250 feet
Range:	559 miles
Armament:	two 30mm Rheinmetall Borsig MK 108 cannon with 135 rounds per gun, and two 20mm Mauser MG 151 cannon with 300 and 350 rounds, all mounted in the nose, plus one 7.9mm MG 81Z twin swiveling machine gun with 800 rounds at the rear of the cabin. Some aircraft with two 20mm Mauser MG 151 or 20mm Oerlikon MGFF drum-fed cannon in *schräge Musik* installation firing upwards
Crew:	pilot, radar operator and radio operator/rear gunner

Bf 110G-4b/R3 cutaway key

1 *Hirschgeweih* (stag's antlers) array for the FuG 220b Lichtenstein SN-2 radar
2 Quad di-pole type antenna for the FuG 212 Lichtenstein C-1 radar
3 Camera gun
4 Cannon muzzles
5 Cannon ports
6 Blast tubes
7 Starboard mainwheel
8 Armor plate (0.4in; 10mm)
9 Twin 30mm Rheinmetall Borsig Mk 103 (Rüstsatz/ Field Conversion Set 3) with 135 rpg
10 Armored bulkhead
11 Supercharger intake
12 Position of nacelle-mounted instruments on day-fighter model
13 Exhaust flame damper
14 Auxiliary tank
15 Three-bladed VDM airscrew
16 Leading-edge automatic slat
17 Pitot tube
18 FuG 227/1 Flensburg homing aerial fitted to some aircraft by forward maintenance units (to home onto Monica tailwarning radar emissions)
19 Stressed wing skinning
20 Starboard aileron
21 Trim tab
22 Slotted flap
23 Hinged canopy roof
24 Armored glass windscreen (2.4 in; 60 mm)
25 Instrument panel
26 Cockpit floor armor (0.16in; 4mm)
27 Twin 20mm Mauser MG 151 cannon with 300 rounds (port) and 350 rounds (starboard)
28 Pilot's seat
29 Control column
30 Pilot's back and head armor (0.315in; 8mm)
31 Cannon magazine
32 Center section carrythrough
33 Radar operator's swivel seat
34 D/F loop
35 Aerial mast
36 Upward-firing cannon muzzles
37 Two 30mm MK 108 cannon in *schräge Musik* (oblique music) installation firing obliquely upward (optional installation supplied as an UmrustBausatz/Factory Conversion Set)
38 Ammunition drums
39 Aft cockpit bulkhead
40 FuG 10P HF R/T set
41 FuB 12F airfield blind-approach receiver
42 Handhold
43 Oxygen bottles
44 Aerials
45 Master compass
46 Starboard tailfin
47 Rudder balance
48 Rudder
49 Tab
50 Starboard elevator
51 Starboard tailplane
52 Variable-incidence tailplane
53 Elevator tab
54 Center section fairing
55 Rear navigation light
56 Port elevator
57 Port tailfin
58 Rudder
59 Hinged tab
60 Tailwheel
61 Fuselage frames
62 Control lines
63 Dipole tuner
64 Batteries
65 Transformer
66 Slotted flap
67 Fuel tank (68.76-gallon capacity)
68 Oil tank (9.24-gallon capacity)
69 Ventral antenna
70 Coolant radiator
71 Radiator intake
72 Hinged intake fairing
73 Aileron tab
74 Aileron construction
75 Wingtip
76 Flensburg aerial (see 18)
77 Port navigation light
78 Leading-edge automatic slat
79 Wing ribs
80 Mainspar
81 Underwing auxiliary fuel tank (79.2-gallon capacity)
82 Landing light
83 Undercarriage door
84 Mainwheel well
85 Supercharger intake
86 Undercarriage pivot point
87 Mainwheel leg
88 Mainwheel
89 Oil cooler
90 Oil cooler intake
91 VDM propeller
92 Pitch-change mechanism
93 Armored ring (0.2in; 5mm)
94 Coolant tank
95 Exhaust flame damper
96 Anti-vibration engine mounting pad
97 Daimler-Benz DB 605B-1 12-cylinder inverted-Vee engine (rated at 1,475hp/1100 kW for takeoff and 1,355hp/1011kW at 18,700ft)
98 Forged engine bearer
99 Fuel tank (99-gallon capacity)
100 Fuselage/mainspar attachment point
101 Fuselage/forward auxiliary spar attachment point
102 Waffenwanne 151Z, a ventral tray housing a pair of 20mm MG 151 cannon (optional)

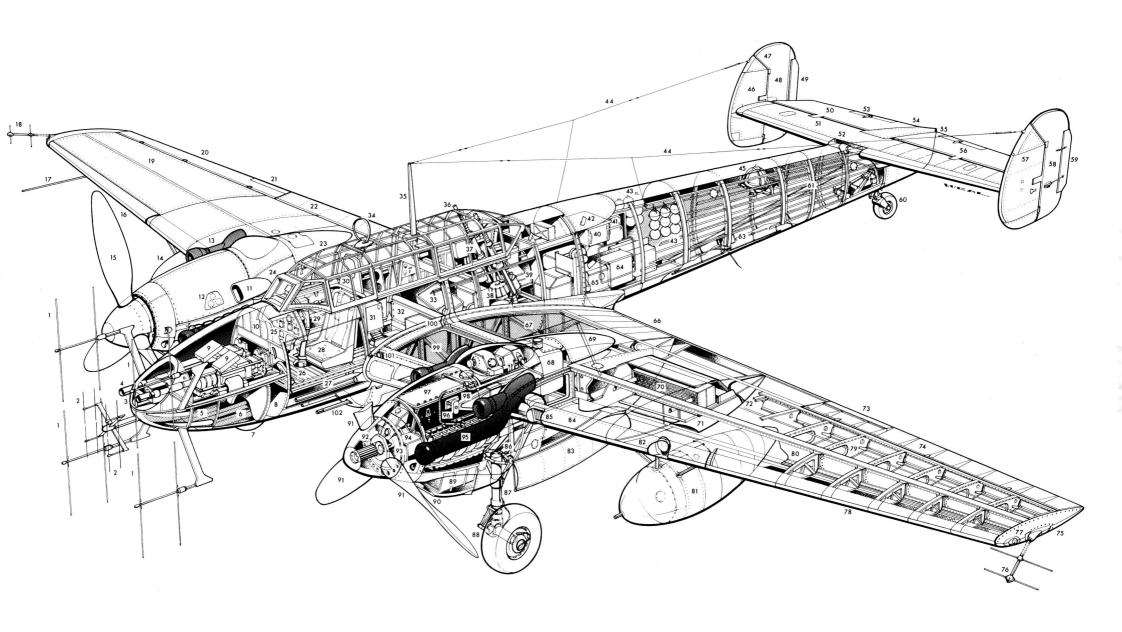

ABOVE: Hermann Göring decreed that his Bf 110 *Zerstörer* (destroyers) would be an elite force, and called them his "Ironsides." Just a handful of fighter pilots were successful on the type by day.

LEFT: A pre-series Bf 110A-0 undergoing manufacturer's trials. A British pilot who flew a captured example described it as flying like a "twin-engined Tiger Moth"! It is uncertain whether this was intended as a compliment.

OPPOSITE: The shortcomings of the Bf 110 were such that even before the war it was scheduled for replacement by the Bf 210. The failure of the latter resulted in the Bf 110F-1s seen here operating as fighter-bombers by default.

OPPOSITE INSET: Successful in Poland, France and Norway, but unable to survive in the skies over England, the Bf 110 was shunted off into less demanding theaters. This is a Bf 110C-4 of ZG 26, operating over the Western Desert.

MESSERSCHMITT Me 262

First flown in April 1941, the German Me 262 was the first jet fighter to be used operationally, although not until the late summer of 1944. It had overwhelming speed, but this was a double-edged sword. It made the Me 262 almost uninterceptable by conventional fighters, but it made attacking much slower bombers very difficult by reducing the time available to line up and fire. Any attempt at hard maneuvering bled off speed at an alarming rate, making the Me 262 vulnerable to counter-attack. Never available in sufficient numbers, the Me 262 made less impact on the war than its performance warranted.

Powered by two Junkers Jumo 109-004B axial-flow turbojets, the Me 262 was the world's first operational swept-wing fighter, although it was in most other ways conventional The engines were mounted outboard on the wings, where they would have been had the Me 262 been a propeller-driven type. Had they been positioned inboard, problems of asymmetric handling with one engine out could have been avoided, and rate of roll improved. No attempt was made to improve pilot view by moving the cockpit forward, ahead of the wings.

The Me 262's wing loading was high (60lb/sq.ft) and this, coupled with the speed, meant that the fighter could not turn tightly. Maneuver combat had to be avoided. Nor could a steep diving attack be used without exceeding the limiting Mach number. Nevertheless, the Me 262 was almost impossible to catch in a straight chase; its speed also prevented Allied ground control radar from tracking it, and the only way of bringing it down was by extremely hazardous power-dives that stressed the best Allied piston-engined fighters to the limit. Moreover, when some Allied pilots followed the jet to its base and attempted to destroy the Me 262 as it landed, when it was at its most vulnerable because of the long and very straight landing approach it needed, they found that German antiaircraft defenses made this tactic almost suicidal.

Like all early jet engines, response time of the Jumos was slow. Once up to speed it was best to leave the throttles alone during combat, and retard them only when it was time to land. Inattention to turbine temperatures easily resulted in the engines catching fire. Another great weakness of the Me 262 was its short endurance, typically less than an hour.

The Me 262 V1, the first prototype, flew on April 18, 1941, but with a piston engine, and this was retained for the aircraft's initial flight with turbojets operating on March 25, 1942. The first flight on turbojets alone was achieved with the Me 262 V3 on July 18, and pre-series aircraft were accepted from April 1944. First production aircraft were delivered the following June, and the fighter had its combat debut in July 1944. The first series production model was the Me 262A-1a single-seat interceptor, semi-officially called *Schwalbe* (Swallow). Total production was about 1,442, including twelve built in Czechoslovakia after the war as the Avia S 92.

There were sub-variants of the Me 262A, including a fighter-bomber and a version with a second crew member who operated a special gyro-stabilized bomb-sight. The Me 262B was a tandem two-seat conversion trainer, with a variant developed as a night fighter, although only seven of the latter appear to have entered service, and the Me 262C was tested as a rocket-boosted version.

ABOVE: The Messerschmitt Me 262 *Schwalbe* was the world's first jet fighter in service. Although much faster than any Allied fighter of the day, it had so many limitations in combat that it was difficult to use effectively.

Me 262A-1a/b cutaway key

1 Flettner-type geared trim tab
2 Mass-balanced rudder
3 Rudder post
4 Tail fin structure
5 Tailplane structure
6 Rudder tab mechanism
7 Flettner-type servo tab
8 Starboard elevator
9 Rear navigation light
10 Rudder linkage
11 Elevator linkage
12 Tailplane adjustment mechanism
13 Fuselage break point
14 Fuselage construction
15 Control runs
16 FuG 25a loop antenna (IFF)
17 Automatic compass
18 Aft auxiliary self-sealing fuel tank (158.4 gallons capacity)
19 FuG 16zy R/T
20 Fuel filler cap
21 Aft cockpit glazing
22 Armoured aft main fuel tank (237.6 gallons capacity)
23 Inner cockpit shell
24 Pilot's seat
25 Canopy jettison lever
26 Armored 0.59in (15mm) head rest
27 Canopy (hinged to starboard)
28 Canopy lock
29 Bar-mounted Revi 16B sight (for both cannon and R4M missiles)
30 Armorglass windscreen 3.54in (90mm)
31 Instrument panel
32 Rudder pedal
33 Armored forward main fuel tank (237.6 gallonscapacity)
34 Fuel filler cap
35 Underwing wooden rack for 12 R4M 2.17in (55mm) rockets (Me 262A-1b)
36 Port outer flap section
37 Frise-type aileron
38 Aileron control linkage
39 Port navigation light
40 Pitot head
41 Automatic leading-edge slats
42 Port engine cowling
43 Electrical firing mechanism
44 Firewall
45 Spent cartridge ejector chutes
46 Four 30mm Rheinmetall Borsig Mk 108 cannon (100rpg belt-fed ammunition for upper pair and 80rpg for lower pair)
47 Cannon muzzles
48 Combat camera
49 Camera aperture
50 Nosewheel fairing
51 Nosewheel leg
52 Nosewheel
53 Torque scissors
54 Retraction jack
55 Hydraulic lines
56 Main nosewheel door (starboard)
57 Compressed air bottles
58 Forward auxiliary fuel tank (44.4 gallons capacity)
59 Mainwheel well
60 Torque box
61 Main spar
62 Mainwheel leg pivot point
63 Mainwheel door
64 Mainwheel retraction rod
65 Engine support arch
66 Leading-edge slat structure
67 Auxiliaries gearbox
68 Annular oil tank
69 Riedel starter motor housing
70 Engine air intake
71 Hinged cowling section
72 Junkers Jumo 004B-2 axial-flow turbojet
73 Starboard mainwheel
74 Wing structure
75 Automatic leading-edge slats
76 Mainspar
77 Starboard navigation light
78 Frise-type ailerons
79 Trim-tab
80 Flettner-type geared tab
81 Starboard outer flap section
82 Engine exhaust orifice
83 Engine support bearer
84 Starboard inner flap structure
85 Faired wing root

Specifications for Messerschmitt Me 262A-1a *Schwalbe*

Dimensions: wingspan 41 feet 0.5 inches, length 34 feet 9.5 inches, height 12 feet 6.75 inches

Power: two Junkers Jumo 109-004B single-spool, axial-flow turbo jets each rated at 1,980lb thrust

Weights: empty 9,742lb, normal takeoff 14,101lb

Speed: max 541mph at 19,685 feet, 500mph at sea level

Ceiling: 37,565 feet

Range: 653 miles

Armament: four nose-mounted 30mm Rheinmetall Borsig MK 108 cannon, two with 100 rounds per gun and two with 80 rounds per gun (some aircraft carried 24 55mm R4M unguided rockets underwing)

Crew: pilot

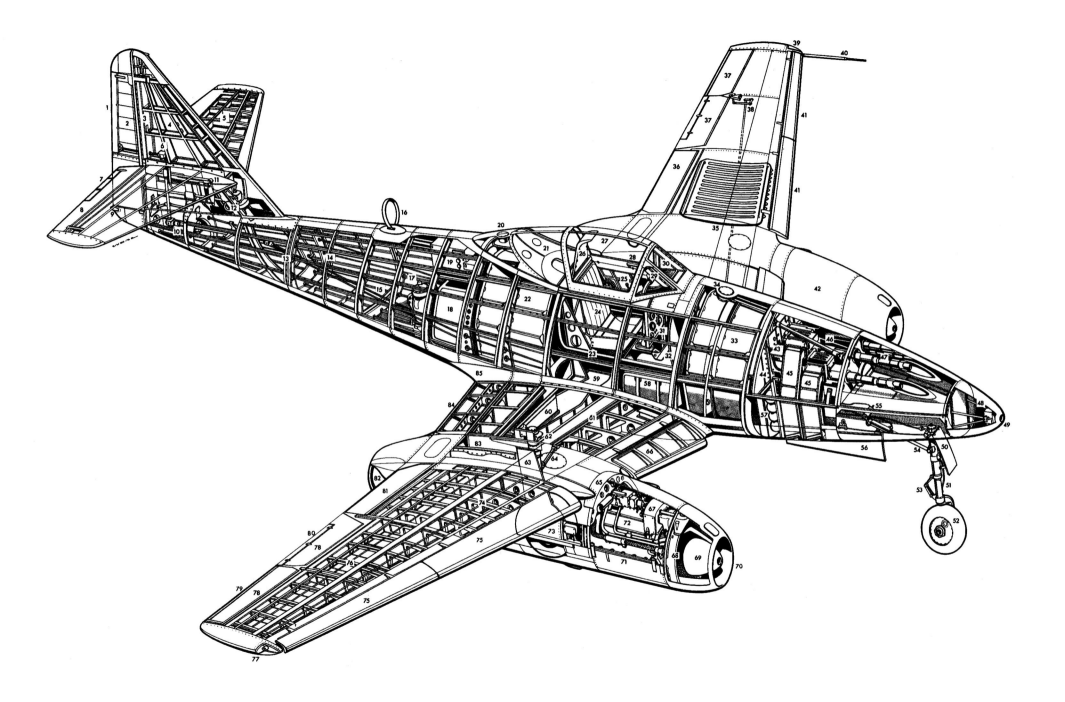

OPPOSITE: Fitted with Neptun radar, with an operator in the back seat, the Me 262B was the only German night fighter with enough margin of performance to catch RAF Mosquitos. Fortunately there were hardly any of them.

OPPOSITE INSET: The presence of just two 30mm MK 108 cannon in the nose is enough to identify this bird as an Me 262-2a/U1 *Sturmvogel* fighter bomber, able to carry a single 2,205 pound or two 1,102 pound bombs.

BELOW: Captured Me 262s were mothballed and taken back to the USA as deck cargo, along with many other German types. Once there, they were restored to flying condition and extensively tested against the Lockheed P-80 jet.

INSET: This Me 262-1a was taken aloft on its maiden flight in April 1945 by a company test pilot. Knowing the war to be as good as lost, he flew it to an Allied airfield and ignominiously surrendered.

MIKOYAN-GUREVICH MiG-21

Left: The Mikoyan and Gurevich MiG-21 has served with more air forces (49), and fought in more conflicts than any other fighter. More than 10,000 have been built in a record 30 variants, and it has held 17 world records. This aircraft is Vietnamese.

The MiG-21, the first Soviet Mach 2 fighter to enter service, was a small, lightweight sports car of an airplane of tailed delta configuration. Initially armed with two 23mm cannon, it was designed as a single-seat, single-engined, fast-climbing point defense interceptor, with maneuverability that allowed it to double as an air combat fighter. With prototypes first flying in 1955, it was built in about 30 main variants in greater numbers than any other jet fighter, set 17 world records, and has served with no fewer than 49 different air forces, making it the world's most used jet fighter. Many nations still fly the type, and of the more than 10,000 produced, far exceeding that of any other supersonic fighter, several hundreds remain in service. Although extremely agile, it had only a limited adverse weather capability, which restricted its usefulness, and it ended on the losing side in many wars. This notwithstanding, in expert hands it proved a worthy opponent to many Western machines.

Following extensive prototype trials with swept and delta-wing configurations, the Mikoyan-Gurevich design bureau ultimately decided that the delta-wing offered marginally superior characteristics. The original 1954 specification was for a Mach 2 maneuverable interceptor that could be built affordably in large numbers, was easy to fly and maintain, was capable of catching fast and high-flying nuclear-armed bombers, had a high rate of climb and an operational ceiling above 65,600 feet, was compatible with air-to-air missiles and range-only radar, and could operate from semi-prepared fields.

What evolved was an austere and agile tactical fighter, whose then-fashionable Mach 2 capability would rarely be relevant or used, and never in turning air combat. Its greatest weaknesses were short endurance, and an appalling or non-existent rear view from the small cockpit, from which the pilot also had inadequate view over the nose, sideways and downwards! Controls were heavy, the fighter was difficult to maneuver below about 250mph or above 585mph, its afterburner was slow to respond, and its gunsight had limitations at more than 3g.

So why was the MiG-21, which was given the NATO reporting name "Fishbed," the subject of so many upgrades, and why were so many built? The main reason is that so many nations found it affordable to buy "second-hand" aircraft, zero-lifing the airframes, and equipping them with new avionics and weapons, certainly cheaper than buying new fighter aircraft.

The first into production was the MiG-21F, which entered service in 1958 and of which just forty were built.

Its delta wing had a 57-degree leading edge sweep, and there were Fowler flaps inboard of the ailerons. A ranging radar was fitted into the three-position shock cones in the pitot-style intake. Its air-to-air armament consisted of two 30mm cannon, each with 60 rounds, and two rocket pods each containing 16 57mm unguided rockets.

Very many variants followed, with engine, fuselage, weapons, avionics and mission changes, the final major and most potent variant being the MiG-21bis which was produced in the Soviet Union between 1972 and 1975, and also license-built in India until 1987. Based on this variant, Israeli Aircraft Industries have developed for export the MiG-21-2000 with service life extension, "glass cockpit" with HOTAS (hands-on-throttle-and-stick) and modern avionics. China, also, has over the years license-built (or pirated) Russian fighter designs, one example being the Chengdu F-7/J7 series of fighters first flown in 1966 and based on the MiG-21F-13, while its twin-engined Shenyang J-8 appears to be a larger variant of the MiG-21.

Specifications for Mikoyan-Gurevich MiG21bis

Dimensions: wingspan 23 feet 5.5 inches, length 48 feet 2.3 inches, height 13 feet 6.5 inches

Power: one Tumansky R-25-300 twin-spool, axial-flow afterburning turbojet rated at 15,653lb max and 9,039lb military thrust, and special short-duration afterburning rating of 21,826lb below 13,125 feet

Weights: empty 13,492lb, normal takeoff 19,235lb, max 21,605lb

Speed: max Mach 2.05/1,352mph at 42,655 feet, Mach 1.2/808mph at sea level

Ceiling: 57,420 feet

Range: 761 miles

Armament: one 23mm GSh-23 cannon with 200 rounds, two or four K-60 air-to-air missiles

Crew: pilot

MiG-21MF "Fishbed-J" cutaway key

1 Pitot static boom
2 Pitch vanes
3 Yaw vanes
4 Conical three-position intake center body
5 "Spin Scan" search-and-track radar antenna
6 Boundary layer slot
7 Engine air intake
8 "Spin Scan" radar
9 Lower boundary layer exit
10 IFF antennas
11 Nosewheel doors
12 Nosewheel leg and shock absorbers
13 Castoring nosewheel
14 Anti-shimmy damper
15 Avionics bay access
16 Attitude sensor
17 Nosewheel well
18 Spill door
19 Nosewheel retraction pivot
20 Bifurcated intake trunking
21 Avionics bay
22 Electronics equipment
23 Intake trunking
24 Upper boundary layer exit
25 Dynamic pressure probe for q-feel
26 Semi-elliptical armor glass windscreen
27 Gunsight mounting
28 Fixed quarterlight
29 Radar scope
30 Control column (with tailplane trim switch and two firing buttons)
31 Rudder pedals
32 Underfloor control runs
33 KM-1 two-position zero-level ejection seat
34 Port instrument console
35 Undercarriage handle
36 Seat harness
37 Canopy release/lock
38 Starboard wall switch pane
39 Rear-view mirror fairing
40 Starboard hinged canopy
41 Ejection seat headrest
42 Avonics bay
43 Control rods
44 Air-conditioning plant
45 Suction relief door
46 Intake trunking
47 Wingroot attachment fairing
48 Wing/fuselage spar-lug attachment points (four)
49 Fuselage ring frames
50 Intermediary frames
51 Main fuselage fuel tank

52 RSIU radio bay
53 Auxiliary intake
54 Leading-edge integral fuel tank
55 Starboard outer weapons pylon
56 Outboard wing construction
57 Starboard navigation light
58 Leading-edge suppressed aerial
59 Wing fence
60 Aileron control jack
61 Starboard aileron
62 Flap actuator fairing
63 Starboard blown flap SPS (*sduva pogranich-novo slova*)
64 Multi-spar wing structure
65 Main integral wing fuel tank
66 Undercarriage mounting/pivot point
67 Starboard mainwheel leg
68 Auxiliaries compartment
69 Fuselage fuel tanks Nos 2 and 3
70 Mainwheel well external fairing
71 Mainwheel (retracted)
72 Trunking contours
73 Control rods in dorsal spine
74 Compressor face
75 Oil tank
76 Avionics pack
77 Engine accessories
78 Tumanskii R-13 turbojet
79 Fuselage break/transport joint
80 Intake
81 Tail surface control linkage
82 Artificial feel unit
83 Tailplane jack
84 Hydraulic accumulator
85 Tailplane trim motor
86 Fin spar attachment plate
87 Rudder jack
88 Rudder control linkage
89 Fin structure
90 Leading-edge panel
91 Radio cable access
92 Magnetic detector
93 Fin mainspar
94 RSIU (*radio-stantsiya istrebitelnaya ultrako-rotkykh vol'n* – very short-wave fighter radio) antenna plate
95 VHF/UHF aerials

96 IFF antennas
97 Formation light
98 Tail warning radar
99 Rear navigation light
100 Fuel vent
101 Rudder construction
102 Rudder hinge
103 Braking parachute hinged bullet fairing
104 Braking parachute stowage
105 Tailpipe (variable convergent nozzle)
106 Afterburner installation
107 Afterburner bay cooling intake
108 Tail plane linkage fairing
109 Nozzle actuating cylinders
110 Tailplane torque tube
111 All-moving tailplane
112 Anti flutter weight
113 Intake
114 Afterburner mounting
115 Fixed tailplane root fairing
116 Longitudinal lap joint
117 External duct (nozzle hydraulics)
118 Ventral fin
119 Engine guide rail
120 ATO assembly canted nozzle
121 ATO assembly thrust plate forks (rear-mounting)
122 ATO assembly pack
123 Ventral airbrake (retracted)
124 Trestle point
125 ATO assembly-release solenoid (front-mounting)
126 Underwing landing light
127 Ventral stores pylon
128 Mainwheel inboard door
129 Splayed link chute
130 23mm GSh-23 cannon installation
131 Cannon muzzle fairing
132 Debris deflector plate
133 Auxiliary ventral drop tank
134 Port forward air brake (extended)
135 Leading-edge integral fuel tank
136 Undercarriage retraction strut
137 Aileron control rods in leading edge
138 Port inboard weapons pylon
139 UV-16-57 rocket pod
140 Port mainwheel

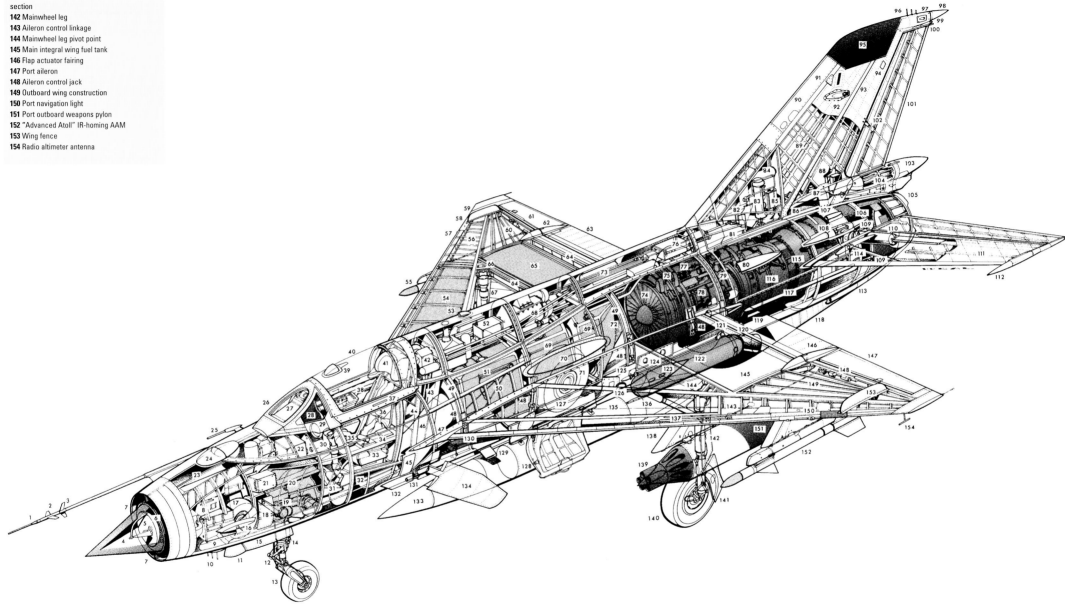

BELOW: Armed with four AAMs, this Russian MiG-21bis, produced between 1972 and 1987, was the definitive type. The MiG-21 series was a light and agile sports car of a fighter and, above all, it was affordable.

INSET: A MiG-21 PFS of the Polish Air Force. From this angle it can be seen that the view from the cockpit is appalling; to the rear it is non-existent, and to the sides and over the nose it is very poor.

LEFT: A formation of Polish MiG-21 PFS fighters, unarmed, but carrying supersonic drop tanks ventrally. The bulged dorsal spine and broad chord fin and rudder are identification features of this model.

ABOVE: First flown in June 1955, the MiG-21 was given the NATO reporting name of Fishbed. This is the MiG-21F; which in 1958 became the first variant to enter service. Aside from the fifteen main variants produced in the Soviet Union between 1958 and 1987, the MiG-21 was license-built in Czechoslovakia, India, and China.

INSET: **A pilot boards his MiG-21MF.** Features are the side-hinged canopy and the heavy windscreen bow. The latter severely impairs the forward view, as does the gunsight. Poor cockpit visibility is a major reason for the lack of air combat success.

LEFT: Finland operated the MiG-21F-13 for many years. Produced in Russia between 1960 and 1965, and in Czechoslovakia until 1972, the F-13 formed the original basis of the Chinese J-7 fighter.

OPPOSITE: A Hungarian MiG-21MF shows its clean lines. Simple to construct, the delta wing has advantages in high speed, high altitude flight, while adding a conventional all-flying tailplane compensates for its drawbacks.

OPPOSITE INSET: An Iraqi defector delivered a MiG-21F to Israel in August 1966. Given the number 007 and Israeli insignia, it was exhaustively evaluated. It later went to the USA, to assist in the development of tactics.

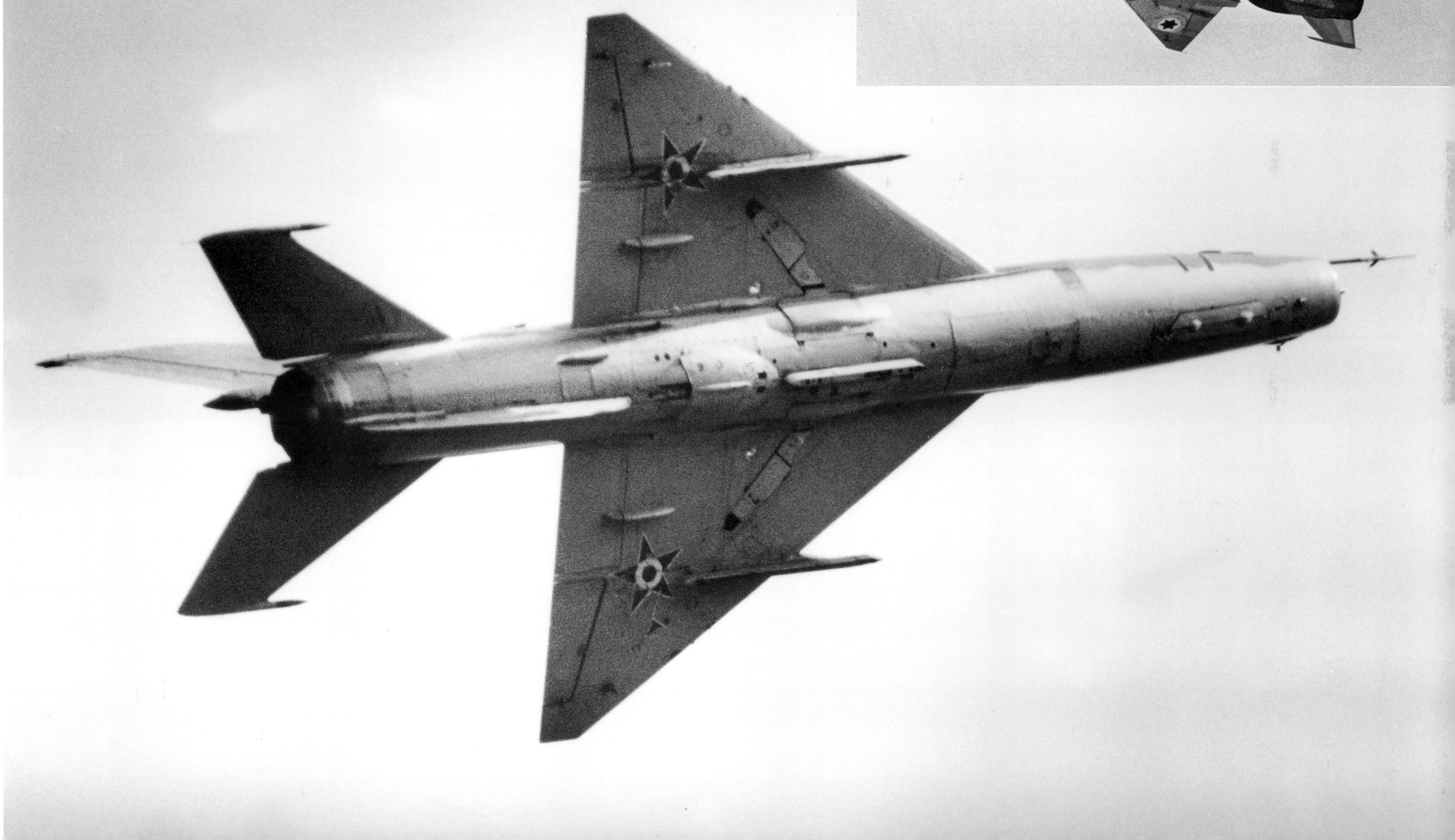

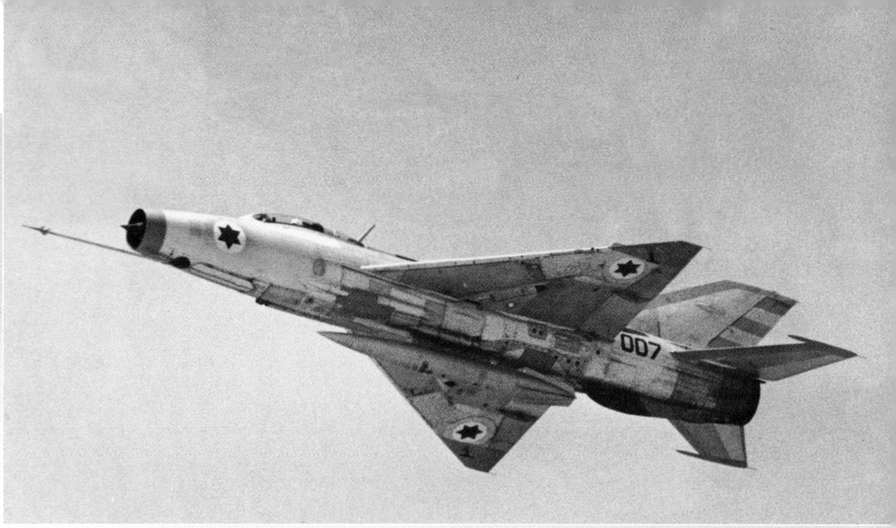
007

MIKOYAN-GUREVICH MiG-25

LEFT: The world's fastest fighter to enter service is the MiG-25A Foxbat. A semi-automated interceptor with a huge and powerful radar, it was designed to operate in typical Russian conditions as seen here.

When the MiG-25 entered service in 1973, it became the fastest combat aircraft ever to do so. Codenamed "Foxbat" by NATO, it was developed to counter the Lockheed A-12 being developed in the United States as a long-range strategic reconnaissance aircraft and the forerunner of the SR-71 Blackbird. The entire design was optimized for the high altitude interception mission, with high speed and rate of climb as priorities, at the expense of maneuverability and endurance. First flown in 1964, it stretched the contemporary Soviet state of the art to its absolute limits. Its flight control system was tied by data link to ground control, which steered it to a collision-course interception. This left the pilot as a systems manager, responsible for takeoff and landing, throttle control and missile selection and launch. In emergencies "Foxbat" could be accelerated to Mach 3.2, but as this wrecked the engines, it was red-lined at Mach 2.83 for normal usage. Of course, maneuver combat was not possible at such speeds, since the aircraft had a turn radius of many miles.

The first prototype of the interceptor, the Ye-155P-1, flew on September 9, 1964, five months after the first flight of a strategic reconnaissance prototype, the Ye-155R. Series production as the MiG-25P began in 1969; special pre-series aircraft (as the Ye-266) had already set a number of world speed and altitude records, and continued to do so.

The MiG-25 was a very large aircraft. Its 5 degree anhedral wing had a compound leading edge swept 42.5 degrees inboard and 41 degrees outboard, and two small fences on each side. Tailerons were differentially moving and swept at 50 degrees, while the twin fins were cropped and outwardly canted at 11 degrees. The twin engines were fed by steeply raked variable lateral intakes.

Fuel consumption was understandably prodigious, since full afterburning was used for takeoff, climb and interception, and therefore 70 percent of the interceptor's total volume was allocated for fuel storage in nine welded-steel tanks. An automatic fuel transfer system was installed to keep the center of gravity within acceptable limits as the fuel was burned off so rapidly. Kinetic heating at the MiG-25's high speeds was a problem, resulting in mostly welded nickle steel having to be used in construction, with only minor use of lighter titanium and other materials.

The MiG-25P was equipped with an RP-25 *Smerch* radar, while armament comprised two radar-guided R-40R and two infrared-homing R-40T air-to-air missiles. In 1978 this version was replaced in production by the up-engined, upgraded MiG-25PD, with improved radar with look-

down/shoot-down capability, two R-40R and four R-60 IR-homing air-to-air missiles. All MiG-25Ps were converted to this standard from 1979, and designated MiG-25PDS.

Some trainer versions were built, designated MiG-25U. This had the instructor cockpit in front of and below the original cockpit (occupied by the pupil), which is not only the reverse of normal procedure but meant that the extra cockpit displaced the radar and other sensors, but not fuel.

More than 1,200 MiG-25s of all versions had been built by the time production ended in 1982, over 900 of them interceptors. Apart from those in service with the Soviet Union/Russia (withdrawn in 1994), users of interceptor MiG-25s have been Algeria, Iraq, Syria and Libya, who all originally received the MiG-25P, although the Libyan aircraft were subsequently upgraded to MiG-25PDS standard. Reconnaissance versions have been used by a few foreign customers. It is believed that five MiG-25s have been lost in conflict in the Middle East, while no successes have been recorded for the aircraft.

Specifications for Mikoyan-Gurevich MiG-25P

Dimensions: wingspan 46 feet, length 64 feet 9.5 inches, height 18 feet 6 inches

Power: two Tumansky R-15B-300 single-spool, axial-flow afterburning turbojets each rated at 22,509lb max and 16,535lb military thrust

Weights: empty 44,000lb, takeoff with four R-40 air-to-air missiles 80,955lb

Speed: max Mach 2.83/1,864mph at 42,655 feet, Mach 0.98/746mph at sea level

Ceiling: 78,090 feet

Range: 777 miles

Armament: four R-60 air-to-air missiles, two SARH and two IR-homing

Crew: pilot

MiG-25 "Foxbat-A" cutaway key

1 Ventral airbrake
2 Starboard tailplane (aluminum alloy trailing edge)
3 Steel tailplane spar
4 Titanium leading edge
5 Tail bumper
6 Fully-variable engine exhaust nozzle
7 Exhaust nozzle actuator
8 Starboard rudder
9 Static dischargers
10 Sirena 3 tail warning radar and ECM transmitter
11 Transponder aerial
12 Twin brake parachute housing
13 Port engine exhaust nozzle
14 Port rudder
15 Static dischargers
16 VHF aerial
17 HF leading-edge aerial
18 Port tailfin (steel primary structure)
19 Rudder actuator
20 Titanium rear fuselage skins
21 Dorsal spine fairing
22 Fireproof bulkhead between engine bays
23 Engine afterburner duct
24 Cooling air intake
25 Tailplane hydraulic actuator
26 Starboard ventral fin
27 VHF and ECM aerial housing
28 Aileron actuator
29 Starboard aileron
30 Static discharger
31 All-steel wing construction
32 Wingtip fairing
33 Sirena 3 radar warning receiver and ECM transmitter
34 Continuous-wave target-illuminating radar
35 AA-6 "Acrid" semi-active radar guided-air-to air missile
36 Missile-launching rail
37 Outboard missile pylon
38 Pylon attachments
39 Wing titanium leading edge
40 Inboard pylon
41 Wing fence
42 Engine access panels
43 Engine accessory gearbox
44 Tumanskii R-31 single-shaft afterburning turbojet engine
45 Port flap
46 Aileron hydraulic actuator
47 Port aileron

48 Fixed portion of trailing edge
49 Sirena 3 radar warning receiver and ECM transmitter
50 Continuous-wave target-illuminating radar
51 Titanium leading edge
52 Port wing fences
53 AA-6 "Acrid" semi-active radar-guided air-to-air missile
54 Infra-red-guided AA-6 "Acrid" missile
55 Stainless steel wing skins
56 Intake flank fuel tanks
57 Controls and systems ducting
58 Main fuel tanks (welded steel integral construction), total system capacity 31,575lb (14,322kg), nitrogen-pressurised
59 Intake bleed air ducts engine bay cooling
60 Engine compressor face
61 Wing spar attachments
62 Main undercarriage leg strut
63 Starboard mainwheel
64 Mainwheel doors
65 Mainwheel stowed position
66 Starboard infra-red guided AA-6 :Acrid" missile
67 Retractable landing/taxiing lamp
68 Intake duct control vanes
69 Steel fuselage primary structure
70 Intake bleed air outlet ducts
71 UHF communications aerials
72 Variable-intake ramp doors
73 Ramp jacks
74 Intake water/methanol injection duct
75 Electric intake tip actuator
76 Variable lower intake lip
77 Nose wheel door/mudguard
78 Twin nose wheels
79 Nose wheel leg doors
80 Starboard navigation light
81 Curved intake inboard sidewall
82 Rear avionics bay, communications and ECM equipment
83 Cockpit canopy cover, hinges to starboard
84 Pilot's ejection seat
85 Cockpit rear pressure bulkhead
86 UHF communications aerial
87 Radar altimeter

88 Pilot's side console panel
89 Control column
90 Instrument panel shroud
91 Stand-by visual sighting system for infra-red missiles
92 Windscreen panels
93 "Odd Rods"' IFF aerials
94 Pitot tube
95 Forward avionics compartment, radar and navigation equipment
96 "Fox Fire" fire control radar system
97 Angle-of-attack probe
98 Scanner tracking mechanism
99 Radar scanner dish, 2ft 9.5in (85cm) diameter
100 Radome
101 "Swift Rod" ILS antenna
102 Pitot tube
103 MiG-25U "Foxbat-C" two-seat operational training variant
104 Student pilot's cockpit enclosure
105 Instructor's cockpit
106 MiG-25R "Foxbat-B" reconnaissance variant
107 Reconnaissance cameras, one vertical and four oblique
108 Sideways-looking airborne radar (SLAR) aperture
109 Ground mapping and Doppler radar antenna
110 "Jay-Bird" forward-looking radar

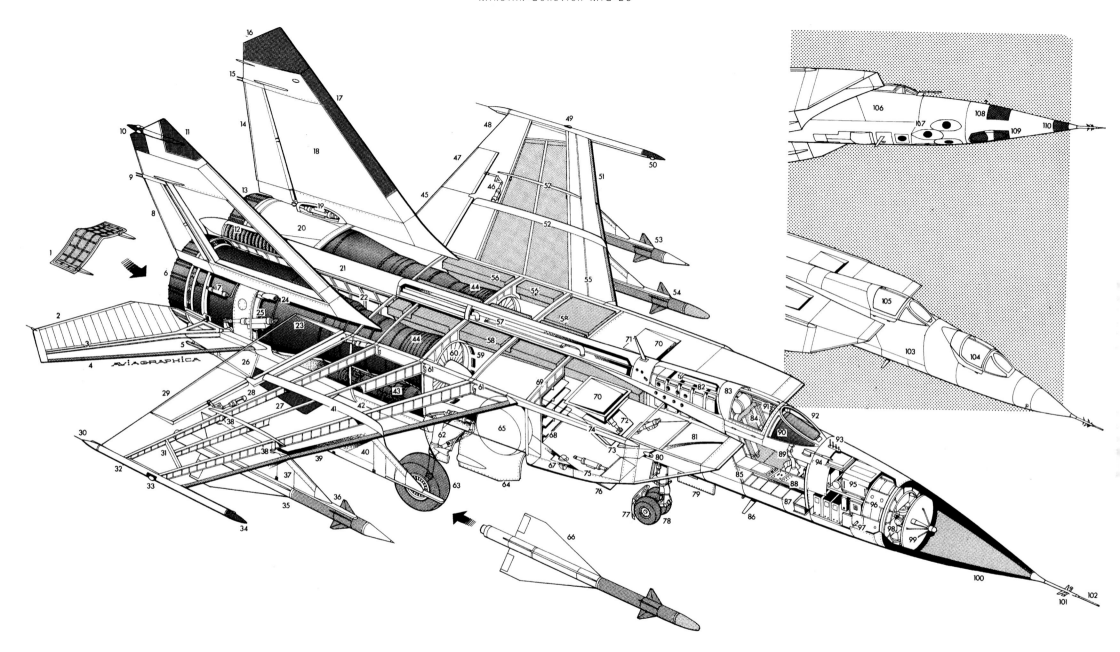

175

MIKOYAN MiG-29

LEFT: Given the NATO reporting name of Fulcrum, the MiG-29 first flew in October 1977, but it was October 1983 before it started to reach the operational units. A twin-engined agile counter-air fighter, it surprised the West.

The MiG-29, given the NATO reporting name "Fulcrum," was developed during the 1970s to fulfill a perceived requirement for a light, highly agile air combat fighter to counter the American F-16 and F-18. It had a number of unusual features, and there were problems with the twin engines and other aspects, such that this single-seater took 19 prototypes, the first of which flew on October 6, 1977, to bring it to the point where production could begin. Operational units did not start to receive aircraft until June 1983, mass-production having begun the previous year.

Construction was mainly from steel and aluminum/lithium, with limited use of composites. The wings were moderately swept at 42 degrees, and there were large leading edge extensions. The leading edges had three-piece computer-controlled maneuver flaps, and trailing edges had slotted flaps inboard and ailerons outboard. There were twin outwardly canted fins, and stabilators were carried on booms outside the engine nacelles. The view from the cockpit was much better than from previous MiG fighters, although the cockpit displays were old-fashioned instrumentation and the flight-control system was hydraulic.

The widely spaced engines were "straight-through" from variable-geometry inlets to nozzles, and were carried in underslung nacelles. One of the unusual features was that the top-hinged perforated inlet doors closed while the aircraft was on the ground, with air being drawn through overwing louvered vents. Apparently this was to prevent ingestion of ice and stones when operating from semi-prepared runways, but the doors could also be closed in flight at speeds up to almost 500mph.

The fire-control system was sophisticated. An IRST featured a laser ranger, providing accurate tracking for the 30mm cannon. The IRST was also linked to the complex Phazotron multi-mode radar, so that if the IRST "lost" the target, the Phazotron took over automatically. Originally, air-to-air armament consisted of six R-60 missiles or two medium-range R-27Rs and four R-60s, but later the agile R-73 replaced the R-60, aided by a helmet-mounted sight for launching at high off-boresight angles.

There have been a number of upgrades, and variants of the type have been exported widely, such that about 25 air arms around the world now fly the Fulcrum. A conversion trainer version, the MiG-29UB, had a cockpit extended forward, displacing the radar, leaving the aircraft with only marginal combat capability. The MiG-29S/SE, flown on December 23, 1980, was the first upgrade, featuring an enlarged dorsal spine carrying extra fuel and avionics, two hardpoints plumbed for external drop tanks, and a more advanced and effective radar compatible with later air-to-air missiles.

The up-engined MiG-29M, first flown on April 25, 1986, was extensively redesigned internally, with analog fly-by-wire system, more fuel capacity, and mesh guards to replace the inlet blanks of earlier models. Externally, differences included modified wing with a new aerofoil section, larger horizontal tails, and a raised cockpit for improved all-round view. This variant did not enter service but did form the basis of other types, including the navalized MiG-29K carrier fighter, whose changes included a strengthened structure and landing gear, folding wings, tail hook, and retractable refueling probe.

The MiG-29SM is similar to the MiG-29S/SE, but with extended air-to-surface capabilities and weapons that include bombs and anti-radiation missiles. The MiG-29SMT has been equipped with a modern "glass cockpit," has more internal fuel, and is more maneuverable than earlier models.

Specifications for Mikoyan MiG-29SM

Dimensions:	wingspan 37 feet 3.2 inches, length 56 feet 10 inches, height 15 feet 6.25 inches
Power:	two Klimov RD-33K twin-spool, axial-flow afterburning turbofans each rated at 19,400lb max and 12,125lb military thrust
Weights:	empty 24,030lb, normal takeoff with six air-to-air missiles 34,392lb, max 44,092lb
Speed:	max Mach 2.30/1,518mph at 39,370 feet, Mach 1.06/808mph at sea level
Ceiling:	55,775 feet
Range:	932 miles
Armament:	one 30mm GSh-30-1 single-barrel cannon with 100 rounds, plus typically six R-77 and four R-73 or R-60 air-to-air missiles
Crew:	pilot

MiG-29 "Fulcrum-A" cutaway key

1 Pitot head
2 Vortex generating nose strake
3 Glass-fiber radome
4 Pulse-Doppler radar scanner
5 Scanner tracking mechanism
6 N-019 (NATO: "Slot Back") radar equipment module
7 Angle-of-attack transmitter
8 ILS aerial fairing
9 SRO-2 (NATO: "Odd Rods") IFF aerial
10 UHF antenna
11 Forward avionics equipment bay
12 Infra-red search and track sensor and laser ranger
13 Dynamic pressure probe
14 Frameless windscreen panel
15 Pilot's head-up-display
16 Instrument panel shroud
17 Rudder pedals and control column
18 Fuselage blended chine fairing
19 Cannon muzzle aperture
20 Cannon barrel
21 Slide-mounted engine throttle levers
22 Canopy latch
23 K-36D "zero-zero" ejection seat
24 Upward-hingeing cockpit canopy cover
25 Electrical distribution centre
26 Cockpit rear pressure bulkhead
27 Cannon bay venting air louvers
28 Nosewheel retraction jack
29 Levered suspension nosewheel leg
30 Twin nosewheels, aft retracting
31 Mudguard
32 ECM aerial panels
33 Cartridge case and link collector box
34 Ammunition magazine
35 Center avionics equipment bay
36 Canopy hinge point
37 Canopy hydraulic jack
38 HF aerial
39 Mechanical control rods
40 Rear avionics equipment bay
41 Air intake louvers/blow-in doors
42 Variable area intake ramp doors
43 Ramp hydraulic actuator
44 Port engine air intake
45 Weapons interlock access
46 Landing lamp
47 Mainwheel door
48 Forward fuselage integral fuel tank
49 Port main undercarriage wheel bay
50 Flight control system hydraulic equipment module
51 ADF aerial
52 Starboard main undercarriage wheel bay
53 Chaff/flare cartridge housing
54 Starboard wing integral fuel tank
55 Starboard wing missile carriage
56 Leading edge manoeuvre flap
57 Starboard navigation light
58 Radar warning antenna
59 Starboard aileron
60 Plain flap
61 Flap hydraulic jack
62 Center fuselage integral fuel tank
63 Engine compressor face
64 Cooling air scoop
65 Top-mounted engine accessory equipment gear boxes
66 Central gas turbine starter/APU
67 Engine bay/tailplane attachment machined main frames
68 Airbrake hydraulic jack
69 RD-33D afterburning turbofan engine
70 Fin rib construction
71 Carbon fiber fin skin panelling
72 Fin tip VHF aerial fairing
73 Radar warning antenna
74 "Swift Rod" ILS aerial
75 Starboard rudder
76 Rudder hydraulic actuator
77 Tailplane hydraulic actuator
78 Starboard all-moving tailplane
79 Airbrake, upper and lower split surfaces
80 Brake parachute housing
81 Variable area afterburner nozzle
82 Port tailfin
83 Tail navigation light
84 Sirena-3 ECM aerial fairing
85 Static discharger
86 Port rudder composite construction
87 Port all-moving tailplane
88 Static dischargers
89 Carbon fibre trailing edge skin paneling
90 Tailplane spar box construction
91 Tailplane pivot point
92 Fuselage side-body fairing construction
93 Artificial feel system pitot heads and control valves
94 Port plain flap composite construction
95 Main undercarriage hydraulic retraction jack
96 Port chaff/flare cartridge
97 Main undercarriage leg pivot fixing
98 Pylon attachment hardpoints
99 Flap hydraulic jack
100 Port wing integral fuel tank
101 Aileron hydraulic actuator
102 Port aileron composite construction
103 Carbon fiber skin panelling
104 Static dischargers
107 Downward identification light and remote compass housing
108 Outer wing panel rib construction
109 Port leading edge maneuver flap
110 Port wing missile pylons
111 Leading edge flap hydraulic jacks
112 Port mainwheel
113 Main undercarriage leg strut
114 Three-spar wing torsion box construction
115 Spar root attachment joints
116 Undercarriage bay pressure refueling connection
117 AA-10 "Alamo" long-range air-to-air missile
118 AA-11 "Archer" intermediate-range air-to-air missile
119 AA-8 "Aphid" short-range air-to-air missile
120 57mm rocket pack
121 Cluster bomb
122 Wing-mounted external fuel tank
123 Tank pylon
124 Center fuselage "tunnel" fuel tank
125 Tank pylon attachment

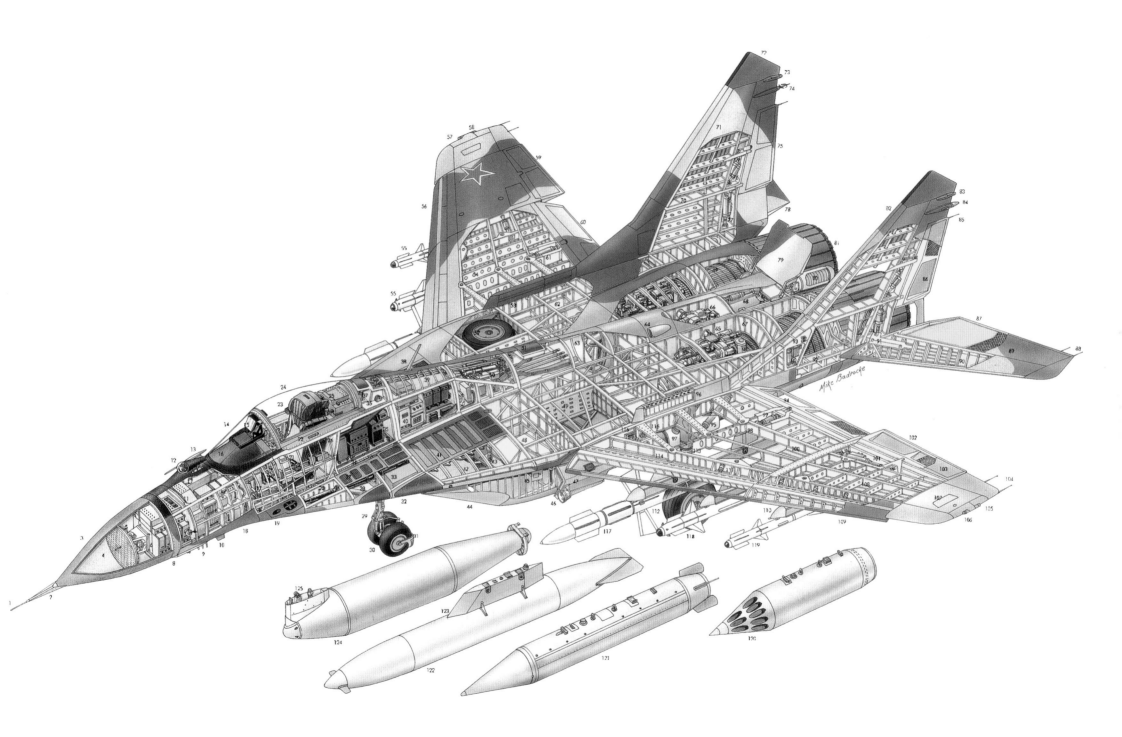

ABOVE: Fulcrum made its Farnborough Air Show debut in 1988. Its layout, with widely spaced turbofans, twin fins, and large leading edge root extensions to a moderately swept, medium aspect ratio wing, aroused a great deal of speculation.

RIGHT: Louvered doors above the intakes, seen here in the closed position, allowed the main intakes to be blanked off at low speeds. Despite rumors that this was a stealth measure, it was actually to prevent foreign object damage.

OPPOSITE: The wide spacing of the Klimov afterburning turbofans gives a "straight-through" line, minimizing the possibility of disturbed airflow. Between the engines can be seen the braking parachute door fairing.

ABOVE: Offset to the right, the IRST/laser ranger is an integral part of the weapons system, and reportedly allows exceptionally accurate shooting with the single 30mm GSh-30-1 cannon mounted in the port wing root.

RIGHT: Since its first appearance, Fulcrum has undergone a process of continuous development. This is the MiG-29SM, with more powerful turbofans, fly-by-wire, "glass" cockpit displays, and a better weapons system.

OPPOSITE: The unification of Germany saw twenty-three MiG-29As of the former East German *Luftstreitkräfte* absorbed by the West German *Luftwaffe*, in whose colors they are seen here. This allowed extensive evaluation against Western fighters.

OPPOSITE INSET: Air-to-air armament carried by this MiG-29A consists of two R-27R-1 medium range radar homing and four R-77 short range dogfight missiles. Fulcrum's air combat record is poor: twelve losses for no victories.

MITSUBISHI A6M ZERO-SEN

LEFT: The Mitsubishi A6M2 Rei-Sen carrier fighter, known to the Allies as the Zeke or Zero, became legendary in the Pacific. Its ability to turn on a dime made it a formidable opponent in a dogfight, while drop tanks extended its endurance.

In 1940 the Japanese sent fifteen of their new single-seat, single-engined A6M Zero fighter to China for trials under operational conditions, and it eliminated all opposition. Although reports of this and its performance had been reported to Washington by General Claire Chennault, commander of the Flying Tigers volunteer force in China, this most famous of all Japanese combat aircraft appeared to come as a complete surprise to U.S. and British planners when war erupted in the Pacific. The first American pilots to encounter the legendary Zero were impressed by its outstanding maneuverability, which at normal combat speeds far outclassed that of their own fighters. Only later did they realize that the Japanese pilots paid a high price for this.

While the Zero had been stressed for the usual combat maneuvers, it had been lightened by leaving off everything regarded as non-essential. This included armor protection, self-sealing fuel tanks, and even the radio. As a direct result the Zero was very vulnerable, and could sustain little battle damage. Another failing was that as speed increased, rate of roll became progressively slower. The Zero was progressively upgraded throughout the war but, failing to keep pace with American fighter developments, was shot from the skies.

Setting out a 1937 specification for a successor to the agile but lightly armed A5M carrier fighter, the Imperial Japanese Navy wanted a faster, longer-ranged, better-climbing, more powerfully armed, and even more maneuverable warplane than any previous fighter. Mitsubishi designers came up with a low-wing cantilever monoplane layout, with retractable wide-set landing gear and enclosed cockpit. Following various prototype testing, the design evolved as a production version accepted as the A6M2 in 1940, the Japanese year 5700, and it became popularly the Zero-Sen, officially codenamed "Zeke" by the Allies. In addition to those sent to China, 48 series aircraft were delivered as the Type 0 Carrier Fighter Model 11.

The design was the subject of continual modifications prior to acceptance and throughout the war. Its radial engines varied: Mitsubishi Zuisei 13 of 875hp on the first two prototypes (A6M1s); a 950hp Nakajima Sakae 12 on the third (A6M2); a 1,130hp Sakei 21 on the A6M3 and A6M5; Sakei 31 on the A6M6 and A6M7, with water/methanol boosting to produce 1,210hp for short periods.

Manually folding wingtips were introduced as the sub-type Model 21 from the 68th aircraft, and 740 of these were built. In 1941 the A6M3 was flown, with folding wingtips discarded, reducing the span by about 39 inches;

343 were built as Model 32s, and then the folding wingtips were reinstated, production continuing as the Model 22.

The Zero was obsolescent by 1943, and was being outclassed by American F4U and F6F fighters flown by pilots who had adopted tactics for dealing with its tight turning and other capabilities, and were exposing its weaknesses: poor performance at high altitude, stiffening ailerons and therefore reduced maneuverability above 205mph, vibration in a prolonged dive – and lack of armor.

The Japanese had no replacement ready, so upgrades of the Type 0 were developed. The A6M5 was built in quantities far greater than any other Japanese warplane, with the Model 52 given more thrust, a revised wing with the reduced span of the A6M3 but rounded rather than cropped, heavier-gauge duralium skinning, armor protection for the pilot, self-sealing tank behind the pilot, and better armament. Speed and dive performance were improved. The A6M6 had a more powerful engine with water-methanol injection, which also powered the A6M7 fighter-bomber, the last production model.

Total production reached over 10,930 of all sub-types, many of which were converted for suicide attacks on Allied forces.

Specifications for Mitsubishi A6M2 Rei-Sen

Dimensions: wingspan 39 feet 4.5 inches, length 29 feet 8.5 inches, height 10 feet

Power: one Nakajima NK1C Sakei 12 14-cylinder twin-row radial engine rated at 950hp at 13,780 feet

Weights: empty 3,704lb, normal takeoff 5,313lb, max 6,164lb

Speed: max 331mph at 14,230 feet

Ceiling: 32,810 feet

Range: 1,162 miles

Armament: two 20mm wing-mounted, drum-fed Type 99 cannon with 60 rounds per gun and two 7.7mm nose-mounted Type 97 synchronized machine guns with 500 rounds per gun

Crew: pilot

A6M2 Rei-Sen cutaway key

1 Tail navigation light
2 Tail cone
3 Tailfin fixed section
4 Rudder lower brace
5 Rudder tab (ground adjustable)
6 Fabric-covered rudder
7 Rudder hinge
8 Rudder post
9 Rudder upper hinge
10 Rudder control horn (welded to torque tube)
11 Aerial attachment
12 Tailfin leading edge
13 Forward spar
14 Tailfin structure
15 Tailfin nose ribs
16 Port elevator
17 Port tailplane
18 Piano-hinge join
19 Fuselage dorsal skinning
20 Control turnbuckles
21 Arrester hook release/retract steel cable runs
22 Fuselage frame/tailplane center brace
23 Tailplane attachments
24 Elevator cables
25 Elevator control horns/torque tube
26 Rudder control horns
27 Tailwheel combined retraction/shock strut
28 Elevator trim tab
29 Tailwheel leg fairing
30 Castored tailwheel
31 Elevator frame (fabric-covered)
32 Elevator outer hinge
33 Tailplane structure
34 Forward spar
35 Elevator trim tab control rod (chain-driven)
36 Fuselage flotation bag rear wall
37 Arrester hook (extended)
38 Arrester hook pivot mounting
39 Elevator trim tab cable guide
40 Fuselage skinning
41 Fuselage frame stations
42 Arrester hook position indicator cable (duralumin tube)
43 Elevator cables
44 Rudder cables
45 Trim tab cable runs
46 Arrester hook pulley guide
47 Fuselage stringers
48 Fuselage flotation bag front
49 Fuselage construction join
50 Wingroot fillet formers
51 Compressed air cylinder (wing gun charging)
52 Transformer

53 "Ku" type radio receiver
54 Oxygen cylinder (starboard) carbon dioxide fire extinguisher cylinder (port)
55 Battery
56 Radio tray support
57 Radio transmitter
58 Canopy/fuselage fairing
59 Aerial mast support/lead-in
60 Aerial
61 Aerial mast (forward raked)
62 Canopy aft fixed section
63 Aluminum and plywood canopy frame
64 Crash bulkhead/headrest support
65 "Ku"-type D/F frame antenna mounting (late models)
66 Canopy track
67 Turnover truss
68 Pilot's seat support frame
69 Starboard elevator control bell crank
70 Aileron control push-pull rod
71 Wing rear spar/fuselage attachment
72 Fuselage aft main double frame
73 Aileron linkage
74 Landing-gear selector lever
75 Flap selector lever
76 Seat adjustment lever
77 Pilot's seat
78 Cockpit canopy rail
79 Seat support rail
80 Elevator tab trim handwheel
81 Fuel gauge controls
82 Throttle quadrant
83 Reflector gunsight mounting (offset to starboard)
84 Sliding canopy
85 Plexiglas panels
86 Canopy lock/release
87 Windscreen
88 Fuselage starboard 0.303in (7.7mm) machine gun
89 Control column
90 Radio control box
91 Radio tuner
92 Elevator control linkage
93 Rudder pedal bar assembly
94 Cockpit underfloor fuel
95 Wing front spar/ fuselage attachment

96 Fuselage forward main double frame
97 Ammunition magazine
98 Ammunition feed
99 Blast tube
100 Cooling louvers
101 Fuselage fuel tank, capacity 40.8 gallons
102 Firewall bulkhead
103 Engine bearer lower attachment
104 Engine bearer upper attachment
105 Oil tank, capacity 15.24 gallons
106 Bearer support struts
107 Cooling gill adjustment control
108 Machine gun muzzle trough
109 Barrel fairing
110 Oil filler cap
111 Fuselage fuel tank filler cap
112 Port flap profile
113 Port fuselage machine gun
114 Port wing gun access panels
115 Port inner wing identification light
116 Port wing flotation bag inner wall
117 Wing spar joins
118 Aileron control rods
119 Port aileron (fabric covered)
120 Aileron tab (ground adjustable)
121 Aileron external counter-balance
122 Control linkage
123 Wing skinning
124 Port inner wing identification light
125 Port navigation light lead conduit
126 Wingtip hinge
127 Wing end rib
128 Port wing flotation bag outer wall
129 Wingtip structure
130 Port wingtip (folded)
131 Port navigation light
132 Port wingtip hinge release catch
134 Wing leading-edge skinning
135 Wing front spar
136 Port wing gun muzzle
137 Port undercarriage visual indicator
138 Undercarriage hydraulics access
139 Nacelle gun troughs
140 Cooling gills
141 Fuselage gun synchronization cable
142 Bearer support strut assembly
143 Carburetor

144 Exhaust manifold
145 Cowling panel fastener clips
146 950 hp Nakajima Sakae 12 radial engine
147 Cowling inner ring profile
148 Cowling nose ring
149 Three-bladed propeller
150 Spinner
151 Propeller gears
152 Hub
153 Carburetor intake
154 Port main wheel
155 Oil cooler intake
156 Exhaust outlet
157 Starboard mainwheel inner door fairing
158 Engine bearer support brace
159 Oil cooler
160 Wingroot fasteners
161 Starboard mainwheel well
162 Front auxiliary spar cutouts
163 Auxiliary fuel tank
165 Intake trunking
166 Front main spar
167 Starboard wing fuel tank,
capacity 51.6 gallons
168 Fuel filler cap
169 Rear main spar
170 Flap actuating
cylinder
171 Access cover
172 Starboard flap structure
173 Starboard inner wing identification light
174 Starboard wing 20mm cannon
175 Access panels
176 Ammunition magazine (underwing loading)
177 Landing gear hydraulic retraction jack
178 Hydraulic lines
179 Starboard undercarriage visual indicator
180 Landing gear pivot axis
181 Undercarriage/spar mounting
182 Starboard wing gun muzzle
183 Starboard undercarriage leg
184 Oleo travel
185 Welded steel wheel fork
186 Wheel uplock latch
187 Starboard mainwheel
188 Wheel door fairing ball and swivel closure
189 Mainwheel door fairing
190 Axle hub
191 Access plate
192 Hinge
193 Left fairing attachments
194 Brake line
195 Leg fairing
196 Leg fairing upperflap
197 Wing gun barrel support collar
198 Wing nose ribs
199 Cartridge ejection chute
200 Wing spar joins
201 Wing outer structure
202 Front spar outer section
203 Inter-spar ribs
204 Rear spar outer section
205 Aileron control access
206 Aileron (ground adjustable)
207 Starboard aileron frame

208 Aileron external counter balance
209 Control linkage
210 Starboard wingtip (folded)
211 Starboard outerwing identification light
212 Aileron outer hinge
213 Starboard wing flotation bag outer wall
214 Wing end rib
215 Starboard wingtip hinge release catch
216 Wingtip structure
217 Starboard navigation light

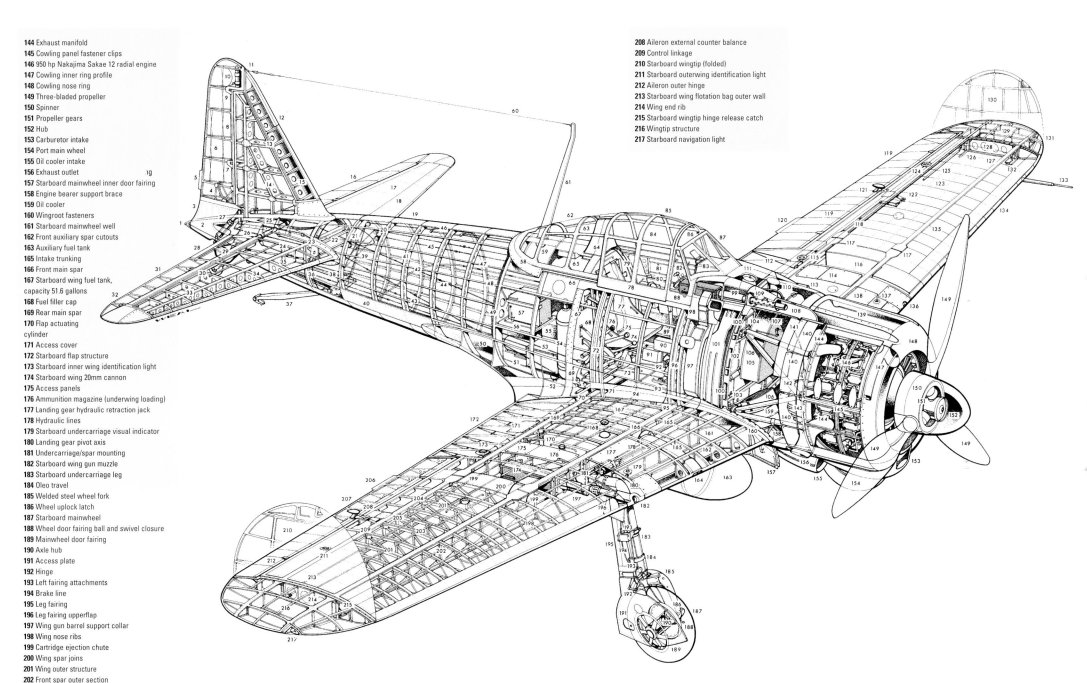

183

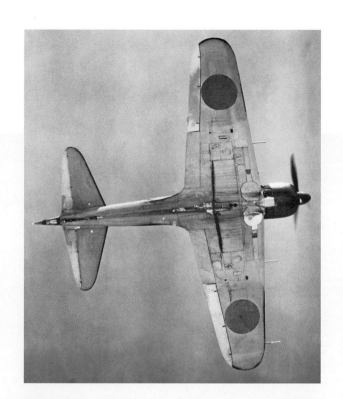

Opposite inset left: False colors! This captured Zero was given U.S. markings while being evaluated against U.S. fighters. These were then crudely overpainted with Japanese "meatballs" for aircraft recognition photographs, of which this is one.

Opposite inset right: The A6M5 Model 52 Zero, which was introduced from late 1943. In an attempt to improve rate of roll, this variant had a reduced wingspan. Unlike former models, it had bullet-proof glass, armor protection, and fire extinguishers.

Opposite: The Zero had been designed for maneuverability above all else. To save weight, self-sealing fuel tanks, armor protection, fire extinguishers, even radios, were all left off. Early Zeros could survive very little battle damage.

This page: Shot down over the Aleutians, this Zero was recovered and restored to flying condition by the U.S. Navy. Combat trials revealed weaknesses that could be exploited, including a sluggish rate of roll and poor handling in a steep dive.

NORTH AMERICAN F-86 SABRE

LEFT: First flown in October 1947, the North American F-86 Sabre was the first production fighter in the world to go supersonic, albeit in a dive. Over Korea, it gained an enviable reputation against Russian-built and -flown MiG-15s.

Armed with World War II German research into the aerodynamic advantages of swept wings for fighter aircraft, the North American Aviation company designed the single-seat, single-engined transonic F-86 Sabre with 35 degrees of wing sweep, flew the first prototype (XP-86) on October 1, 1947, and the first production model (F-86A) on May 18, 1948, thereby creating a legend. It entered service with the U.S. Air Force from February 1949, just weeks before its contemporary, the MiG-15, joined its Soviet units. The first flight of the F-86 had predated that of the similarly swept-wing MiG-15 by three months.

Like the Russian fighter, it had a nose inlet, although the horizontal tail surfaces were mounted rather lower. Overall, the Sabre was considerably larger and heavier, while its systems were considerably more sophisticated. Whereas the MiG carried a simple gyro gunsight, that of the Sabre had radar ranging, a considerable asset in combat. American flight control systems were also superior.

With a General Electric J47 axial-flow turbojet, the Sabre was underpowered, and its armament of six fast-firing 0.50 caliber Colt-Brownings, with 267 rounds per gun, giving over 13 seconds of firing time, was light compared with that of the MiG-15, but the American fighter was a far more stable gun platform, especially at very high speeds. Its rate of roll was faster at all speeds and altitudes, enabling the Sabre to change direction faster, and its general handling was vice-free, so that it could be flown to its absolute limit. In a dive it could exceed Mach 1 with little difficulty, becoming the first production fighter capable of attaining supersonic speed in a dive.

When the Russian-built and -flown MiG-15 was committed to the Korean conflict USAF sent the F-86A to counter it. It was quick to achieve success. The first victory of one swept-wing jet over another came on December 17, 1950, when a Sabre downed a MiG-15. It was the first of hundreds. At the armistice in July 1953, USAF Sabres claimed a victory/loss ratio of 14 to 1, but this was officially amended to 7.5 to 1, the actual figures being 757 victories to 103 losses.

The Sabre was the subject of continual development, there being more than a dozen major model changes, adaptation for five different turbojets, versions being license-built in four countries, and more than 25 nations flying the type. The F-86 was the first swept-wing design to serve with NATO forces.

Manufacture continued for 13 years until February 1961, by which time the total reached 8,732 land-based Sabres, and 1,112 navalized versions (FJ-2, -3, and -4 Fury

carrier fighters) with beefed-up landing gear, wing folding, and arrester hook for service with the U.S. Navy and Marine Corps. The Canadian-built Sabres (1,815 made by Canadair) mostly had home-grown Orenda turbojets rated at 6,355lb or 7,275lb compared with 5,200lb for the U.S. machines, and the Australian version had the British Avon engine of even greater power, as well as two 30mm cannon.

When air-to-air missiles were first used in combat on September 14, 1958, it was by Taiwan-based Chinese Nationalist F-86F Sabres which clashed with PRC MiG-15s over Qemoy and Matsu Islands. They claimed 10 MiGs shot down, four with Sidewinders.

The F-86F had four pylons and so could undertake long-range attack missions with drop tanks and two 1,000lb bombs. The F-86D, the fastest of the Sabre family, and armed with rockets instead of guns, was fitted with an advanced target-finding and tracking collision-course system. German and Italian companies collaborated to build an F-86D variant, the F-87K, armed with four 20mm cannon. Later, all these all-weather Sabres were also given Sidewinder heat-homing missiles, and served with many air forces.

Specifications for North American F-86F Sabre

Dimensions:	wingspan 39 feet 1.5 inches, length 37 feet 6.5 inches, height 14 feet 9 inches
Power:	one General Electric J47-27 single-spool, axial-flow turbojet rated at 5,910lb thrust
Weights:	empty 11,125lb, normal takeoff 15,198lb, max 20,611lb
Speed:	max 678mph at sea level, 599mph at 35,000 feet
Ceiling:	47,000 feet
Range:	785 miles, 926 miles with drop tanks
Armament:	six 0.50in nose-mounted Browning M-3 machine guns with 300 rounds per gun, two 1,000lb bombs or eight 5in rockets carried underwing
Crew:	pilot

F-86E Sabre cutaway key

1 Radome
2 Radar antenna
3 Engine air intake
4 Gun camera
5 Nosewheel leg doors
6 Nose undercarriage leg strut
7 Nosewheel
8 Torque scissor links
9 Steering control valve
10 Nose undercarriage pivot fixing
11 Sight amplifier
12 Radio and electronics equipment bay
13 Electronics bay access panel
14 Battery
15 Gun muzzle blast troughs
16 Oxygen bottles
17 Nosewheel bay doors
18 Oxygen servicing point
19 Canopy switches
20 Machine gun barrel mountings
21 Hydraulic system test connections
22 Radio transmitter
23 Cockpit armored bulkhead
24 Windscreen panels
25 A-1CM radar gunsight
26 Instrument panel shroud
27 Instrument panel
28 Control column
29 Kick-in boarding step
30 Used cartridge case collector box
31 Ammunition boxes (267 rounds per gun)
32 Ammunition feed chutes
33 0.5in (12.7mm) Colt Browning machine guns
34 Engine throttle
35 Starboard side console panel
36 North American ejection seat
37 Rear view mirror
38 Sliding cockpit canopy cover
39 Ejection seat headrest
40 ADF sense aerials
41 Pilot's back armor
42 Ejection seat guide rails
43 Canopy handle
44 Cockpit pressure valves
45 Armored side panels
46 Tailplane trim actuator
47 Fuselage/front spar main frame
48 Forward fuselage fuel tank (total internal fuel capacity 435 gallons)
49 Fuselage lower longeron
50 Intake trunking
51 Rear radio and electronics bay

52 Canopy emergency release handle
53 ADF loop aerial
54 Cockpit pressure relief valve
55 Starboard wing fuel tank
56 Leading-edge slat guide rails
57 Starboard automatic leading-edge slat, open
58 Cable drive to aileron actuator
59 Pitot tube
60 Starboard navigation light
61 Wingtip fairing
62 Starboard aileron
63 Aileron hydraulic control unit
64 Aileron balance
65 Starboard slotted flap, down position
66 Flap guide rail
67 Upward identification light
68 Air conditioning plant
69 Intake fairing starter/generator
70 Fuselage/rear spar main frame
71 Hydraulic system reservoirs
72 Longeron/main frame joint
73 Fuel filter de-icing fluid tank
74 Cooling air outlet
75 Engine equipment access panel
76 Heat exchanger exhaust duct
77 Engine suspension links
78 Fuselage skin plating
79 Engine withdrawal rail
80 Starboard side oil tank
81 General Electric J47-GE-27 turbojet
82 Bleed air system primary heat exchanger
83 Ground power connections
84 Fuel filler cap
85 Fuselage break point sloping frame (engine removal)
86 Upper longeron joint
87 Engine bay air cooling duct
88 Cooling air outlet
89 Engine firewall bulkhead
90 Engine flame cans
91 Rear fuselage framing
92 Fuel jettison pipe
93 Fuselage top longeron
94 Fin/tailplane root fillet fairing
95 Control cable duct
96 Fin spar attachment joint

97 Tailplane/rudder control cables
98 All-moving tailplane hydraulic jack
99 Tailfin construction
100 Flush HF aerial panel
101 Starboard tailplane
102 Fintip dielectric aerial fairing
103 ADF aerial
104 Rudder construction
105 Rudder trim tab
106 Tail navigation light
107 Port elevator/ tailplane flap
108 All-moving tailplane construction
109 Engine exhaust nozzle
110 Fuel jettison pipe
111 Heat-shrouded jet pipe
112 Power control compensator
113 Emergency hydraulic valves
114 Airbrake housing
115 Airbrake hydraulic jack
116 Port airbrake (open)
117 Hydraulic system emergency pump
118 Cooling air intake
119 Lower longeron joint
120 Trailing-edge root fillet
121 Aft main fuel tank
122 Main undercarriage wheel bay
123 Hydraulic retraction jack
124 Main undercarriage pivot fixing
125 Hydraulic flap jack
126 Flap shroud ribs
127 Port slotted flaps
128 Port aileron construction
129 Aileron hydraulic power control unit
130 Gyro compass remote transmitter
131 Wingtip fairing
132 Port navigation light
133 Port automatic leading-edge slat, open position
134 Leading-edge slat rib construction
135 Front spar
136 Wing rib and stringer construction
137 Wing skin/leading-edge piano hinge attachment joint
138 120-gallon drop tank
139 Drop tank pylon
140 Port main wheel

141 Fuel filler cap
142 Main undercarriage leg strut
143 Fuel tank bay corrugated double skin
144 Port wing fuel tank
145 Tank interconnectors
146 Skin panel attachment joint strap
147 Slat guide rails
148 Fuel feeders
149 Aileron cable drive

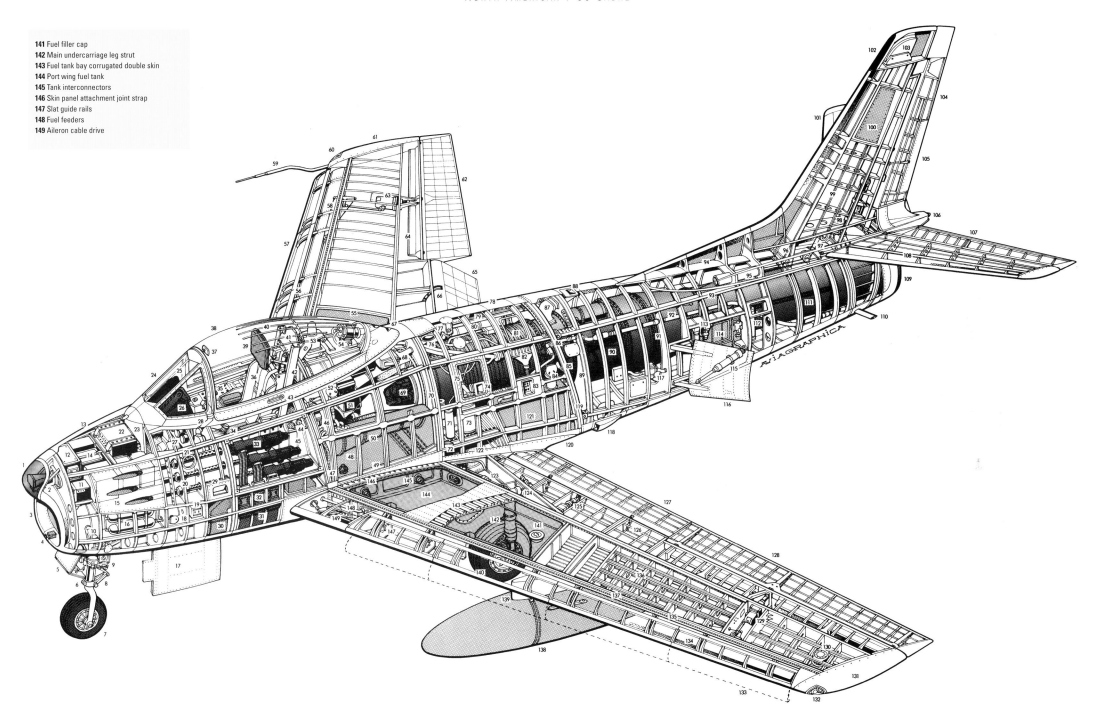

OPPOSITE: Developed in several variants, the Sabre was the mainstay of many air forces from the 1950s and beyond. Seen here with the almost obligatory underwing tanks is an F-86F of the Japanese Self Defense Force.

LEFT: Sabres served with no fewer than twenty-seven overseas air forces. This is a Royal Netherlands Air Force example, sporting a blue (practice) Sidewinder under the starboard fuselage, and an empty missile rail under the port wing.

INSET CENTER: An F-86D carrying out trials at Edwards AFB in 1954. The Dogship Sabre, as it was known, was a radar-equipped all weather fighter armed with a box of twenty-four folding fin aircraft rockets, but carrying no guns.

INSET LEFT: By the markings, this appears to be an Imperial Iranian Air Force F-86E. As this service is not listed as operating the type, it is possible that this particular aircraft was taking part in a North American sales pitch.

INSET RIGHT: In the 1950s, accident rates, in all air forces and on all fast jets, were on the high side. This led the USAF to adopt high visibility markings in day-glo red on the wings and tails of these F-86 Sabres.

RIGHT: The rocket armament of the F-86D Sabre was designed to give a high probability of knocking down a bomber with a collision course attack. Against enemy fighters, the system was next to useless.

OPPOSITE: While USAF Sabres were generally left in natural aluminum finish, those of other nations, including Canada and most European air forces, sported camouflage of various patterns, as seen here.

OPPOSITE INSET: Canadair license-built Sabres were designated CL-13, powered by the indigenous Avro Canada Orenda turbojet. The definitive model was the CL-13B, seen here, which in many ways was superior to the North American machine.

NORTH AMERICAN F-100 SUPER SABRE

LEFT: The world's first genuinely supersonic fighter to enter service, and the first of the American "Century" series was the North American F-100 Super Sabre, seen here launching an AGM-12 Bullpup missile.

The F-100 Super Sabre was the first supersonic fighter to enter service anywhere in the world. A single-seat, single-engined, swept-wing fighter, the first of the U.S. Air Force "Century" series and nicknamed "Hun," it exceeded the speed of sound on its maiden flight on May 25, 1953. It was an advanced offspring of the F-86 Sabre with more sweep (45 degrees), more fuel capacity, a 15,000lb afterburning engine, and four new guns. It could fly at more than 800mph, and later versions introduced underwing loads of offensive stores, an autopilot (later with toss-bomb capability for nuclear bombs) and flight refueling. There were over 2,290 built, hundreds serving with NATO and other air forces, as well as with the USAF, and their versatility gave them a leading role during the Vietnam War, where it did well in ground attack as well as flying top cover as a fighter.

During design development, to avoid a problem of wing-twisting by aileron movement at transonic speeds, large two-piece ailerons were mounted inboard. There were no flaps, and the only lift devices were full-span automatic leading edge slats. The shape continued to evolve even after production aircraft were ordered. The original plain nose intake was made wider and flatter, the canopy was made longer and was faired into a dorsal spine, and the all-moving slab tailplane was repositioned at the bottom of the rear fuselage.

The avionics equipment was somewhat crude, not much more than a ranging gunsight similar to that used on the predecessor, the F-86. The main armament comprised four 20mm Pontiac M-39 fast-firing revolver cannon set under the cockpit, and if truth be told the F-100's greatest failing as a fighter was its all-gun armament.

Before the full flight test program had been completed the Hun was rushed into service, even though Air Force project pilot Pete Everest had warned of certain handling problems. This proved almost a portent of disaster, which occurred on October 12, 1954 – just two weeks after the fighter's service entry – when the last, and most demanding, structural test (a 7.5g pull out at maximum indicated air speed) resulted in the aircraft breaking up and killing the test pilot. The F-100A was grounded while extensive modifications were made to overcome the cause of the problem: overstressing its yaw design limits. Directional stability was improved by increasing the span by almost two feet, and wing area was increased, as was the height of the fin.

Whereas the F-100A had been designed as an air superiority fighter, the next variant to go into production could double as a fighter-bomber, the F-100C. It had substantially increased fuel capacity, particularly in the wings, an enlarged vertical tail, and a more powerful engine. This flew on January 17, 1955. It kept the four cannon armament, but six underwing stores were added for bombs and rockets.

The F-100C was a dual role aircraft, but the F-100D, first flown January 24, 1956, was dedicated to the fighter-bomber mission. It had the same wing stores stations and gun armament, but was slightly longer than the C and had increased wing and tail surface area, inboard landing flaps, and improved avionics. About a year later there followed the F-100F, a tandem two-seat version, some aircraft of which acted as combat proficiency trainers while others were fitted out with electronic gear and flew "Wild Weasel" defense suppression missions over North Vietnam between November 1965 and May 1966. They were later used as fast forward air controllers, although all USAF F-100s were withdrawn from front line service in 1972. Denmark, France Taiwan and Turkey also flew versions of the Super Sabre.

Specifications for North American F-100A Super Sabre

Dimensions: wingspan 38 feet 9.5 inches, length 47 feet 0.75 inches, height 15 feet 4 inches

Power: one Pratt & Whitney J57-P-7 twin-spool, axial-flow afterburning turbojet rated at 14,800lb max and 9,700lb military thrust

Weights: empty 19,270lb, normal takeoff 27,587lb

Speed: max Mach 1.26/830mph at 35,000 feet, Mach 1.01/770mph at sea level

Ceiling: 48,000 feet

Range: 572 miles, 926 miles with drop tanks

Armament: four fuselage-mounted 20mm Pontiac M-39 cannon with 200 rounds per gun, plus air-to-surface stores

Crew: pilot

F-100D Super Sabre cutaway key

1 Pitot tube, folded for ground handling
2 Engine air intake
3 Pitot tube hinge point
4 Radome
5 IFF aerial
6 AN/APR-25(V) gun tracking radar
7 Intake bleed air electronics cooling duct
8 Intake duct framing
9 Cooling air exhaust duct
10 Cannon muzzle port
11 UHF aerial
12 Nose avionics compartment
13 Hinged nose compartment access door
14 Inflight refueling probe
15 Windscreen panels
16 A-4 radar gunsight
17 Instrument panel shroud
18 Cockpit front pressure bulkhead
19 Rudder pedals
20 Gunsight power supply
21 Armament relay panel
22 Intake ducting
23 Cockpit canopy emergency operating controls
24 Nosewheel leg door
25 Torque scissors
26 Twin nosewheels
27 Nose undercarriage leg strut
28 Pontiac M39 20mm cannon (four)
29 Kick-in boarding steps
30 Ejection seat footrests
31 Instrument panel
32 Engine throttle
33 Canopy external handle
34 Starboard side console panel
35 Ejection seat
36 Headrest
37 Cockpit canopy cover
38 Ejection seat guide rails
39 Cockpit rear pressure bulkhead
40 Port side console panel
41 Cockpit floor level
42 Control cable runs
43 Gun bay access panel
44 Ammunition feed chutes
45 Ammunition tanks, 200 rpg
46 Power supply amplifier
47 Rear electrical and electronics bay
48 Cockpit pressurisation valve
49 Anti-collision light
50 Air-conditioning plant
51 Radio compass aerial
52 Intake bleed air heat exchanger

53 Heat exchanger exhaust duct
54 Secondary air turbine
55 Air turbine exhaust duct (open)
56 Starboard wing integral fuel tank, capacity 208.8 gallons
57 Starboard automatic leading-edge slat, open
58 Slat guide rails
59 Wing fence
60 Starboard navigation light
61 Wingtip faring
62 Fixed portion of trailing edge
63 Starboard aileron
64 Aileron hydraulic jack
65 Starboard outer plain flap
66 Flap hydraulic jack
67 UHF aerial
68 Engine intake centerbody
69 Wing attachment fuselage main frames
70 Fuselage fuel tanks, total internal capacity 769.2 gallons
71 Wing spar center section carry through beams
72 Engine intake compressor face
73 Main engine mounting
74 Pratt & Whitney J57-P-21A afterburning turbojet engine
75 Dorsal spine fairing
76 Fuel vent pipe
77 Engine oil tank
78 Fuselage upper longeron
79 Engine accessory gearbox
80 Compressor bleed air blow off valve
81 Fuselage break point
82 Rear fuselage attachment bolts (four)
83 Finroot filet
84 Engine turbine section
85 Engine rear mounting ring
86 Afterburner fuel spray manifold
87 Fin attachment sloping frame
88 Rudder hydraulic jack
89 Fin sub attachment joint
90 Tailfin construction
91 Fin leading edge
92 Fintip aerial fairing
93 Upper UHF aerial
94 Fixed portion of trailing edge
95 AN/APR-26(V) radar warning antenna

96 Tail navigation light
97 Fuel jettison pipe
98 Rudder construction
99 Rudder trim control jack
100 Externally braced trailing-edge section
101 Brake parachute cable fixing
102 Variable-area afterburner exhaust nozzle
103 Parachute cable "pull-out" flaps
104 Afterburner nozzle control jacks
105 Brake parachute housing
106 Port all-moving tailplane
107 Tailplane spar box construction
108 Pivot fixing
109 Tailplane mounting fuselage double frames
110 Engine afterburner duct
111 Tailplane hydraulic jack
112 Fuselage lower longeron
113 Rear fuselage fuel tank
114 Port inner plain flap
115 Flap rib construction
116 Main undercarriage wheel bay
117 Undercarriage leg pivot fixing
118 Flap hydraulic jack
119 Flap interconnecting linkage
120 Port outer flap
121 Flap hydraulic jack
122 Aileron jack
123 Wing fence
124 Port aileron
125 Fixed portion of trailing edge
126 Wingtip fairing
127 Port navigation light
128 Compass master transmitter
129 750lb (340kg) M117 HE bomb
130 SUU-7A CBU 19-round rocket pod and bomblet dispenser
131 Outboard wing pylon
132 Leading-edge slat rib construction
133 Hinged leading-edge attachment joint
134 Outboard pylon fixing
135 Wing rib construction
136 Rear spar
137 Port wing integral fuel tank, 208.8 gallons
138 Multi-spar inner wing panel construction
139 Center pylon fixing
140 Multi-plate disc brake
141 Port mainwheel

142 Main undercarriage leg strut
143 Undercarriage mounting rib
144 Front spar
145 Wing/fuselage attachment skin joint
146 Aileron cable control run
147 Inboard pylon
148 Airbrake hydraulic jacks (two)
149 Retractable landing/taxiing lamps, port and starboard
150 Ventral airbrake
151 199.8-galon napalm container
152 AGM-12C Bullpup B tactical missile
153 Center wing pylon
154 334.8-gallon air refuelable supersonic fuel tank
155 Tank side bracing strut

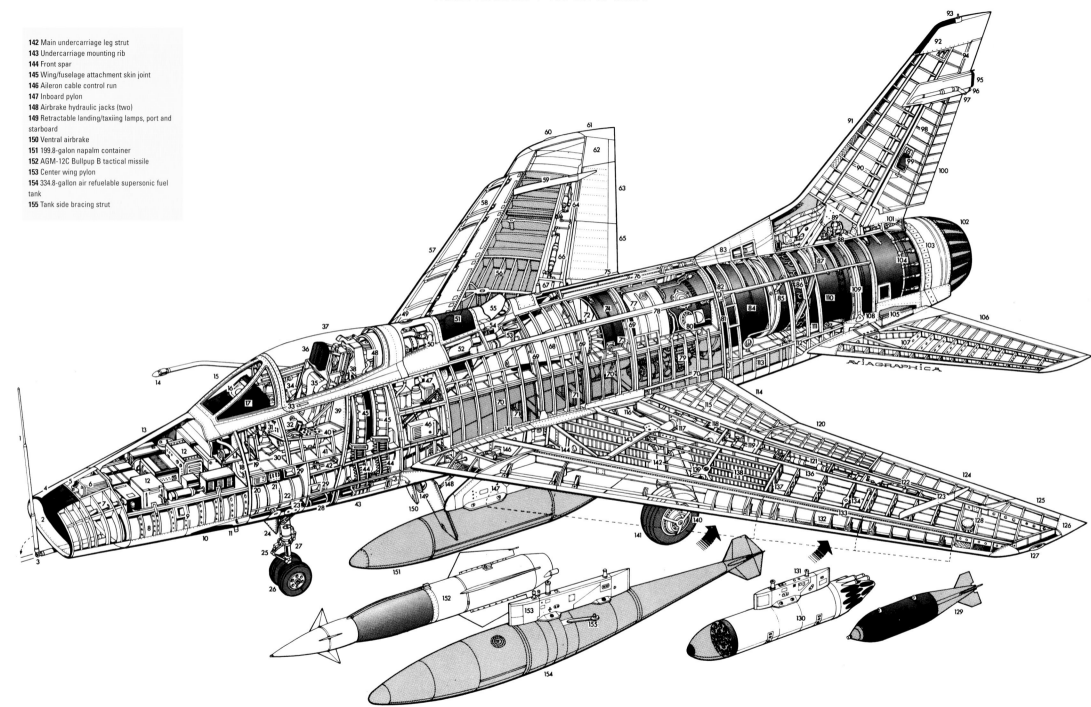

RIGHT INSET: Having failed as an escort fighter, the F-100D served in Vietnam with USAF's 35th Tactical Fighter Wing at Phan Rang until 1971. Here two F-100Ds stand alert, loaded and ready to take off when a target is located.

RIGHT MAIN PICTURE: First flown in May 1953, the "Hun," as the F-100 was widely known, had too many compromises to make an effective air superiority fighter. As a fighter-bomber, it was widely used in Southeast Asia.

OPPOSITE: The tail fin marks this aircraft as an F-100C dual role fighter and fighter-bomber, with a "wet" wing for increased fuel, an enlarged fin, and the more powerful J57-P-21 engine. In all, 476 F-100Cs were built.

OPPOSITE INSET: One of many experimental paint jobs tried on the Hun. A hot ship by reputation, it was generally popular with its pilots, and in Vietnam it was even used for dive bombing point targets at night.

NORTH AMERICAN P-51 MUSTANG

LEFT: The North American Mustang was a happy marriage of an American airframe and a British engine to make a superb fighter. This is a P-51D-5 of the 374th Fighter Squadron, of the 361st Fighter Group, in 1944.

Although it took just 122 days from initial concept to first flight of the prototype on October 26, 1940, the P-51 Mustang became arguably the best all-round, single-seat, piston-engined fighter of World War II, and the core of the most successful fighter program in history. Ultimately, some 15,586 P-51s of all variants were produced, more than 55 nations flew them, and some new and remanufactured versions were still in service beyond 1980.

Initially commissioned for Britain's RAF, this American fighter was at first powered by the Allison V-1710 engine. Aerodynamically very clean, with a low-drag laminar-flow wing, it lacked high altitude performance. Re-engined with the Rolls-Royce Merlin, it became the best long-range fighter of the war, able to escort American heavy bombers all the way from England to Berlin, and gradually establishing Allied air superiority over the heart of Germany.

The original P-51B was armed with just four 0.50-inch Brownings, and these often jammed during heavy maneuvering. The later P-51D, fitted with a tear-drop canopy to give a first-class all-round view, was slightly slower, but was armed with six heavy machine guns. In combat the Mustang was a match for any of its German or Japanese opponents, and it comfortably outranged them all.

The RAF received 820 Mustangs (a mix of I, IA and II variants) while the U.S. Army initially adopted 500 of the A-36A attack bomber version and 310 P-51A fighters. The first production Mustangs to reach Britain, with Allison engines, handled well, and were found to be faster at low and medium altitudes than the Spitfire VB, dived better, but had inferior rate of climb, did not turn as well, and were slower at altitude. The RAF decided not to use them in the air superiority role, but for low-level armed reconnaissance. However, once Rolls-Royce Merlin 61 engines were installed into the type in 1942, creating the P-51B, the bulged-hood C (Mustang III) and teardrop-canopy D (Mustang IV), the upgrade in performance was dramatic, with rate of climb almost doubling.

For the long-range bomber escort role, hundreds of the last P-51Bs and Cs were fitted with a large fuselage fuel tank, and with two drop tanks the type could protect bombers from England to Berlin. Such long-range missions posed problems, of course, including tricky handling with full fuel load, engine overheating, even structural failure in a high-speed dive as ammunition bay doors sometimes bulged and distorted the wing. But, when everything worked well, the P-51B proved faster than the Luftwaffe's Fw 190A and Bf 109G, was better in the turn, had equal rate of climb, and could out-dive both.

The P-51D, with its one-piece, sliding, teardrop, all-round-vision canopy, and cut-down rear fuselage to accommodate this, is regarded as the definitive Mustang, many of which saw extensive service in the Pacific Theater from the end of 1944, and from April 7, 1945, were flying long and exhausting escort missions to Japan, some being 1,500 mile return trips lasting often eight hours.

Later Mustang versions were built, including the P-51H with longer fuselage, taller fin, and more powerful engine that made it the fastest propeller-driven fighter of the war. A further development was the Twin Mustang created by mating two P-51H fuselages to a central wing to produce a two-seat, twin-engined escort fighter which saw service after the war with the U.S. Air Force as the F-82E escort fighter and F-82F and F-82G all-weather night fighters.

After World War II Mustangs were gradually replaced in U.S. service by jet fighters, although they served well as fighter-bombers in the Korean War, and in other conflicts such as with Israel (War of Independence, 1948) and El Salvador (in the so-called "World Cup War" of 1969).

Specifications for North American P-51D

Dimensions: wingspan 37 feet, length 32 feet 3 inches, height 13 feet 8 inches

Power: one Rolls-Royce/Packard Merlin V-1650-7 liquid-cooled V-12 with two-speed, two-stage supercharging, rated at 1,450hp for takeoff and 1,695hp war emergency

Weights: empty 7,635lb, normal takeoff 10,100lb, max takeoff 12,100lb

Speed: max 437mph at 25,000 feet, 395mph at 5,000 feet

Ceiling: 40,000 feet

Range: 950 miles, with drop tanks 1,650 miles

Armament: six 0.50in wing-mounted Browning MG53-2 machine guns, two with 400 and four with 270 rounds per gun; two 1,000lb bombs or 10 5-inch HVAR rockets underwing

Crew: pilot

P-51B Mustang cutaway key

1 Plastic (Phenol fiber) rudder trim tab
2 Rudder frame (fabric covered)
3 Rudder balance
4 Fin front spar
5 Fin structure
6 Access panel
7 Rudder trim-tab actuating drum
8 Rudder trim-tab control link
9 Rear navigation light
10 Rudder metal bottom section
11 Elevator plywood trim tab
12 Starboard elevator frame
13 Elevator balance weight
14 Starboard tailplane structure
15 Reinforced bracket (rear steering stresses)
16 Rudder operating horn forging
17 Elevator operating horns
18 Tab control turnbuckles
19 Fin front spar/ fuselage attachment
20 Port elevator tab
21 Fabric-covered elevator
22 Elevator balance weight
23 Port tailplane
24 Tab control drum
25 Fin root fairing
26 Elevator cables
27 Tab control access panels
28 Tailwheel steering mechanism
29 Tailwheel mount
30 Tailwheel leg assembly
31 Forward-retracting steerable tailwheel
32 Tailwheel doors
33 Lifting tube
34 Fuselage aft bulkhead/break point
35 Fuselage break point
36 Control cable pulley brackets
37 Fuselage frames
38 Oxygen bottles
39 Cooling-air exit flap actuating mechanism
40 Rudder cables
41 Fuselage lower longeron
42 Rear tunnel
43 Cooling-air exit flap
44 Coolant radiator assembly
45 Radio and equipment shelf
46 Power supply pack
47 Fuselage upper longeron
48 Radio bay aft bulkhead (plywood)
49 Fuselage stringers
50 SCR-695 radio transmitter-receiver (on upper sliding shelf)
51 Whip aerial
52 Junction box
53 Cockpit aft glazing
54 Canopy track
55 SCR-552 radio transmitter-receiver
56 Battery installation
57 Radiator supercharger coolant pipes
58 Radiator forward air duct
59 Coolant header tank/radiator pipe
60 Coolant radiator ventral access cover
61 Oil-cooler air inlet door
62 Oil radiator
63 Oil pipes
64 Flap control linkage
65 Wing rear spar/fuselage attachment bracket
66 Crash pylon structure
67 Aileron control linkage
68 Hydraulic hand pump
69 Radio control boxes
70 Pilot's seat
71 Seat suspension frame
72 Pilot's head/back armor
73 Rearward-sliding clear-vision canopy
74 Rearview rear-view mirror
75 Ring and bead gunsight
76 Bullet-proof windshield
77 Gyro gunsight
78 Engine controls
79 Signal-pistol discharge tube
80 Circuit-breaker panel
81 Oxygen regulator
82 Pilot's footrest and seat mounting bracket
83 Control linkage
84 Rudder pedal
85 Tailwheel lock control
86 Wing center-section
87 Hydraulic reservoir
88 Port wing fuel tank filler point
89 Port Browning 0.5in (12.7mm) guns
90 Ammunition feed chutes
91 Gun-bay access door (raised)
92 Ammunition box troughs
93 Aileron control cables
94 Flap lower skin (Alclad)
95 Aileron profile (internal aerodynamic balance diaphragm)
96 Aileron control drum and mounting bracket
97 Aileron trim-tab control drum
98 Aileron plastic (Phenol fiber) trim tab
99 Port aileron assembly
100 Wing skinning
101 Outer section sub-assembly
102 Port navigation light
103 Port wingtip
104 Leading-edge skin
105 Landing lamp
106 Weapons/stores pylon
107 500lb (227kg) bomb
108 Gun ports
109 Gun barrels
110 Detachable cowling panels
111 Firewall/integral armor
112 Oil tank
113 Oil pipes
114 Upper longeron/ engine mount attachment
115 Oil-tank metal retaining straps
116 Carburetor
117 Engine bearer assembly
118 Cowling panel frames
119 Engine aftercooler
120 Engine leads
121 Packard V-1650 (R-R Merlin) 12-cylinder liquid-cooled engine
122 Exhaust fairing panel
123 Stub exhausts
124 Magneto
125 Coolant pipes
126 Cowling forward frame
127 Coolant header tank
128 Armor plate
129 Propeller hub
130 Spinner
131 Hamilton Standard Hydromatic propeller
132 Carburettor air intake, integral with (133)
133 Engine-mount front-frame assembly
134 Intake trunk
135 Engine-mount reinforcing tie
136 Hand-crank starter
137 Carburettor trunk vibration-absorbing connection
138 Wing center-section front bulkhead
139 Wing center-section end rib
140 Starboard mainwheel well
141 Wing front spar/fuselage attachment bracket

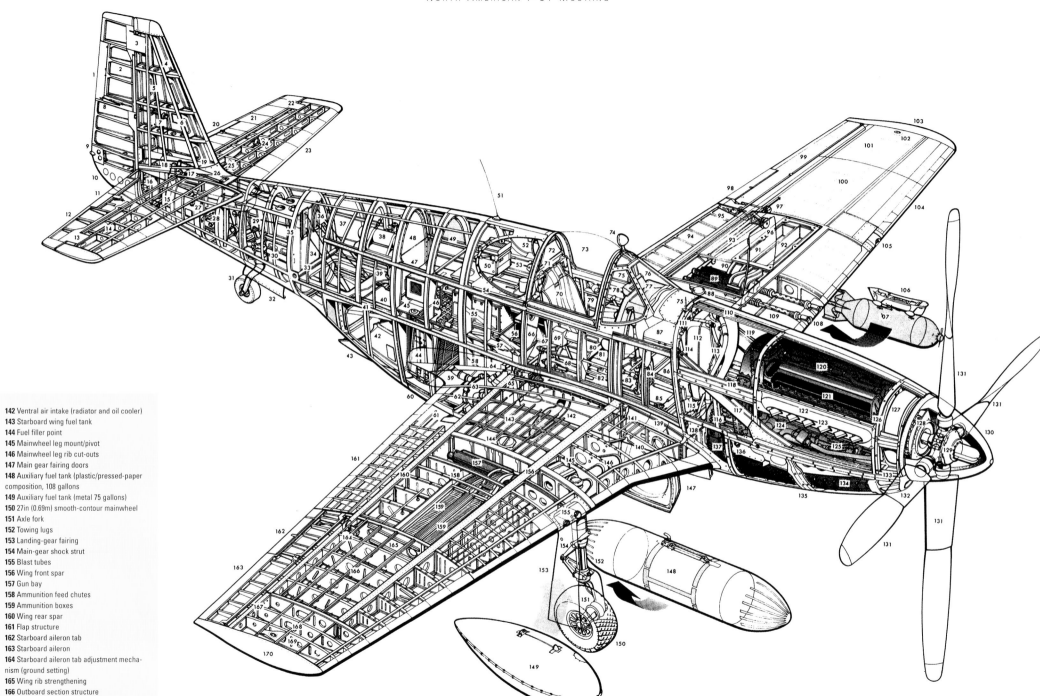

142 Ventral air intake (radiator and oil cooler)
143 Starboard wing fuel tank
144 Fuel filler point
145 Mainwheel leg mount/pivot
146 Mainwheel leg rib cut-outs
147 Main gear fairing doors
148 Auxiliary fuel tank (plastic/pressed-paper composition, 108 gallons)
149 Auxiliary fuel tank (metal 75 gallons)
150 27in (0.69m) smooth-contour mainwheel
151 Axle fork
152 Towing lugs
153 Landing-gear fairing
154 Main-gear shock strut
155 Blast tubes
156 Wing front spar
157 Gun bay
158 Ammunition feed chutes
159 Ammunition boxes
160 Wing rear spar
161 Flap structure
162 Starboard aileron tab
163 Starboard aileron
164 Starboard aileron tab adjustment mechanism (ground setting)
165 Wing rib strengthening
166 Outboard section structure
167 Outer section single spar
168 Wingtip sub-assembly
169 Starboard navigation light
170 Detachable wingtip

RIGHT: A P-51B Mustang sports a bulged Malcolm canopy which gave improved rearward visibility. This machine belongs to the 354th Fighter Squadron, 355th Fighter Group, flying from East Anglia, England, as part of USAAF 8th Air Force.

RIGHT INSET: Apart from the Rolls-Royce Merlin engine, the greatest factor in increasing the range of the Mustang was the laminar flow wing, seen on this P-51D-5, although this was less efficient in a sustained climb.

OPPOSITE: A factory-fresh P-51D, showing the bubble canopy which gave the best possible view to the vulnerable rear quadrant. The slight extra drag of this caused a marginal reduction in maximum speed.

OPPOSITE INSET: The standard cockpit configuration of the P-51B is seen here on this Mustang of the 355th Squadron, 354th Fighter Group, a tactical rather than an escort unit that was part of USAAF 9th Air Force.

OPPOSITE: Mustangs served in Korea in the close air support role, but by then were redesignated F-51s. Seen taxiing out at the dusty Taegu airstrip in South Korea, these F-51Ds are armed with unguided rockets.

OPPOSITE INSET: Australian and South African squadrons flew Mustangs over Korea. Armed with six air-to-surface rockets, this South African Mustang pilot is about to set out on a close air support mission.

LEFT: Ranging high above the clouds, Mustangs controlled the skies deep into Germany. From March 1944, no German fighter pilot could ever feel entirely safe from attack even over his own homeland.

LEFT INSET: This unmarked P-51D is configured to carry a battery of three rocket tubes under each wing, probably during the weapons clearance phase. Although not terribly accurate, these weapons were widely used in 1944/45.

PANAVIA TORNADO F.3

The Tornado ADV (Air Defense Variant) two-seat, twin-engined, bisonic interceptor was an unusual development of a dedicated fighter derivative of the long-range Tornado IDS (Interdictor Strike) aircraft. The latter was tasked with the accurate delivery of ordnance at very high speed at extremely low altitude, and was produced in the 1970s by a multi-national consortium for the air forces of Britain, Germany and Italy. The ADV version, which possessed 80 percent commonality with the Tornado IDS, was developed not as an agile dogfighter but specifically to meet an RAF Cold War perceived requirement for a fighter that would operate autonomously 500nm over the sea to the north of the United Kingdom to intercept mass long-range missile-armed Soviet bombers in the worst conditions that darkness, poor weather and intense electronic countermeasures can create. It was designed for high speed and long endurance while carrying a full load of air-to-air missiles.

Like the IDS version, the Tornado ADV (which entered service as the F.2 in November 1984, while production continued with the definitive F.3 from 1985) was designed with variable-sweep wings to provide a balance between good short-field performance, rapid acceleration and sustained high speed, agile rate of roll and economic high-altitude cruising.

Tornado IDS was quite a small airplane, with an overall length of 54 feet 9.5 inches; to accommodate the ADV variant's medium-range Skyflash missiles, that were to be semi-submerged beneath the fuselage to minimise drag, the fuselage had to be lengthened with an extra bay astern of the cockpit. This, together with a new, lengthened and reshaped nose housing the GEC-Marconi AI.24 multi-mode radar, produced an overall length for the fighter of 61 feet. This shifted the center of gravity, necessitating an increase in the sweep angle of the wing glove from 60 degrees on the IDS to 68 degrees on the ADV.

Wing sweep and flap/slat positions are varied automatically by the flight control system to match the aircraft's angle of attack. Four basic angles of wing sweep are normally used: 25 degrees at speeds up to Mach 0.73, 45 degrees up to Mach 0.88, 58 degrees up to Mach 0.9, and 67 degrees at higher speeds. The Tornado F.2/F.3 is reported to be easy to fly and highly maneuverable. On one test flight the fighter was pushed into a 4g 360-degree turn directly over the airfield, barely exceeding the field boundaries. The Tornado may not have the agility of dedicated dogfighters, but it clearly has the ability to outmaneuver virtually everything else.

The AI.24 radar was designed to track up to forty targets simultaneously, displaying the ten greatest threats, and to be capable of detecting low-level fighter-sized targets out to 115 miles. Whereas the IDS version had two Mauser cannon, Tornado ADV is fitted with one. For short-range combat the F.2 and F.3 carry four AIM-9 Sidewinder air-to-air missiles on pivoting underwing pylons, to be replaced by Asraams. The long-range weapon is the BAe Skyflash AAM, being replaced by the AIM-120 Amraam.

During the 1991 Gulf War, the F.3 was held back from the front line and made no contact with enemy fighters during its 700 air defense missions, while it also operated over Bosnia in the 1990s. The Tornado is set to be replaced by the Eurofighter Typhoon by 2008.

LEFT: A Panavia Tornado F.2 of the RAF's 229 Operational Conversion Unit based at Coningsby, launches a Skyflash medium range AAM during trials. Developed from the interdiction Tornado, this is a dedicated bomber interceptor.

Specifications for Panavia Tornado F.3

Dimensions: max wingspan 45 feet 7 inches, minimum wingspan 28 feet 2 inches, length 61 feet, height 19 feet 8 inches

Power: two Turbo-Union RB 199 Mk 104 three-spool, axial-flow afterburning turbofans each rated at 9,656lb military and 16,920lb max thrust

Weights: empty 31,800lb, normal takeoff 50,200lb, max takeoff 61,700lb

Speed: max Mach 2.20 at altitude, Mach 1.21at sea level

Ceiling: 50,000 feet

Range: subsonic combat radius 1,036 miles, supersonic combat radius 230 miles

Armament: one 27mm Mauser BK 27 cannon with 180 rounds, four Skyflash/AIM-120 Amraam and four AIM-9 Sidewinder/Asraam air-to-air missiles

Crew: pilot and weapons systems officer

Tornado F.Mk 3 cutaway key

1 Starboard taileron construction
2 Honeycomb trailing-edge panels
3 Compound sweep taileron leading edge
4 Taileron pivot fixing
5 Afterburner ducting, extended 14in (36cm)
6 Thrust-reverser bucket door actuator
7 Afterburner nozzle jack
8 Starboard fully-variable engine exhaust nozzle
9 Thrust-reverser bucket doors, open
10 Dorsal spine and fairing
11 Rudder hydraulic actuator
12 Honeycomb rudder construction
13 Rudder
14 Fuel jettison pipes
15 Tail navigation light
16 Aft passive ECM housing/radar warning antenna
17 Dielectric fin tip antenna housing
18 VHF aerial
19 Fuel jettison and vent valve
20 ILS aerial, port and starboard
21 Underside view showing semi-recessed missile positions
22 Extended fuselage section
23 Extended radar equipment bay
24 Radome
25 Secondary heat exchanger intake
26 Wing pylon-mounted missile rails
27 External fuel tanks
28 Port taileron
29 Fin leading edge
30 Fin integral fuel tank
31 Tailfin construction
32 Vortex generators
33 Heat shroud
34 Fin spar root attachment joints
35 Engine bay central firewall
36 Starboard airbrake, open
37 Airbrake hydraulic jack
38 Taileron actuator, fly-by-wire control system
39 Turbo-Union RB.199-34R Mk 104 three-spool afterburning turbofan
40 Hydraulic reservoir
41 Hydraulic system filters
42 Engine bay bulkhead
43 Bleed air duct
44 Heat exchanger exhaust duct
45 Primary heat exchanger
46 Ram air intake
47 HF aerial fairing
48 Engine compressor faces
49 Rear fuselage bag-type fuel tank
50 Intake trunking
51 Wing root pneumatic seal
52 KHD/Microtecnica/ Lucas T312 APU
53 Engine-driven auxiliary gearbox
54 APU exhaust
55 Flap drive shaft
56 Starboard full-span double-slotted flaps, extended
57 Spoiler housings
58 Starboard wing fully-swept position
59 Flap guide rails
60 Flap screw jacks
61 Wingtip fairing
62 Starboard navigation light
63 Structural provision for outboard pylon attachment
64 Full-span leading-edge slats, extended
65 Starboard external fuel tank, capacity 594 gallons
66 Fuel tank-stabilising fins
67 Wing weapons stores pylon
68 Missile launching rail
69 AIM-9L Sidewinder air-to-air missiles
70 Leading-edge slat screw jacks
71 Slat guide rails
72 Wing rib construction
73 Two-spar wing torsion box construction
74 Swiveling pylon mounting
75 Starboard wing integral fuel tank
76 Main undercarriage leg strut
77 Starboard mainwheel
78 Mainwheel door
79 Undercarriage breaker strut
80 Wing pivot sealing fairing
81 Telescopic control linkages
82 Pylon swiveling link
83 Main undercarriage hydraulic retraction jack
84 Wing sweep actuator attachment joint
85 Starboard wing pivot bearing
86 Flexible wing seals
87 Wing pivot carry-through (Electron beam welded titanium box construction)
88 Wing pivot box integral fuel tank
89 Pitch and roll control non-linear gearing mechanism
90 Air-conditioning supply ducting (Normalair Garrett system)
91 Dorsal spine fairing
92 Anti-collision light
93 UHF aerials
94 Port wing pivot bearing
95 Flexible trailing-edge seals
96 Spoiler actuators
97 Port spoilers, open
98 Port wing fully swept back position
99 Full-span double-slotted flaps, extended
100 Port wing fully forward position
101 Wing tip fairing
102 Port navigation light
103 Full-span leading-edge slats, extended
104 Port wing integral fuel tank
105 Swiveling pylon mounting
106 Pylon angle control link
107 Port wing sweep actuator
108 Wing flap and leading-edge slat drive motors
109 Starboard wing sweep actuator
110 Hydraulic drive motor and gearbox
111 Extended wingroot glove fairing
112 Forward radar-warning receiver, port and starboard
113 Supplementary "blow-in" intake doors
114 Landing lamp, port and starboard
115 Starboard fully-variable engine air intake
116 Navigation light
117 Variable-intake ramp
118 Ramp control linkage
119 Ramp hydraulic jack
120 Bleed air exit louvres
121 Boundary layer spill duct
122 Enlarged forward fuselage bag-type fuel tank
123 Cockpit canopy pivot mounting
124 Air and fuel system ducting
125 Port intake bleed air outlet fairing
126 AIM-9L Sidewinder air-to-air missiles
127 Missile launching rail
128 Port external fuel tank
129 Intake lip
130 Navigator's cockpit enclosure
131 Navigator's ejection seat (Martin-Baker Mk 10A "zero-zero" seat)
132 Canopy jack strut
133 Cockpit rear pressure bulkhead

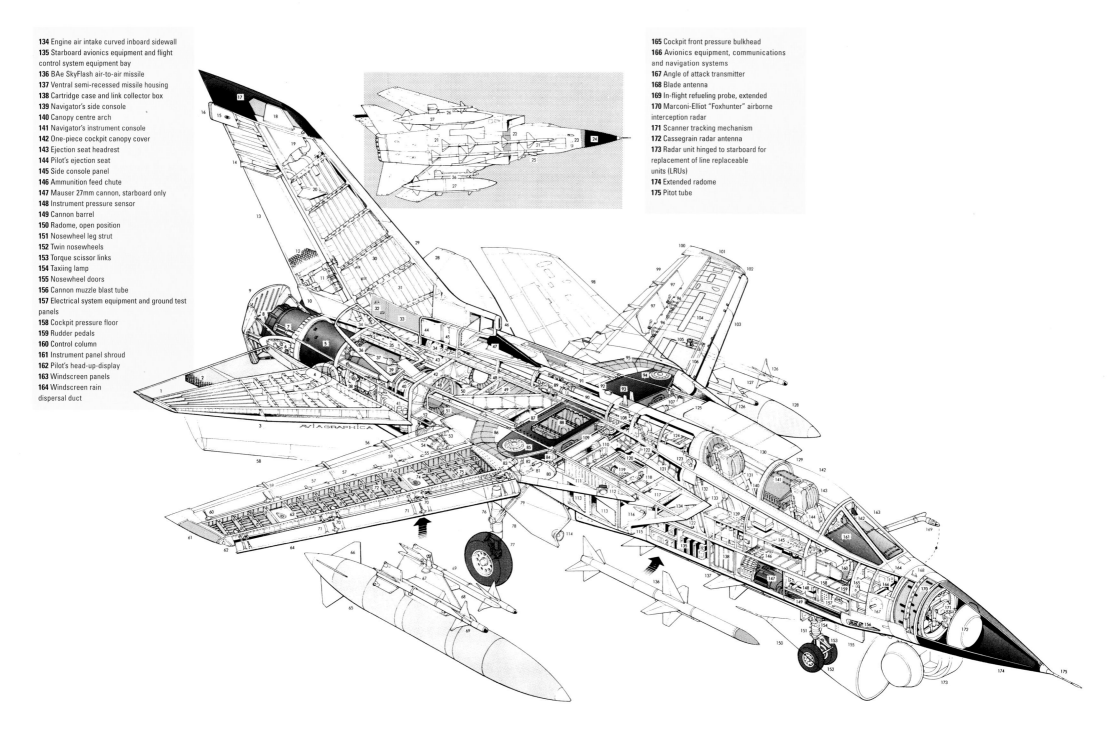

134 Engine air intake curved inboard sidewall
135 Starboard avionics equipment and flight control system equipment bay
136 BAe SkyFlash air-to-air missile
137 Ventral semi-recessed missile housing
138 Cartridge case and link collector box
139 Navigator's side console
140 Canopy centre arch
141 Navigator's instrument console
142 One-piece cockpit canopy cover
143 Ejection seat headrest
144 Pilot's ejection seat
145 Side console panel
146 Ammunition feed chute
147 Mauser 27mm cannon, starboard only
148 Instrument pressure sensor
149 Cannon barrel
150 Radome, open position
151 Nosewheel leg strut
152 Twin nosewheels
153 Torque scissor links
154 Taxiing lamp
155 Nosewheel doors
156 Cannon muzzle blast tube
157 Electrical system equipment and ground test panels
158 Cockpit pressure floor
159 Rudder pedals
160 Control column
161 Instrument panel shroud
162 Pilot's head-up-display
163 Windscreen panels
164 Windscreen rain dispersal duct

165 Cockpit front pressure bulkhead
166 Avionics equipment, communications and navigation systems
167 Angle of attack transmitter
168 Blade antenna
169 In-flight refueling probe, extended
170 Marconi-Elliot "Foxhunter" airborne interception radar
171 Scanner tracking mechanism
172 Cassegrain radar antenna
173 Radar unit hinged to starboard for replacement of line replaceable units (LRUs)
174 Extended radome
175 Pitot tube

OPPOSITE: A Tornado F.2 carrying a full external load poses for the camera, deploying its speed brakes and flaps to stay in position. As can be seen, Tornado is really quite a small airplane.

LEFT: Full house! A Tornado F.2 carries a full load of four Skyflash, two Sidewinders, and two long range tanks. Carried semi-submerged for low drag, the Skyflash AAMs have to be staggered to fit in.

BELOW: Wings fully swept, a fully armed Tornado F.3 heads for the heavens. This angle really shows how much the Skyflash AAMs have had to be staggered to shoehorn them in. The critical dimension is actually width rather than length.

RIGHT: Glowing afterburners indicate the power of the RAF Tornado's Rolls-Royce RB 199 turbofans. The engines and the airplane have served in the Gulf for many years now. Aside from the F.3 air defense variant (ADV), the RAF fields two other variants: the GR.4 interdictor/strike (IDS) and the GR.4A, although a few GR.1s and GR.1As remain available.

OPPOSITE: A Tornado F.3 of 111 (F) Squadron based at RAF Leuchars in Scotland dispenses chaff and flares over the North Sea. It carries four Matra BAe Dynamics Sky Flash medium range air-to-air missiles and four Sidewinder short range AAMs.

REGGIANE RE 2000

The Reggiane Re 2000 single-seat, single-engined fighter was designed just prior to World War II and is interesting in many ways. Only 25 of the approximately 170 built served with Italian forces, and the aircraft even attracted a potential order for 300 from Britain's RAF, until Italy's entry into the war scuppered the deal. Hungary and Sweden bought 70 and 60 examples, respectively, with the former acquiring a manufacturing license and in 1942 building over 200 of a slightly longer version with a lighter, smaller engine, and actually pressing it into combat with an Independent Fighter Group before Hungary's capitulation.

The Re 2000 was designed by Roberto G. Longhi, who had spent some time in the USA studying manufacturing techniques and was inspired by the Seversky P-35 which introduced the U.S. Army Air Corps fighter fraternity to the enclosed cockpit, constant-speed propeller, and retractable undercarriage. The Re 2000 was a low-wing monoplane with retractable landing gear. It was unusual, for an Italian machine, in having a five-spar semi-elliptical wing embodying integral fuel tankage. Construction was virtually all-metal – aluminum alloy – with stressed skin, except for the fabric-covered rudder and elevators.

It was a nimble airplane, extremely maneuverable, but lightly built, and Italian reports claimed that trials against the Messerschmitt Bf 109E proved it was superior in close combat performance, although no match for the German fighter in a dive.

What really let the Italian fighter down, however, were its slow speed and its relatively weak armament, only two 12.7mm SAFAT machine guns, with which it hardly packed sufficient punch.

The aircraft was first flown on May 24, 1939, and an initial pre-series production order was placed by the *Regia Aeronautica* in September of that year, but this was cancelled in April 1940, with the Italian air force claiming that the lack of self-sealing wing tanks made the aircraft too vulnerable. *Regia Aeronautica* did order a few of the fighters and accepted seventeen into service from spring 1941, mainly as convoy escorts. Sixteen of these were fitted with additional fuel tankage in the fuselage, these being designated Re 2000 GA (*Grande Autonomia*, or Long Range). A further eight served with the *Aviazione Ausiliaria per la Regia Marina*, fitted with catapult pick-up points for use from battleships. Five actually served aboard battleships, but three were lost in attacks on the ships, and one crashed on landing at an airfield.

There were adaptations of the Re 2000. The Reggiane Re 2001 had a redesigned wing structure, the five-spar

arrangement being replaced by a three-spar construction, and the integral fuel tankage being eliminated. This aircraft was powered by the Daimler-Benz DB 601A liquid-cooled engine and first flew on July 14, 1940. Some 237 fighters of this type served with the *Regia Aeronautica* as the Ariete (Ram), and variants were upgunned. The similarly constructed Re 2002 Ariete II was a single-seat ground attack fighter fitted with a 14-cylinder radial Piaggio engine, and was ordered into production in September 1941, although only 147 of 200 reached the *Regia Aeronautica* before the Armistice. Later, production continued on behalf of the *Luftwaffe*, although only 35 of 76 completed entered German service. The Re 2005 was considered a superior fighter and 34 pre-series and 750 production aircraft were ordered, but only the pre-series aircraft were completed, just 20 of them seeing brief combat with the *Regia Aeronautica*.

LEFT: The Reggiane Re 2000 suffered from an unreliable engine and lack of hitting power. The type served with Sweden (as depicted) and Hungary, as well as Italy. Its wartime career was undistinguished.

Reggiane Re 2000 G.A. cutaway key

1 Pitot head
2 Starboard navigation light
3 Wing tip fairing
4 Starboard fabric-covered aileron
5 Aileron hinge control linkage
6 Corrugated inner wing skin panel
7 Bottom skin/stringer panel
8 Three-bladed variable pitch P.100 propeller
9 Carburetor air intake
10 Engine cooling air intake
11 Spinner
12 Spinner fixing belt
13 Propeller hub pitch-change mechanism
14 Propeller reduction gearbox
15 Cowling nose ring
16 Starboard mainwheel
17 Oil cooler intake
18 Oil radiator
19 Detachable engine cowling panels
20 Piaggio P.Xbis R.C. 40 14-cylinder two-row radial engine
21 Machine gun port
22 Machine gun muzzle blast tube
23 Carburetor intake ducting
24 Oil filler cap
25 Forward oil tank
26 Cowling air flaps
27 Engine mounting ring frame
28 Exhaust collector ring
29 Exhaust stub
30 Cartridge case collector box
31 Cartridge case chute
32 Engine bearer struts
33 Engine accessory equipment compartment
34 Port Breda-SAFAT 12.7mm machine gun
35 Gun synchronizing drive
36 Ammunition tank (300 rounds per gun)
37 Engine compartment bulkhead
38 Wing front spar/fuselage attachment joint
39 Center section integral fuel tank
40 Rudder pedals
41 Control column linkage
42 Link collector box
43 Secondary instrument panel
44 Upper engine bearer support longeron
45 Main instrument panel
46 Stand-by ring-and-bead gunsight
47 Flap operating shaft
48 Starboard split trailing edge flap
49 Windscreen panel
50 Reflector sight
51 Machine gun cocking lever
52 Oxygen regulator

53 Engine throttle, propeller and mixture control levers
54 Fuel cock controls
55 Footboards
56 Flap and undercarriage gearbox
57 Trim control handwheels
58 Fire extinguisher handle
59 Milliameter
60 Sliding cockpit canopy cover
61 Headrest
62 Pilot's seat
63 Safety harness
64 Radio control box
65 Adjustable seat mounting
66 Flap drive torque shaft
67 Reserve fuel tank
68 Flap operating rod rack-and-pinion drive
69 Radio transmitter/receiver
70 Sloping cockpit bulkhead
71 Fuselage oil tank
72 Flap and undercarriage drive electric motor
73 Fuselage fuel tank
74 Sliding canopy rail
75 Turn-over crash support frame
76 Canopy tail fairing construction
77 Aerial mast
78 Fuel filler cap
79 Rearward vision cut-out
80 Aft fuselage frame-and-stringer construction
81 Elevator control linkage
82 Tailwheel retraction torque shaft and screw jack
83 Rudder trim tab actuator
84 Starboard tailplane
85 Starboard fabric-covered elevator
86 Fin rib construction
87 Sloping fin spar
88 Sternpost
89 Aerial cable
90 Fin tip fairing
91 Fabric-covered rudder
92 Rudder rib construction
93 Rudder trim tab
94 Tail navigation light
95 Rudder and elevator hinge controls
96 Port elevator
97 Elevator trim tab
98 Elevator rib construction

99 Tailplane tip fairing
100 Tailplane rib construction
101 Elevator trim tab actuator
102 Castoring tailwheel
103 Tailwheel forks
104 Tailwheel doors
105 Tailplane spar attachment joint
106 Tailwheel shock absorber strut
107 Fin/tailplane spar attachment bulkhead
108 Fuselage lifting bar
109 Tailwheel steering linkage
110 Trim control cables
111 Rudder cable
112 Hydraulic reservoir
113 Battery
114 Fire extinguisher bottle
115 Electrical terminal panel
116 Fuselage lower longeron
117 Wing root trailing edge fillet
118 Center-section split trailing edge flap
119 Flap shroud ribs
120 Inboard split trailing edge flap segment
121 Outboard split trailing edge flap segment
122 Flap operating rod
123 Aileron control linkage
124 Aileron trim tab
125 Port fabric-covered aileron
126 Aileron rib construction
127 Wing tip fairing construction
128 Wing tip edge member
129 Port navigation light
130 Pitot head
131 Leading edge nose ribs
132 Wing rib construction
133 Multi-spar wing torsion box
134 Mainwheel housing
135 Undercarriage retraction torque shaft
136 Retraction screw jacks
137 Undercarriage position indicator
138 Mainwheel leg fairing
139 Leg fairing doors
140 Mainwheel leg pivot fixing
141 Retraction linkage/drag strut
142 Leading edge access panel
143 Mainwheel leg strut
144 Hydraulic brake pipe
145 Mainwheel door
146 Port mainwheel

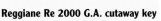

Specifications for Reggiane Re 2000

Dimensions: wingspan 36 feet 1 inch, length 26 feet 2.75 inches, height 10 feet 6 inches

Power: one Piaggio P.XI RC 40D 14-cylinder two-row radial rated at 1,040hp

Weights: empty 4,564lb, normal takeoff 6,349lb

Speed: max 329mph at 16,400 feet, 255mph at sea level

Ceiling: 36,7500 feet

Range: 339 miles

Armament: two nose-mounted, synchronized, belt-fed 12.7mm Breda-SAFAT machine guns with 300 rounds per gun

Crew: pilot

Copyright Mike Badrocke – 2004

REPUBLIC P-47 THUNDERBOLT

LEFT: The Republic P-47 Thunderbolt was the largest single-engined fighter of World War II. What made it so large was the need to install a turbocharger in the fuselage to give good high altitude performance.

For a fighter of the World War II period, the P-47 Thunderbolt was huge, the largest single-seat, single-engined fighter of the war. Its size was determined by the quest for high-altitude performance during long-range bomber escort duties, which led American designers to come up with turbo-supercharging, whereby air from the intake was ducted to the rather large turbo-supercharger, the turbine of which was driven by exhaust gases ducted from the engine. The intake air, having been compressed in the turbo-supercharger, was then ducted back to the engine aspiration system. While the benefits of this system were undeniable, it was so heavy and bulky that it virtually demanded that the airframe be designed to suit.

In 1940, the very powerful Pratt & Whitney Double Wasp 18-cylinder radial engine was selected for Republic Aviation's new fighter design. The engine offered enough power for a single-engined layout, and the turbo-supercharger was located in the fuselage behind the pilot. This involved a tremendous amount of ducting to lead air and gases back and forth, and the airframe of what became the P-47 Thunderbolt was designed around it.

First flying on May 6, 1941, the P-47B Thunderbolt became operational with the USAAF 56th Fighter Group in Europe in April 1943, and was quickly dubbed "Juggernaut," or "Jug." At first it looked a loser. It was out-climbed and out-turned by both the Bf 109G and Fw 190A, but when combat was joined its finely harmonized controls gave it a very fast rate of roll, which in part compensated for its mediocre turning ability. In a dive the Thunderbolt could even outpace the Fw 190. Its armament of eight wing-mounted 0.50in Browning machine guns gave it a very heavy punch, and it could survive an amazing amount of battle damage.

However, even with drop tanks, early Thunderbolts could barely reach the German border from England, and German fighters could wait until the Allied bombers passed beyond the range of their escorts before attacking. Gradually, the reach of the Thunderbolt was extended, using drop tanks under the wings as well as beneath the fuselage.

The Thunderbolt needed a four-bladed propeller to utilize the engine output. To provide enough ground clearance the main gear legs had to be long. They retracted inwards, being telescopic to shorten them to allow for the wing-mounted guns. Wings were semi-elliptical in planform, with large ailerons outboard and flaps inboard.

The main variant was the P-47D, with water injection and other changes, including heavier armor protection and

a bubble canopy. P-47Ds served throughout Europe and the Pacific Theater until the end of the war, but were largely switched to close air support during the closing stages.

Total production of the "Jug" was 15,660, with Republic's output of D models (12,602) being the largest total of one sub-type of any fighter in history. The lightweight P-47M was too late for its intended role of chasing flying bombs, but did score successes against the Me 262 and Ar 234 jets, while the long-range P-47N matched the M fuselage with a bigger wing for Pacific operations. There were also many experimental versions. The P-47 was phased out of USAAF service as jet fighters emerged, but many were still serving with other air forces until the 1970s.

Specifications for Republic P-47D Thunderbolt

Dimensions: wingspan 40 feet 9 inches, length 36 feet 1 inch, height 14 feet 2 inches

Power: one Pratt & Whitney R-2800-59 Double Wasp 18-cylinder two-row radial developing 2,000hp for takeoff and 2,300hp at 31,000 feet with turbo-supercharging

Weights: empty 10,700lb, normal takeoff 14,600lb, max 17,500lb

Speed: max 426mph at 30,000 feet, 350mph at sea level

Ceiling: 40,000 feet

Range: 950 miles

Armament: eight wing-mounted, belt-fed 0.50in Browning machine guns with 425 rounds per gun, and provision for 2,000lb bombload or ten 5in high velocity rockets

Crew: pilot

P-47D cutaway key

1 Rudder upper hinge
2 Aerial attachment
3 Fin flanged ribs
4 Rudder post/fin aft spar
5 Fin front spar
6 Rudder trim tab worm and screw actuating mechanism (chain-driven)
7 Rudder center hinge
8 Rudder trim tab
9 Rudder structure
10 Tall navigation light
11 Elevator fixed tab
12 Elevator trim tab
13 Starboard elevator structure
14 Elevator outboard hinge
15 Elevator torque tube
16 Elevator trim tab worm and screw actuating mechanism
17 Chain drive
18 Starboard tailplane
19 Tail jacking point
20 Rudder control cables
21 Elevator control rod and linkage
22 Fin spar/fuselage attachment points
23 Elevator
24 Aerial
25 Port tailplane structure (two spars and flanged ribs)
26 Tailwheel retraction worm gear
27 Tailwheel anti-shimmy damper
28 Tailwheel oleo
29 Tailwheel doors
30 Retractable and steerable tailwheel
31 Tailwheel fork
32 Tailwheel mount and pivot
33 Rudder cables
34 Rudder and elevator trim control cables
35 Lifting tube
36 Elevator rod linkage
37 Semi-monocoque all-metal fuselage construction
38 Fuselage dorsal "razorback" profile
39 Aerial lead-in
40 Fuselage stringers
41 Supercharger air filter
42 Supercharger
43 Turbine casing
44 Turbosupercharger compartment air vent
45 Turbo-supercharger exhaust hood fairing (stainless steel)
46 Outlet louvers
47 Intercooler exhaust doors (port and starboard)

48 Exhaust pipes
49 Cooling air ducts
50 Intercooler unit (cooling and supercharged air)
51 Radio transmitter and receiver packs (Detrola)
52 Canopy track
53 Elevator rod linkage
54 Aerial mast
55 Formation light
56 Rearward-vision frame cut-out and glazing
57 Oxygen bottles
58 Supercharger and cooling air pipe (supercharger to carburetor) port
59 Elevator linkage
60 Supercharger and cooling air pipe (supercharger to carburetor) starboard
61 Central duct (to intercooler unit)
62 Wingroot air louvres
63 Wingroot fillet
64 Auxiliary fuel tank (100 gallons)
65 Auxiliary fuel filler point
66 Rudder cable turnbuckle
67 Cockpit floor support
68 Seat adjustment lever
69 Pilot's seat
70 Canopy emergency release (port and starboard)
71 Trim tab controls
72 Back and head armor
73 Headrest
74 Rearward-sliding canopy
75 Rear view mirror fairing
76 "Vee" windshields with central pillar
77 Internal bulletproof glass screen
78 Gunsight
79 Engine control quadrant (cockpit port wall)
80 Control column
81 Rudder pedals
82 Oxygen regulator
83 Underfloor elevator control quadrant
84 Rudder cable linkage
85 Wing rear spar/fuselage attachment (tapered bolts/bushings)
86 Wing-supporting lower bulkhead section
87 Main fuel tank (205 gallons)
88 Fuselage forward structure

89 Stainless steel/Alclad firewall bulkhead
90 Cowl flap valve
91 Main fuel filler point
92 Anti-freeze fluid tank
93 Hydraulic reservoir
94 Aileron control rod
95 Aileron trim tab control cables
96 Aileron hinge access panels
97 Aileron and tab control linkage
98 Aileron trim tab (port wing only)
99 Frise type aileron
100 Wing rear (No. 2) spar
101 Port navigation light
102 Pitot head
103 Wing front (No. 1) spar
104 Wing stressed skin
105 Four gun ammunition troughs (individual bays)
106 Staggered gun barrels
107 Removable panel
108 Inter spar gun bay access panel
109 Forward gunsight bead
110 Oil feed pipes
111 Oil tank (28.6 gallons)
112 Hydraulic pressure line
113 Engine upper bearers
114 Engine control correlating cam
115 Eclipse pump (anti-icing)
116 Fuel level transmitter
117 Generator
118 Battery junction box
119 Storage battery
120 Exhaust collector ring
121 Cowl flap actuating
122 Exhaust outlets to collector ring
123 Cowl flaps
124 Supercharged and cooling air ducts to carburetor (port and starboard)
125 Exhaust upper outlets
126 Cowling frame
127 Pratt & Whitney R-2800-59 18-cylinder twin-row engine
128 Cowling nose panel
129 Magnetos
130 Propeller governor
131 Propeller hub
132 Reduction gear casing

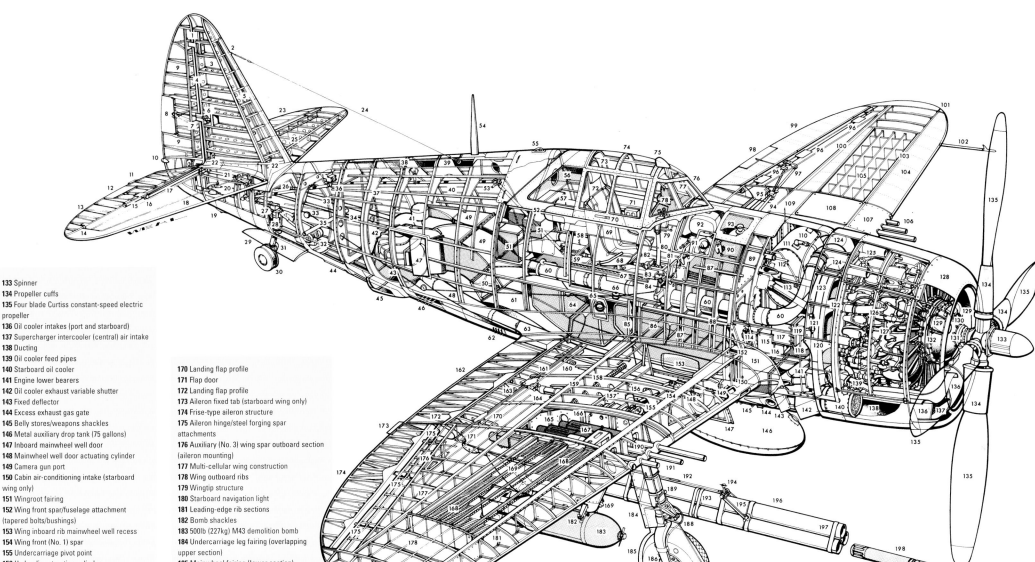

133 Spinner

134 Propeller cuffs

135 Four blade Curtiss constant-speed electric
propeller

136 Oil cooler intakes (port and starboard)

137 Supercharger intercooler (central) air intake

138 Ducting

139 Oil cooler feed pipes

140 Starboard oil cooler

141 Engine lower bearers

142 Oil cooler exhaust variable shutter

143 Fixed deflector

144 Excess exhaust gas gate

145 Belly stores/weapons shackles

146 Metal auxiliary drop tank (75 gallons)

147 Inboard mainwheel well door

148 Mainwheel well door actuating cylinder

149 Camera gun port

150 Cabin air-conditioning intake (starboard
wing only)

151 Wingroot fairing

152 Wing front spar/fuselage attachment
(tapered bolts/bushings)

153 Wing inboard rib mainwheel well recess

154 Wing front (No. 1) spar

155 Undercarriage pivot point

156 Hydraulic retraction cylinder

157 Auxiliary (undercarriage mounting)
wing spar

158 Gun bay warm air flexible duct

159 Wing rear (No. 2) spar

160 Landing flap inboard hinge

161 Auxiliary (No. 3) wing spar inboard section
(flap mounting)

162 NACA slotted trailing-edge landing flaps

163 Landing flaps center hinge

164 Landing flap hydraulic cylinder

165 Four 0.5in (12.7mm) Browning machine guns

166 Inter-spar gun bay inboard rib

167 Ammunition feed chutes

168 Individual ammunition troughs

169 Underwing stores/weapons pylon

170 Landing flap profile

171 Flap door

172 Landing flap profile

173 Aileron fixed tab (starboard wing only)

174 Frise-type aileron structure

175 Aileron hinge/steel forging spar
attachments

176 Auxiliary (No. 3) wing spar outboard section
(aileron mounting)

177 Multi-cellular wing construction

178 Wing outboard ribs

179 Wingtip structure

180 Starboard navigation light

181 Leading-edge rib sections

182 Bomb shackles

183 500lb (227kg) M43 demolition bomb

184 Undercarriage leg fairing (overlapping
upper section)

185 Mainwheel fairing (lower section)

186 Wheel fork

187 Starboard mainwheel

188 Brake lines

189 Landing gear air-oil shock strut

190 Machine-gun barrel blast tubes

191 Staggered gun barrels

192 Rocket launcher slide bar

193 Centre strap

194 Front mount (attached below front spar
between inboard pair of guns)

195 Deflector arms

196 Triple tube 4.5in (11.5cm) rocket
launcher (Type M10)

197 Front retaining band

198 4.5in (11.5cm) M8 rocket projectile

LEFT: Armorers replenish the wing-mounted 12.7mm Browning heavy machine guns. With eight of these weapons, the Thunderbolt had enough firepower to chew up any German fighter it encountered, with some to spare.

ABOVE: Although designed to perform at altitude, it was ironic that the Jug (short for Juggernaut) as the P-47 was affectionately known, did its best work lower down. Here, a P-47D is loaded with bombs on a temporary airfield in Southern England.

OPPOSITE: Too heavy to climb well, the Thunderbolt was unbeatable in the dive, as many German pilots found to their cost. While it did not turn well, it had a remarkable rate of roll, giving an advantage in three-dimensional maneuvering.

RIGHT INSET: **The RAF used Thunderbolts in Burma. Three birds return from a sortie in December 1944, while others are serviced and made ready. The closely packed flight line shows that a counterattack by the Japanese is considered to be unlikely.**

RIGHT MAIN PICTURE: **A P-47B Thunderbolt on an escort mission. Even with drop tanks it had insufficient range to stay with the bombers, and was later superseded by the Mustang. But whatever its failings, it produced a lot of aces.**

OPPOSITE: **P-47D-25 fighter-bombers outbound. The lines beneath the cockpit of the nearest aircraft indicate successful bombing and strafing missions carried out. The total to date appears to be a hundred.**

OPPOSITE INSET: **The portly lines of this P-47B Thunderbolt of the USAAF 8th Air Force are clearly evident. Not only could it survive a lot of battle damage, it was one of the safest fighters to belly-land.**

REPUBLIC F-84 THUNDERJET

Left: Early F-84 Thunderjets having lacked the agility for air combat, the F-84E seen here was developed as a fighter-bomber. First flown in May 1949, it featured a beefed-up wing, increased fuel, and greater load-carrying.

Design of the Thunderjet began in October 1944, and it became the second American jet fighter (after the F-86 Sabre) to be built in large numbers, while also being the last of the subsonic straight-wing jet fighters to see USAF operational service. It was the first turbojet-powered fighter to offer a radius of action permitting penetration missions. However, when it was deployed to Korea (as the F-84E), it was found to be generally inferior to the communist MiG-15s in fighter-versus-fighter combat, was ineffective as an escort fighter, but performed with distinction as a fighter-bomber.

Built around the J35-A-15C turbojet engine located just astern of the cockpit, the Thunderjet used a straight-through airflow concept. A simple pitot-type intake combined maximum flow efficiency with the highest possible critical Mach number, minimum fuselage cross-section and comparatively high fineness ratio. This resulted in very low drag, but resulted in all internal fuel being carried in the wings, which were in the mid-low position to minimize interference drag and were straight, with a constant thickness/chord ratio of 12 percent, leading to the nickname "plank-wing." To allow for maximum space for fuel, the inward-retracting main gear legs were positioned towards the rear of the wings, while the nose gear was hinged under the very front of the nose, and a tail bumper was fitted to the rear of the fuselage.

The first of three prototypes flew on February 28, 1946, with the first production model, the F-84B, flying in June 1947 and entering service two months later. Some 226 F-84Bs were built, followed by 191 F-84Cs with minor changes.

The Thunderjet was not the easiest of aircraft to fly. It was demanding of runway length, being difficult to lift off particularly in hot weather, and, while accelerating rapidly because of its low drag characteristics, it was subject to sudden and uncontrollable pitch-up below 15,000 feet, and extreme buffeting at higher altitudes, where the F-84B was relatively unmaneuverable.

An improved-thrust engine, the J35-A-17D, was fitted to the F-84D, which had general structural strengthening and thicker wing skinning, but only 154 of this model were built as a major rework of the design eventually emerged as the F-84E. This featured a 12-inch longer fuselage, stronger wing structure, increased internal fuel capacity, provision for underwing drop tanks, radar-ranging gunsight, and provision for two JATO (jet-assisted takeoff) rockets.

The F-84E flew its first combat mission over Korea on December 6, 1950, and it was not long before its true

strengths – exceptional load-carrying capability, stable weapons platform, good instrument flying characteristics, and ability to withstand battle damage and rough field conditions – saw it switched to fighter-bomber duties. The last of 843 F-84Es was completed in July 1951, with 100 of these being assigned to other NATO air forces.

The final "plank-wing" Thunderjet variant was the F-84G, which started to reach squadrons in 1951. Some 789 were delivered to the USAF, and a further 2,236 to foreign air forces under the Mutual Defense Assistance Program up to July 1953. The F-84G differed from the E mainly in having an uprated engine (J35-A-29), provision for a tactical nuclear store, multi-paned canopy, and in-flight refueling capability – the first production fighter to be built with this facility.

Specifications for Republic F-84E Thunderjet

Dimensions: wingspan 36 feet 5 inches, length 38 feet 6 inches, height 12 feet 10 inches

Power: one Allison J35-A-17D single-spool, axial-flow turbojet rated at 5,000lb military thrust

Weights: empty 10,995lb, normal takeoff 16,685lb, max 22,463lb

Speed: max 587mph at 4,000 feet

Ceiling: 40,750 feet

Range: 1,198 miles with tip tanks

Armament: six belt-fed 0.50in Colt-Browning M-3 machine guns, four in the nose, two in wing-roots, with 300 rounds per gun; provision for 2,000lb external ordnance

Crew: pilot

F-84G Thunderjet cutaway key

1 Engine air intake
2 Gun laying radar seeker
3 Machine gun muzzles
4 Pitot tube
5 Main undercarriage leg strut
6 Steering control
7 Nosewheel
8 Shimmy damper
9 Taxiing lamp
10 Nosewheel retraction strut
11 Nosewheel doors
12 Bifurcated intake ducting
13 Nosewheel hydraulic retraction jack
14 Machine gun barrels
15 Gyro compass unit
16 Ballast weights
17 Ammunition tanks (300 rounds per gun)
18 M3 0.5in (12.7mm) machine guns
19 Spent cartridge case collector chute
20 Nosewheel bay between intake ducts
21 Battery
22 Servicing access panels
23 Gun bay access panel latch
24 Oxygen converter
25 Hydraulic system header tank
26 Gun bay access panel
27 Armored bulkhead
28 Cockpit front pressure bulkhead
29 Rudder pedals
30 Instrument panel
31 Control column
32 Instrument panel shroud
33 Sperry radar gunsight
34 Bullet-proof windscreen
35 Cockpit canopy cover
36 Canopy framing
37 Starboard side console panel
38 Pilot's ejection seat
39 Engine throttle control
40 Cockpit floor level
41 Intake suction relief door
42 Intake trunking
43 Port side console panel
44 Cockpit rear pressure bulkhead
45 Canopy external latch
46 Ejection seat headrest
47 Pilot's back and head armor
48 Cockpit air system
49 Starboard wing fuel tank bays, total internal fuel system capacity 450 gallons
50 Fuel tank interconnecting piping
51 Starboard navigation light

52 Fixed tip tank, capacity 230 gallons
53 Tip tank stabilising fin
54 Rear identification light
55 Starboard aileron
56 Aileron aerodynamic seal
57 Fixed tab
58 Aileron hinge control
59 Starboard Fowler flap
60 Hydraulic flap jack
61 Starboard main undercarriage pivot fixing
62 D/F loop aerial
63 Cockpit air system vent
64 Sliding canopy cover electric motor and rail
65 Fuselage top longeron
66 Main fuselage fuel tank
67 Intake center fairing accessory compartment
68 Fuselage/main spar attachment frame
69 Wing root machine gun ammunition tank (300 rounds)
70 Ammunition feed chute
71 Allison J35-A-29 axial-flow turbojet
72 Fuselage/rear spar attachment main frame
73 Rear fuselage break point (engine removal)
74 Engine flame cans
75 Cooling air vent
76 Radio and electronics equipment bay
77 VHF radio transmitter and receiver
78 Jet pipe cooling air intake
79 Jet pipe heat shroud
80 Control cable runs
81 Fin root fillet
82 Fin/tailplane attachment joints
83 Starboard tailplane
84 Starboard elevator
85 Tailfin construction
86 Fin tip VHF aerial fairing
87 Rudder hinge post
88 Rudder construction
89 Fixed ruddertab
90 Tail navigation light
91 Elevator trim tab
92 Jet exhaust nozzle
93 Port elevator
94 Tailplane construction
95 Elevator hinge control
96 Fin/tailplane fixing main frames
97 Ventral fin/tail bumper

98 Fuel system vent
99 Jet pipe
100 Fuselage skin plating
101 Rear fuselage framing
102 Wing root trailing-edge fillet
103 Wing walkway
104 Spar attachment joint
105 Rearspar
106 Flap shroud ribs
107 Main undercarriage hydraulic retraction jack
108 Undercarriage leg pivot fixing
109 Flap hydraulic jack
110 Port Fowler flap
111 Aileron trim tab
112 Port aileron construction
113 Fixed tab
114 Port rear identification light
115 Tip tank stabilising fin
116 Fuel filler cap
117 Port navigation light
118 Fixed tip tank, capacity 230 gallons
119 Port wing fuel tank bays
120 Wing stringers
121 Mainspar
122 Fuel tank interconnecting piping
123 Leading edge nose ribs
124 Mainwheel doors
125 Port mainwheel
126 Hydraulic brake unit
127 Main undercarriage leg strut
128 In-flight refueling probe (alternative to item 133)
129 Leading-edge fuel tank
130 Main undercarriage wheel well
131 Mainwheel door
132 Wing root M-3 0.5in (12.7mm) machine gun
133 Boom type in-flight refueling probe (alternative to item 128)
134 Stores pylon
135 Airbrake hydraulic jack
136 Perforated ventral airbrake
137 Drop tank, capacity 230 gallons
138 500lb (227kg) HE bomb
139 "Tiny Tim" 30cm air-to-ground rocket
140 Rocket fixing shackles
141 HVAR ground attack rockets

Mike Badrocke

LEFT: Pitot-type nose intake and a straight "plank-type" wing were the main features of the Thunderjet, the prototype of which first flew in February 1946. The badly underpowered F-84B was dubbed the Groundhog.

ABOVE: A difficult shot for any cameraman as, ahead of his cockpit, a Thunderjet looses off HVAR ground attack rockets from underwing pylons. When it was decided that the F-84's agility wasn't up to competing in fighter-versus-fighter combat, emphasis changed to enhancement of its fighter-bomber capabilities.

RIGHT: The final Thunderjet was the F-84G seen here. Flight refueling extended endurance, and the F-84E was used in the bomber escort role over Korea. Outclassed by the MiG-15, it recorded few victories.

RIGHT: Uninspiring as a fighter, the straight-winged F-84 Thunderjet was operated is an attack aircraft by a dozen overseas nations in all, seven of them European, and perhaps surprisingly, communist Yugoslavia.

ABOVE: An F-84E Thunderjet, with the then fashionable tip tanks. The framed canopy suggests that the bubble canopy, so much in use in the latter days of World War II, was unable to withstand jet speeds.

OPPOSITE: In the nuclear age, the vulnerability of runways became apparent. To overcome this, experiments were made with ZELL (Zero Length Launch). The first jet fighter to carry a nuclear weapon, the Thunderjet was an obvious choice for this.

ROYAL AIRCRAFT FACTORY S.E. 5

LEFT: A Royal Aircraft Factory design, this S.E. 5a was originally built by Wolseley, and fully restored to flying condition in 1972. First flown in November 1916 as the S.E. 5, total production of the type was 5,205.

The S.E. 5 entered service with Britain's Royal Flying Corps in the spring of 1917, at a time when the service was taking heavy losses against superior German fighters over the Western Front in Europe, and it was largely responsible for reversing the situation. It was fast, climbed well, and was rugged and reliable. Although not the most agile of fighters of the day, its outstanding performance, coupled with dive and zoom tactics, enabled it to more than hold its own. Its cockpit, although open, was warm, which increased fighting efficiency.

With major components of conventional wood construction, with fabric covering, the S.E. 5 was a compact, single-bay biplane with equal-span wings that had raked tips, a similarly raked tailplane, triangular fin, and almost rectangular rudder, with a small ventral fin and a V-strut undercarriage. A large windshield was provided over the front of the cockpit, although this was removed from some production models in the field, since pilots felt it was a hazard in the event of crash-landing, which was not uncommon. Planned armament comprised a Lewis gun above the top wing, on a Foster mounting that enabled it to be slid down for reloading and for firing upwards, and a forward-firing synchronized Vickers gun, although early S.E. 5s had a Vickers gun offset to port in the front fuselage and the Lewis above the center section.

It was intended that the S.E. 5 would have a 200hp geared Hispano-Suiza engine, but two of the three prototypes and some production examples were fitted with the earlier Hispano 8Aa version of the engine, a basic direct-drive 150hp unit. Thus powered, the first prototype flew on November 22, 1916, followed by the second on December 4, similarly powered. The third, introducing the 200hp engine, effectively became the prototype for the S.E. 5a. The first of 24 S.E. 5 production aircraft was completed in March 1917, followed by a second batch of 50; some of these became the S.E. 5a version, while others in service were also modified to receive 200hp engines.

Based on experience with the first batch of S.E. 5s, airframe modifications were made. The wing rear spars were shortened at the tips to add strength, blunting the previously raked tips and reducing overall wingspan; a smaller windscreen was fitted; a small fabric-covered head fairing was fitted behind the cockpit. Together with the 200hp engine and the Vickers-plus-Lewis armament as standard, this became the S.E. 5a, which went into large scale production, with the total built by five companies reaching over 5,300 in less than 18 months. Because engine production could not maintain this pace, some S.E. 5a aircraft

were fitted with available alternatives.

There were twenty-two squadrons of the Royal Flying Corps and U.S. Air Service flying the S.E. 5a by the end of the war. It was a favorite mount of many of the Allies' aces, including the British Edward Mannock (73 victories) and James McCudden (57 victories), and the Canadian William Bishop (72 victories). One regarded by many as the greatest was the British Albert Ball (44 victories, 10 in an S.E. 5a), who made several modifications to his personal aircraft, including stripping out the Vickers gun and using the space for extra fuel.

Specifications for Royal Aircraft Factory S.E. 5a

Dimensions:	wingspan 26 feet 7.5 inches, length 20 feet 11 inches, height 9 feet 6 inches
Power:	(most aircraft) one Hispano-Suiza 8B liquid-cooled V-8 of 200hp driving a four-bladed propeller
Weights:	empty 1,531lb, normal takeoff 1,940lb
Speed:	max 138mph at sea level, 126mph at 10,000 feet, 116mph at 15,000 feet
Ceiling:	17,000 feet
Range:	345 miles
Armament:	one fixed, drum-fed 0.303in Lewis gun on a Foster mount above the top wing with four 97-round drums, and one fixed, synchronized belt-fed 0.303in Vickers machine gun mounted above the nose, with 400 rounds
Crew:	pilot

Royal Aircraft Factory S.E. 5a cutaway key

1 Fixed-pitch laminated wooden propeller
2 Radiator filler cap
3 Aluminum engine top cowling panel
4 Auxiliary fuel tank
5 Cylinder head fairing
6 Wolsley Viper 200hp (149kW) direct drive engine
7 Carburetor
8 Exhaust stubs
9 Propeller hub bolted attachment
10 Radiator
11 Main engine bearer
12 Engine mounting bulkheads
13 Engine sump
14 Cooling air louvers in hinged bottom cowling panel
15 Port upper aileron
16 Spruce wing spars, spindled for lightness
17 Double compression rib
18 Aileron control horn
19 Aileron balance cable pulley
20 Wing panel internal wire bracing
21 Wing tip edge member
22 Port interplane struts
23 Diagonal wire bracing
24 Leading edge riblets
25 Aileron drive cable pulley
26 Auxiliary spar
27 Wing rib construction
28 Port lower aileron
29 Aileron rib construction
30 Lower aileron control horn
31 Aileron interconnecting cable
32 Interplane strut attachment fittings
33 Port mainwheel
34 Wheel spoke fabric cover
35 Elastic cord shock absorber
36 Undercarriage leg V struts
37 Trailing edge ribs
38 Axle fairing
39 Starboard mainwheel
40 Wing spar bolted root attachments
41 Fuselage lower main longeron/wing mounting beam
42 Rudder pedal bar
43 Priming pump
44 Constantinesco C.C. gun interrupted gear drive
45 Cartridge case ejection chute
46 Vertical frame member
47 Wing spar mounting tubular cross-member
48 Cooling air vent

49 Sloping bulkhead
50 Engine oil tank
51 Oil filler cap
52 Fuel tank supports
53 Main fuel tank
54 Machine gun cut-out
55 Center section cabane struts
56 Machine gun ring-and-bead sight
57 Upper wing panel bolted spar joints
58 Fuel contents gauge
59 Vickers 0.303in machine gun
60 Ammunition magazine, 400-rounds
61 Instrument panel
62 Engine throttle and compensator
63 Compass
64 Map pocket
65 Plywood top decking
66 Windscreen panel
67 Aldis sight
68 Gun firing cable
69 Lewis gun elevating track
70 Trailing edge cut-out
71 Wing panel center section construction
72 Foster sliding gun mounting
73 0.303in Lewis machine gun
74 Interchangeable ammunition drum, 97-rounds
75 Starboard upper wing panel rib construction
76 Compression rib
77 Wing panel fabric covering
78 Aileron control cable and horn
79 Starboard upper aileron
80 Interconnecting cable
81 Starboard lower aileron
82 Interplane struts
83 Diagonal wire bracing
84 Landing wires
85 Flying wires double
86 Starboard fabric-covered lower wing panel
87 Cockpit coaming
88 Radiator shutter lever
89 Ignition switches
90 Control column handgrip with engine cut-out and gun triggers
91 Lewis gun spare ammunition drum
92 Exhaust pipe
93 Cockpit floor boards
94 Elevator trim handwheel
95 Boarding step

96 Seat mounting
97 Pilot's seat
98 Seat back sloping bulkhead
99 Headrest fairing
100 Personal equipment locker
101 Locker hatch
102 Fuselage fabric covering
103 Dorsal fairing frames and stringers
104 Fin front attachment
105 Fabric-covered fin structure
106 Tailplane bracing wires
107 Hollow sternpost with internal tailplane trim adjustment
108 Rudder control horn
109 Starboard fabric-covered tailplane
110 Starboard elevator
111 Elevator control horn and cable
112 Fabric-covered rudder
113 Steerable tail skid
114 Shock absorber spring
115 Tailplane trim adjustment screw jack and sprocket drive
116 Ventral fin
117 Port elevator rib construction
118 Tailplane rib construction
119 Leading edge riblets
120 Compression rib
121 Elevator control horns
122 Elevator drive cables and pulleys
123 Tailplane internal wire bracing
124 Hinged spar attachment joint
125 Fuselage upper longeron
126 Vertical spacers
127 Tailplane control cables
128 Fabric lacing (taped and doped)
129 Diagonal wire bracing
130 Fuselage lower longeron
131 Rear fuselage longeron joints

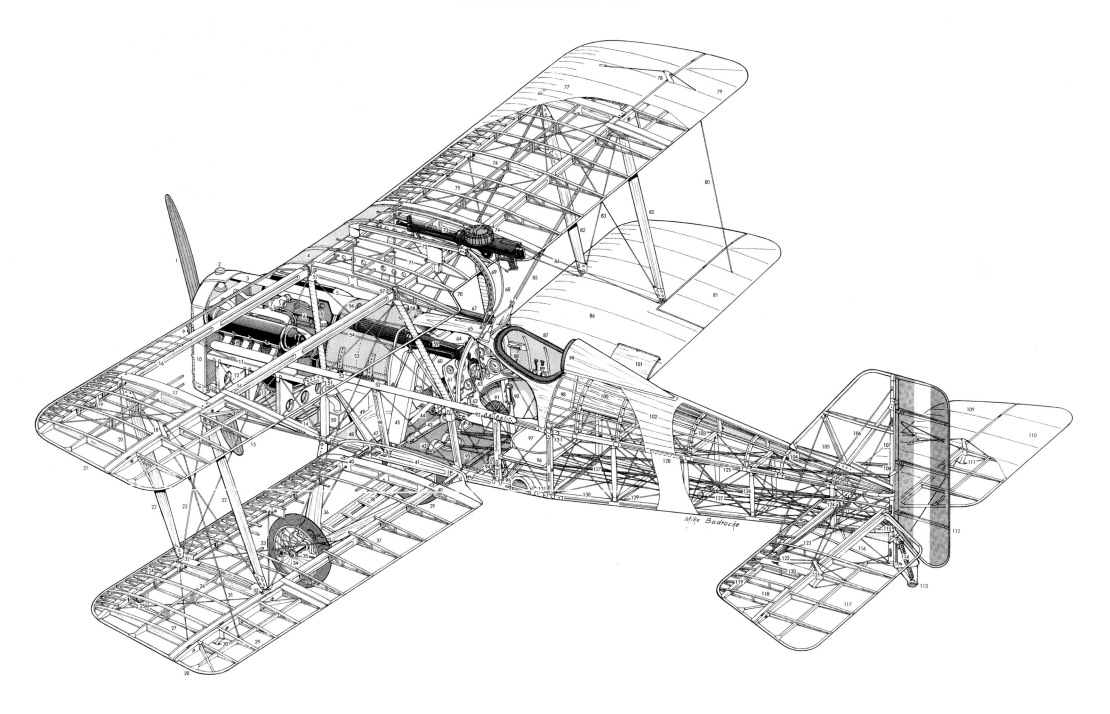

Mike Badrocke

Copyright Mike Badrocke – 2004

THIS PAGE: The S.E. 5 made its combat debut in "Bloody April" 1917 with No 56 Squadron RFC, but was quickly superseded by the improved S.E. 5a. Seen here is G. H. Lewis of No 40 Squadron, in his personal aircraft.

INSET: The S.E. 5a was flown by many of the top-scoring RFC and RAF aces, including Mannock, McCudden and Bishop. This is Roderic Dallas, the Australian top scorer with fifty-one victories. He was killed in action in June 1918.

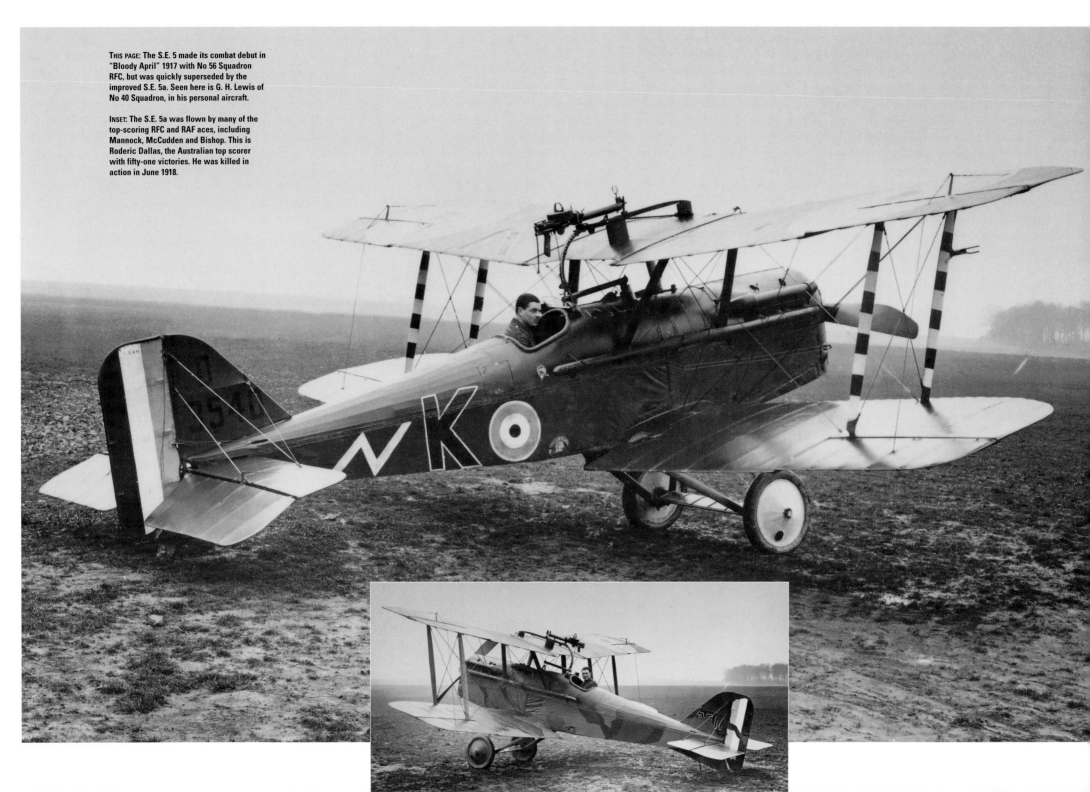

THIS PAGE: For its day, the S.E. 5a was a high performance fighter, with a maximum speed of 138mph, and could reach 200mph in a dive without pulling the wings off. A stable airplane, it was easy to fly.

INSET: The Lewis gun on the top plane could be pulled down for the drum to be changed. Aiming was via the tubular Aldiss sight. Seen in July 1918, the pilot, of No 1 Squadron RAF, holds the Very pistol used for signaling.

SAAB 37 VIGGEN

Sweden is a militarily neutral country, but its defense forces still have a duty to protect its people and land, and when, in the late 1950s, it was decided to build a fleet of advanced multi-role jet fighters to replace its aging J35 Draken and the A32 Lansen fighter-bomber, the air force (*Flygvapen*) posed the Saab designers a whole range of problems. The new fighter, to be called Viggen (Thunderbolt), was intended to cope with low-altitude strike and reconnaissance missions involving Mach 1 flight at sea level, have powerful acceleration and climbing ability, plus a Mach 2 top speed, while still having good high-altitude performance for the interception role. For good measure, *Flygvapen* demanded short takeoff and landing (STOL) performance so that the new aircraft could operate from short runways and strips of strengthened roads. Following initial studies in 1961, it was decided that four basic variants were required for air superiority and interception, attack, reconnaissance, and training.

What emerged was an aircraft that was remarkable in many ways, not least the fact that it came from a home-grown program developed by a nation of fewer than nine million people. The most dramatic aspect, though, was its shape. The double-delta layout of the Draken had already displayed the Swedish designers' ability to devise unique planforms tailored to national requirements; now Saab came up with an even more revolutionary concept for the Viggen. Instead of plumping for perhaps the rather more obvious variable-geometry solution, Saab decided on a canard layout, with a cranked delta wing and, ahead of it, mounted on the air intakes, large fixed canards with moving control surface on their trailing edges. The canards provided extra lift required for short field performance, and also produced vortices across the main wing surface at high angles of attack, affording required stability. The wing is of compound-sweep form, and incorporates hydraulically actuated elevons designed to work differentially or in unison. Little wonder that the Viggen has been described as virtually a supersonic biplane.

Most of the fuselage is made from aluminum alloy, with titanium restricted to critical areas of the engine bay. Extensive use of honeycombed-bonded components in the fuselage, moving surfaces in the wing, canard and fin, and also in the undercarriage doors. Fuel is carried in six tanks.

The powerplant chosen for early Viggens was the Pratt & Whitney JT8D airliner turbofan engine, modified into the JT8D-22 by Volvo Flygmotor for supersonic flight and for hauling heavy ordnance loads out of short strips. For the fighter version of the Viggen, the JA 37, the more powerful

RM8B was developed from the P&W engine.

The JA 37 fighter version was armed with a 30mm Oerlikon KCA cannon, plus Skyflash semi-active homing (SARH) and Sidewinder infrared homing air-to-air missiles; more recently it has carried the Amraam fire-and-forget missile.

Development and production initially concentrated on the AJ 37 attack version, which first flew on February 8, 1967, the first of 110 production examples flying on February 23, 1971. There followed 70 SF 37 and SH 37 reconnaissance aircraft and two-seat SK 37 trainers. The JA 37 fighter was essentially an extensively re-engineered "second generation" Viggen, optimized for the interceptor fighter role, and this first flew on December 15, 1979, entering service from 1980. A total of 329 of all variants had been built by the time production ended in June 1990. Replacement of the Viggen by the Saab JAS 39 Gripen began in October 1995, but a few upgraded Viggens will remain in service until 2007.

ABOVE: Sweden's Viggen was an ingenious attempt by Saab to produce an airframe that could be customized for various roles. First flight of the prototype took place in February 1967. This is the JA 37 dedicated fighter/interceptor variant, which first flew in December 1979; service entry began in 1980.

Specifications for Saab JAS 37 Viggen

Dimensions: wingspan 34 feet 9.25 inches, length 53 feet 9.75 inches, height 19 feet 4.25 inches

Power: one Volvo Flygmotor RM8B (based on Pratt & Whitney JT8D) two-spool, axial-flow, afterburning turbofan rated at 28,110lb max and 16,208lb military thrust

Weights: empty 23,655lb, normal takeoff 37,478lb, max 44,092lb

Speed: max 1,364mph Mach 2.1 at 36,100 feet, 840mph at 1,000 feet

Ceiling: 60,040 feet

Range: tactical radius 620 miles

Armament: one 30mm Oerlikon KCA cannon with 150 rounds, two Rb74 Sidewinder missiles and either two Rb71 Skyflash or four Rb99 Amraam air-to-air missiles

Crew: pilot

Saab 37 Viggen cutaway key

1 Pitot head
2 Glass-fiber radome
3 Radar scanner housing
4 LM Ericsson PS-37/A radar equipment module
5 Incidence probe
6 Cockpit pressure bulkhead
7 Forward avionics equipment bay
8 Rudder pedals
9 Instrument panel shroud
10 One piece frameless windscreen panel
11 Pilot's head-up display
12 Upward-hinging cockpit canopy
13 Ejection seat arming lever
14 Saab rocket-powered ejection seat
15 Engine throttle lever
16 Boundary layer splitter plate
17 Port air intake
18 Landing/taxiing lamp
19 Twin nosewheels, forward retracting
20 Hydraulic steering control
21 Red Baron multisensor reconnaissance pod
22 Centerline external fuel tank
23 Electro-luminescent formation lighting strip
24 Central avionics equipment bay
25 Intake ducting
26 Boundary layer spill duct
27 Forward fuselage integral fuel tank
28 Dorsal avionics equipment bay
29 Starboard canard foreplane
30 Canard flap
31 SATT AQ31 ECM jamming pod
32 SSR transponder aerial
33 Anti-collision light
34 Air-conditioning equipment bay
35 Heat exchanger air exhaust
36 Intake flank fuel tankage
37 Engine compressor face
38 Accessory equipment gearbox
39 Foreplane spar attachment joint
40 Fuselage flank avionics equipment bays, port and starboard
41 Emergency ram air turbine
42 Port canard foreplane flap honeycomb panel
43 Hydraulic reservoirs
44 Formation lighting strip
45 Centre fuselage integral fuel tankage
46 Main engine mounting
47 Volvo Flygmoto RM8A afterburning turbofan engine
48 Engine bleed air pre-cooler
49 Fuel-cooled engine oil cooler
50 Wing spar attachment fuselage main frame
51 Fuel system recuperators
52 ADF aerial
53 Starboard wing panel
54 Outboard missile pylon
55 ECM antenna fairing
56 Extended-chord outboard leading edge
57 Starboard navigation light
58 Starboard elevon panels
59 Artificial feel system pressure head
60 Fin tip aerial fairing
61 Multi-spar fin construction
62 Rudder hydraulic actuator
63 Fin spar attachment joints
64 Hydraulic hand pump for hangaring fin folding
65 Port lateral airbrake
66 Airbrake hydraulic jack
67 Afterburner ducting
68 Variable area afterburner nozzle control jack
69 Exhaust duct ejector seal (closed at speeds above Mach 1)
70 Ejector seal screw jack
71 Thrust reverser door pneumatic actuator
72 Radar warning antennas
73 Engine/afterburner exhaust nozzle
74 Thrust reverser blocker doors
75 Tail navigation light
76 Lower thrust reverser door pneumatic actuator
77 Port inboard elevon
78 Elevon hydraulic actuators
79 Elevon honeycomb construction
80 Port outboard elevon
81 Port navigation lights
82 Outboard elevon hydraulic actuator
83 Saab Bofors Rb 24 (license-built Sidewinder) air-to-air self-defense missile
84 Missile launch rail
85 ECM antenna fairing
86 Bofors BOZ-9 flare launcher pod
87 Wing stores pylon
88 Honeycomb wing skin panels
89 Multispar wing panel construction
90 Wing panel integral fuel tank
91 Main spar
92 Main undercarriage wheel bay
93 Side breaker strut
94 Hydraulic retraction jack
95 Main undercarriage mounting rib
96 Mainwheel leg strut
97 Torque scissor links
98 Tandem mainwheels
99 Starboard fuselage pylon
100 Long-range camera pod
101 Rb 05A air-to-surface missile
102 Rb 04E air-to-surface anti-ship missile
103 Missile launch adaptor

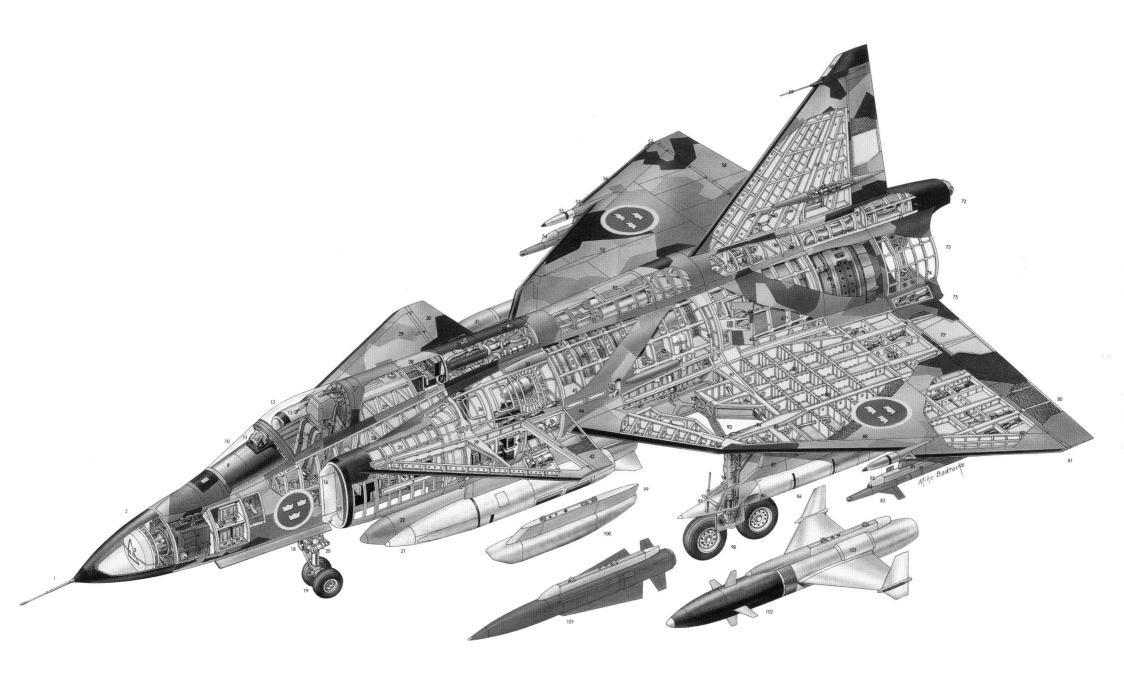

Mike Badrocke

LEFT: Short field performance was a primary consideration for all Viggens. This is reflected by the unusual delta wing, with the sharpest sweep outboard, and the fixed canards, which have moving trailing edges.

BELOW: Afterburner blasting, this Viggen lifts off after a very short ground run. This is actually an AJ 37 attack aircraft, as is shown by the straight trailing edge of the vertical fin and rudder.

OPPOSITE: Three JA 37 Viggens of F13 Wing based at Norrkoping. The two nearest the camera are finished in air superiority gray, but the third appears to have an experimental white paint job. This was not adopted.

SAAB IG JAS 39 GRIPEN

LEFT: For such a small nation, Sweden has a remarkable record of producing advanced fighters. The latest is the multi-role JAS 39 Gripen, the first of three new European canard deltas to enter service, in June 1996.

By 1979, a successor to the radical Viggen (described elsewhere) was under consideration for the Royal Swedish Air Force (*Flygvapen*) and a consortium made up of Saab-Scania, Volvo Flygmotor, Ericsson and FFV Aerotech was formed as Industri Gruppen JAS to designa and produce the JAS (*Jakt/Attack/Spåning*, or fighter/attack/reconnaissance) Gripen. It needed the latest technology: fly-by-wire (FBW), relaxed stability, a high thrust-to-weight ratio with moderate wing loading, composite construction, a modern multi-mode radar, and a sophisticated suite of avionics. While the payload/range had to be at least equal to that of the Viggen, it had to be affordable in sufficient numbers. Therefore it had to be smaller than the Viggen. Studies suggested that advances in technology would make possible a lightweight fighter with full capability. The fighter variant took precedence over attack and reconnaissance versions.

The engine selected for the new single-engined fighter was the General Electric F404 turbofan which had been selected for the twin-engined F/A-18 Hornet, but developed by Volvo Flygmotor and GE to form the increased-thrust RM12.

A tail-less delta wing planform was adopted, set in the mid position, mainly to optimize wing/body blending, but with the additional advantage that it provided plenty of clearance for external stores. The dogtooth leading edge has two flaps, while two elevons make up the trailing edge. All-moving canard foreplanes are mounted on the outside of the intake ducts, behind the pilot's line of sight. These can be tilted at a steep angle after touchdown to provide aerodynamic braking, the download increasing the effectiveness of the main braking system for a short landing run, essential for offsite braking.

The advanced-technology cockpit is fitted with HOTAS (hands-on-throttle-and-stick), a wide-angle HUD (head-up display), three multi-function head-down displays, and a steeply raked Martin-Baker ejection seat. The look-down shoot-down radar is the Ericsson PS-05/A pulse-Doppler set, with an estimated detection range out to 50 nautical miles, while the fighter is also equipped with an Ericsson electronic warfare suite. Mission profiles can be amended after takeoff using on-board programmable software and integrated weapons systems. Armament consists of a 27mm Mauser cannon, two Skyflash or Amraam missiles, and four Sidewinders. The aircraft can also carry a wide range of air-to-surface ordnance.

Overall, the Gripen is about two-thirds the size of the Viggen, less than half its weight, but with similar performance. It has an extremely small radar cross-section, giving some stealth characteristics.

First flight of the prototype took place on December 9, 1988. Early flight-testing was protracted, with two crashes occurring in 1989, one on landing and the other during a public display. The JAS 39 first entered service with the *Flygvapen* in June 1996, with initial operational capability being achieved in late 1997.

Sweden has ordered 176 single-seat JAS 39As and 28 two-seat, fully combat-capable trainer Bs. An upgraded version, the JAS 39C/D, with more powerful engine and a flight-refueling probe is due to enter service up to 2006. Thrust-vectoring is also planned for future versions. South Africa is expected to take delivery of 28 Gripens. Total orders are expected to be in excess of 200.

Specifications for Saab JAS 39A Gripen

Dimensions:	wingspan 27 feet 7 inches, length 46 feet 3 inches, height 14 feet 9 inches
Power:	one Volvo Flygmotor RM12 afterburning two-spool turbofan rated at 18,105lb max and 12,141lb military thrust
Weights:	empty 14,595lb, normal takeoff 19,225lb, max 30,865lb
Speed:	max Mach 1.8 at altitude, supersonic at low level
Ceiling:	50,000 feet
Range:	497 miles
Armament:	one 27mm Mauser BK 27 cannon, two AIM-120 Amraam and four Rb 74 Sidewinder or MICA air-to-air missiles, plus provision for a range of air-to-surface weapons
Crew:	pilot

Saab JAS 39A Gripen cutaway key

1 Pitot head
2 Vortex-generating strakes
3 Glass-fiber radome
4 Radar scanner
5 Scanner mounting and tracking mechanism
6 Radar mounting bulkhead
7 ADF antenna
8 Ericsson/GEC-Marconi Avionics PS-05A multi-mode pulse Doppler radar equipment racks
9 Yaw vane
10 Cockpit front pressure bulkhead
11 Lower UHF antenna
12 Incidence vane
13 Electro-luminescent formation lighting strip
14 Rudder pedals (digital flight control system)
15 Instrument panel, three Ericsson head-down CRT displays
16 Instrument panel shroud
17 Single-piece frameless windscreen panel
18 Hughes wide-angle head-up-display (HUD)
19 Ericsson ECM pod
20 Starboard intake stores pylon
21 Cockpit canopy, hinged to port
22 Canopy breaker detonating cord
23 Starboard air intake
24 Martin-Baker S10LS "zero-zero" ejection seat
25 Sloping cockpit rear pressure bulkhead
26 Slide mounted engine throttle lever, hands-on-throttle-and-stick (HOTAS) controls
27 Side console panel
28 Cockpit section honeycomb composite structure
29 Door-mounted taxiing light
30 Nosewheel leg door
31 Twin-wheel nose undercarriage, aft retracting
32 Hydraulic steering unit
33 Cannon muzzle
34 Port engine air intake
35 Boundary layer splitter plate
36 Air conditioning system heat exchanger intake duct
37 Avionics equipment bay, access through nosewheel bay
38 Boundary layer spill duct
39 Cockpit rear avionics shelf
40 Starboard canard foreplane
41 UHF antenna
42 Heat exchanger exhaust ducts
43 BAe environmental control system equipment for cabin conditioning, pressurisation and equipment cooling
44 Self-sealing fuel tank between intake ducts
45 Canard foreplane hydraulic actuator
46 Foreplane hinge-mounting trunnion
47 Port intake ducting
48 27mm Mauser BK27 cannon barrel, single gun offset to port
49 Temperature probe
50 Port navigation light
51 Centerline external fuel tank
52 Ammunition loading door
53 Ground test panels
54 Formation lighting strips
55 Port canard foreplane carbon-fiber composite structure
56 Cannon ammunition magazine
57 Center fuselage aluminum alloy structure and skin pane1ing
58 Upper fuselage strakes
59 VHF antenna
60 Dorsal spine fairing
61 TACAN antenna
62 Bleed air and cable ducting
63 Fuselage integral fuel tankage
64 Hydraulic reservoir, dual system port and starboard
65 Forged and machined wing attachment fuse-lage main frames
66 Engine compressor intake
67 IFF antenna
68 Wing attachment carbon-fiber composite cover panel
69 Starboard wing integral fuel tank
70 Pylon hardpoints
71 Starboard stores pylons
72 Leading edge dog-tooth
73 Leading edge maneuvering flap
74 Carbon-fiber composite wing skin paneling
75 Combined wing tip EW pod and missile launch rail
76 Wing tip missile installation
77 Rear position light, port and starboard
78 Starboard outboard elevon
79 Inboard elevon
80 Inboard elevon actuator housing fairing
81 Bleed air spill duct
82 Formation lighting strips
83 Pneumatic flight control system equipment
84 Fin root attachment joints
85 Rudder hydraulic actuator
86 Carbon-fiber composite skin paneling with honeycomb substrate
87 Flight control system dynamic pressure sensor
88 Forward radar warning antenna
89 ECM equipment fairing
90 UHF antenna
91 Glass-fiber fin tip antenna housing
92 Strobe light/anti-collision beacon
93 Carbon-fiber composite rudder
94 Variable area afterburner nozzle
95 Nozzle control actuator (3)
96 Port airbrake panel, open
97 Airbrake hinge fairings
98 Airbrake hydraulic jack
99 Afterburner ducting
100 General Electric/Volvo Flygmotor RM12 (F404-GE-400) afterburning turbofan engine
101 Rear equipment bay, port and starboard
102 Microturbo Auxiliary Power Unit (APU)
103 Airframe mounted accessory equipment gearbox bay
104 Titanium wing root attachment fittings
105 Port wing integral fuel tank
106 Multi-spar wing panel primary structure
107 Inboard elevon actuator
108 Port inboard elevon
109 Elevon carbon-fiber skin paneling with honeycomb substrate
110 Port outboard elevon
111 Port rear quadrant radar warning antenna
112 Rb 74/AIM-9L Sidewinder, close range air-to-air missile
113 Wing tip missile launch rail
114 Port forward oblique radar warning antenna
115 Port leading edge maneuvering flap
116 Leading edge flap carbon-fiber composite construction
117 Outboard pylon hardpoint
118 Rb 75 Maverick air-to-surface anti-armor missile
119 Missile launch rail
120 Outboard stores pylon
121 Port mainwheel
122 Leading edge flap powered hinge actuator
123 Inboard pylon hardpoint
124 Mainwheel leg mounted landing light
125 Shock absorber mainwheel leg strut
126 Mainwheel leg pivot mounting

127 Hydraulic retraction jack
128 Leading edge flap drive motor and torque shaft
129 Mainwheel leg drag/breaker strut
130 Mainwheel door, closed after cycling of undercarriage
131 Inboard stores pylon
132 Wing mounted external fuel tank
133 MBB/DWS 39 sub-munitions dispenser
134 Saab RBF 15F anti-shipping missile
135 Meteor future medium-range air-to-air missile (Fmraam)
136 AIM-120 advanced medium-range air-to-air missile (Amraam)
137 Matra Mica EM close-range air-to-air missile
138 Bofors M70 six-round 135mm rocket pack

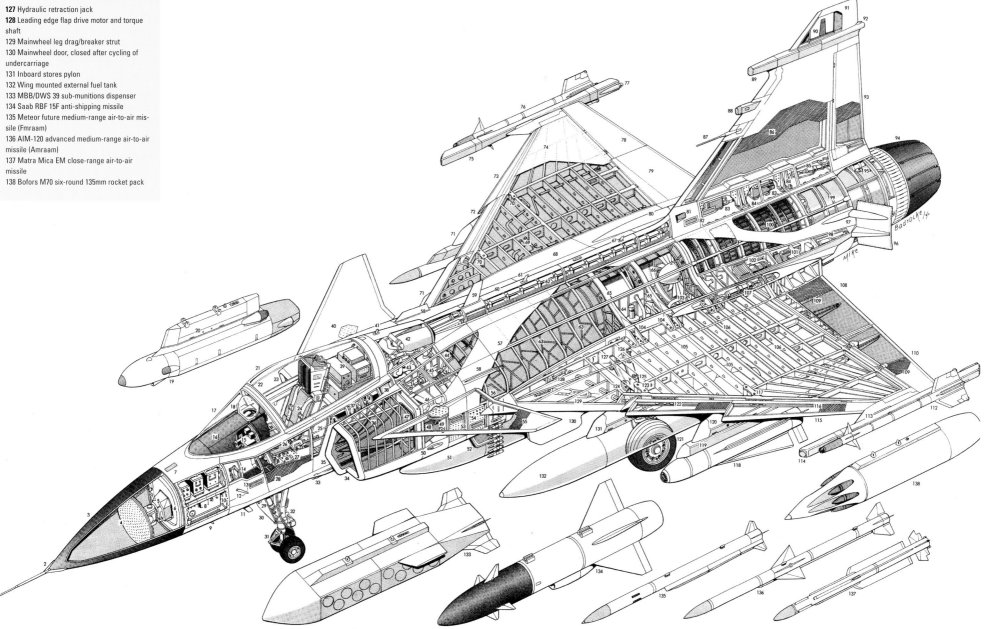

Copyright Mike Badrocke – 2004

ABOVE: The keynote for Gripen was capability with affordability, both for the Swedish Air Force and for potential export customers. In essence, this meant small. By contemporary standards, Gripen is tiny.

RIGHT: From head-on, Gripen almost appears to have been tailored around the pilot. In fact it was sized around the RM-12 turbofan, a developed General Electric F404, the thrust of which determines weight, payload, etc.

LEFT : The canard foreplanes deploy to give aerodynamic braking after touchdown, to aid short field performance. A chin inlet would have been preferable, but ground clearance would have been insufficient. The mid wing location was chosen to give enough ground clearance for stores.

ABOVE: Gripen was built by a consortium called Industri Gruppen JAS AB, consisting of Saab-Scania, Volvo Flygmotor, Ericsson, and AFV Aerotech. Gripens began replacing Viggens in *Flygvapen* (Swedish Air Force) service in 1996-7.

SOPWITH SCOUT (PUP)

The Sopwith Scout, affectionately known as the Pup, is considered by many to have been the finest flying machine ever built. Initially flown in February 1916, and entering service from August that year, it was the first British single-seat aircraft designed to bring a synchronized gun to bear as a fighter. It was a very small, simple airplane of mainly fabric-covered wooden construction with two-spar main-planes forming a single-bay wing cellule and wire-braced box girder fuselage. Although it was fitted with an under-powered French rotary engine, it was a robust aircraft with impeccable handling qualities, and had an aerobatic prowess that earned it countless combat victories. Its armament was a single, centrally mounted machine gun synchronized to fire through the propeller disc by means of an interrupter system.

The Scout/Pup served with both the Royal Naval Air Service (RNAS) and the Royal Flying Corps (RFC) and by the end of 1916 was fighting in France, where it was found to be more than a match for the early German opposition, such as the Albatros D I and D II, having a tighter turning circle and being capable of maintaining height in turns, even at considerable altitudes. However, within a few months it was outclassed by more powerful German machines, and the RNAS began to phase out the Pup early in 1917, although the RFC soldiered on with it until the end of that year.

By that time, however, it had started a new career – in the development of aircraft carriers, in the modern sense of the term, in which Britain led the way. This followed experiments aimed at permitting the operation of wheeled airplanes from ships, which would not then have to heave-to in order to launch and recover their seaplanes.

Early in 1917 both Royal Navy vessels *Campania* and *Manxman* were issued with Pup fighters after Flight Commander F. J. Rutland had shown that the Sopwith air-craft could be flown off the seaplane decks of these ships. Rutland demonstrated that the Pup could take off after a fif-teen-foot run at a speed of about 23mph. As a result, some twenty-two British light cruisers, starting with HMS *Yarmouth*, were fitted with twenty-foot flying-off platforms and issued with fighters. On August 21, 1917, a Pup launched by the *Yarmouth* and flown by Flight Sub-Lieutenant B. A. Smart intercepted and shot down the Zeppelin *L.23*.

To overcome the objection that the ships had to turn into the wind to launch their aircraft, Rutland evolved a technique for flying off platforms attached to the swiveling gun turrets of battle cruisers, which then adopted two fighters each as standard equipment.

This still left the problem of landing back aboard the ship. Hair-raising experiments were made in August 1917 on HMS *Furious*, a light battle cruiser converted in con-struction to carry seaplanes and wheeled airplanes, which were launched from a flying-off deck some 228 feet long ahead of the bridge structure. Combining a ship speed of about 21 knots and a wind speed of 25 knots or more, the airflow over the flight deck could match the landing speed of the Pup. Squadron Commander E. H. Dunning took advantage of this to show how the aircraft could be landed on this early "carrier." Flying alongside the *Furious*, he side-slipped in ahead of the bridge and virtually hovered over the deck while men grabbed the aircraft as he cut the throttle. A successful landing – the first on board a warship under way – was made on August 2, 1917. Less than a week later, Dunning was killed in a further attempt.

LEFT: When it entered service late in 1916, the new Sopwith Scout bore a distinct family resem-blance to the two-seater 1½ Strutter. The joke became that the Strutter had pupped, and the name Pup stuck.

Sopwith Pup cutaway key

1 Fabric-covered port elevator
2 Fabric-covered rudder
3 Light tubular steel fin and rudder construction
4 Rudder post
5 Rudder operating crank
6 Tailskid elastic cord shock absorber
7 Wooden tailskid
8 Tailskid hinge mounting
9 Steel tailskid shoe
10 Starboard elevator
11 Elevator hinge bar
12 Elevator operating crank
13 Tailplane rib construction
14 Tailplane bracing wires
15 Elevator cables
16 Fabric-covered rear fuselage top decking
17 Elevator cable guide panel
18 Top longeron
19 Vertical spacers
20 Rudder cables
21 Bottom longeron
22 Fuselage cross bracing
23 Entry step, port
24 Plywood top decking
25 Port lower mainplane fabric
26 Port lower aileron
27 Aileron connecting cable
28 Interplane struts
29 Diagonal wire bracing
30 Light steel tube trailing edge
31 Rear spar
32 Wing ribs
33 Diagonal bracing wires
34 Spar bracing strut
35 Port upper aileron
36 Aileron operating crank
37 Wingtip diagonal bracing frame
38 Front spar
39 Leading edge construction
40 Port upper wing spar joints
41 Wing center section struts
42 Trailing edge cut-out
43 Fixed synchronized 0.303in Vickers machine gun
44 Gun synchronizing drive
45 Padded pilot's face guard
46 Gun cocking lever
47 Padded cockpit coaming
48 Instrument panel
49 Control column
50 Pilot's seat
51 Cartridge elector chute
52 Rudder bar
53 Ammunition tank
54 Ammunition feed chute
55 Fuel tank
56 Engine bearer frame
57 Engine bulkhead
58 80hp Le Rhone rotary engine
59 Aluminum engine cowling
60 Propeller hub
61 Two-bladed wooden propeller
62 Starboard upper wing ribs
63 Leading edge stiffeners
64 Front spar
65 Spar bracing strut
66 Wing internal wire bracing
67 Wingtip diagonal bracing frame
68 Aileron balance cable
69 Aileron operating crank
70 Starboard upper aileron
71 Interplane bracing wires
72 Light steel tube trailing edge
73 Engine cooling air duct
74 Fabric-covered fuselage framework
75 Footboards
76 Lower wing/fuselage attachment rib
77 Port mainwheel
78 Undercarriage V strut
79 Axle beam
80 Half axle pivot fixing
81 Undercarriage bracing wires
82 Starboard mainwheel
83 Axle hub
84 Wing internal bracing wires
85 Interplane struts
86 Diagonal bracing wires
87 Spar bracing strut
88 Lower wing ribs
89 Aileron connecting cable
90 Starboard lower aileron
91 Aileron operating crank
92 Wingtip diagonal bracing frame
93 Light steel tube wingtip

Specifications for Sopwith Scout (Pup)

Dimensions: wingspan 26 feet 6 inches, length 19 feet 4 inches, height 9 feet 6 inches

Power: one 9-cylinder Le Rhone 9C rotary engine rated at 80hp

Weights: empty 787lb, normal takeoff 1,099lb

Speed: max 111.5mph at sea level, 94mph at 15,000 feet

Ceiling: 17,500 feet

Range: endurance 4 hours

Armament: one 0.303in belt-fed, nose-mounted, synchronized Vickers machine gun with 400 rounds, or one drum-fed Lewis gun with 291 rounds mounted on top plane (some aircraft carried eight Le Prieur unguided rockets on interplane struts)

Crew: pilot

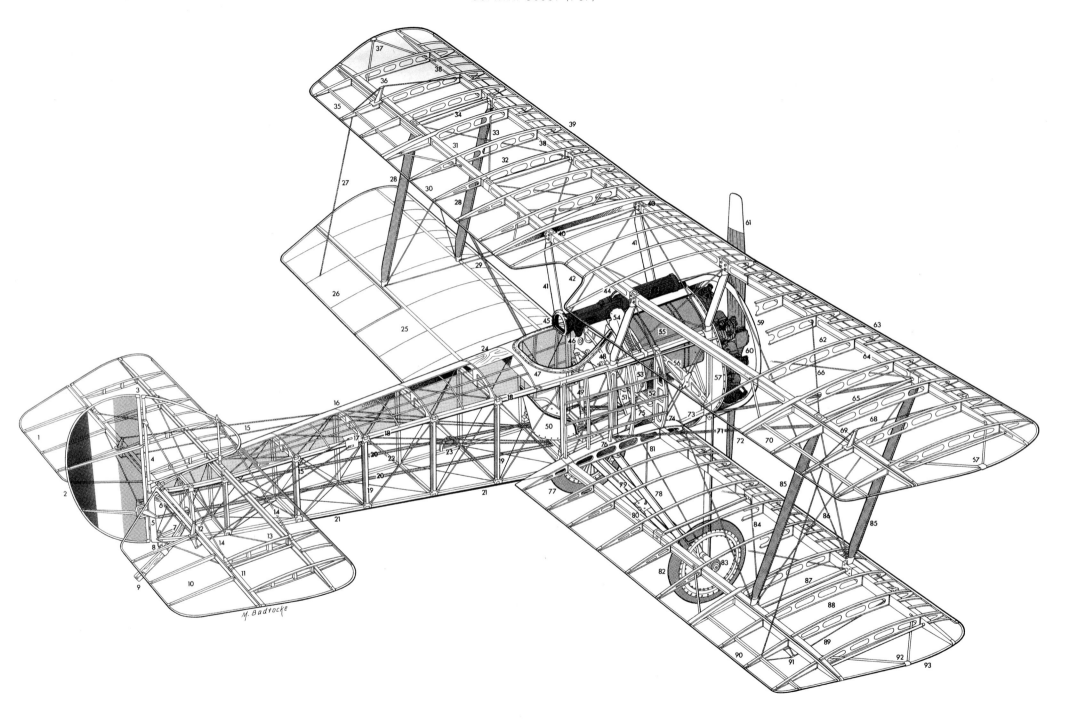

M. Badrocke

Copyright Mike Badrocke – 2004

RIGHT: The Pup was probably unique in that it could be looped directly after takeoff, and would continue to gain height during a series of loops. But, outperformed and outgunned by its German opponents, it was withdrawn at the end of 1917.

RIGHT INSET: Although underpowered, the Pup was one of the most agile fighters ever built, due to its light wing loading. It was operated on the Western Front by Britain's Royal Naval Air Service as well as the Royal Flying Corps.

OPPOSITE: "The best flying machine ever built," was one opinion of the Pup, but perhaps not to go to war in. It could out-turn any opponent near its ceiling, but its advantages were progressively lost as altitude was reduced.

OPPOSITE INSET: This is believed to be Lt. Cdr. Dunning making the first ever deck landing on a carrier under way, on HMS *Furious*, August 2, 1917. Forward way, wind over deck, and low stalling speed combined to make the relative speed of the Pup almost zero.

SPAD S. VII

The Spad VII was a rugged high-performance fighter of only moderate maneuverability, which nevertheless was the mount of several distinguished French aces of World War I. (The ace fighter pilot was first recognized by the French and defined as a pilot who had shot down five enemy aircraft. The Germans were rather more conservative, dubbing those who had accounted for ten enemy aircraft as aces, or *Obercannone*.) These included Georges Guynemer (destined to become France's greatest air hero, with 54 victories), René Fonck (75 victories), and Charles Nungesser (45 victories). The fighter was officially designated Spa. VII C1, and was named after the design organization Société anonyme pour l'Aviation et ses Dérivés, and first flew in April 1916.

The tempo of fighter development was frantic at that stage of World War I, with both sides vying for the advantage provided by more powerful engines giving higher speeds. Thus it was that the Spad reflected the demand for increased emphasis on level speed and dive capabilities at some expense of maneuverability that had resulted from actual combat experience over the Western Front. Just a few months later, however, despite having made an impact on the air war, the Spad VII had lost its edge as faster, more heavily armed adversaries gained air superiority.

It was a single-gunned, single-bay braced biplane with two sets of interplane struts, giving it the appearance of a twin-bay aircraft. It had a steeply raked low aspect ratio fin/rudder, and all trailing edges were braced with steel wire, giving a scalloped appearance. Many accounts indicate that it was not easy to fly, although it was more maneuverable than Britain's S.E. 5a (described elsewhere), and equal to it in a dive. Low-speed handling was apparently poor, and landing necessitated flying it into the ground with power on – just as well, then, that it was strong enough to withstand heavy grounding.

The first fighter units to receive the Spad S. VII were the elite *Les Cicognes*. Unlike the British, the French and Germans believed in recruiting their best fighter pilots into elite units. The most celebrated French units went under the generic term of *Les Cicognes*, or The Storks. These units embodied the finest pilots of the French air service from 1916 to the end of the war. Some would argue that such practice tended to denude other units of the leadership and example that might have improved them. Units of *Les Cicognes* could be recognized by the flying stork emblem usually painted along the fuselage.

In French service, the Spad S. VII quickly replaced the slower Nieuport 17 from September 1916. It was, in turn, replaced in front line French service by the up-engined, larger Spad S. XIII from summer 1917. Some 5,500 S. VIIs were built by several factories in France, a further 120 in Britain and more than 100 in Russia. The fighter was flown by pilots of at least seventeen nations, including Britain, Italy, Russia and the United States, and many remained in service until 1923.

Specifications for Spad S. VII

Dimensions: wingspan 25 feet 8 inches, length 19 feet 11 inches, height 7 feet 2.75 inches

Power: one Hispano-Suiza HS 8Aa liquid-cooled V-8 engine of 150hp

Weights: empty 1,102lb, normal takeoff 1,552lb

Speed: max 119mph at 6,560 feet

Ceiling: 18,045 feet

Range: endurance 2 hours 15 minutes

Armament: one 0.303in belt-fed, nose-mounted, synchronized Vickers machine gun with 400 rounds (some Russian aircraft carried Le Prieur unguided rockets)

Crew: pilot

ABOVE: First flown in April 1916, the SPAD S. VII was a very rugged aircraft, replacing the rather delicate Nieuport 17s which had equipped most French fighter squadrons (and not a few British) from later that year.

Spad S.VII cutaway key

1 Steel wire trailing edge
2 Rudder construction
3 Rudder post
4 Sternpost
5 Rudder hinge control
6 Starboard elevator
7 Elevator construction
8 Elevator hinge control
9 Tailplane construction
10 Fin construction
11 Tailskid
12 Steel shoe
13 Elastic cord shock absorber
14 Port elevator
15 Port tailplane
16 Fin attachment
17 Fuselage fabric covering
18 Dorsal construction
19 Dorsal stringers
20 Top longeron
21 Tailplane control cables
22 Vertical spacers
23 Bottom longeron
24 Fuselage stringers
25 Diagonal wire bracing
26 Headrest fairing
27 Plywood decking
28 Headrest
29 Padded cockpit coaming
30 Fuel filler cap
31 Used cartridge belt storage drum
32 Exhaust pipe tail fairing
33 Control cable pulleys
34 Pilot's seat
35 Safety harness
36 Underfloor fuel tank
37 Starboard upper wing panel construction
38 Upper wing spars
39 Compression rib
40 Internal wire bracing
41 Aileron horn control
42 Starboard aileron
43 Leading edge carry-round
44 Leading edge stiffeners
45 Interplane strut
46 Aileron control rod
47 Aileron rod crank
48 Lower wing spars
49 Compression rib
50 Internal wire bracing
51 Leading edge rib construction
52 Flying wire bracing

53 Flying wire support strut
54 Spar root fixing
55 Fuselage wing root rib
56 Cockpit floor panel
57 Rudder pedal bar
58 Fuselage keel member
59 Control column
60 Instrument panel
61 Gun cocking lever
62 Engine throttle
63 Center section strut
64 Windscreen
65 Padded trailing edge section
66 Service fuel tank
67 Steel wire trailing edge
68 Port aileron
69 Aileron horn
70 Port upper wing panel construction
71 Spar section joint
72 Interplane strut
73 Flying wires
74 Flying wire bracing strut
75 Lower wing panel fabric covering
76 Radiator header tank
77 Ammunition drum
78 Ammunition belt feed chute
79 Engine compartment bulkhead
80 0.303in Vickers machine gun
81 Engine blister fairing
82 Radiator filler cap
83 Engine access panel
84 205hp Hispano-Suiza 8Ab Vee-engine
85 Exhaust pipe
86 Engine bearer construction
87 Ventilation air intake panel
88 Nose cowlings
89 Radiator cowling wing
90 Water radiator

91 Radiator shutters
92 Propeller fixing bolts
93 Propeller hub
94 Two-bladed wooden propeller
95 Port mainwheel
96 Laminated wooden main undercarriage legs
97 Undercarriage leg top fixing
98 Undercarriage bracing wires
99 Fixed axle beam
100 Swing axle fixing
101 Elastic cord shock absorber
102 Wheel hub fixing
103 Fabric wheel disc fairing
104 Tire inflation valve
105 Starboard mainwheel

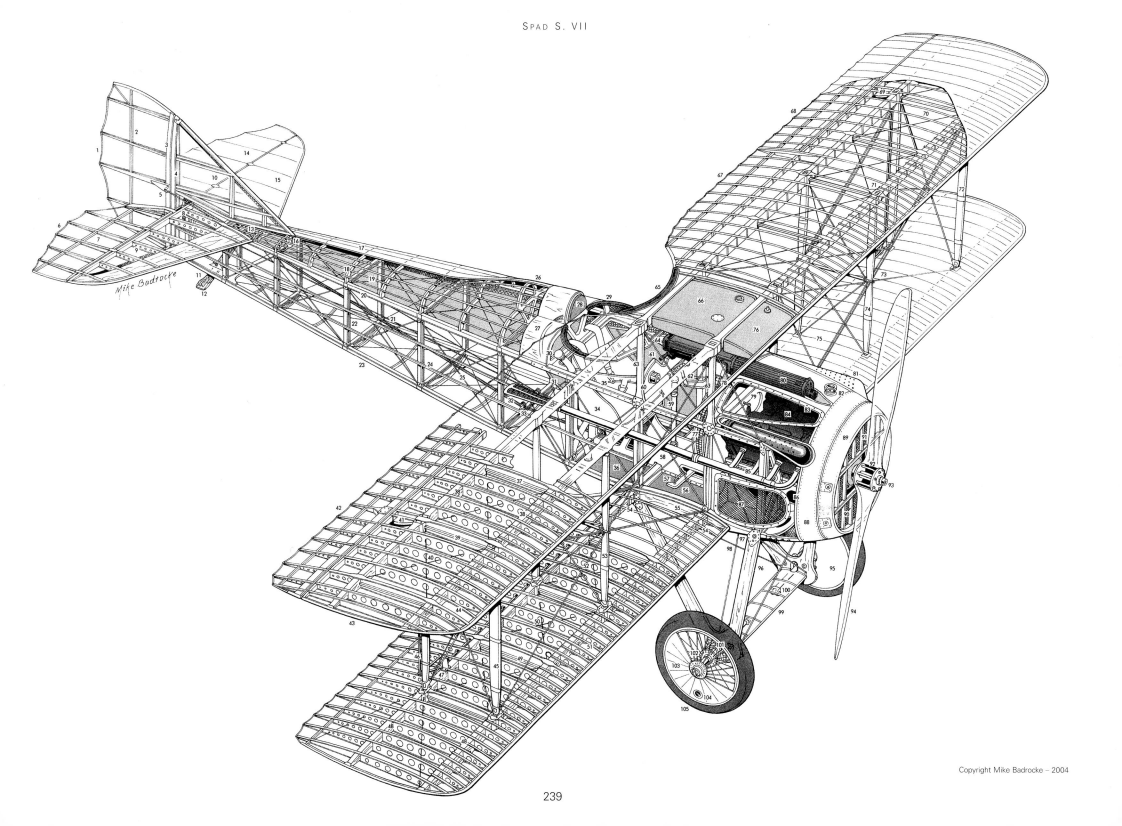

Mike Badrocke

Copyright Mike Badrocke – 2004

Opposite: Rugged or not, the Spad S. VII was not invulnerable. This machine was one of the elite *Cicognes.* Most high scoring French aces flew Spads at one time or another, including Guynemer, Fonck, and Nungesser.

Opposite inset: A ground crewman rather nervously prepares to swing the propeller of this Spad S. VII of SPA 99. The circular cowling is misleading; the engine was actually a water-cooled Hispano-Suiza V-8 with a circular radiator.

Below: Pictured in Seattle in March 1919, this Spad S. VII was built in England by Mann Egerton. The unrivaled exponent of the two Spad types was René Fonck, who scored 73 of his 75 victories with them.

Inset: The Spad was slightly more maneuverable than the S.E. 5a. Far from easy to handle, it had to be powered onto the ground to land. It was replaced from mid-1917 by the similar but more powerful S.XIII.

SUKHOI Su-27

Concerned that its standard tactical fighter, the MiG-23 Flogger, would be totally outclassed by the United States' evolving F-15 Eagle, the Soviet Union in 1969 had an urgent need for a high-performance fighter with outstanding combat persistence, with exceptional endurance and a heavy load of air-to-air missiles. Sukhoi's T-10 heavy fighter project was accepted in 1971, and what emerged was a huge, very capable fighter able to carry up to ten AAMs, and with massive internal fuel capacity, giving very long range without having to use drag-producing external tanks. It had two widely spaced turbofan engines, a wing of moderate sweep and high-aspect ratio, leading edge root extensions (LERX), low-set horizontal all-moving tails, and twin fins set forward on top of the engine nacelles.

The T-10-1 first flew on May 20, 1977, and handling problems were immediately obvious, with drag and fuel consumption being higher than predicted. The triplex analog fly-by-wire (FBW) flight control system demonstrated faults, and the crash of the second prototype, in which the pilot was killed, was attributed largely to this. In addition, computer studies showed that the T-10, which by then had been given the NATO reporting name of Flanker A, was far inferior to the F-15.

Without a realistic alternative, the fighter underwent almost total redesign, and the new aircraft, T-10-7, took to the air on April 20, 1987, entering production as the Su-27 in 1983. Changes included: much larger wing area; reduced wing sweep; squared tips with missile rails; full-span leading edge slats that could also operate as maneuver flaps; enlarged tailplane with cropped tips; increased-height vertical fins, now located outboard on booms; extended spine, with a long "sting" replacing the "beaver tail" between the engine exhausts; large dorsal speed brake; and forward-retracting nosewheel set further aft than the original, to improve ground handling.

Under the skin, the T-10-1's triplex FBW system was replaced by a quadruplex analog system, cockpit displays were analog, and the control column and throttle levers had numerous switches in Russia's first attempt at hands-on-throttle-and-stick (HOTAS). The pilot sat high under a two-piece bubble canopy that afforded him a 360-degree view. Fuel tankage was huge, and all internal, leaving the ten (later twelve) hardpoints free for ordnance.

Weapons were a 30mm cannon for close-range combat in the starboard wing root, and a combination of short- and medium-range air-to-air missiles. A huge multi-mode pulse-Doppler radar was housed in a massive radome.

After a long period of development and problem fixing,

production commenced in 1982, but service entry did not occur until 1986, when the big fighter was designated Flanker B by NATO. About 500 have been delivered to the Russian air forces. There have been many variants, including: the Su-27UB Flanker C fully combat capable conversion trainer; Su-27SK export version with downgraded avionics; Su-27K Flanker D carrier fighter with ski-jump takeoff and arrested landing capability, wing and tail folding, movable canards, full-span trailing edge flaps and ailerons, and flight refueling probe; and various attack and interdiction variants.

One important development was the highly maneuverable Su-35, widely known as the Super Flanker, which first flew as the T-10M-1 on June 28, 1988. It was equipped with a quadruplex digital FBW system, coupled with moving canard surfaces. Compared with the Su-27 it had square-topped fins, wingtip pods housing electronic warfare equipment, higher rated engines, "glass cockpit," fourteen hardpoints, and improved radars. Developed from the Su-35 Super Flanker was the Su-37, which was first flown on April 2, 1996, and introduced, among other things, thrust-vectoring engines, enabling the aircraft to perform "impossible" maneuvers which appear to have been more air show crowd-pleasers than valid combat maneuvers.

Flankers have flown with or have been ordered by at least nine air forces outside Russia, including China and India, where some have been license-built.

Specifications for Sukhoi Su-27 Flanker B

Dimensions:	wingspan 48 feet 3 inches, length 71 feet 11 inches, height 19 feet 6 inches
Power:	two Ly'ulka Saturn AL-31F twin-spool afterburning turbofans each rated at 16,755lb military and 27,558lb max thrust
Weights:	empty 36,112lb, normal takeoff 51,015lb, max takeoff 62,391lb
Speed:	max 1,553mph Mach 2.35 at 39,370 feet, 870mph Mach 1.14 at sea level
Ceiling:	60,700 feet
Range:	combat radius 677 miles on internal fuel with 10 missiles
Armament:	one 30mm single-barrel GSh-301 cannon with 150 rounds, up to 10 short- and medium-range air-to-air missiles
Crew:	pilot

Su-27K (Su-33) cutaway key

1 Pitot head
2 Upward-hinging radome
3 Radar scanner
4 Scanner mounting
5 Radome hinge point
6 Infra-red search and tracking scanner
7 Refueling probe housing
8 Radar equipment module; tilts down for access
9 Lower SRO-2 "Odd-Rods" IFF aerial
10 Incidence transmitter
11 Cockpit front pressure bulkhead
12 Retractable spotlight, port and starboard
13 Cockpit side console panel
14 Slide-mounted throttle levers
15 Flight-refueling probe, extended
16 Instrument panel shroud
17 Pilot's head-up display
18 Upward-hingeing cockpit canopy
19 K-36MD "zero-zero" ejection seat
20 Canopy hydraulic jack
21 Dynamic pressure probe, port and starboard
22 Cockpit rear pressure bulkhead
23 Temperature probe
24 Nosewheel door
25 Twin nosewheels, forward-retracting
26 ASM-MSS long-range ramjet and rocket-powered anti-shipping missile
27 Missile folding fins
28 Nosewheel hydraulic steering jacks
29 Deck approach "traffic-lights"
30 Leading-edge flush EW aerial
31 Avionics equipment bay
32 Ammunition magazine, 149 rounds
33 HF aerial
34 Starboard fuselage GSh-30-1 30mm cannon
35 Canard foreplane
36 Starboard wing missile armament
37 Dorsal airbrake
38 Gravity fuel filler cap
39 Center fuselage fuel tank
40 Forward lateral fuel tanks
41 ASM-MSS missile carrier on fuselage centerline station
42 Variable-area intake ramp doors
43 Ramp hydraulic jack
44 Foreplane hydraulic actuator
45 Port canard foreplane
46 Engine air intake
47 Boundary layer bleed air louvers
48 Segmented ventral suction relief doors
49 Retractable intake FOD screen

50 Mainwheel door
51 Door hydraulic jack
52 Port mainwheel bay
53 Intake trunking
54 Wing panel attachment joints
55 Engine compressor face
56 Wing center-section integral fuel tanks
57 ADF antenna
58 Airbrake hydraulic jack
59 Starboard mainwheel, stowed position
60 Fuel tank access panels
61 Wing-fold hydraulic jack
62 Leading-edge flap, down position
63 Starboard outer, folding, wing panel
64 Outboard plain flap, down position
65 Starboard wing, folded position
66 Inboard double-slotted flap segments
67 Engine bleed air pre-cooler air intake
68 Engine accessory equipment gearbox
69 Central auxiliary power unit
70 Chaff/flare launchers
71 Rear fuselage integral fuel tank
72 Engine oil tank
73 Fin structure
74 Leading-edge HF aerial
75 Rudder hydraulic actuator
76 Fintip UHF/VHF aerial
77 ILS aerial
78 Tail navigation light
79 Radar warning antenna
80 Starboard rudder
81 Starboard tailplane folded position
82 AL-31F afterburning turbofan engine
83 Port tailfin
84 ILS aerial
85 ECM antenna

86 Upper SRO-2 "Odd Rods" IFF aerial
87 Tailcone fairing
88 Rear EW antenna fairing
89 Deck arrester hook
90 Variable-area afterburner nozzle
91 Port tailplane
92 Tailplane fold joint rotary actuator
93 Tailplane pivot bearing
94 Hydraulic actuator
95 Hydraulic accumulator
96 Ventral fin
97 Port inboard double-slotted flap segments
98 Flap hydraulic actuators
99 Wing-fold hydraulic jack
100 Outer wing panel structure
101 Outboard plain flap segment
102 Port navigation light
103 Wingtip missile launch rail
104 Vympel R-73 (AA-11 "Archer") air-to-air missiles
105 Leading-edge flap
106 Pylon attachment hardpoints
107 Port wing integral fuel tank
108 Wing-fold locking mechanism jack
109 Main undercarriage hydraulic retraction jack
110 Mainwheel leg strut
111 Wing-fold hinge joint
112 Leading-edge flush EW aerial panels
113 Missile pylon
114 Vympel R-27 (AA-10 "Alamo-B") IR-homing air-to-air missile
115 Port mainwheel
116 Vympel R-27 (AA-10 "Alamo-C") RHAAM

ABOVE: Given the NATO reporting name of Flanker B, the Sukhoi Su-27 is without doubt the most outstanding modern Russian fighter. A twin-engined single seater, it is huge, even larger than the F-15. This is the Su-27SK.

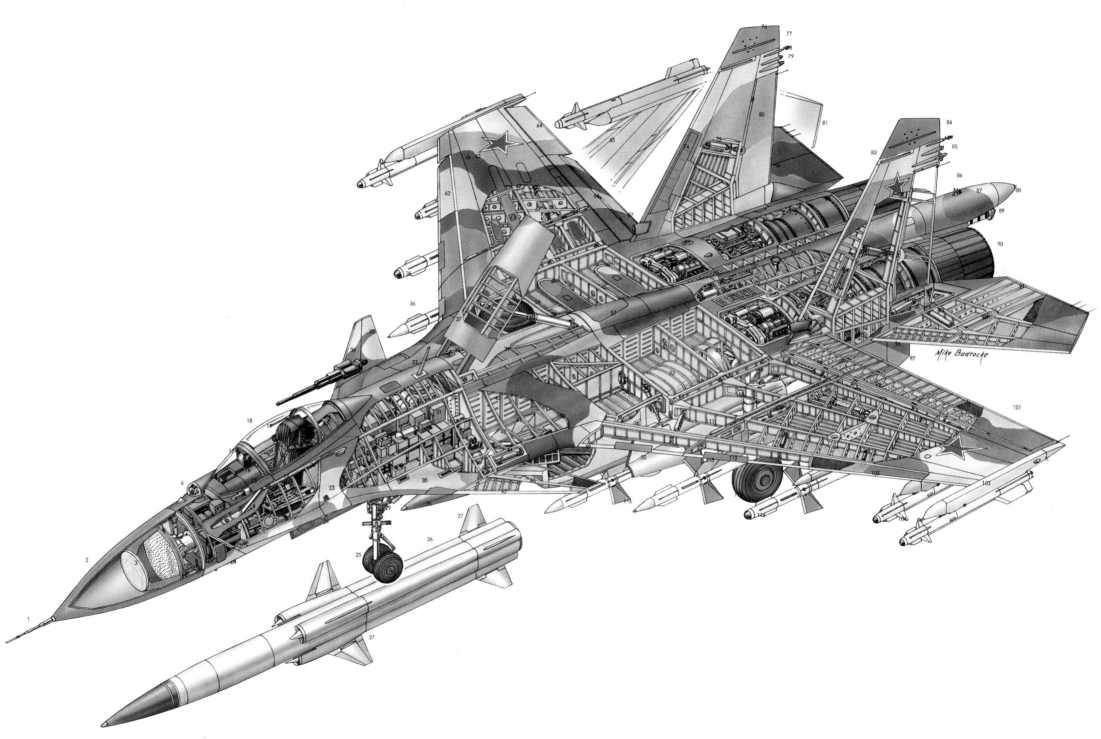

LEFT: Flanker first amazed the West at the Paris Air Show in 1989. Arriving virtually unheralded, and flown by chief test pilot Viktor Pugachev, the aircraft here performed the Cobra maneuver, something never before seen. Starting at level flight, he suddenly hoiked the fighter onto its tail, briefly passing an angle of attack of 100 degrees, before pitching back into a slight nose-down position.

ABOVE: As the Flanker's pilot seat level is high, all-round visibility is excellent. Even the IRST ball, seen here in front of the cockpit, is not obtrusive. Quadruplex analog (digital in later models) fly-by-wire contributes to its amazing maneuverability.

OPPOSITE : Developed from the two-seater combat trainer, the Su-30MK is a dedicated attack aircraft, able to carry more than eight tons of munitions on its twelve hardpoints. Unlike in the Su-34, the crew is seated in tandem.

OPPOSITE INSET: The Su-34, commonly known as the Platypus, is a dedicated all-weather attack aircraft. With a two-man crew seated side by side, it is limited to Mach 1.8. Canard foreplanes add to its maneuverability.

SUPERMARINE SPITFIRE

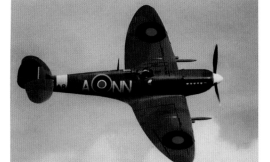

LEFT: The Spitfire is arguably the world's most famous fighter. First flown in March 1936, it remained in RAF service until 1957. This example is still flown by the Battle of Britain Memorial Flight.

Probably the most famous warplane in history, the Spitfire is widely regarded as the greatest fighter of World War II. It was first flown in March 1936 and entered large-scale production just in time for the war. Over Dunkirk in 1940, and during the Battle of Britain, it established a reputation second to none. Its ability to hold tight turns was outstanding, and later models were fitted with progressively more powerful engines and cannon armament. Such was the excellence of the original design that development continued through many variants until the end of the war, by this time with the more powerful Griffon engine in place of the Merlin. It served in every theater of the war with fifteen nations, was tropicalized for desert and jungle, and navalized for carrier operations as the Seafire.

The Spitfire had impeccable breeding, having been developed from a series of successful racing floatplanes, including the S.6B which, in 1931, had won the Schneider Trophy outright. It had the smallest practicable airframe that could be designed around its pilot, the selected engine and specified armament. It was of all-metal stressed-skin monocoque structure (the first such to enter production in Britain), with a thin wing of elliptical planform that had the lowest lift/drag ratio of any shape. Main gear legs retracted outboard into the wings, and the armament (initially four and later eight machine guns) was located in the wing roots. Its original fixed-pitch, two-bladed wooden propeller was replaced first by a two-pitch metal one and then by a three-bladed propeller.

The production Spitfire I first flew on May 14, 1938, and began reaching RAF squadrons in August 1939. There followed intensive and continuous development and incremental redesign resulting in three distinct generations based around the availability of more powerful engines, and also in answer to evolving service requirements to match different conditions and enemy warplane developments.

Total Spitfire production was in excess of 20,330, in addition to more than 2,550 Seafires. The Merlin-powered Spitfire Mk V was the most numerous variant and was produced in many subtypes. It was the main fighter version from 1941-42 in three forms, all with centerline rack for 500lb bomb or drop tank: VA with eight 0.303in guns; VB with two 20mm and four 0.303in guns; and VC with a choice of guns and two 250lb bombs.

Probably the most advanced of the Merlin-engined Spitfires was the VIII, with two-speed, two-stage supercharging, which entered service in August 1943 and saw action in Italy, Russia and the Far East but not the West.

The Spitfire IX was the second most numerous subtype built, and was a hybrid produced by fitting a Merlin 60 engine to a VC airframe.

The more powerful Griffon engine was being developed from an early stage, even before the war, and the major Spitfire variant powered by it to see action was the Mk XIV. It, too, was a hybrid, with a VIII airframe strengthened and modified to the Griffon 65 which had a five-bladed propeller. Late (and final) Mk XIVs had a teardrop canopy and cut-down rear fuselage.

The Spitfire XVIII was the final development of the original airframe, but it arrived too late to see action during World War II. The final Spitfire variant was the Mk 24, which was used by only one squadron.

Seafires, many variants of which featured wing-folding, were not particularly successful as carrier fighters, their main gear being generally far too delicate for carrier operations.

Specifications for Supermarine Spitfire Mk 1A

Dimensions:	wingspan 36 feet 10 inches, length 29 feet 11 inches, height 12 feet 7.75 inches
Power:	one Rolls-Royce Merlin II supercharged, liquid-cooled V-12 rated at 1,030hp
Weights:	empty 4,517lb, normal takeoff 5,844lb
Speed:	max 346mph at 15,000 feet
Ceiling:	30,500 feet
Range:	415 miles
Armament:	eight wing-mounted 0.303in belt-fed Browning Mk 2 machine guns with 300 rounds per gun
Crew:	pilot

Spitfire Mk VB cutaway key

1 Aerial stub attachment
2 Rudder upper hinge
3 Fabric-covered rudder
4 Rudder tab
5 Sternpost
6 Rudder tab hinge
7 Rear navigation light
8 Starboard elevator tab
9 Rear navigation light
10 Elevator balance
11 Tailplane front spar
12 IFF aerial
13 Castoring non-retractable tailwheel
14 Tailwheel strut
15 Fuselage double frame
16 Elevator control lever
17 Tailplane spar/fuselage attachment
18 Fin rear spar (fuselage frame extension)
19 Fin front spar (fuselage frame extension)
20 Port elevator tab hinge
21 Port elevator
22 IFF aerial
23 Port tailplane
24 Rudder control lever
25 Cross shaft
26 Tailwheel oleo access plate
27 Tailwheel oleo shock-absorber
28 Fuselage angled frame
29 Battery compartment
30 Lower longeron
31 Elevator control cables
32 Fuselage construction
33 Rudder control cables
34 Radio compartment
35 Radio support tray
36 Flare chute
37 Oxygen bottle
38 Auxiliary long-range fuel tank
39 Dorsal formation light
40 Aerial lead-in
41 HF aerial
42 Aerial mast
43 Cockpit aft glazing
44 Voltage regulator
45 Canopy track
46 Structural bulkhead
47 Headrest
48 Plexiglass canopy
49 Rear-view mirror
50 Entry flap (port)
51 Air bottles (alternative rear fuselage stowage)

52 Sutton harness
53 Pilot's seat (moulded Bakelite)
54 Datum longeron
55 Seat support frame
56 Wingroot fillet
57 Seat adjustment lever
58 Rudder pedal frame
59 Elevator control connecting tube
60 Control column spade grip
61 Trim wheel
62 Reflector gunsight
63 External windscreen armor
64 Instrument panel
65 Main fuselage fuel tank (57.6 gallons)
66 Fuel tank/longeron attachment fittings
67 Rudder pedals
68 Rudder bar
69 King post
70 Fuselage lower fuel tank (68.4 gallons)
71 Firewall/bulkhead
72 Engine bearer attachment
73 Steel tube bearers
74 Magneto
75 "Fishtail"/exhaust manifold
76 Gun heating intensifier
77 Hydraulic tank
78 Fuel filler cap
79 Air compressor intake
80 Air compressor
81 Rolls-Royce Merlin 45 engine
82 Coolant piping
85 Port cannon wing fairing
84 Flaps
85 Aileron control cables
86 Aileron push tube
87 Bellcrank
88 Aileron hinge
89 Port aileron
90 Machine gun access panels
91 Port wingtip
92 Port navigation light
93 Leading-edge skinning
94 Machine gun ports (protected)
95 20mm cannon muzzle
96 Three-blade constant-speed propeller
97 Spinner

98 Propeller hub
99 Coolant tank
100 Cowling fastening
101 Engine anti-vibration mounting pad
102 Engine accessories
103 Engine bearers
104 Main engine support member
105 Coolant pipe
106 Exposed oil tank
107 Port mainwheel
108 Mainwheel fairing
109 Carburetor air intake
110 Stub/spar attachment
111 Mainwheel leg pivot point
112 Main spar
113 Leading-edge ribs (diagonals deleted for clarity)
114 Mainwheel leg shock-absorber
115 Mainwheel fairing
116 Starboard mainwheel
117 Angled axle
118 Cannon barrel support fairing
119 Spar cut-out
120 Mainwheel well
121 Gun heating pipe
122 Flap structure
123 Cannon wing fairing
124 Cannon magazine drum (120 rounds)
125 Machine gun support brackets
126 Gun access panels
127 0.303in (7.7mm) machine gun barrels
128 Machine gun ports
129 Ammunition boxes (350 rounds per gun)
130 Starboard aileron construction
131 Wing ribs
132 Single-tube outer spar section
133 Wingtip structure
134 Starboard navigation light

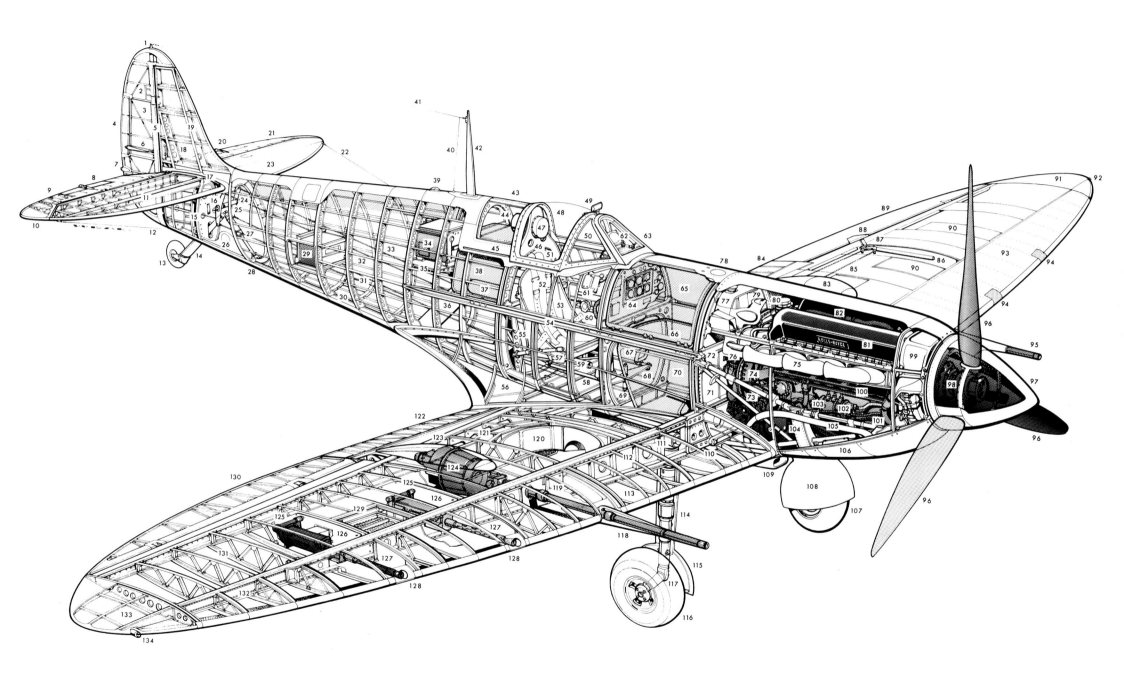

ABOVE: Spitfire IAs of No 610 Squadron, led by "Big Jim" McComb in 1940. As can be seen, they are still using the outdated Vic formations, although the various sections certainly seem to be well spread out.

RIGHT: An exciting moment for this RAF No 222 Squadron pilot as flames pour from his engine exhausts on startup. This is a rare color picture of a Spitfire VB, taken in May 1942.

OPPOSITE BELOW RIGHT: Identifiable by the four-bladed propeller and pointed fin, the Spitfire VIII was one of the nicest handling Spitfires of all, but is largely unsung since it never operated from England. This is RAF No 136 Squadron in the Cocos Islands in 1945.

RIGHT: The Spitfire VB had a more powerful engine than earlier models, and carried wing armament of two 20mm Hispano cannon and four .303 inch caliber Browning machine guns. A match for the Bf 109F, it was outclassed by the Fw 190A.

OPPOSITE: Reconnaissance Spitfires were unarmed and stripped of all unnecessary weight to improve performance. Most photo birds were painted blue, as is this Mk XI, but other colors were used, including pink!

OPPOSITE INSET: Short-legged for offensive operations, Spitfires were able to reach Germany for the first time in April 1944. A Spitfire IX, which was little more than an up-engined Mk V, is seen preparing to take off for this sortie.

RIGHT INSET: A Spitfire VC with a tropical intake with a filter for sandy and dusty conditions, and a long range slipper tank. With this and an extra tank in the fuselage, they were able to reach Malta from Gibraltar.

BELOW: A Spitfire IX shares its airfield with a P-51B Mustang of the USAAF. One is reminded of the German saying: if they are camouflaged they are British; if they are silver, they are American; if you can't see them at all, they are German!

VOUGHT F-8 CRUSADER

LEFT: The last force to operate the Vought F-8 Crusader, seen here aboard the carrier Clemenceau, was France's l'Aeronavale. A unique feature of the Crusader was its ability to adjust the incidence of the wing for takeoff, as seen here.

The first carrier fighter to enter service, in March 1957, with genuine supersonic level flight performance, the F-8 Crusader was also the last U.S. fighter to be equipped with guns as its primary armament. It was also unique in having a two-position variable-incidence wing. This, hinged on the rear spar and hydraulically operated, could be raised seven degrees to give the optimum angle of attack during takeoff and landing, keeping the fuselage as near horizontal as possible. The single-piece wing was mounted level with the top of a slab-sided fuselage, and had hinged leading edges with inboard flaperons and conventional flaps which lowered 25 degrees to increase effective camber. It would have been virtually impossible for the main gear to have retracted into the wing, so it retracted into the fuselage instead, allowing very short but robustly constructed legs to be used. This arrangement provided ample space for a significant volume of fuel, while allowing for low deck clearance which was of advantage when loading underwing stores.

One of the initial design aims was to give the pilot the best possible view from the cockpit during carrier landings. The cockpit was therefore placed as far forward as possible, just behind the nose, which carried a small radar, and the plain chin engine inlet below. This gave the pilot excellent forward and sideways view, but, since the canopy was faired into the fuselage for the sake of optimum performance, he could see little or nothing behind him. At the rear were a sharply swept fin and rudder, all-moving low-set tail surfaces and small ventral strakes. Powerplant was a single Pratt & Whitney J57 afterburning turbojet, which, unusually for the time, included extensive use of titanium around the nozzle.

The first Crusader prototype was flown on March 25, 1955, when the aircraft went supersonic. Deliveries of the initial clear-weather day air superiority version, the F-8A, commencing two years later, and for ten years the type was the U.S. Navy's standard carrier fighter. It first saw combat over Southeast Asia on March 2, 1965, and racked up a favorable record against communist MiG fighters, although most of its twenty victories were scored with Sidewinder air-to-air missiles.

Successive improvements were introduced, including more powerful engine, upgrades in armament, radar and avionics. Whereas the F-8A was fitted with a retractable belly pack of 78 Mighty Mouse rockets in addition to the cannon, these were deleted in favor of two Sidewinders. The F-8B was fitted with the APS-67 radar, giving it limited all-weather capability, while the F-8C had a higher rated

engine, ventral fins for added yaw stability at high altitude, and could carry four Sidewinders. The F-8D was even more powerful, could carry more internal fuel, and had improved avionics. The final new-production model was the F-8E, which could carry increased air-to-surface weapons, and was fitted with the superior APQ-94 radar.

Manufacture ended in early 1965, by which time 1,261 Crusaders of all types had been built, although some 550 were remanufactured and upgraded. Crusaders served with the U.S Navy and Marine Corps, being phased out of front line service in 1976, although the RF-8 reconnaissance version carried on in reserve units for another ten years. Some much modified F-8E(FN)s were used by France's L'Aeronavale until mid-2000, and twenty-five ex-U.S. Navy F-8Hs (previously F-8Ds) were delivered to the Philippine Air Force.

Specifications for Vought F-8D Crusader

Dimensions: wingspan 35 feet 8 inches, length 54 feet 3 inches, height 15 feet 9 inches

Power: one Pratt & Whitney J57-P-20 twin-spool, axial-flow afterburning turbojet rated at 10,700lb military and 18,000lb max thrust

Weights: empty 17,541lb, normal takeoff 27,550lb, 34,000 max

Speed: max 1,228mph Mach 1.6 at 36,000 feet, 762mph Mach 1.00 at sea level

Ceiling: 42,900 feet

Range: combat radius 455 miles

Armament: four fuselage-mounted 20mm Colt-Browning Mk 12 cannon with 125 rounds per gun, four cheek-mounted AIM-9 Sidewinder air-to-air missiles

Crew: pilot

F-8E Crusader cutaway key

1 Fintip VHF aerial fairing
2 Tail warning radar
3 Tail navigation light
4 Rudder construction
5 Rudder hydraulic jack
6 Engine exhaust nozzle
7 Variable-area nozzle flaps
8 Afterburner cooling air duct
9 Nozzle control jacks
10 Starboard all-moving tailplane construction
11 Tailplane spar box
12 Leading-edge ribs
13 Tailplane pivot fixing
14 Tailplane hydraulic control jack
15 Tailpipe cooling air vents
16 Fin attachment main frame
17 Afterburner duct
18 Rudder control linkages
19 Fin leading-edge construction
20 Port all-moving tailplane
21 Fin-root fillet construction
22 Rear engine mounting
23 Fuselage break point double frame (engine removal)
24 Afterburner fuel spray manifold
25 Tailplane autopilot control system
26 Deck arrester hook
27 Starboard ventral fin
28 Rear fuselage fuel tank
29 Pratt & Whitney J57-P-20A afterburning turbojet
30 Engine bay cooling air louvers
31 Wingroot trailing-edge fillet
32 Bleed air system piping
33 Engine oil tank (85 gallons)
34 Wing spar pivot fixing
35 Hydraulic flap jack
36 Starboard flap
37 Control rod linkages
38 Rear spar
39 Engine accessory gearbox compartment
40 Inboard wing panel multi-spar construction
41 Starboard wing integral fuel tank, total fuel system capacity 1,348 gallons
42 Aileron power control unit
43 Starboard drooping aileron construction
44 Hydraulic wing fold jack
45 Trailing-edge ribs
46 Fixed portion of trailing edge
47 Wingtip fairing
48 Starboard navigation light
49 Leading-edge flap, lowered position

50 Leading-edge flap rib construction
51 Outer wing panel spar construction
52 Leading-edge flap hydraulic jack
53 Wingfold hinge
54 Front spar
55 Leading-edge flap inboard section
56 Leading-edge dog-tooth
57 Wing pylon
58 AGM-12B Bullpup A air-to ground missile
59 Starboard mainwheel
60 Main undercarriage leg strut
61 Shock absorber strut
62 Hydraulic retraction jack
63 Landing lamp
64 Wheel bay doors
65 Main undercarriage pivot fixing
66 Wing spar/front engine mounting main bulkhead
67 Engine compressor intake
68 Wingroot rib
69 Center-section fuel tank
70 Wing spar carry-through structure
71 Dorsal fairing
72 Port flap jack
73 Port plain flap, lowered position
74 Port drooped aileron, lowered position
75 Aileron power control unit
76 Fuel system piping
77 Wing-fold hydraulic jack
78 Fixed portion of trailing edge
79 Port wing folded position
80 Wingtip fairing
81 Port navigation light
82 Port outboard leading-edge flap, lowered
83 Outboard flap hydraulic jack
84 Leading-edge dogtooth
85 Wing-fold hinge
86 Inboard leading-edge flap hydraulic jacks
87 Port wing integral fuel tank
88 Anti-collision light
89 Missile system avionics
90 Two-position variable-incidence wing, raised position
91 Intake trunking
92 Wing incidence hydraulic jack
93 Fuselage upper longeron
94 Air system exhaust heat shield

95 Main fuselage fuel tank
96 Airbrake hydraulic jack
97 Airbrake housing
98 Ventral airbrake, lowered
99 Rocket launch tubes
100 Rocket launcher pylon adaptor
101 Zuni folding-fin ground attack rockets (8)
102 Emergency air-driven generator
103 Liquid oxygen bottle (LOX)
104 Fuselage stores pylon
105 Intake duct
106 Heat exchanger air exhaust
107 Air-conditioning plant
108 Dorsal fairing
109 Upper fuselage access panels
110 Electronics bay and electrical power system
111 Fuselage pylon adaptor
112 Missile launch rails
113 AIM-9 Sidewinder air-to-air missiles (4)
114 Inflight-refueling probe, extended
115 Refueling probe housing door
116 Ammunition tanks (144 rounds per gun)
117 Avionics system inertial platform
118 Ammunition feed chutes
119 Gun bay gas vent panel
120 Mk 12 20mm cannon
121 Spent cartridge case/link collector chutes
122 Gun compartment access panel
123 Nosewheel doors
124 Nosewheel
125 Pivoted axle beam
126 Nose undercarriage leg strut
127 Cannon barrels
128 Radio and electronics equipment bays
129 Canopy hinge point
130 Cockpit rear pressure bulkhead
131 Ejection seat rails
132 Pilot's Martin-Baker ejection seat
133 Face blind-firing handle
134 Cockpit canopy cover
135 Safety harness
136 Canopy emergency release
137 Pilot's starboard side console panel
138 Cockpit floor level
139 Cannon muzzle blast troughs
140 Intake duct framing
141 Radar cooling air piping

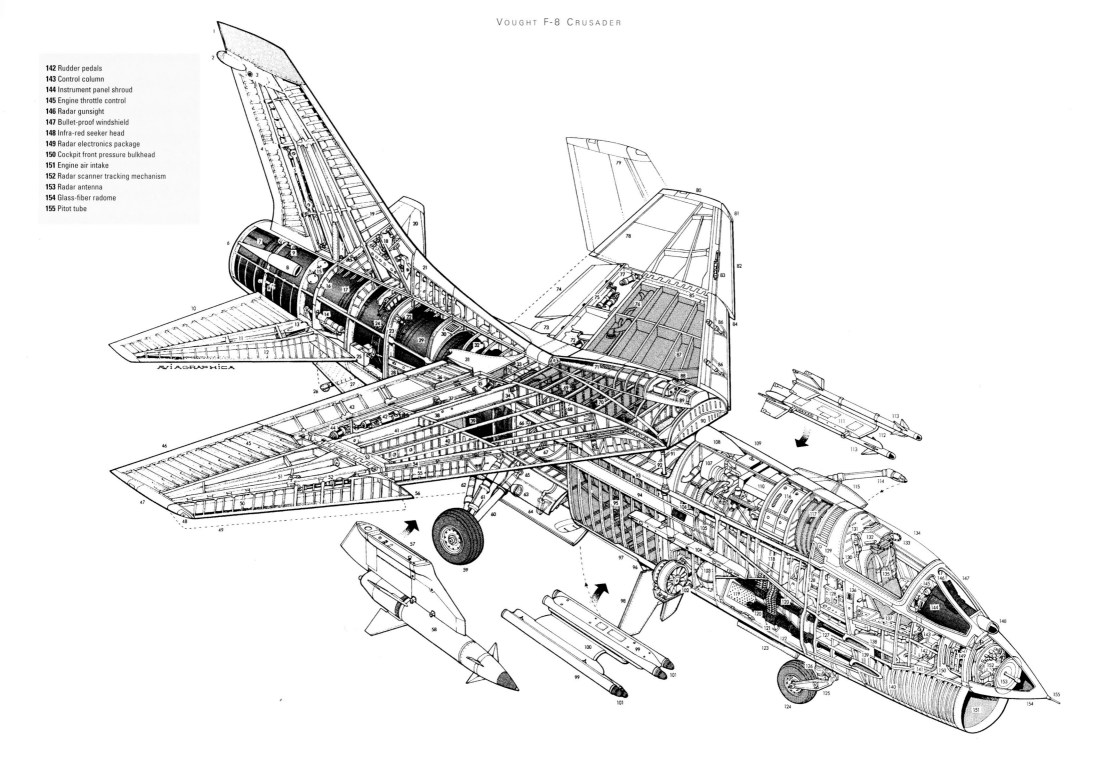

AVIAGRAPHICA

24
18

147010
NAVY
145566
NAVY
VC-10
147029
NAVY
VC 10
145549
NAVY
VC-10

OPPOSITE: F-8K Crusaders were actually rebuilt F-8Cs. Mainly operated by the U.S. Navy and Marine Corps, the Crusader was used in the early years of the Vietnam War, where it was touted as "The Last of the Gunfighters."

OPPOSITE INSET: Two F-8E(FN)s of *l'Aeronavale*, in which they were used not only for air defense, but in the anti-shipping role. For this mission they carried the Matra R.530 anti-shipping missile.

BELOW INSET: The primary armament of four 20mm cannon was mechanically unreliable, and the sighting system also had defects. Most of the twenty Crusader victories in Vietnam were scored with Sidewinders, carried on cheek rails.

MAIN PICTURE: In a 1966 remanufacturing program involving modifications that included strengthened wings and main undercarriage, and lengthened nosewheel strut, some 448 Crusaders were upgraded: 89 F-8Ds were rebuilt as F-8Hs (as here), 136 F-8Es became F-8Js, 87 F-8Cs were restored to U.S. Navy service as F-8Ks, and 61 F-8Bs became F-8Ls.

ACKNOWLEDGMENTS

The author and publishers are grateful to Mike Spick for his assistance with the photograph captions; to Stasz Gnych and Keren Harragan of Amber Books, and to Mike Badrocke for supplying the excellent cutaway drawings (as itemised in the credits); and to Philip Jarrett for supplying the photographs that appear on pages 6, 7, 10, 12, 20, 25 inset, 29 inset, 36, 38, 40, 42, 43, 44, 46, 47, 52, 58 top and bottom, 66, 68, 69 inset, 72 main picture, 73, 76, 77, 79, 80, 84 inset, 85 main picture, 89 top and bottom, 98 inset, 99 left, 99 right, 100, 102 left, 103, 104 both insets, 108, 109, 113 main picture, 116, 118 top, 119, 124, 128 inset, 132, 134, 135, 139 left, 140 main picture, 141 inset, 154, 156 main picture, 158 main picture, 159 inset, 162, 163, 164, 166, 172 main picture, 173, 181, 184, 189 main picture, 198 inset, 208, 213, 214 inset, 216, 218 right, 219, 220 inset, 222, 224, 225 main picture, 234, 236, 237 main picture, 238, 240, 241, 246, 249, 250 inset, 251 inset, 255. All other photographs were provided by the author.

Designed as a close air combat fighter without compromise to offset the agile Soviet MiGs, the Fighting Falcon was first deployed to USAFE based at Hahn in Germany in 1982-83, with the 50th Tactical Fighter Wing.